84   85.00
            75u

ÉLITES AND POWER IN
TWENTIETH-CENTURY SPAIN

D0204987

Sir Raymond Carr

ÉLITES AND POWER IN TWENTIETH-CENTURY SPAIN

Essays in Honour of
SIR RAYMOND CARR

Edited by
FRANCES LANNON
and
PAUL PRESTON

CLARENDON PRESS · OXFORD

1990

Oxford University Press, Walton Street, Oxford OX2 6DP

Oxford   New York   Toronto
Delhi   Bombay   Calcutta   Madras   Karachi
Petaling Jaya   Singapore   Hong Kong   Tokyo
Nairobi   Dar es Salaam   Cape Town
Melbourne   Auckland

and associated companies in
Berlin   Ibadan

Oxford is a trade mark of Oxford University Press

Published in the United States
by Oxford University Press, New York

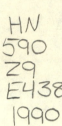

© Oxford University Press, 1990

All rights reserved. No part of this publication may be reproduced,
stored in a retrieval system, or transmitted, in any form or by any means,
electronic, mechanical, photocopying, recording, or otherwise, without
the prior permission of Oxford University Press.

British Library Cataloguing in Publication Data
Élites and power in twentieth-century Spain: essays in
honour of Sir Raymond Carr
1. Spain. Elites history
I. Lannon, Frances II. Preston, Paul 1946– III. Carr,
Raymond
305.520946
ISBN 0–19–822880–5

Library of Congress Cataloging in Publication Data
Élites and power in twentieth-century Spain: essays in honor of Sir
Raymond Carr/edited by Frances Lannon and Paul Preston.
p.   cm.
Includes bibliographical references.
1. Elite (Social sciences) — Spain — History — 20th century.
2. Spain — Politics and government — 20th century. 3. Spain — Social
conditions — 1886–1939. 4. Spain — Social conditions — 1939–1975.
5. Carr, Raymond. I. Lannon, Frances. II. Preston, Paul, 1946–.
III. Carr, Raymond.
HN590.Z9E438   1990
305.5'2'09460904 — dc20   90–34109
ISBN 0–19–822880–5

Typeset by Wyvern Typesetting Ltd
Printed and bound in
Great Britain by Biddles Ltd.,
Guildford and King's Lynn.

PREFACE

In the preface to his monumental work *Spain 1808–1939* (1966), Raymond Carr described modern Spain as being still 'in terms of modern historical scholarship, largely an unmapped region' and noted 'the immensity of the unexplored'. Sixteen years later, introducing the expanded second edition, *Spain 1808–1975* (1982), he paid tribute to the revolution in Spanish historiography that had occurred since the first appearance of his history. With characteristic modesty, he refrained from commenting on his own contribution to sparking off that revolution. Like all revolutions, the great leap forward in Spanish historiography has been exciting, untidy, and incomplete. It was presaged both in Gerald Brenan's classic *The Spanish Labyrinth* (1943) and in the new social history fostered in Catalonia in the 1950s and 1960s by Jaime Vicens Vives. Carr himself has always generously acknowledged his debts to both Brenan and Vicens. In fact, given the difficulties imposed upon the Spanish historical profession by the censorship apparatus of a dictatorship determined to avoid close scrutiny of its own origins, the course of the revolution was influenced by several French, American, and British scholars.

Among them, however, no one individual enjoyed the influence exercised by Raymond Carr. When he began to work on Spain, its modern history was considered in British universities to be something of a backwater—less significant than, for instance, that of Italy. Through his supervision of numerous doctoral theses, he created an Oxford 'school' of historians of contemporary Spain. As a result of his own work and then that of his English pupils, Carr has ensured that the study of modern Spanish history and politics is a flourishing academic activity in a number of British universities. In the peninsula itself, his Spanish pupils obtained university chairs. More importantly, the translation of his ambitious Oxford history established itself as *the* basic text on the modern period.

The remarkable influence of *Spain 1808–1939* in Spanish circles was a consequence of several factors. It covered 131 years; in the 1982 revision, 163. The book presented Spain's twentieth-century disasters in terms of the long-term historical failure of the middle classes to overcome the resistance of a recalcitrant landed oligarchy to the political, economic, and intellectual modernization of the country. In doing so, Carr examined rainfall and railways, population structure and property relations, farming and freemasons, schooling and military strategy, as well as the constitutional conflicts, revolutions, civil wars, and periods of reconstruction that have characterized Spanish political history in the nineteenth and twentieth centuries. Work on the contemporary period of such sweeping vision and long historical span was virtually unknown in Franco's Spain. That was largely due to the activities of the censorship. However, it was also a reflection of the fact that such an adventurous approach ran contrary to an academic tradition which placed greater value on the massive accumulation of empirical data on relatively narrow topics than on interpretative or methodological boldness. In the 1960s, Spain's historians wrote largely for their fellow professionals. In contrast, the graceful readability and teeming insights of Carr's work ensured that it would be read by a large number of students.

Spain 1808–1939 was based on enormous reading, a deeply sensitive knowledge of modern Spanish literature, particularly the works of Galdós, and indefatigable travel. Indeed, the uncommon humanity which is a hallmark of Carr's work derived partly from his avid consumption of the novels of both nineteenth- and twentieth-century Spain. It was a reflection too of his incessant journeys through the highways and byways of Spanish towns and villages during which he met many of the protagonists of his own books. In *The Spanish Tragedy* (1977) and *Spain, Dictatorship to Democracy* (written with J. P. Fusi, 1979) Carr was able to give freer rein to his sensitivity to the shifting preoccupations and kaleidoscopic variety of Spanish popular culture. Football and bullfighting, television and soap operas were as likely to be fruitful sources as the memoirs of politicians. In these works too, concerned as they were with the contemporary period, he was able to make more of his uncanny feel for the grandeurs and miseries of a Spanish political life as often characterized by suicidal idealism as by creeping corruption. However, it was the sheer range of Carr's 1966 Oxford history which established him as a generous guide and it is an essential framework for the general student of Spanish history. At the same time, it posed a series of questions with which many historical researchers have been grappling ever since.

Eventually, the historiographical revolution which Carr helped inspire was to gather force and depth with the innovative work of many Spanish historians during the last years of the Franco regime and particularly since the re-establishment of democracy in the second half of the 1970s. In the political and economic spheres especially, our knowledge of modern Spain has gained in both comprehensiveness and sophistication. Studies of political parties and political culture, elections, the unions, regional affairs, and agrarian and industrial structure have proliferated since Raymond Carr first produced his great history. Government and administration, institutions, popular and local culture, women's history and social history in general, have followed, albeit more slowly. This ongoing revolution in the historiography of modern Spain boasts, if not revolutionary heroes, at least great figures whose creative discontent with the old world and vision of wider possibilities helped construct a new one. It is in recognition of the eminence among them of Sir Raymond Carr that these essays are written and now presented with admiration and affection.

One of Raymond Carr's abiding preoccupations has been the analysis of power in modern Spain. The questions that he has raised continue to provoke discussion. Why did political liberalism not establish itself as the accepted orthodoxy in the nineteenth or early twentieth centuries? Why was liberal constitutionalism unable to foster genuine mass parties, or permeate mass culture? What exactly has been the political role of the army? Why has the central state remained weak, and why have the regions (particularly Catalonia and the Basque country) and the great urban centres of Spain so often proved resistant to governmental control? Why has religion been so politically divisive? Can one fully account for the dogged and violent opposition to reform of the local holders of rural power and property, especially in the south of Spain? How could Primo de Rivera's dictatorship disintegrate, and Franco's disappear so swiftly? What were the economic, social, and ideological sources of the new democratic hegemony?

Because of the importance of these questions, and the issues of authority and legitimacy from which they arise, it seemed appropriate to take as the theme for this collection of essays the uses of political, social, and economic power in twentieth-century Spain. This implies no disillusionment with the history of the popular masses, so crucial and so rapidly developing in Spain. Indeed, the élites studied here include anarchist leaders, trade unionists, and local Catholic women activists as well as politicians, industrial bosses, landowners, bishops, and generals. The analysis of the exercise of power in small things and in great has lost none of its fascination or its urgency. On the contrary, it is again a timely focus precisely because of the greater understanding gained from recent scholarship of the socio-economic and administrative contexts of local and national élite groups of all kinds. The emphasis is therefore on the particular role within the power structure of soldiers and churchmen, entrepreneurs and rural grandees, falang-ists and socialists, reformers and revolutionaries, rather than any theoretical speculations on the nature of élites.

This volume deals with only one aspect of Raymond Carr's work. It does not touch upon his influence on the study of Latin American history, nor upon his interest in fox-hunting. Even within the chosen theme of the book—the exercise of power in twentieth-century Spain—the essays collected here are by no means comprehensive; nor could they be with so vast a topic. They represent, nevertheless, an attempt to explore from a variety of perspectives a question that Raymond Carr has never tired of asking. Where does real power lie, and with what justifications, and within what limits? They are presented to Sir Raymond, in the hope that he will find them interesting, by grateful former students, colleagues, and friends.

CONTENTS

x   *Contents*

NOTES ON CONTRIBUTORS

SEBASTIAN BALFOUR is a Senior Lecturer in Spanish, Goldsmiths' College, University of London. He is the author of *Dictatorship, Workers, and the City* (1989) and a forthcoming biography of Fidel Castro.

SHLOMO BEN-AMI is the Israeli Ambassador to Spain and Professor of History at the University of Tel Aviv. His books include *The Origins of the Second Republic in Spain* (1978) and *Fascism from Above: The Dictatorship of Primo de Rivera* (1983).

MARTIN BLINKHORN is a Professor of European History and Head of Department of History in the University of Lancaster and editor of *European History Quarterly*. His publications include *Carlism and Crisis in Spain 1931–1939* (1975) and (ed.) *Spain in Conflict* (1986).

BURNETT BOLLOTEN, who died on 27 October 1987, was a United Press Correspondent in Spain during the Civil War. He was the author of *The Grand Camouflage* (1961) and *The Spanish Revolution* (1979). The Bolloten collection of Civil War materials is held by the Hoover Institution, Stanford.

MALCOLM DEAS is Fellow and Sub-Warden of St Antony's College, Oxford. His publications include *Eloy Alfaro: Narraciones Históricas* (1984).

GEORGE ESENWEIN is a Librarian at the Hoover Institution, and the author of *Anarchist Ideology and the Working-Class Movement in Spain 1868–1898* (1989).

JUAN PABLO FUSI AIZPÚRUA is the Director of the Biblioteca Nacional and Professor of Contemporary History at the University of Madrid. His books include *Politica obrera en el país vasco 1880–1923* (1975), *Franco* (1985), and (with Raymond Carr) *Spain: Dictatorship to Democracy* (1979).

HELEN GRAHAM is a Lecturer in the Department of Spanish, Portuguese, and Latin American Studies, University of Southampton, and editor (with Paul Preston) of *The Popular Front in Europe* (1986) and (with Martin Alexander) of *The French and Spanish Popular Fronts: Comparative Perspectives* (1989).

JOSEPH HARRISON is Senior Lecturer in Economic History at the University of Manchester. He is the author of *An Economic History of*

Modern Spain (1978) and *The Spanish Economy in the Twentieth Century* (1985).

SANTOS JULIÁ is a Professor in the Spanish Open University. His publications include *La izquierda del PSOE* (1977), *Los orígenes del Frente Popular* (1979), and *Madrid 1931–34: De la fiesta popular a la lucha de clases* (1984).

FRANCES LANNON is a Fellow of Lady Margaret Hall, Oxford, and author of *Privilege, Persecution, and Prophecy: The Catholic Church in Spain 1875–1975* (1987).

ROBERT A. MCNEIL is Head of the Hispanic Section in the Bodleian Library, Oxford. He is the editor of *Latin American Studies: A Basic Guide to Sources* (1989).

CHARLES POWELL is A. J. Pye Junior Research Fellow at University College, Oxford. His doctoral thesis was a study of the politics of the transition to democracy in Spain.

PAUL PRESTON is Professor of History and Director of the Centre for Contemporary Spanish Studies, Queen Mary & Westfield College, University of London. His books include *The Coming of the Spanish Civil War* (1978), *The Triumph of Democracy in Spain* (1986), and *The Spanish Civil War* (1986).

TIMOTHY REES is a Lecturer in History at the University of York. He is completing a doctoral thesis on agrarian politics in Badajoz during the Second Republic.

MARY VINCENT is a Lecturer in History at the University of Sheffield. She is completing a doctoral thesis on Catholic culture in Salamanca province 1931–9.

1. RAYMOND CARR: APPROACHES TO THE HISTORY OF SPAIN

Malcolm Deas

I guess that many of his old friends would be surprised to realize how little they know for certain about Raymond Carr—surprised because they would all agree about the strength of his personality: once encountered, never forgotten.[1] I have known him for thirty years, but found myself with few facts. I therefore interviewed him.

Raymond Carr was born in Bath on 11 April 1919, the son of Reginald Carr and Ethel Graham. His forebears were 'manual labourers, domestic servants, bricklayers, porters, butlers'. One of his grandfathers was a grocer's assistant. His mother was a clerk in a post office, and his father was a schoolteacher.

He was an only child in a religious household. Though the family background was Wesleyan or Primitive Methodist, his father became 'low Church of England—a village schoolmaster always competes a bit with Methodists'. Once he had learnt to read, Raymond was expected to read the Bible aloud every night. He did so when he was at home until he went up to Oxford.

He remembers his father as 'an austere self-improver', but more interested in horticulture than in books. There were not many books in the house at Winfrith, Dorset, where for most of Raymond's childhood his father was master of the village school. This 'straight patriotic imperialist' possessed a set of Kipling, Sir James Jeans's *The Mysterious Universe*, and Hendrik Van Loon's *The Story of Mankind*. The young Carr read no novel until he was 'about seventeen', when he bought a copy of *The Idiot* in W. H. Smith's, Southampton, supposing it to be about mental illness. His ordinary secondary education he received at Brockenhurst County Secondary School—his father was by then headmaster at Wootton, New Milton. By 1936 he had begun to play the tenor saxophone, for he remembers that he was out playing it the night George V's life was drawing peacefully to its close, which

[1] For a typical encounter see Mary Killen's 'Don Quixotic', *Tatler*, 282/9 (Oct. 1987), 176–9, 200.

distressed his father. His childhood memories are mostly rural: stables, farms, carthorses. He has ploughed a field with horses.

This background was not rich, but nor was it conventional. Perhaps Raymond Carr's resistance to the simpler sociological generalizations derives first from his own experience, for these religious, politically conforming parents sent him abroad to learn languages. He first attended a course at the University of Besançon—the Spanish Civil War was being fought at the time, though it made no particular impression on him. Later, he was sent to Germany, to Freiburg-im-Breisgau, in 1937. There he 'learnt German, more or less'. He regards himself as having no natural gift for languages, and is forever grateful to his parents for having given him these advantages.

He has more to say about his time in Germany than about France. He read more there. He had two particular friends, one Jewish, one a member of the Hitler Youth. His father was later instrumental in helping this Jewish friend to get out of Germany, and he was eventually to have a distinguished academic career in England. His friend in the Hitler Youth gave him Plato's *Republic* as a good introduction to the Third Reich.

He did well in his school certificate, except in algebra. He was not good at mathematics, though otherwise fond of science. He then sat for a 'County Major Scholarship' hoping to read history—at Brockenhurst he had had an exceptional history master—at Southampton University. Professor Betts of Southampton read his papers, and advised him that he 'ought to try for something better'.

He looked at a list of the Oxford colleges, and taking them in alphabetical order wrote to All Souls. As All Souls has no undergraduates, he received only a short letter from Sir Charles Oman advising him to try elsewhere. He chose to try Christ Church, which gave him a scholarship. He went up with that, his 'county major', and a measure of help from his parents. In the Oxford of 1938 this was to enable him to live 'a rather vivid social life'.

His abiding memories of the 1930s are of 'the shaming waste of talent' of those times, of clever companions in school who came to nothing, who never got the exceptional chances he thinks came his way through his parents and good fortune.

At Christ Church he thinks he must have been 'a scholarship boy through and through'. He worked hard, from early morning. Nobody noticed. The 'vivid social life' could then be led in the evening. He made friendships 'which no doubt had a profound social influence'. He is uncomplicatedly fond of his first college. His memories of his tutors—Keith Feiling, J. C. Masterman, J. N. L. Myers, Patrick Gordon-Walker—are benign but not powerful.

He remembers books better: Pirenne's *Mohammed and Charlemagne*—his ambition at this time was to be a medievalist; Tawney's *Religion and the Rise of Capitalism*—'capitalism', and the future independence of India, were bones of contention with his father; Namier's *Structure of Politics on the Accession of George III*—its lasting influence visible in his work on Spain. He grew interested in theories of history through Meinecke and Dilthey, and at one time began projecting a history of history. He admired Elie Halévy's *A History of the English People in the Nineteenth Century*, particularly for what then struck him as an adventurous range of sources, including pamphlets and newspapers. He started reading novels 'pretty intensely', though he has never much liked modern novels. The only course of lectures he can remember attending were those of R. G. Collingwood: he still admires *The Idea of History*. He liked military history, which he thinks teaches precision: 'it is no good saying so-and-so was on the left if in fact he was on the right'. He thinks that the strictly military history of the Spanish Civil War has been neglected for its political history.

Though Raymond strikes his friends as physically strong, tireless, careless of health, indestructible, he had early on given up games on account of a particular heart condition. He graduated with a first-class degree in 1941, and was then rejected for military service on medical grounds. He spent the rest of the Second World War teaching at a public school, Wellington College.

There he taught the sixth form history and English, and he regards this as 'one of the happiest and most fulfilled parts of my life'. He found his pupils responsive and malleable. At the end of the war, when orthodox schoolmasters came back on the market, the headmaster called him in: 'I don't think you're really the sort of man to make a career as a public-school master'. Raymond did not disagree—while at Oxford he had resolved one day to become a don—and found himself for a while unemployed.

He cannot remember exactly how he got back to Oxford. He failed to get a studentship at his old college, though he had at some point held a Gladstone Research Exhibition. He thinks he saw a newspaper advertisement for the All Souls Prize Fellowship. He sat the examination—a large field returning from the war—and was elected. He entered the competition as a medievalist—again, he feels his German was a great advantage.

He intended however to work on Sweden: the road to All Souls is paved with later unrealized intentions. He had a contract to write a life of Gustavus Adolphus for A. L. Rowse's 'Teach Yourself History' series. His interest in Sweden derived from his youthful stay in Freiburg-im-Breisgau. On a cycling or vandervogeling expedition he had met a Swedish girl in a youth hostel who had 'helped sew a button on my coat'. This 'started a sort of amorous affair'. Raymond had learnt Swedish. He had been in Sweden when the Second World War broke out. He began to work on Swedish history at Wellington 'as a means of getting some professional credentials'.

He admired Eli Heckscher's *Mercantilism* and besides writing the brief life of Gustavus Adolphus he intended to translate Heckscher's work on Swedish economic history into English. He was encouraged to do so by R. H. Tawney himself, from whom he also received a piece of advice for economic historians: 'I wouldn't bother with any economists after Marshall'. The life of Gustavus was written, but Rowse found it boring—'quite rightly'. It has recently been burnt. Heckscher's Swedish work was the subject of a short piece by Raymond in the *Economic History Review*: the translation had been done by another hand.[2]

The late 1940s were an uncertain period in Raymond's life. Chance, he will say, governed his courses. At one time he wished to study brigandage in Naples, but found himself anticipated by Eric Hobsbawm. For a time he was a lecturer at University College, London, where he taught 'General History' and 'British Constitution' under the eye of Sir John Neale. He was uncertain what to do or where to go. Stuart Hampshire advised him to stick out for an Oxford tutorial fellowship. B. H. Sumner, Warden of All Souls, alarmed at his mounting bills, asked him 'if he had ever thought of Canada'—the Warden seemed to have in mind some sort of frontier-land for bankrupts and remittance-men.

Having failed to get a fellowship at Queen's and at Worcester, he was elected a fellow of New College in 1952.

---

[2] 'Essays in Bibliography and Criticism XXXIII, Heckscher's Economic History of Sweden', *Economic History Review*, 9/1, pp. 132–3. Other articles on Sweden were 'Gustavus IV and the British Government, 1804–9', *The English Historical Review*, 60/236 (Jan. 1945), and 'Two Swedish Financiers: Louis de Geer and Joel Gripenstierna', in H. E. Bell and R. L. Ollard (eds.), *Historical Essays 1600–1750 Presented to David Ogg* (London, 1963). Their author now dismisses these works as 'archetypes of the useless historical article'. He is too severe, but more than usually few English readers can have had the necessary grasp of context to make much sense of them: 'It was in the interstices of an ill-ordered financial system that the private financier inserted himself

In 1950 he had married Sara Strickland. It was on their honeymoon that Raymond first went to Spain, to the 'fishing village of Tor-remolinos', which then had one hotel. Of his first impressions, he remembers the seasonal workers in the railway station at León 'with their sickles and sacks'. The problems of this European/un-European country dimly began to interest him. It did not strike him as exotic, but 'poor beyond belief when you think of it now'. He began reading Spanish history in a desultory way.

Alan Bullock and Bill Deakin commissioned him to ask Gerald Brenan to write the Spain volume for the Oxford History of Modern Europe. He drove to visit Brenan with Julian Pitt Rivers. Brenan did not want then to write any more history; at that time he thought 'the truth was better got at by writing novels'. Driving away with Julian, Raymond confessed that he did not want to go on with Sweden or Italy. He decided that he would do the book on Spain.

Spain 1808–1936 appeared in 1966. The research was done in vacations, never in a period of 'long immersion'. He studied and trav-elled on his own resources—'it was very cheap'—took no sabbaticals, and received no aid from any committee, foundation, or council. (He made one application for a grant, to the Leverhulme Foundation. It was unsuccessful.) Impressed from his first stay, and from his first reading of Brenan's *The Spanish Labyrinth*, by Spain's diversity, he travelled all over the country. He knows every province, and finds that a visit anywhere, however short, works wonders for his curiosity.

He bought a lot of books, read in the Biblioteca Nacional ('full of students, catalogue hopeless, no seats'), the Chamber of Commerce ('much interesting stuff'), the Instituto de Reformas Sociales, the Ateneo, and the Archivo Militar, to which last he was introduced by the former Nationalist artillery chief, General Martínez Campos ('a wasted opportunity—I don't think I got a dozen sentences out of it'). He found no ideal place to work.

He had gone to Spain with conventional anti-Franco views and a simple picture of a regime that rested on the three pillars of army, church, and falange. He and Sara had given the views some frivolous expression in Ronda, where their stay in a café was disturbed by a loud Catholic mission denouncing atheists and reds. They wrote '¡Abajo

for his own gain. . . . The whole atmosphere of the Treasury is one of intrigue. It was such a deterioration that gave Gripenstierna his chance and the deterioration is reflected in the corruption of Gripenstierna himself.' The future historian of Spain at least gained some practice in working in an unfashionable field.

Franco!' and 'iAbajo la Iglesia!' on bills and napkins. When they got back to their hotel they found a plain-clothes policeman in their room. He had already been through their luggage and told them simply that they should either behave like normal tourists or leave Spain and never come back. They went back to the café and collected up all the incriminating bits of paper they could find.

Meetings with all sorts of Spaniards altered and complicated this picture. He remembers how surprised he was by a series of meetings with the monarchist opposition, whose members talked freely in the vain hope that their views might be relayed to the Foreign Office. He had many long conversations with the Duque de la Torre, General Martínez Campos, and the Infante de Orleans, and with General Kindelán of the Nationalist Air Force. He greatly regrets that he kept no sort of diary, but he can remember how astonished he was by their fierce criticisms of Franco. Of another quarter, he recalls one promi-nent Falangist who 'really wanted to murder Franco'. He also sought out Republicans, as he was thinking of a separate book on the Civil War. He had interviews with General Aranda, who was under some form of house arrest, while his guards went out to lunch. He found General Rojo living in a meagre flat; Martínez Campos asked to be introduced to his old opponent, but Rojo refused to meet him.

Thinking of the Spain of the 1950s, he reflects: 'The English have no idea at all of what life is like in authoritarian societies. They think only of repression—of course there was repression, terrible repression, but there is much more to it than that.' The general acquiescence was produced in so many other ways, by so much else that the English imagination rarely encompasses. He recommends reading Carlos Bar-ral's *Años de penitencia*, Francisco Umbral's *Memorias de un niño de derechas*. The atmosphere of the 1950s was not so different from the 1940s: the great change came in the 1960s.

He worked largely in isolation. Of the historians he met, the one who had the greatest influence on him—and he would say on modern Spanish historiography—was Jaime Vicens Vives. There was not much current interest in the nineteenth century, which in Francoist orthodoxy was regarded as a disaster. Much of the best work then was being produced on 'safe' remoter periods, though traditional right-wing historians did from time to time produce 'useful stuff'. A book he singles out as having been more than ordinarily useful to him was J. Pabón's *Cambó*. His readers know that he has the talent for finding 'useful stuff' practically anywhere.

He is not a keen attender at professional congresses. He had little contact with France—he has never been invited to lecture by the French[3]—or with the United States.

This background to the writing of *Spain 1808–1936* perhaps helps account for some of its characteristics: its originality, its range, its wide rapport, its argumentativeness—the product of long internal wrangling over unfamiliar problems. Its lack of parochialism was maybe achieved through his obligations as a teacher of much else besides Spain at that time, not in spite of them. He is no romantic; he is impatient with quests for the unique essence of Spain, whether undertaken by Spaniards or by foreigners. He thinks that Napoleon said somewhere that 'Spaniards are just like any other people,' and he would incline to agree.

Of course the background is only a partial explanation. The book's sense of situations, its judgement of the possibilities and limitations of circumstances, its understanding of all sorts and conditions, is no accident of timing, but a product of the author's vast curiosity, and of his ability to imagine that he himself might have drawn any sort of ticket in the lottery of life. He is not given to sententious quotations, but when pressed produced a memory of Hegel: 'tragic is the conflict, not between right and wrong, but between right and right'.

The smaller virtues of his writing are the easiest to illustrate. The anonymous reviewer in *The Economist* inexplicably referred to his footnotes as 'disappointingly erudite and unamusing', a verdict so wrong that it itself deserves a footnote in the history of reviewing. The reader can learn that the banker Aguado not only charged a 73 per cent commission on a royal loan but that he was a friend of Rossini and a former fruit-wholesaler, and that the first English-style flat-race held in Spain was won by a gypsy. The text too is enlivened with sudden colour, as when General Quesadas's severed hand is 'passed round the tables of the Café Nuevo'. Analysis is helped with strange example: Javier de Burgos's proposed reforms include the castration of merino sheep, chairs of arithmetic, and free soap; Madrid's occupational structure includes five guitar-string manufacturers and six manufacturers of false teeth. Something seen not only conveys a point, but the author's enjoyment: 'Diego de León's noble conduct to the soldiers who shot him entered romantic mythology; the cigars he had distributed to his escort now repose, with his uniforms, in the Madrid Military Museum'.

Such touches never interrupt a continuous flow of hypothesis and

[3] Nor by the British Council.

judgement. He never wrote a thesis himself, he has never written a scholarly monograph, and thinks he would have been incapable of doing either. He has never squeezed an archive to the last footnote, though his work draws on much more original material than his modest use of footnotes lets on. He would not, I feel, claim or desire to be called 'definitive', yet he has the quality of leaving no subject, no theme, the same as when he came fresh to it. That is true not only of *Spain 1808–1936*—his first book, published when he was 47—but of all his work, on Spain, on fox-hunting, on Puerto Rico, on what he writes about as a reviewer. In the classification of his old friend Isaiah Berlin—the living thinker who has influenced him most—he is a fox, one who knows many things, and a fox ahead of the field. 'I have no enemies,' he quotes General Narváez, 'I have had them all shot.' He would not want it said that on the history of modern Spain he has no rivals, for he is a generous admirer of the contributions that others—Spanish, French, British, North American—have made to Spanish historiography in its vast expansion since his first book appeared, but he surely has no rival as the master of many debates.[4]

These thoughts are provoked by rereading *Spain 1808–1936*. If the book looks less original now than when it appeared, that is because of the impact it has had on so much thinking. Though the book baffled some lesser reviewers, his few peers never doubted its importance. Gerald Brenan, the unwitting cause of its having been written at all, hailed it as a masterpiece in the *New York Review of Books*: for a while, he wanted to resume his own historical studies under the guidance of this new master. Looking at the book again in its solemn English format, I remember I once visited the parish church of Virginia Water, Surrey, and found there a handsome marble monument to the Carlist General Ramón Cabrera, dead in exile, reminding an indifferent congregation of conflicts they can never have had much inkling about. The book is as grand and as surprising as that memorial.[5]

Most of the essays in this collection are by his grateful pupils in

---

[4] For some recent views of his own on the course of Spanish historiography see his 1987 speech at the Universidad Internacional Menéndez Pelayo, printed as 'Reflexiones sobre la historia de Espana', *Vuelta* (Mexico City), 133/4 (Dec. 1987–Jan. 1988), 34–6.

[5] Ramon Cabrera (1806–77), 'The Tiger of the Maestrazgo'. At one point he shot '1110 prisoners of war, 100 officers and many civilians, including the wives of four leading *isabellinos*', to avenge his mother, who had been held as a hostage and executed. After the second Carlist war he made his way to London and in 1850 married Miss Marianne Catherine Vaughan-Richards; they resided at Wentworth House (now Wentworth Golf Club) and in Eaton Square. He refused to take up arms again in 1872, and in 1875 published his allegiance to Alfonso XII: 'an old man, long accustomed to a

Spanish history. While their authors studied, Raymond was successively Fellow of New College, Fellow of St Antony's College, Professor of the History of Latin America, and Warden of St Antony's
College. He has been responsible for an unprecedented academic
exchange between Oxford and Spain.[6] Latin American as well as
Spanish history is in his debt—he more than anyone established the
study of Latin America in Oxford. If this book deals exclusively with
the history of Spain, it is partly for the sound reason that a book should
have a theme, and partly because, despite his incursions into Latin
American history, he has remained first and foremost a historian of
Spain. Latin America, he swiftly realized, was no simple extension of
Iberia. His work on it further demonstrates his gifts of sympathy and
curiosity, his intellectual energy, his ability to worry any expert with a
sudden insight. His book on Puerto Rico—written for the Twentieth
Century Fund: 'the only thing I ever did for money'—has become a
subject of perpetual dispute in that ever disputatious island. Yet Spain
is his abiding subject.

'Subject' may seem too cold a word. Why not 'love'? He has been
heard to argue that you can study a country just as well detesting it as
loving it, and loving does not quite fit his cerebral and unromantic
approach to all countries, Spain included. One loves people, or dogs,
or fox-hunting, not countries—which does not of course preclude an
immense and abiding liking. He likes as much as anything the conver-
sational quality of Spanish intellectual and political life—'there is no
intellectual social life in Oxford'—even though as one slightly deaf he
finds it now impossible to carry on a decent conversation amid the
noise of the average Spanish restaurant. He has still much more to say
on Spanish politics and history and culture, and he will continue to
visit Spain and to write on Spain. His devotees should therefore in
future take him to eat in private rooms; from the more audible
exchange of ideas with this singular and generous spirit, they will not
emerge the poorer.

---

comfortable exile in England, he had lost faith in the simple creed of Carlism'—*Spain*,
p. 338. He was a substantial landowner in the Virginia Water district; as one of his
memorial inscriptions reads, 'There the wicked cease from troubling, and the weary be
at rest' (Job 3: 17). (My thanks to R. G. Davis Esq. of the Egham-by-Runymede Historical Society.)

[6] I do not list the names in this traffic for three reasons: (i) because the list would be
too long; (ii) because I am afraid of leaving someone out; (iii) because Raymond never
sought to form a school, and his help and influence have been acknowledged by many
historians who would not be on such a formal list.

2. AN ÉLITE OF GRACE: THE SPANISH BISHOPS IN THE TWENTIETH CENTURY

Frances Lannon

Twentieth-century Spanish bishops owed and still owe their most characteristic and enduring influence to their traditional role as leaders of dioceses within the Roman Catholic Church. The pivotal position between the diocesan faithful and the ultimate ecclesiastical authority in Rome was established by episcopal consecration. It could be enhanced by a man's gifts of leadership and—for much of the century —by political office, but the pivot remained consecration and appointment to a particular see. In the course of this century, however, the Spanish hierarchy has also emerged as an organized élite with both the means and the will to act collectively in national politics. Internal ecclesiastical factors, including more frequent communication between bishops, improved bureaucratic resources, and new ideas about how the episcopacy should function, contributed decisively to this new phenomenon. It seems that the bishops acquired the group consciousness, coherence, and common will to action often identified as necessary by the major classical theorists of effective élite formation.[1] Often they intervened dramatically and controversially in national policies.

It would be misleading, however, to see the development of this élite role as steady and continuous. It was also shaped by the peculiar problems of successive political systems in Spain, and was often provoked by national crisis. Moreover, collective decisions have rarely been unanimous, and differences of opinion have sometimes been fundamental. The pastoral relationship of each bishop with his own diocese has remained important, as has the Church's varying success in impressing its values and beliefs on Spanish society. In so far as the bishops have been a powerful élite in Spanish political life, their

---

[1] The classic texts are V. Pareto, *The Rise and Fall of the Elites* (first publ. in article form, 1901); G. Mosca, *The Ruling Class* (first publ. 1896, enlarged 1923); R. Michels, *Political Parties* (first publ. 1911). For a useful survey of these and later writers, see G. Parry, *Political Elites* (London, 1969).

influence has varied with both political opportunity, and also—in the long term—with the irresistible growth of cultural as well as political pluralism. However frequent their meetings, professional their bureaucratic backing, and effective their channels of communication, their role as a national élite in the 1980s as necessarily more circumscribed than in some earlier periods this century.

At the beginning of the century there were nine metropolitan sees headed by archbishops (Toledo, Burgos, Granada, Santiago, Seville, Tarragona, Valencia, Saragossa, and Valladolid), each with a group of dioceses round it. There were forty-seven such suffragan sees, making a total of fifty-six bishops in charge of Spanish dioceses and archdioceses, with an occasional auxiliary bishop added when local circumstances required. This total remained fairly constant until the 1950s and 1960s, when various circumstances combined to increase it. Firstly, a handful of new dioceses were created to meet the pastoral needs of particular Spanish provinces; for example San Sebastián and Bilbao were carved out of the diocese of Vitoria in 1950. Then two new metropolitan sees, Oviedo and Pamplona, were established to permit a regrouping of ecclesiastical provinces. And Madrid and Barcelona, although remaining within the ancient divisions of Toledo and Tarragona respectively, became archbishoprics in recognition of the obvious importance of these two cities.[2] Finally, during the 1960s and early 1970s a rapidly growing number of auxiliary bishops were appointed to heavily populated sees, bringing the usual total of active bishops to about eighty, an increase of one-third over the earlier tally of approximately sixty.

These men were named directly by the Vatican during the Second Republic—which unilaterally abrogated the concordat of 1851—and after 1976, when King Juan Carlos renounced the crown's right of presentation to bishoprics only months after Franco's death and his own accession to the throne.[3] Before 1931, and from the agreement reached between Franco and the Vatican in 1941 until 1976, episcopal appointments emerged after complex processes of recommendation and scrutiny by both the Spanish government and the Holy See.[4] Such

---

[2] For a useful table showing the evolution of diocesan sees in Spain 1850–1970s, see V. Cárcel Ortí (ed.), *Historia de la Iglesia en España*, v (Madrid, 1979) (henceforth *HIE*), 199–201.

[3] Agreement of 28 July 1976, in *HIE* 771–2.

[4] According to the *convenio* of 7 June 1941, the apostolic nuncio in Madrid sent to the pope a list of at least six names whenever a vacancy arose. The pope then selected three, from which the head of state chose one. There were provisions, however, for the pope to

changes in the source of appointment immediately reveal conflicting views on the role of the episcopacy. For the first thirty years of the twentieth century, there was wide agreement that political as well as ecclesiastical criteria had to be satisfied before a man was consecrated bishop. In the 1930s, politicians on the left imposed their contrary opinion that religion was a private matter, and that the naming of bishops, like the funding of the Church's pastoral work, had nothing to do with the Spanish state. The Franco regime reverted to Spain's traditional regalist claims and eventually succeeded in gaining the reluctant agreement of Pius XII, who would have preferred to guard against possible political manipulation of the Spanish Church by the state, through securing for the Vatican greater independence in the appointment of Spanish bishops.[5] This discrepancy became much more radical after the Second Vatican Council's insistence on the Church's autonomy relative to all political systems, and in 1968 Pope Paul VI asked Franco to renounce the right of presentation. Although this request was refused, and wider bi-lateral negotiations about strained Church–state relations were proposed instead, it was evident that it was only a matter of time — and perhaps of a change in regime — before Spain fell into line with the post-conciliar Vatican norm. In January 1973 the Spanish bishops themselves formally asked the Spanish state to reconsider its position.[6] Since the 1976 *convenio*, the Vatican has merely informed Spanish governments of its forthcoming episcopal nominations.

For most of this century, then, the Spanish episcopacy as an ecclesiastical élite was created partly by the Vatican and partly by Spanish governments, with the Vatican eventually winning greater and then total control. The turning point was undoubtedly the papacy of Paul VI (1963–78). When Franco declined his invitation to withdraw from the presentation to bishoprics, Paul VI outmanoeuvred him by appointing auxiliary or coadjutor bishops, or apostolic administrators — categories not covered by the 1953 concordat. Whereas there were five auxiliary bishops in 1966, there were no fewer than seventeen in 1973, representing over 20 per cent of the total of seventy-nine

---

substitute candidates he preferred to those on the original list, and for the head of state to raise objections 'of a general political character' (*HIE* 740–1).

[5] The essential study, printed with all the relevant documents, is A. Marquina Barrio, *La diplomacia vaticana y la España de Franco (1936–1945)* (Madrid, 1983).

[6] *Sobre la iglesia y la comunidad política*, para. 59, in J. Iribarren (ed.), *Documentos colectivos del episcopado español 1870–1974* (Madrid, 1974), 548–9.

active bishops.[7] In these crucial years when the teaching of the Second Vatican Council had to be promulgated in Spain, the Vatican had found a way of rapidly making the episcopacy younger and more sympathetic to its orientation. But it was always true that the bishops, while a Spanish élite, were dependent on and answerable to Rome. By vocation, education, and hierarchical position, they formed an élite within the Church before and more profoundly than they were an active élite within the political structures of the Spanish state.

A study made in 1973 concluded that of the sixty-five bishops about whose background adequate information was available, fifty came from lower and lower-middle classes—categories taken to include occupations ranging from unskilled manual work to small peasant farming and primary school teaching. Another thirteen were the sons of men in the liberal professions, army officers, or the middle ranks of commerce and industry. Only two had been born into families of higher social status. Equally clear was the distribution by place of birth. Of seventy-nine bishops, only fourteen had been born in Madrid, Barcelona, or provincial capitals; the other sixty-five came from lesser population centres, often small rural towns or villages. The seventy-nine were amply provided with first degrees and often doctorates, but overwhelmingly in theological and ecclesiastical subjects studied in Church seminaries, although there was a greater sprinkling of qualifications in secular subjects taken at Spanish universities than would have been the case earlier in the century. Like the diocesan clergy from which they are almost all selected (there were just two bishops from the religious orders in the 1973 survey), the occupants of Spanish episcopal sees have characteristically been of rural or small town origin, from modest or moderately comfortable families, and educated from the age of 11 or 12 entirely in ecclesiastical establishments, almost exclusively by priests.[8] The recent trend towards later vocations and a longer secular education is now modifying this pattern, but slowly.

Similar social and cultural as well as intellectual formation must have contributed to a sense of shared identity by the bishops. Nor does their modest social background appear to have disadvantaged them when representing the Church's interests among the holders of politi-

[7] J. M. Vázquez, F. Medín, L. Méndez, *La iglesia española contemporánea* (Madrid, 1973), 107.
[8] Ibid. 107–31.

cal power, wealth, and status.[9] They derived their authority and prestige not from birth and social connection but from office.

Priests were consecrated bishop when ecclesiastical authorities—often the papal nuncio—and for most of the century civil authorities too, perceived in them qualities of piety, intelligence, and leadership. The dioceses to which they were appointed varied enormously. In 1968, for example, the archbishop of Barcelona had responsibility for a population of about two and a half million, and the archbishop of Madrid for over three million, while their colleagues in Barbastro, Ibiza, Menorca, and Tudela counted fewer than 50,000 residents each in their dioceses. In the same year, the archbishop of Pamplona could draw on the resources of over twice as many priests as the archbishop of Seville to minister to a diocese only half as extensive, and with less than a quarter the number of inhabitants.[10] Being a bishop meant very different things in different parts of Spain. It could mean presiding over intensely Catholic parts of Spanish society or struggling to make the Church's presence felt in areas of low religious practice and few priests; it could place a man at the heart of political strife or urban problems, or it could dispatch him to depopulated rural wastelands. The actual diocese was the essential factor and, given the contrasts they provided, it cannot always have been easy for the sixty or so bishops at the beginning of the century or their more numerous successors in the 1980s to experience as a felt reality the group identity, coherence, and common will to action theoretically desirable in an effective élite.

Each bishop was separately accountable to the pope in periodic *ad limina* visits and reports, and enjoyed almost unlimited powers within his own diocese. He supervised seminary education, appointed the staff, ordained new priests, and then placed them and moved them at his discretion; he approved or blocked pastoral initiatives; he was ultimately responsible for diocesan finances and buildings and schools; he was the final authority on spiritual and moral affairs for the laity. He was monarch in his own kingdom, or—in more usual ecclesiastical language—shepherd of his flock. But whether as monarch with its emphasis on power, or shepherd with its stress on pastoral care, he was sole and undisputed. His episcopal consecration, his mitre and crook,

---

[9] Mosca considered such 'democratic' recruitment a major disadvantage for the Roman Catholic Church, but he concentrated on the organization and prestige of an élite group, rather than its institutional base, which was in this case the key factor. G. Mosca, *The Ruling Class* (New York and London, 1939), 425.
[10] *Guía de la iglesia en España* (Madrid, 1970), 34–5.

marked him out as uniquely in charge, at the head of the complex hierarchy within his own diocese.

It could be argued that the Spanish bishops became a coherent, organized élite precisely during this century, as the structures and practice of joint action gradually counter-balanced the individual and separate role of each one. There had been occasional earlier instances of bishops within the same ecclesiastical province addressing themselves jointly to the monarch, government, or pope, but communications from the whole hierarchy began when the Spanish bishops in Rome for the Vatican Council in 1870 protested to the Constituent Cortes about the proposed legalization of civil marriage. Nearly thirty years passed before the Catholic hierarchy again thought it appropriate to express its views openly and formally to the civil authorities, when in 1896 it reminded the government of its duty to abide by the terms of the 1851 concordat. But even this communication was not from the whole hierarchy, but only twenty-two bishops who had met at a Eucharistic Congress and decided to act. In the intervening years a few short joint messages had been sent to the pope, and one exhortation to the faithful in 1886 on the rather distant subject of the lack of respect being shown to Pope Leo XIII in Italy, and the necessity of returning to him the papal lands lost during Italian unification. In the early years of the twentieth century joint communications to the king or government became more numerous, as the bishops grew alarmed at the whittling away of ecclesiastical privileges, especially in education. But there was no document addressed to the faithful in Spain until 1917, nearly thirty years after the attempt to engage public opinion on the unpromising question of the papal states.[11]

The 1917 letter marked the real beginning of the collective action by all the bishops of Spain relative not just to pope and government, but to the Spanish people. It was provoked by the military, political, and social crisis that came close to undermining the monarchy and threatened disorder on a revolutionary scale. Faced by what they recognized as a 'tremendous crisis', the bishops felt it their duty to address the nation on the need for social peace and justice as well as a return to law and order.[12] In 1923 another important step was taken when a junta of the metropolitan archbishops was constituted to speak on behalf of the whole hierarchy. Clearly there was a need for

[11] All in Iribarren (ed.), *Documentos colectivos*, which also has a useful survey of the emergence of collective action, in the Introduction.

[12] *Documentos colectivos*, 105–11.

authoritative statements to be formulated without always convening sixty men from all over the country. As the dissemination of information speeded up, the Church needed appropriate means of joining in public debate. From the 1920s to the 1960s, either the metropolitan archbishops, or the episcopacy as a whole, collectively addressed the Spanish people both at moments of crisis—especially during the Second Republic's attempts to close Catholic schools and weaken the Church's moral and social influence—and more generally to express official Catholic teaching on matters of faith and morals. It was in these years that the bishops gradually acquired the institutional means of exercising their influence as a national élite rather than simply as separate officials each powerful in his own diocese, or as—in some cases—individual occupants of a political post.

This slow development received an enormous boost from the Second Vatican Council held in Rome between 1962 and 1965. Because its major theme was the nature and mission of the Church, it considered the role and organization of the episcopacy at some length. The pivotal concept in the Council's understanding was that the bishops formed a 'college', or corporate body. This was true of all bishops everywhere, united with the pope and called upon to take joint responsibility for the universal Church. The Council therefore decided to inaugurate regular meetings or synods that 'will be representative of the whole Catholic episcopate, [and] will bear testimony to the participation of all the bishops in hierarchical communion in the care of the universal Church'.[13] It also pertained at diocesan level, since the Council proposed the consecration of co-adjutor and auxiliary bishops to assist the diocesan where numbers justified it, especially in big cities.[14] In Spain as elsewhere episcopal teams within a single diocese have since become common. But most dramatic in its effects was the intermediate level of the national episcopacy. Here the Council enjoined the creation of the episcopal conference, 'a form of assembly in which the bishops of a certain country or region exercise their pastoral office jointly in order to enhance the Church's beneficial influence on all men'.[15] The Spanish Episcopal Conference was duly established in 1966, with a standing council, permanent secretariat, and numerous sub-committees with particular

[13] Quotation from *Decree on the Pastoral Office of Bishops in the Church*, 28 Oct. 1965, in A. Flannery (ed.), *Vatican Council II: The Conciliar and Post-Conciliar Documents* (Leominster, 1981), 566.

[14] Ibid. 576–9.   [15] Ibid. 587.

responsibility for matters like education, the clergy, religious orders, or the apostolic work of the laity. For the first time, bishops in Spain acquired the institutional apparatus to act permanently and not just on special occasions as a coherent ecclesiastical élite, able to put forward agreed views (on the basis of a two-thirds majority) on a wide variety of topics, and to publish those views effectively. Since 1966 the Spanish Episcopal Conference and its committees have produced vast quantities of material on just about every aspect of Spanish social and political, as well as religious life. Moreover, the relevant committee with its store of information and research has been available and ready to negotiate or argue with appropriate bodies. In 1983, for example, when the Ministry of Education found unacceptable the wording on abortion in catechisms approved by the Episcopal Conference for use in secondary schools, its officials were immediately confronted by the permanent staff of the bishops' education committee, who challenged the state's right to intervene.[16]

The bishops now had a national organization and a permanent, centralized bureaucracy. They had every opportunity to attain or reinforce the group consciousness necessary for concerted action, whether in relation to government, or papacy, or Spanish Catholics. To some extent they jointly controlled the orientation of policy through their participation in debate and vote, and through the election of the president of the Conference every three years. This has enabled the bishops to bypass the leadership traditionally exercised by the archbishop of Toledo; it meant they could and did elect Paul VI's candidate, Archbishop Tarancón, to take the Church in the direction of post-conciliar reform for the decade from 1971; and they elected Tarancón's disciple Gabino Díaz Marchán, archbishop of Oviedo, in 1981 and again in 1984 when Pope John Paul II would probably have preferred a more conservative leader. In 1987 their choice of Archbishop Suquía eventually reflected the general trend towards ecclesiastical traditionalism encouraged by the pope.

The experience of a similar education and ecclesiastical experience, often roughly similar social background, and shared work in recent collegial structures have not necessarily, however, created a united and decisive élite, better able than in earlier years to assume joint leadership in the Church. On the contrary, some of the most important issues have been taken out of the bishops' hands altogether. Much the

---

[16] See a blow by blow account in A. Hernández, *Crónica de la Cruz y de la Rosa (Los Socialistas y la iglesia, hoy)* (Barcelona, 1984), 158–85.

most dramatic example of this is the series of agreements negotiated between the Vatican and the Spanish state which replaced the outdated 1953 concordat. These five agreements were reached in 1976 and 1979 and signed by the Spanish Foreign Minister and the Vatican Secretary of State. They regulated the procedures for episcopal nominations, guaranteed the freedom of action of the Church in the field of welfare, recognized the Church's right to found schools and colleges, and promised that students at Church schools would not be excluded from state grants. They recognized the juridical rights of religious communities, stipulated that religious instruction would be available in all state schools and its content determined by the bishops, affirmed that Catholic sentiments would be respected by state-owned mass media, and committed the state to the economic support of the Church and its ministry. In other words, these agreements comprehensively regulated relations between Church and state, and also secured the institutional bases for the Church's presence and activity in Spanish society. But they were not negotiated by the Spanish bishops. The bishops were consulted, and their advocacy of a series of agreements rather than a new concordat—which is what the government had initially wanted—was no doubt powerful. But their role was consultative and secondary, as they themselves clearly recognized.[17]

Princes of the Church though they be, the bishops inevitably find their authority circumscribed by the absolute monarch in the Vatican. To some extent their sphere of operation is what he permits it to be— the ideals of 'collegiality' notwithstanding—and papal decisions often pre-empt them. Probably the best recent example of this was John Paul II's dramatic award to the Opus Dei in 1982 of a privilege not even conceded to the more venerable religious orders, namely that it should form a kind of scattered 'diocese' of its own, under the jurisdiction of its own bishop. Since the Opus Dei is a world-wide organization, it is understandable that its ecclesiastical status should be determined by the Vatican. But its Spanish origins, its numerical strength in Spain, and its controversial role in both the Spanish Church and Spanish public life necessarily meant that the hierarchy there was peculiarly interested in its fortunes. And it was no secret that the pope's decision was taken against the advice of most of the Spanish bishops.[18]

[17] Accords in *HIE* 771–86. Also in *Iglesia Viva*, 79 (1979) together with commentaries. On the role of the Episcopal Conference, see F. Gil Delgado, *Conflicto Iglesia–Estado* (Madrid, 1975), 297–301.

[18] For an account of the emergence of the 'personal prelature', see D. Le Tourneau, *El Opus Dei* (Barcelona, 1986), 61–89.

The exact nature of the authority enjoyed by the Spanish Episcopal Conference remains unclear. On the one hand its 'collegial' exercise of responsibility alongside the pope depends on his willingness to permit it; on the other, it has no formal authority over individual bishops within Spain. The Second Vatican Council pointed to the joint exercise of pastoral office by episcopal conferences, but without defining any specific way in which this would or could override the authority of the individual bishop within his own diocese. The sacred rights given by episcopal consecration could be neither diminished nor enhanced by group meetings and majority decisions. Although the Spanish Episcopal Conference since its foundation over twenty years ago has been able to gather information, discuss policy, communicate ideas, and speak for the Church to the Spanish state and to Spanish society, it has not modified in any essential way the sovereignty of each bishop. In 1973, for example, the Spanish bishops issued a very important and long-awaited statement on the relationship between Church and state, explaining in detail the need for disengagement from the Franco regime.[19] This document marked the existence for the first time of a majority in favour of the orientation given by the Second Vatican Council, including separation of Church and state. It argued that, in consequence, it was inappropriate for priests and bishops to hold political office. But this solemn declaration was powerless to constrain bishops who disagreed with it, as was evident in, for example, the continuance as a nominated member of the Cortes of Bishop Guerra Campos who, moreover, published his view that decisions of the Episcopal Conference taken over against a dissenting minority lacked authority and would not be accorded normative status within his diocese.[20] Whatever the size of the majority in the Episcopal Conference—the vote in favour of the Church–state relations document was fifty-nine to twenty—it was also powerless to prevent Guerra Campos monopolizing the religious slots on state television, and becoming 'the television bishop' presenting opinions approved by Franco's governments but deplored by most of his colleagues. The bench of bishops had been institutionalized and provided with modern bureaucratic facilities, but while this improved communication and made the bishops as a body more visible and audible, it could not assure cohesion or solidarity.

[19] *Documentos colectivos*, 520–54.
[20] Gil Delgado, *Conflicto Iglesia–Estado*, 233.

The crucial bases of a bishop's authority remained what they had always been, his own see and his consecration. No one could undo the latter, and in normal circumstances it was difficult for anyone other than the pope to insist that a bishop abandon his diocese. Although translation from one see to another was very common, providing the normal method of promotion within the hierarchy, it was possible for a bishop to choose to stay put. In 1914, for example, Bishop Torras i Bages preferred to remain in the Catalan see of Vich rather than become archbishop of Valencia. In the 1920s Primo de Rivera attempted to transfer Cardinal Vidal i Barraquer, archbishop of the Catalan see of Tarragona, out of the region, first to Granada or Saragossa, then later to Burgos. No promotion was entailed, although all three sees were richer than Tarragona. The motive behind the attempted move was clearly political, since the government was involved at the time in a trial of strength with the Catalan bishops about the use of Catalan in catechesis and preaching. Vidal i Barraquer declined to go, and could not be moved.[21]

A very different incident fifty years later again demonstrated how hard it was to separate a bishop from his diocese. In February 1974 Bishop Añoveros of Bilbao authorized the reading of a prepared homily in all churches of his Basque diocese, which covered the troubled province of Vizcaya. The defence of the rights and customs of ethnic minorities which it contained infuriated a regime whose prime minister, Admiral Carrero Blanco, had been assassinated by Basque terrorists just two months earlier. Carrero Blanco's successor, Arias Navarro, ordered Añoveros out of the country, but he refused, specifically on the grounds that no one but the pope had the right to make a bishop abandon his see. Earlier in the century the Vatican had agreed in exceptionally fraught circumstances to the exile and replacement of bishops regarded as undesirable by governments—Cardinal Segura under the Republic, and Cardinal Vidal i Barraquer and Bishop Múgica early in Franco's dictatorship—but on this occasion no agreement was forthcoming. It is also instructive to note that the Spanish hierarchy publicly supported Añoveros, even though the president of the Episcopal Conference, Cardinal Tarancón, had tried to dissuade him from authorizing material that was orthodox in content but inflammatory in context and timing. A united but embarrassed hierarchy

---

[21] R. Muntanyola, *Vidal i Barraquer, Cardenal de la pau* (Montserrat, 1976), 136–9, 180–4.

rallied to the defence of one of their number, not because of agreed policy reached through the new group methods, but because of the ancient tie between bishop and his see, and bishop and pope.[22]

Even when concerted policy-making and planning by a group of bishops was deemed useful by all of them, the question remained as to whether the appropriate unit was the entire hierarchy. Were they a national ecclesiastical élite addressing the people or government of Spain, or a more local élite with peculiarly local pastoral concerns? This question arose insistently in Catalonia and the Basque provinces. After the appointment of Vidal i Barraquer to the metropolitan see of Tarragona in 1919, joint initiatives by all the bishops of Catalonia on pastoral matters became common. Plans for youth programmes, liturgy, and lay associations were co-ordinated at regional level, because there were common circumstances and problems that could be discussed more effectively there than at either national or diocesan level. A proposed Catalan ecclesiastical council did not survive the advent of Primo de Rivera's centralizing dictatorship, but the Catalan bishops continued to meet periodically and issue joint statements on specifically Catalan pastoral issues.[23] This development was pragmatic, not political, although it was regarded with suspicion for political reasons by the government. What defined the Catalan bishops as a group within Catalonia and within the Spanish hierarchy was their experience as ecclesiastical leaders in a region with a well-developed identity and culture. It is not surprising that Spanish governments under the monarchy up to 1931, and under the Franco regime, often ensured that Catalan sees were occupied by non-Catalan incumbents.[24] An organized and consciously regional ecclesiastical élite was bound to seem troublesome in a centralist state.

In the last years of the Franco regime the Basque provinces were the most unsettled and violent region of Spain, with Basque terrorists and a militarized police force engaged in constant conflict from 1968.[25] Church leaders could not escape involvement, accused as they were on the one hand of complicity with a Catholic but unchristian political system committed to the use of torture and repression, and on the

---

[22] Gil Delgado, *Conflicto Iglesia–Estado*, 259–62.

[23] Muntanyola, *Vidal i Barraquer*, 111–22.

[24] J. Massot i Muntaner, 'El Vaticà i Catalunya', *Qüestions de vida cristiana*, 109 (Montserrat, 1981), 43–63.

[25] That year marked the escalation of conflict between ETA and the state into armed violence on both sides, with the killing of an ETA man by the Civil Guard, and the assassination by ETA of a police chief in San Sebastián.

other of defending terrorism.[26] In these circumstances, the bishops of the two Basque provinces where political and armed confrontation was most acute, Vizcaya and Guipúzcoa, issued joint statements. In December 1969, for example, Bishop Cirarda of Bilbao and Bishop Argaya Goicoechea of San Sebastián wrote a joint pastoral letter about political violence in the area, condemning both terrorism and police infringements of basic civil rights.[27] The following November they published another joint pastoral letter as the trial began in Burgos, before a military tribunal, of Basque defendants—including two priests charged with terrorism. This was a brief communication of only a few pages offering to the people of their dioceses an account of the efforts made by the two bishops to have the trial held in an open, civil court, and to have any eventual death penalties commuted.[28] Between 1969 and 1979 no fewer than twelve official joint communications were issued on Basque problems, with the participation in later years of the bishops of the other Basque sees of Pamplona and then Vitoria.[29]

This combined action depended upon incumbents with a common view of the crisis in the Basque provinces, but it also reflected a social and political reality peculiar to the region, and especially to two provinces within the region. Joint statements seemed more appropriate sometimes than individual ones, because the problems addressed did not stop at the boundaries of one diocese. But detailed statements from the whole of the Spanish hierarchy would obviously have been inappropriate. Cirarda and Argaya Goicoechea and their successors had something to say together, not because they formed part of a Spanish ecclesiastical élite, but because they were bishops of particular Basque dioceses with particular traditions and conflicts. It is not surprising that Basque priests who were dissatisfied with the links between the Church and Franco's dictatorship should call explicitly— though unsuccessfully—for the creation of a Basque Episcopal Conference that would remove the four Basque dioceses from the ambit of the Spanish hierarchy.[30] The kind of leadership they wanted in the

---

[26] For a fuller discussion, see F. Lannon, *Privilege, Persecution, and Prophecy: The Catholic Church in Spain 1875–1975* (Oxford, 1987), 107–13, 251–2.

[27] The letter, dated 26 Oct. 1969, in *Boletín Eclesiástico del Obispado de Bilbao (BEOB)*, 231 (Dec. 1969), 581–602.

[28] Letter dated 21 Nov. 1970 in *BEOB* 242 (Dec. 1970), 500–3.

[29] Catalogued in special issue of *BEOB* 326 (Jan.–Feb. 1979).

[30] Text in P. Iztueta, *Sociología del fenómeno contestatorio del clero vasco 1940–75* (San Sebastián, 1981), 420–33.

local Church had nothing to gain and much to lose, in their view, from identification with a Spanish élite.

In other areas too, for example Andalusia, bishops grouped together to study and comment on regional problems in the 1970s, applying the Second Vatican Council principle of rooting pastoral initiatives in social reality.[31] Everywhere this tendency was encouraged by the fostering of regional autonomy in the new democratic constitution of the Spanish state, promulgated in 1978. With regional parliaments and governments suddenly emerging, there was also pressure on bishops to function at regional, as well as diocesan and national, level. This is still a very recent development, however, of uncertain results. It is not clear how effective bishops can be as a regional élite when they are so often appointed from outside the area and can be promoted away again, when diocesan boundaries invariably do not coincide neatly with regional or provincial ones, and when the political ramifications of local autonomy are so often themselves controversial.[32] But it remains true that regionalism, like the traditional importance of the individual see, necessarily modifies the capacity of the Spanish hierarchy to act consciously as a cohesive national élite.

In so far as the bishops have acted as a national élite in the twentieth century, they have done so in unusual circumstances, and on special issues of major importance for the Spanish state and Spanish society as well as for the Church. They first issued a document called a 'collective declaration' in the turbulence of 1917, when they were convinced that 'the very existence and future' of the social life of the nation was at stake, and their message was one of instruction and exhortation to politicians and people. This provided a marked contrast with, for example, the protests written specifically to King Alfonso XIII in 1905 and 1906 over attempts by Liberal governments to curtail, respectively, ecclesiastical courts and the expansion of the religious orders. Whereas both of these, and a similar address to Prime Minister Antonio Maura in 1909 about lay schools, presented a formal episcopal view on matters directly concerning the Church, the 1917 document laid claim to a wider, more general responsibility before the whole people on a crisis that was not specifically ecclesiastical at all. It was followed in 1922 by a collective letter explicitly 'to the nation' on

---

[31] Andalusian bishops issued collective letters, e.g. on emigration (1973), regional unemployment (1975), and Andalusian autonomy (1980).

[32] For an early survey of some of the problems and initiatives, see special issue of *Misión abierta* (June 1981).

social conflicts that were seen as a threat to both Church and country.[33]

In calmer times, when Church leaders felt more confident of government sympathy, the tone and subject-matter of statements made by the bishops changed, as they reverted to preoccupation with individual piety and morality, and the safeguarding of ecclesiastical interests. Primo de Rivera's dictatorship from 1923 to 1930 was on the whole very favourable to the Church. In these years the bishops—or rather the new junta of metropolitan archbishops on their behalf—contented themselves with an exhortation to the faithful on modesty (1926) and a request to the government to increase priests' pay and help repress immorality and maintain Sunday as a day of rest (1928). Similarly, in the first decade of the Franco regime the committee of archbishops produced only two formal statements, one on Protestant propaganda (1948) and one on the defence of Catholic values in the press, cinema, theatre, and radio (1950).[34]

Larger claims were made, inevitably, when there was a sense of crisis as in 1917 and bishops undertook to speak to and for the nation on matters that concerned the Church but were not narrowly ecclesiastical. It is therefore not surprising that no fewer than six major, and often lengthy, documents were issued by the bishops or in their name in the first two years of the Second Republic, when the Constitution and subsequent legislation set about not just separating Church and state but also undermining the Church's traditional position in Spanish society.[35] This is not to say that all bishops interpreted these events in exactly the same way, or agreed on precisely what the appropriate response might be. Vidal i Barraquer, for instance, asked —too late—that Cardinal Segura should not publish on behalf of the hierarchy the trenchant attack on the draft Constitution that he wrote in exile in July 1931. But all the bishops were bound to view the Constitution with alarm, especially the attack on Catholic education in general and the schools of the religious orders in particular. And there could be no fundamental disagreement about the need to oppose such measures and offer an alternative interpretation of the proper role of the state relative to Spanish society and the Church. In the careful and solemn criticism of the new Constitution which the bishops issued in December 1931, it is instructive that they explained their duty as that

---

[33] All in *Documentos colectivos*.
[34] Ibid. 117–23, 125–30, 242–57.
[35] Ibid. 130–212.

of ecclesiastical leaders, defending the doctrine and rights of the Church, and emphatically also as that of citizens, committed to the public well-being of the nation.[36] When the issues were sufficiently clear and profound, the Catholic hierarchy spoke to, and in its own view for, the nation rather than just the Church. Circumstances of crisis made it into a national élite in a different sense from its role in gentler times, and its voice was powerful, notwithstanding the polemical and contested nature of its claim to speak for Spain.

Of all the statements by the Spanish hierarchy this century, the collective letter of 1 July 1937 *On the Spanish War* was the most controversial. Prepared by Archbishop Gomá with Franco's encouragement, it was addressed, most unusually, not to the Spanish faithful or civic or military authorities, but to the Catholic bishops of the whole world. It stated that the account it gave of the origins and nature of the Civil War was 'not the demonstration of a thesis, but the simple exposition, in broad outline, of the facts', and that the bishops wrote out of patriotic and humanitarian duty as well as pastoral responsibility. Gomá clearly thought he and his episcopal colleagues were by virtue of their office authoritative interpreters of Spanish politics and history. His view of the war, as a conflict between atheistic materialism and religion, identified the Church with the true Spain, and true Spain with the cause of Franco. As the letter recognized, Catholic Basque Nationalists on the 'wrong' side spoilt this neat division, but they were dismissed as misguided. Spanish bishops acted as a national élite only by excluding from their definition of the nation all left-of-centre political and union movements and their supporters, and all anti-centralist dissident Catholics. Twelve of them were killed, offering their lives for Spain as well as for God. But it was significant that the signatures of Mateo Múgica, Basque bishop of the Basque see of Vitoria, and the Catalan Cardinal Vidal i Barraquer were missing. Even in the extreme circumstances of a bitter Civil War, there was disagreement about the appropriateness of assuming the public role of a national élite committed to the victory of one side in the war in order to defend Catholic interests.[37]

During the early years of the Franco regime, a renewed and purged hierarchy (neither Múgica nor Vidal i Barraquer was allowed back to his see) experienced little conflict between the political aims of the

[36] *Documentos colectivos*, 161, 170.
[37] Ibid. 219–42. On the missing signatories, see Lannon, *Privilege, Persecution, and Prophecy*, 204–6.

dictatorship and the pastoral aims of the Church. On the contrary, the Church powerfully legitimated a regime whose military victory it had staunchly supported. In 1939 Gomá suffered the indignity of having a pastoral letter, *Lessons of the War and the Duties of Peace*, banned because it stressed the limitations of state authority and the need for widespread political participation. But there were no collective statements until the two in 1948 and 1950 on more narrowly religious matters. In circumstances of ideological harmony, the bishops as a collective body kept a low profile, while individual prelates concentrated on using to the full, each in his own diocese, the new opportunities for religious restoration. It is likely that bishops in the first post-war decade had a strong sense of common identity and shared mission, but little need or inclination to express these as a group.

The gradual emergence of a new public role for the hierarchy in the 1950s and 1960s was analysed many years ago by Guy Hermet.[38] He pointed out that religious leaders were able to criticize aspects of the political system on social and economic rather than strictly religious grounds, and to defend particular groups not defined primarily by Church membership—striking workers, the low-paid, the unemployed—who lacked formal structures for representation and protest. It is interesting to note, however, that this 'tribune' function of limited political criticism and informal representation of vulnerable groups involved some bishops but not others. Indeed, by widening the interpretation some bishops made of their pastoral role into spheres that others considered inappropriately political, it made it extremely difficult to achieve a common view. This was especially obvious in the first years of the new Episcopal Conference, established in 1966, which set out to contain and channel the radical Catholic Action lay organizations in industry and agriculture that were mobilizing working-class protest over wages, working conditions, and the lack of proper trade union representation. The first leaders of the Episcopal Conference, particularly Morcillo the vice-president, and Guerra Campos the secretary, were out of sympathy with the developments within the lay organizations and expelled some chaplains, placed restrictions on the lay leaders, and devised constricting new constitutions that were quite unacceptable to them. A substantial majority of bishops approved their actions, but a minority of thirteen voted against the new statutes in

[38] G. Hermet, 'Les Fonctions politiques des organisations religieuses dans les régimes à pluralisme limité', *Revue française de science politique*, 23/3 (June 1973), 439–72.

1967. Within a few years—too late to be of use to working-class radicals—the balance had shifted the other way as new appointments and the permeating influence of the Second Vatican Council had their effect.[39] But on whichever side the majority fell, the underlying issue was divisive. Bishops no longer agreed, as they had done in the 1940s, about how lay Catholics, or priests, or they themselves, should relate to the Catholic Spanish state, its political structures, and its social policy. Until Franco's death in 1975 controversy continued within the Conference over whether Spain should remain a confessional Catholic state, over the legitimacy of political protest, and the desirability of political pluralism. Between 1966 and 1975 bishops were rarely out of public sight, but there was no consensus among them. The very debate about the political future that engulfed them and demanded a series of public statements also by its nature made unanimity unlikely. The more political circumstances in these tense years required the bishops to take a stand—on the Constitution, the economy, civil rights—the further they moved from narrowly devotional or ecclesiastical preoccupations. They became an institutional élite committed to political reform, but a divided élite.

In the first years after Franco's death Spanish bishops, like all their compatriots, were preoccupied by major constitutional issues. The direction was set by the homily of Cardinal Tarancón, archbishop of Madrid and president of the Episcopal Conference, at the accession of King Juan Carlos.[40] This in turn was the culmination of many recent episcopal documents—dating back to the crucial collective statement, *On the Church and the Political Community* of 1973—that looked towards democratic and pluralist politics. Disengagement not just from the confessional state, but from the authoritarian regime was evident. Not all bishops were convinced by the arguments, and a minority would have preferred instead to perpetuate the political and institutional outlines of 'Catholic Spain'.[41] The official line, however, was clear and consistent; the hierarchy was on the side of some kind of democratic transition.

With the transition progressing well in the general elections of 1977 and the debates on the new Constitution, and many long-standing problems in Church–state relations being settled in the Vatican–

---

[39] For a fuller discussion, see Lannon, *Privilege, Persecution, and Prophecy*, 231–8.

[40] Text in V. E. y Tarancón, M. González, and N. Jubany, *Iglesia y política en la España de hoy* (Salamanca, 1980), 137–43.

[41] See e.g. the contribution of Cardinal González Martín, archbishop of Toledo in ibid. 85–112.

Spanish accords of 1976–9, the bishops entered a prolonged period of controversy that was both new and traditional. The new issues notoriously centred on Catholic education, sexual morality, and the family. It was as though, after the extraordinary circumstances of the last years of the Franco regime and the first of the monarchy, the Church's leaders could return to their permanent preoccupations with the transmission of Catholic culture and the defence of Catholic morality and doctrine.[42] Probably the strongest indication that the new state would not do this job on the Church's behalf, even when the Christian Democrat UCD was still in power, was the legalizing of divorce in July 1981. The Socialist victory in the general elections of 1982 inevitably heralded further changes of which many bishops disapproved, notably Education Minister Maravall's reforms of secondary education. Important and contentious as these questions were, however, it was nevertheless true that the bishops were once again busy about the promotion and defence of confessional, ecclesiastical matters, arguing their case in a way that they had not done since the incomparably more difficult days of the Second Republic. In the new democratic politics, the religious hegemony of the 1940s and 1950s was impossible, the tribune role of the 1960s and early 1970s unnecessary. The role of the bishops changed, because their political and social context changed.

It is ironic that the Episcopal Conference was strongly criticized for not denouncing the attempted coup by Tejero on 23 February 1981. While Tejero brandished his gun in the Cortes, the Conference was in deepest retreat, pondering the election of a successor to Tarancón, whose term of office as president had ended that very morning. When the bishops were informed of the Cortes drama, no denunciation was forthcoming, only a promise that they 'would pray'. It is probably the case, as Tarancón later claimed, that they were caught temporarily leaderless and almost in abeyance, rather than that their silence denoted any sinister willingness to accept a threatened new dictatorship.[43] The irony is that they were widely expected to issue a statement immediately in defence of democracy, at just the time when such transcendent constitutional issues seemed to be disappearing from their agenda and the bishops were adapting to the more limited role

---

[42] The change in emphasis is charted in FOESSA, *Informe sociológico sobre el cambio social en España 1975–1983* (Madrid, 1983), 575–80.

[43] J. L. Martín Descalzo, *Tarancón, el cardenal del cambio* (Barcelona, 1982), 248–50.

that democracy itself imposed on them, that of spokesmen for Catholic moral and social values.

The kind of influence exercised by the bishops as a group, and its extent, has always depended not just on the inner cohesion of the hierarchy, the efficacy of its structures for decision-making and communication, and its will to action but also, and decisively, on the scope permitted by Spanish society and politics. It has functioned visibly as an organized political élite most successfully at times when both political consensus and adequate methods for expressing and mediating disagreement were lacking, during the Second Republic, the Civil War, and the closing years of the Franco regime. Under the protection of authoritarian governments with few significant opponents, that is during both Primo de Rivera's and much of Franco's dictatorships, bishops tended to see little need for joint action, concentrating instead on pastoral affairs within their own dioceses and ritual legitimation of official Catholic Spain. If the role of the bishops since 1977–8 as an active élite arguing for Catholic social and moral doctrine within an accepted, constitutional pluralism has any precedent this century, it is the inexact one of the pleas against the erosion of the Church's influence made to Liberal governments in the Alfonsine monarchy.

While shaped to a considerable extent by its own changing membership, theologies, and structures, the Spanish episcopacy as an élite in public life has also acted as circumstances allowed or demanded. The underlying, irreducible concern has been the promotion of ecclesiastical interests and Catholic values as variously understood at different times. What has become apparent in a political system that is neither confessional nor hostile, and in which the bishops are not required specifically as spokesmen for anything but Church interests, is that their role depends ultimately on their pastoral success. The hierarchy's voice echoes as boomingly or as faintly as Catholic conviction in Spanish society determines. It appears that the extra magnification provided so often this century either by an elaborately maintained cultural hegemony or by political crisis has faded. It is truer now than at any earlier point this century that the strength of the bishops as an élite in Spanish social and political life depends on their influence on their own clergy and faithful within the Roman Catholic Church. Intra- rather than extra-ecclesial factors are the essential determinants. With an established Episcopal Conference and bureaucracy, bishops will not revert to the purely diocesan role of many of their predecessors before the institutional changes that began in 1917, yet the ancient links of bishop and pope, bishop and faithful, inside the Church remain fundamental. The greatest threat to the bishops' influence is simply the marked decline in religious practice, and the gradual detachment of many sectors of the Spanish population from religious traditions and loyalties.

3. CENTRE AND PERIPHERY 1900–1936: NATIONAL INTEGRATION AND REGIONAL NATIONALISMS RECONSIDERED

Juan Pablo Fusi Aizpúrua

Regional nationalisms have been in Spain like the Anglo-Irish question in British politics, 'One of those desperate problems of internal government which admit of no smooth and satisfying solutions', to put it in H. A. L. Fisher's classic words. This became evident in the years between 1900 and 1936 and has remained so ever since. Basque nationalism constituted the main obstacle to political stability in the transition towards democracy after General Franco's death in 1975.

The problem has a long history. Historians tend to put the blame on the centralizing efforts of the Spanish state after the establishment of the Bourbon dynasty in the eighteenth century. This is a view which ignores the many weaknesses of Spain's central state in both the eighteenth and nineteenth centuries. It somehow disregards the complexities which surround the emergence of national consciousness on both the national and regional levels. Besides, we still lack adequate information about questions which are essential for understanding the complex problems involved in the construction of Spain as a modern nation. The study of nationalisms in Spain has revolved around ideological and political aspects of regional nationalisms, and has dealt in detail with the politics and economics of the different regions (particularly Catalonia, the Basque country, and Galicia). But questions such as the formation of the Spanish state, the evolution of its central and local administrations, the growth of state bureaucracy, the history of the Spanish legal and judicial systems, have not received yet the attention they surely deserve. In short, most of what in sociological jargon would be called the process of socialization and modernization of Spanish politics and society is scarcely known.

These are processes which are crucial to an understanding of Spanish nationalisms. To study them in depth would obviously exceed the length and purpose of this essay, which focuses on the years 1900 to 1936. But there are a number of questions which seem worth mentioning. At least two points have not in my view been sufficiently emphasized. On the one hand, and contrary to the view which holds state centralism responsible for the emergence of peripheral nationalisms, it should be remembered that the unity of Spain remained highly artificial until well into the nineteenth century. It was late in this century that social and technological changes began to turn Spain into a cohesive national system. Throughout the eighteenth century and for most of the nineteenth, the social and economic fragmentation of Spain remained considerable. Far from being an integrated social unity, Spain appeared as a social network of insufficiently united 'natural' regions. Regional differences were conspicuous in the eighteenth century. José Cadalso, writing in the 1770s, pointed to the 'incredible variety' in the character of the Spanish provinces: 'Andalusians', he wrote, 'have nothing to do with the Basques; Catalans are entirely different from Galicians; the same would apply to someone from Valencia and someone from Santander.' In his *Gatherings from Spain*, published in 1846, Richard Ford underlined the fact that Spain was actually made up of several different regions and stated that their original differences in language, costumes, social traditions, and local character remain unaltered. State centralism was slow, therefore, to overcome the secular fragmentation of Spain's territory. In terms of the classical French distinction between *pays légal* and *pays réal*, the Spanish state was marked almost up to the twentieth century by the remarkable contrast between legal centralism and real localism.

On the other hand, it is doubtful that Spanish or state nationalism could have been an operative force in Spanish politics before the twentieth century. The elements of Spanish nationalism were certainly there long before. The change from a mainly geographical to a 'national' perception of Spain was well on its way in the eighteenth century, as the works of reformers like Campomanes, Jovellanos, and Floridablanca show. To mention only one example, the Napoleonic invasion in 1808 prompted an explosion of popular, if fragmented and localist, nationalism. Patriotic concerns and Spanish national preoccupations permeate the thoughts and programmes of nineteenth-century politicians and ideologues—both conservatives and liberals—and the books and works of contemporary poets, historians, novelists, and playwrights.

But the construction of a central and centralized state was not the work of political nationalism. It was, rather, the result of a long, unplanned, and changing process of adjustment of an ever-growing machinery of government to the also growing and changing problems of Spanish society. It is certainly significant that a major reform in the territorial structure of the state, the creation of the Spanish provinces in 1833, was the work of Spain's foremost 'administrativist', Javier de Burgos. Burgos was an eighteenth-century enlightened reformist, not a nineteenth-century nationalist. His provincial scheme was based on bureaucratic and administrative notions rather than on political considerations. His aim was efficient administration, not the implementation of a national ideal. Nineteenth-century Spain witnessed the crystallization of both a national political language and a national political culture. It also saw the emergence of different 'theories' about Spain. Liberals (Jovellanos, Giner, Costa), Republicans and Democrats (Pi y Margall, Galdós), Catholics (Balmes, Menéndez Pelayo) — to mention just a few names — held their own particular views about Spain and its history. All this was highly significant in both historical and political terms. But it was still a long distance away from modern political nationalism, in the two main meanings of the term: as an emotional exaltation of the traditions and glories of the nation, and as a political mass movement aimed at establishing a political order based on national unity and national 'grandeur'.

It could hardly be otherwise. Modern nationalism is the result of a long social process of national assimilation which culminates in the formation of a common perception of nationality. This required, in Spain as elsewhere, the growth of both regional and national markets, a certain degree of urbanization, a unified system of education, and the expansion of mass communications. In Spain, as in France, the process took at least the whole of the nineteenth century. A number of developments helped. The integration of the Spanish economy was accelerated after institutions such as the Madrid stock exchange (1831), and the Bank of Spain (1856) with a monopoly of monetary issue, were established, and after both taxation (1845) and the currency (1868) were unified on a national basis. Social communications multiplied with the extension of the road network and the construction of railways in mid-century. No fewer than 9,000 kilometres of roads and another 6,000 of railways were built between the 1840s and the 1860s. Telegraphs were first available to the public in 1855. Urbanization, if still comparatively low, grew considerably in those years: seventeen provincial capitals doubled their population between 1851 and 1866. State control over society was put on a firm basis with the creation of the Civil Guard in 1844 and the Penal Code of 1848, even if the compilation of a Civil Code had to wait until 1889. The introduction of national systems of both secondary and higher education, in 1845 and 1857 respectively, promoted cultural homogeneity: so did the growing development of a national press throughout the century. Central administration grew with the definitive establishment in 1823 of a ministerial system of government under the authority of a prime minister. Local government became unified after the reform of 1833. The socialization of politics advanced after 1833, even if erratically, with constitutional government, party politics, and elections.

It was only after the combined effects of these developments changed the political perceptions and preoccupations of Spaniards that Spanish nationalism began to play a part in the political culture of Spain. This was a slow and gradual process whose political effects began to be clearly felt only around the turn of the century. Thus, Spaniards seem not to have mourned the loss of their American empire in the 1820s. Things certainly changed in the next forty years. The wars fought by Spain in the 1860s in North Africa, Mexico, and the Far East raised waves of national sentiment throughout the country: they were 'an unifying political emotion', in Raymond Carr's words. But it was around 1900 that those national sentiments appeared definitively to have matured. At least, the loss of Cuba, Puerto Rico, and the Philippines in 1898 gave rise to the most serious crisis of national consciousness ever experienced by the Spanish intelligentsia. Spain had finally become a cohesive national entity.

In short, there was no state (or Spanish) nationalism in Spain in the nineteenth century; the Spanish state remained poor, weak, and inefficient throughout that century (which helps to explain the formidable extension of private and local networks of clientelism and patronage); localism dominated both social and political life in nineteenth-century Spain.

The emergence of peripheral nationalisms can hardly be attributed, therefore, to strong state centralism. The opposite seems closer to the truth. It was because the Spanish central state was weak and inefficient that centrifugal tendencies appeared in some of the more developed and culturally differentiated regions of the periphery. In both Catalonia and the Basque provinces there existed the pre-conditions of nationalism: a separate language and a separate history in Catalonia; a singular ethnicity, a particular language, and distinct institutions in the case of the Basques. Against this background, the actual emergence of nationalist movements in both Catalonia and the Basque country was most likely the result of slow, gradual processes of modernization and socialization of their own internal politics. Their study would again exceed these pages. For purposes of this essay, however, one thing seems significant. It was also around 1900, and not before, that the growth of nationalist consciousness and sentiments in some Spanish regions was completed. This was certainly the case in Catalonia and to a lesser degree in the Basque country, where Basque nationalism became the dominant political force in the 1930s. In other provinces, the growth of nationalist sentiments was still slow and limited; but it was also beginning to gain some momentum.

We are in a position now to understand why the regional question became a desperate problem of internal government in Spain in the first thirty years of the twentieth century. First, it was between 1900 and 1936 that the full 'nationalization' of both social and political life finally took place. The nation as a whole, and not the town or the region, became the centre of political and social action, even if localism still retained part of its secular strength, as Ortega y Gasset argued in his famous essay *La redención de las provincias* (The Redemption of the Provinces), written in 1927. Second, it was also in those years that the cultural unity of Spain was completed as a result of the greater national integration brought about by the growth of state control over society, the development of mass education, higher newspaper circulation, and the increase in social communications.

It might be argued that the vertebration of Spain as a nation was still not fully achieved: significantly Ortega y Gasset wrote his celebrated *Invertebrate Spain* in 1920. But the change that had taken place since the nineteenth century had been formidable (to the extent that ironically one might well say that never had Spain been so 'vertebrate' as when Ortega wrote about 'invertebrate' Spain). Around 1920, the emergence of a common Spanish nationality was clearly completed. In many ways, the Spain of 1900–36 was a fully integrated community.

This is precisely what gave the regional question its political singularity in the years under consideration. The Spanish case between 1900 and 1936—and ever since—was marked by a 'confrontation of nationalisms', that is by the antagonism of Spanish nationalism on the one hand, and peripheral nationalisms on the other.

I denied earlier that anything like state or Spanish nationalism existed in nineteenth-century Spain. But the twentieth century was

different. Spanish nationalism did appear after 1900. This was political nationalism in the full sense of the word: it was integral, unitarian
nationalism. As such, it reflected a fervent devotion to an idealized,
abstract concept of the Spanish fatherland, and gave rise to the formulation of a number of nationalist theories and doctrines. Spanish
nationalism of the early twentieth century was not centred around a
single political party. It permeated a variety of élites, movements, and
ideologies. Elements of this new nationalist mood were clearly present
in the writings and ideas of representatives of right-wing traditionalism
like Vazquez de Mella and Victor Pradera; in the language and
ideology of the Maurist Youth, the organization of young conservatives
that gathered around the charismatic figure of Maura after 1913; in
the editorials and articles published in conservative newspapers such
as *ABC* and *El Debate*; in the ideologues of Primo de Rivera's dictatorship; in the programmes of Catholic organizations such as the
National-Catholic Association of Propagandists, founded in 1909 (and
in right-wing Catholic thought); and, finally, in the army, particularly
in the young officers of the Moroccan army of the so-called military
generation of 1915.

We shall come back to the nature of twentieth-century Spanish
nationalism later. Let us now turn briefly to 'nationalist' movements.
Peripheral nationalisms made their entry into the political arena at the
turn of the century. Catalan nationalism won a resounding victory in
the 1901 general election. Arana, founder of Basque nationalism, won
a seat in the provincial council of Vizcaya in 1898. One of his followers
became mayor of Bilbao in 1907.

Events such as these completely changed the regional question.
This took a new development whose historical significance might best
be grasped in the light of the different circumstances which
accompanied it in the years up to 1931. Four of those circumstances
seem prominent:

1 The growing tension between Spanish nationalism and peripheral
   nationalisms, first made evident in 1905 when military officers
   stationed in Barcelona attacked a radical Catalan publication, the
   Cu-Cut, and in the intense debates on Catalan home rule and on
   Basque nationalism which erupted in the years between 1917 and
   1920, both in Parliament and the national press. In January 1919,
   the monarchist parties of the Basque country united in a common
   front — the League of Monarchist Action — to fight Basque 'separat-

ism'. A number of intellectuals gathered in the same years around Bilbao's daily *El Pueblo Vasco*: men like Ramiro de Maeztu, José Calvo Sotelo, the Count of Rodezno, Eduardo Aunós, Victor Pradera, Rafael Sánchez Mazas, and others formulated the ultra-nationalist concept of Spain that was later to inspire the dictatorships of both Primo de Rivera and Franco.

2 The gradual extension of political regionalism to provinces other than Catalonia and the Basque country—to regions like Galicia or Andalucia, and to a lesser extent Valencia, where regional sentiment, if previously existent, seemed to have been confined to literature. In Galicia, where cultural regionalism went back to the 1880s, the emergence in 1916 of a movement called *Irmandade da Fala* (Brotherhood of Speech) marked the beginning of political nationalism. At its 1919 Congress, the Brotherhood demanded the right of Galicia to self-determination. In 1920, Vicente Risco wrote the most thorough exposition of Galician ideology in his *Teoria do nacionalismo gallego* (Theory of Galician nationalism). In 1915, Blas Infante, the founding father of Andalusian nationalism, wrote *Ideal andaluz* (The Andalusian Ideal), the Bible of the movement. In 1916, Infante issued the programme and the manifesto of Andalusian regionalism.

3 The dual process of radicalization and left-wing realignment of most peripheral nationalisms, due to changes in ideology and strategy after intense self-examination in their respective search for political identity. In Catalonia, the conservative Catalan League which had dominated Catalan politics since 1900 saw its leadership seriously eroded after 1914, in favour of more radical nationalist groups: the Republican Left of Catalonia was to become the undisputed leader of Catalan nationalism between 1931 and 1936. In the Basque country, the hegemony of the Catholic and moderate Basque Nationalist Party (PNV) suffered, however lightly, when an independentist group split off in 1921, and later in 1930 when a liberal, republican faction left the PNV to found a new party, Basque Nationalist Action (ANV). In Galicia, an unbridgeable gap would open between the authoritarian, non-democratic nationalism of Risco, and the federal, progressive views of Villar Ponte, the founder of the Brotherhood. The Andalusian ideal of Infante had always had a mildly left-wing tinge.

4 The increasing sympathy of the Spanish left for the demands of regionalist and nationalist movements.

It is this last point which should retain our attention at this juncture, since it was a left-leaning regime, the Second Republic proclaimed in 1931, which was to be the first regime in Spanish history to try to solve the regional question by granting regions the right to full political autonomy.

This was by no means a minor change. The intellectual tradition from which the Spanish left had historically derived its views and ideals had been obsessed with the problem of Spain, and deeply imbued in the rhetoric of national regeneration, as reflected in the thoughts and books of Giner, Galdós, Unamuno, and Ortega y Gasset. With the exception of the Federal Party, neither Republicans nor Democrats had considered the Spanish problem in territorial terms. They believed that what had failed in Spain in such critical circumstances as 1898 or 1917 had been the political form of the state (i.e. the monarchy), not its territorial organization. The problem of Spain was in their view the replacement of an old, archaic monarchy by a modern republic; the question of state centralism (or decentralization) was secondary.

The Spanish left, with few exceptions, showed scarce sympathy for the peripheral nationalisms when these first appeared. The rising star of the Republican left at the beginning of the century, Alejandro Lerroux, broke away from the Republican ranks when in 1905 the old Republican guard joined with Catalan nationalists in a common front to oppose military laws that threatened the freedom of the press. Anti-Catalanism became one of the dominant features of the Radical party that Lerroux founded in 1907.

This was not an isolated case. Moderate Republicans like Melquíades Alvarez and old-style liberals like Montero Ríos opposed both the 1907 Law of Local Administration, which contemplated some measure of decentralization, and the formation in 1914 of the *Mancomunidad Catalana*, which unified the four provincial councils of Catalonia. The Socialist Party (PSOE) was not more favourable. It had no influence whatsoever in Catalonia, was extremely hostile to nationalism in the Basque country—one of the party's strongholds— and saw a strong central state as the instrument for social change and social reform.

The change began to take place around the end of the First World War. Two factors seem to have been decisive: the international recognition of the right to self-determination for oppressed nationalities, and the emergence in Catalonia of left-wing, Republican nationalist élites. It was significant that *España*, the journal that expressed the views of the democratic intelligentsia between 1916 and 1923, should include articles and comments in favour of Catalan autonomy. The Socialist Party Congress held in November 1918 recognized the right of Spanish nationalities to self-government. A speech in Parliament by the leader of the Basque Socialists, Prieto, delivered in April, had indicated that the PSOE was even prepared to take a conciliatory stand towards reactionary Basque nationalism. Later, Socialist parliamentary deputies defended Catalan autonomy. It was under the dictatorship of Primo de Rivera (1923–30), when left-wing Catalan nationalists fought together with Republicans and Socialists to demand a democratic republic, that the change was completed. Democracy became identified with republicanism and with home rule for 'national' regions. A book written by Ortega y Gasset in 1927 (but published in 1931) entitled *La redención de las provincias* revealed the changes that were taking place among liberal intellectuals when confronted with the regional issue. (It also uncovered many of their ambiguities.) In his book, Ortega pleaded for a reform of the territorial structure of the Spanish state. He argued that Spain should be divided into ten 'big regions', all of them endowed with a large degree of self-government that included the right to elect their own separate government and their own legislative assembly. Ortega wanted to construct a new Spain, a Spain built up, as he wrote, by the provinces and for the provinces.

The so-called 'great reform' of Ortega amounted to what in constitutional terms became known as a 'regional state'. Ortega pointed to a Spanish state based on what he considered to be the ultimate social and territorial reality of Spain—the province. This was something new among liberal intellectuals: one should remember the uncompromisingly unitary view of Spain held by Unamuno—the intellectual 'conscience' of the Spanish liberal intelligentsia—in the same years. To a certain extent, Ortega's book was a landmark. His thesis meant that Spanish liberal intellectuals were prepared to acknowledge the regional plurality that lay hidden beneath the apparent secular unity of the country.

The book was also significant for its ambiguities. The ethnic, linguistic, historical, and cultural particularities of the regions were not Ortega's concern. Indeed, in his book he neither dealt with 'nationalities' nor cared about the 'historical' rights of the regions. His main and only concern was Spain. Ortega turned his attention towards provinces and regions because he thought they were truly the ultimate reality of Spain, because he saw them as the real centre of social life for the average Spaniard. Ortega rejected the modern Spanish state not because of its centralism but because of its artificiality; in his view the *official* state did not represent the *real* Spain. But let us make no mistakes about Ortega's ultimate aim. He wanted a Spain built upon the provinces. He was quite prepared to see them endowed with a greatly increased political power. However, his aim was the 'renaissance' of Spain. Ortega's intellectual ambition was the definition of a new common national will based on the strong localism of both provinces and regions.

To a certain extent, Ortega's evolution was paradigmatic. In 1931, his generation, the generation of 1914, was to come to power. It was a generation ready to accept regional autonomy. But it was also a generation obsessed by the vertebration of Spain as a unified nation. This duality explains the attitude of the Second Republic (1931–6) towards the regional problem. The Republic followed a very cautious and sensible line. When the Civil War broke out in July 1936, only one region, Catalonia, had been granted political autonomy. Basque autonomy was recognized in October (and lasted only until the fall of Bilbao in June 1937). A referendum on Galician autonomy was held in June 1936: but the triumph of military rebellion in Galicia one month later destroyed all hopes for Galician nationalism.

The great contribution of the Second Republic was the so-called 'integral' state, an alternative both to federalism and to centralism. The 1931 Constitution recognized the rights of the provinces to full autonomy, but it did not grant it automatically to all of them (as in a federal state). Behind the idea of the 'integral' state there lay a clear conception of Spain. Spain was seen as a unitary nation with a common culture. But it was somehow accepted that there were three particular cultures within it—Catalonia, the Basque country, and Galicia—and more or less vague local sentiments in almost all regions. In fact, the Second Republic of 1931 opened the way to a regional state. Regions had the right to self-government. But the procedure to achieve it was not easy. Above all, sovereignty lay in the Spanish Parliament; thus, the right to self-determination was rejected. In short, the legislators of 1931 recognized the 'legitimate' rights of the regions to organize their collective life within the unity of the state. But the concept of an integral state meant the ratification of Spain as a historical, national unity.

The constitutional solution adopted in 1931 for the regional problem seemed both reasonable and responsible. Yet it was anathema to
the Spanish nationalists, whose ultra-unitary ideology lay behind the
military rebellion of 1936 (and behind Franco's forty-year dictatorship). This was due to the nature of twentieth-century Spanish
nationalism, one of whose fundamental tenets was the firm advocacy
of national unity against both Catalan and Basque nationalisms
(or 'separatisms'). This is important. Twentieth-century Spanish
nationalism did not develop into a mass movement led by a single party
(like Italian Fascism or German National Socialism). Instead, because
of its unitary, anti-regionalist stand, it appealed to large sectors of the
Spanish army.

This resulted in part from the 1898 crisis, when Spain lost the last
remnants of its overseas empire (Cuba, Puerto Rico, and the Philippines) after a short war with the USA. The 1898 disaster and its aftermath had profound effects on Spanish politics, bringing in its wake a
deep crisis in national consciousness, the political emergence of
Catalan nationalism, and the frustration of a defeated colonial army.
The crucial fact was that the army turned towards military action in
Morocco—where a full-scale war would be waged from 1912 to
1926—as a means to avenge the defeat suffered in Cuba. A new military mentality appeared that would gradually identify parliamentary
and party politics with Spain's international decline, and would see in
peripheral nationalisms a sort of internal enemy wholly incompatible
with the idea of national unity as embodied by the army.

Militarism and anti-regionalism became the major components of
twentieth-century Spanish nationalism. It is in this light that my
previous statement that there was no Spanish nationalism in
nineteenth-century Spain must be understood. There were national
perceptions and preoccupations, patriotic sentiments, different
national traditions, different ways to define Spain's past and Spanish
identity. But nationalism as the enthusiastic exaltation of the unity of
Spain, as an almost mystical faith in her destiny, as a glorification of
her military and religious past, only emerged in the twentieth century.
Twentieth-century Spanish nationalism was based on a national-
military theory that saw in the army both the symbol and the pillar
of national unity, and aimed at the establishment of a strong,
authoritarian, unitary state. This kind of nationalism rejected the
aspirations of peripheral nationalisms, and opposed any conception of
Spain reasonably sympathetic to those aspirations. When democracy

became identified with regional autonomy, Spanish nationalism condemned democracy. Thus, the way was paved for a confrontation of
nationalisms. This confrontation is what gives the Spanish regional
case its special historical significance.

4. THE CATALAN INDUSTRIAL ÉLITE, 1898–1923*

Joseph Harrison

When Antonio Cánovas, architect of the Restoration system, set about his task of reinstalling the previously discredited Bourbon monarchy in 1875, he soon secured the approval of the majority of the *fuerzas vivas* (the so-called productive forces) of Catalonia.[1] At first sight perhaps, Cánovas's achievement of introducing a system of limited pluralism— in which a narrow oligarchy of agrarian and financial interests alter- nated in power, represented in two artificial parties, Conservatives and Liberals—might seem to have little appeal to representatives of Spain's foremost industrial region. Catalan politicians, it should be remem- bered, played no small part both in the ousting of the unpopular Isabel II and in the administration of the ill-fated Federal Republic. Was it not a Catalan, Laureano Figuerola, who, as Minister of Finance, championed the cause of free trade in 1869 when he led the assault on the country's high tariff barriers? However, Barcelona in the second half of the nineteenth century was not Manchester: the textile manufacturers of the *ciudad condal* were protectionists to a man. Figuerola, with his Cobdenite ideas, attracted only antipathy from the owners of a plethora of small, undercapitalized, and uncompetitive mills who clamoured for even greater customs duties to be imposed on imported goods whenever market forces turned against them.[2]

In marked contrast to other sections of the Catalan community, business interests invariably portrayed themselves as profoundly *españolista*. As a reward for their strident patriotism they sought from Madrid not only measures to restrict the entry of foreign manufactures

* The author wishes to thank the British Academy and the Leverhulme Foundation for grants to carry out research in Barcelona and Madrid.

[1] On political support for the Restoration regime in Catalonia, following some initial reluctance, see especially Borja de Riquer, 'El conservadorisme polític català: Del fracàs del moderantisme al desencís de la Restauració', *Recerques*, 11 (1981), 29–80.

[2] For a background to the longstanding protectionist campaign in Catalonia see Manuel Pugés, *Como triunfó el proteccionismo en España: La formación de la política arancelaria española* (Barcelona, 1931), *passim*.

but expected that at moments of revolutionary 'excesses' the central authorities would place the forces of law and order at their disposal.[3] During the Isabelline period (1840–68), when the *petite bourgeoisie* of the Principality gave their enthusiastic support to the Progressives in opposition to the system of political and administrative centralization introduced into Spain from north of the Pyrenees, the industrial élite of Catalonia threw in their lot with the Moderates, precursors of Cánovas's Conservative Party, who imported the poorly fitting French model.[4] At a time of embryonic interest in Catalan nationalism, particularly amongst the region's intellectuals, during the early years of the Restoration, the hard-nosed men of the textile industry, the leading sector of the Catalan economy, looked to Cánovas for the reestablishment of social order throughout the Peninsula after the indiscipline of the *sexenio revolucionario* (1868–74).[5] Before long, in the throes of the nationwide agricultural crisis of the 1880s and 1890s, when the arrival of cheap grain from Russia and North America further depressed the pathetically low spending power of the great mass of rural consumers, bringing in its wake falling profits, bankruptcies, and unemployment to the mill towns of Catalonia, the politicians in Madrid offered a small consolation prize. This concession took the form of the Law of Commercial Relations with the Antilles of 1882 which, for customs purposes, considered the overseas provinces as part of the Spanish mainland and initiated a gradual reduction in duties paid by Spanish exporters over the next decade.[6]

Such a piece of legislation in defence of the industrial interests of Catalonia followed strong lobbying from industrial groups in Barcelona after the suppression of the Cuban revolt in 1878. Petitions from Catalan manufacturers for a bigger portion of the Cuban market,

[3] Factory burnings in Barcelona in 1836 and 1854 were a cause of great concern to the millowners; see Guillermo Graell, *Historia del Fomento del Trabajo Nacional* (Barcelona, 1911), 55–6.

[4] On how fears of anarchism in Catalonia contributed to the hegemony of the Moderates see Raymond Carr, *Spain: 1808–1939* (Oxford, 1966), 227–46.

[5] The desire for law and order at this time is conveyed in Borja de Riquer, 'Burguesos, polítics i cacics a la Catalunya de la Restauració', *L'Avenç*, 85 (Sept. 1985), 16–33.

[6] On the importance of this Act to the Catalan cotton textile industry see Carles Sudrià, 'La exportación en el desarrollo de la industria algodonera española, 1875–1920', *Revista de Historia Económica*, 1 (1983), 371–3, and Joseph Harrison, 'Catalan Business and the Loss of Cuba, 1898–1914', *Economic History Review*, 2nd ser., 27 (1974), 431–41. For a wider view of the problems of the Catalan economy see Jordi Maluquer de Motes, 'La historia económica de Cataluña', *Papeles de Economía Española*, 20 (1984), 268–81.

which pre-date the outbreak of the damaging agricultural crisis, are best seen in the context of the region's struggle for protectionism. Indeed, it was largely through its longstanding campaign to protect its business interests that the Catalan bourgeoisie acquired a political identity of its own. From the late eighteenth century onwards, the leading pressure groups of the Principality, the Comisión de Fábricas, the Fomento de la Producción Nacional, and later the most influential of them all, the Fomento del Trabajo Nacional, founded in 1889, all cut their political teeth on the tariff question, which was to dominate their affairs.[7] With its 2,000 members at the turn of the century, the Fomento del Trabajo Nacional was without doubt the most important economic organization in the whole of Spain. According to Borja de Riquer, over half of its subscribers were manufacturers. Together they represented the key sectors of Catalan industry. Included among its membership were 70 per cent of the largest cotton textile producers. The list of its presidents read like a *Who's Who* of the industrial middle classes of Catalonia: Ferrer Vidal, Sert, Caralt, Sedó, Sallarés, Rusiñol, Muntadas, etc. Its research department, directed by Guillem Graell and Frederic Rahola was generally considered the best informed on economic issues in Spain, while the organization's magazine, *El Trabajo Nacional* enjoyed enormous prestige and a readership of over 3,000.[8]

In the sphere of Spanish politics, the industrial élite of late nineteenth-century Catalonia has frequently been accused of accepting a subordinate position as uncritical supporters of the two corrupt parties of the Restoration, Cánovas' Conservatives and Sagasta's Liberals, who maintained themselves in power by a variety of dubious electoral practices, not least *caciquismo* or boss rule.[9] During the period 1875–99, eleven out of thirteen presidents of the Fomento served as either deputies or senators. More dramatically, of the forty-four deputies elected to the Cortes in 1899 for the four Catalan provinces of Gerona, Lérida, Barcelona, and Tarragona, no fewer than fourteen were known members of the Fomento.[10] Perhaps the most representative figure of Catalan Conservatism during the last two decades of the

---

[7] See Pierre Vilar, *La Catalogne dans l'Espagne moderne: Recherches sur les fondements économiques des structures nationales* (Paris, 1962), i. 147–9.

[8] Borja de Riquer, *Lliga Regionalista: La burguesia catalana i el nacionalisme, 1898–1904* (Barcelona, 1977), 36.

[9] Ibid. 31. Albert Balcells, *Historia contemporánea de Cataluña* (Barcelona, 1983), 103–6.

[10] Riquer, *Burguesos, polítics i cacics*, p. 31.

nineteenth century was Manuel Duran i Bas, founding president of the Círculo Conservador Liberal of Barcelona in 1883, who resigned from that office eight years later after levelling charges of political corruption and *caciquismo* against other leading members. This distinguished lawyer went on to join the dissident Conservative Francisco Silvela in his tireless crusade to clean up Spanish political life. Meanwhile, Catalan cotton manufacturers, who sat on the Conservative benches, although frequently voicing criticisms of political skulduggery and administrative inefficiency, made no serious attempt to bring about a reform of the centralist state.[11] Similar criticisms can be levelled at the woollen interests of Sabadell and Terrassa who demonstrated a greater affiliation to the Liberal party and whose best-known spokesman was Alfons Sala, the ever-present deputy for Terrassa.[12]

As mostly acquiescent, if sometimes vociferous, representatives of capitalist Catalonia in the Spanish Parliament, the industrial lobby generally kept its powder dry for debates on economic matters. Above all, during the early Restoration they campaigned for additional tariff protection for the embattled textile industry and the reservation of the Cuban and Puerto Rican markets for domestic producers. In 1891, two years after the formation of the Fomento del Trabajo Nacional, this approach seemed to have been vindicated. In response to demands from the Catalan millowners, together with the steelmasters of Vizcaya and the cereal growers of Old Castile, their livelihoods threatened by cheap imports, the Cánovas government introduced what was generally considered an ultra-protectionist tariff. At the same time, after studying the report of a commission whose membership included Duran i Bas, the Conservatives imposed substantial duties on goods entering the markets of the Antilles from outside the metropolis. As Carles Sudrià shows, the years 1890–8, largely as a result of these initiatives, witnessed a phase of considerable prosperity for Catalan textile manufacturers. On the eve of Spain's disastrous conflict with the United States in 1898, which resulted in the loss of her last

---

[11] On the split of Duran i Bas from Catalan Conservatism see Borja de Riquer, 'Del dinastisme al catalanisme: sobre el fracàs del Círculo Conservador Liberal de Barcelona', in Manuel González Portilla, Jordi Maluquer de Motes, and Borja de Riquer (eds.), *Industrialización y nacionalismo: Análisis comparativos* (Barcelona, 1985), 415–29.
[12] On Sala, who, despite his emotional Catalanism, remained as Liberal deputy for Terrassa from 1893 to 1920, apart from 1907 when he did not stand, see Josep Puy, *Alfons Sala i Argemí: Industrial i polític, 1863–1945* (Terrassa, 1983), *passim*.

remnants of empire, Cuba and Puerto Rico accounted for approximately one-fifth of the output of the cotton textile industry.[13]

The loss of Cuba came as a profound shock to the Catalan business
community. With so much at stake they had made loud jingoistic
noises during the three-year Cuban campaign (1895–8). The
Fomento, in particular, rarely missed the opportunity to attack the
fickleness of reformist politicians such as the Minister of Colonies,
Antonio Maura, who argued the case for the island's autonomy.[14]
When General Valeriano Weyler was relieved of his command as Captain General of Cuba for opposing the autonomy decree issued by the
Sagasta administration in October 1897 the Fomento organized a protest campaign in his defence.[15] Upon his return to Barcelona, General
Camilo García Polavieja, former Captain General of the Philippines
and victor over the rebels at Cavite in Spring 1897, was given a triumphal reception. Crowds lined the Ramblas to greet the 'Christian
General' who was soon to play a prominent role in the political life of
the Catalan bourgeoisie.[16]

THE FAILURE OF POLAVIEJISMO

Once the armistice was signed on 12 August 1898 there arose among
all sections of the Catalan business community a firm belief that the
time had come for changes to be made. The politically bankrupt
parties of the so-called *turno político*, which they had once supported
without great reservations, had not only dragged Spain into a costly
colonial campaign but the resulting débâcle had deprived the
Principality of its most lucrative markets. How ironical that three years
later the region's businessmen, who had so vociferously opposed the
granting of a mild form of autonomy to the island of Cuba, should find
themselves in the forefront of a regionalist movement whose prime
objective was home rule for Catalonia. In the intervening months, both
the aims and overall strategy of the Catalan industrial élite were in a
state of almost continuous turmoil.

[13] Sudrià, 'La exportación', pp. 374–5. The author calculates that about two-fifths of
the increase was due to colonial demand and three-fifths to the recovery of the home
market consequent upon the 1891 tariff.
[14] See especially Carlos Serrano, *Final de imperio: España, 1895–8* (Madrid, 1984),
50–2, and Carr, *Spain*, pp. 379–88.
[15] Riquer, *Lliga Regionalista*, p. 79.
[16] On Polavieja's triumphal return see Carlos Seco Serrano, *Militarismo y civilismo en
la España contemporánea* (Madrid, 1984), 225–6.

In November 1898, Albert Rusiñol, soon to become president of the Fomento, represented the Barcelona Chamber of Commerce at a well-attended assembly of its sister organizations held in Saragossa. Here a succession of delegates railed against the inefficiency and corruption of the Restoration system before elaborating a detailed manifesto which advocated a series of political and economic measures aimed at the regeneration of the Spanish nation. Among their long list of demands were calls for administrative and economic decentralization, increased expenditure on education and public works, cuts in military spending, and a reform of the taxation system.[17] For his part, Rusiñol was elected one of the four secretaries of the Assembly which was to have a strong impact on Spanish political life over the next few years. Yet joint action with what were known as the 'neutral classes', i.e. those groups previously excluded from dynastic politics, was only one of the options open to the *fuerzas vivas* of Barcelona. Throughout the summer of 1898 representatives of the Fomento, including Joan Sallarés, its president, and Joan Costa, held talks with General Polavieja who was posing as a potential saviour of the fatherland, a regenerator who, without seizing power, would institute reforms from above (*desde arriba*). In September 1898 the 'Christian General' and his advisors issued a manifesto, set out in typical regenerationist rhetoric—a lengthy list of what were deemed to be 'the ills of the country' along with the requisite remedies. Along with others of his ilk, including Silvela, Polavieja focused his attacks on the politicians of the *turno* parties whom he blamed for the crisis which afflicted Spain in the wake of humiliating defeat at the hands of the United States. Among his solutions to the *fin de siècle* crisis were the eradication of *caciquismo*, decentralization, a reorganization of the armed forces, and the incorporation of the 'neutral masses' into active politics.[18] Polavieja's manifesto was immediately greeted with a telegram of solidarity and support from the Fomento, which finally emerged from its narrow focus on economic issues.[19] In a series of letters to the Barcelona newspaper *La Vanguardia*, Sallarés contended that only Catalonia had been truly concerned about the problems of the colonies. Thanks to

---

[17] For the proceedings of the Saragossa Assembly see *Asamblea de las Cámaras de Comercio de Zaragoza, 20–7 noviembre de 1898* (Saragossa, 1899), *passim*. On the wider impact of regenerationism see my article 'The Regenerationist Movement in Spain after the Disaster of 1898', *European Studies Review*, 9 (1979), 1–27.

[18] On Polaviejismo and its reception in Barcelona see especially Joaquín Romero Maura, *'La Rosa de Fuego': El obrerismo barcelonés de 1899 a 1909* (Barcelona, 1974), 9–41.   [19] Riquer, *Lliga Regionalista*, p. 115.

the mistaken policies of the central authorities, these territories, instead of enriching Spain, had been destroyed by war. Defeat and the loss of the colonies had left Spain in ruins, saddled with a massive debt.[20] On 12 November 1898 Costa and Sallarés organized the Junta Regional de Adhesiones al Programa del General Polavieja which comprised leading figures of industry, commerce, and intellectual life in the *ciudad condal*. Yet the backbone of support was the Fomento del Trabajo Nacional.[21]

The Fomento's own views were set out in its famous message to the Queen Regent of 14 November 1898 which was seconded by a number of other local organizations including the Instituto Agrícola Catalán de San Isidro, the Sociedad Económica de Amigos del País, the Liga de Defensa Industrial y Comercial, and the Ateneo Barcelonés. This document called for administrative decentralization and an economic agreement (*concierto económico*), similar to that enjoyed by the Basque region since 1878, whereby each Catalan province would be able to collect its own taxes and distribute the revenue as it saw fit.

In March 1899, unable to form an administration of his own, Polavieja was appointed War Minister in the self-styled 'Government of National Regeneration' led by Francisco Silvela. To placate public opinion in Catalonia, Duran i Bas was given the justice portfolio. Among its first initiatives, the new government announced the appointment of the Catalanist Josep Morgades as bishop of Barcelona. More significantly, Morgades was replaced in the see of Vic by Josep Torras i Bages, the notorious canon and well-known defender of the Catalan language and culture. Later, under pressure from Polavieja and Duran i Bas, Dr Bartomeu Robert, president of the Sociedad Económica de Amigos de País, and one of the signatories of the message to the Queen Regent, was nominated as Mayor of Barcelona. This last appointment drew a blast of disapproval from the anti-Catalanist press in Madrid since Robert had recently delivered a lecture in which he was judged to have argued the superiority of the Catalan race.[22]

Within cabinet Polavieja did his best to pursue the often conflicting claims of Catalan business and the Spanish army. Briefed by represen-

---

[20] *La Vanguardia*, 18–24 Sept. 1898, cited in Riquer, *Lliga Regionalista*, p. 116.

[21] Romero Maura, *'La Rosa de Fuego'*, p. 23; Riquer, *Lliga Regionalista*, p. 123.

[22] Melchor Fernández Almagro, *Historia política de la España contemporánea*, iii. *1897–1902* (Madrid, 1968), 222.

tatives of the large contingent of Catalan industrialists who took their seats in the Cortes after the elections of 16 April 1899, and armed with a welter of documentation prepared by the Fomento,[23] he reiterated the call of the business community for a *concierto económico*. However, the rejection of this proposal out of hand by Silvela's Finance Minister, Raimundo Fernández Villaverde, together with the latter's proposed cuts in defence spending, left the politically inexperienced general with no other alternative than to resign. Villaverde, meanwhile, announced his intention of introducing a form of income tax based on industrial contributions.[24] Against a general diatribe of catalanophobia in the Madrid press, the middle classes of the Principality, represented in their guilds (*gremios*), retaliated by declaring a taxpayers' strike and the closure of all shops, a movement which became known as the *tancament de caixes*. While leaders of the Fomento tried to stand aloof from the conflict, the merchants of Barcelona seized the initiative. A visit of members of the French fleet to the Tivoli theatre resulted in the audience singing *Els Segadors* and the *Marseillaise*, while the Spanish anthem was roundly booed. To deal with the unrest in Barcelona, Silvela unwisely chose to employ repressive measures. On 24 October 1899 he suspended the normal application of public order regulations for the whole of the province. This decision led to the departure from his government of a disillusioned Duran i Bas. Robert had earlier tendered his own resignation rather than hand over a list of defaulters. In an atmosphere of mounting excitement, the Fomento, together with other business groups, was no longer able nor willing to distance itself from the grass-roots protest. On 4 November 1899 the presidents of the five organizations which had petitioned the Queen Regent one year before wrote again arguing that only the immediate concession of a *concierto económico* would put an end to the conflict in Barcelona. Yet Silvela was not in a conciliatory mood. The *cinc presidents* therefore decided to issue a final warning on 30 November 1899. 'If you leave us isolated in our patriotic task,' they threatened, 'we can only defend ourselves by gaining the right to look after our own interests.'[25] The heavy-handed treatment of the Catalan rebels by the Silvela

---

[23] See especially Fomento del Trabajo Nacional, *Exposición elevada al presidente del Congreso con motivo del proyecto de ley de presupuestos para el ejercicio 1899–1900* (Barcelona, 1899), *passim*.

[24] For a wider discussion see Joseph Harrison, 'Financial Reconstruction in Spain after the Loss of the last Colonies', *Journal of European Economic History*, 9 (1980), 317–49.

[25] J. Marian Pirretas, *El tancament de caixes* (Barcelona, n.d.), 222.

administration had finally pushed the business community into the regionalist camp.

THE LLIGA REGIONALISTA

After their split with Silvela, the *Junta Regional* which had actively encouraged the candidacy of Polavieja formally dissolved itself. Thereupon, the disappointed leaders of the Fomento, among them Lluís Ferrer Vidal, Frederic Rahola, and Albert Rusiñol, joined forces with other leading personalities, including Dr Robert, to form a new organization known as the Unión Regionalista. Feeling themselves betrayed by the old order in the aftermath of the failure of Silvela's *aperturismo*, the business community of Barcelona now saw no other way forward than a complete break with the political system of the Restoration. As a result, talks took place with the Unió Catalanista, the most 'possibilist' section of the Catalanist movement, on the prospects of drawing up a common slate of candidates to fight the dynastic parties in the forthcoming elections. Thus the conservative manufacturers of the Fomento were reinforced by a group of young intellectuals and aspiring politicians, among them Enric Prat de la Riba and Francesc Cambó.[26]

The triumph of the *quatre presidents* in the elections to the Cortes of 19 May 1901 marked a turning point in Catalan politics. The victors, who all represented Barcelona constituencies, were four of the five signatories of the original document to the Queen Regent in November 1898. They were Albert Rusiñol, president of the Fomento del Trabajo Nacional, Bartomeu Robert, ex-president of the Sociedad Económica de Amigos del País of Barcelona, Lluís Domènech i Montaner, former president of the Ateneo Barcelonés, and Sebastiá Torres, president of the Liga de Defensa Industrial y Comercial. The fifth president, the Marqués de Camps of the Instituto Agrícola Catalán de San Isidro, previously elected on a regionalist ticket in 1899, was beaten in Olot. Despite the efforts of Sagasta and Moret to fix the election results, not only the four Catalanists but also the republicans Lerroux and Pi y Margall were returned in Barcelona. Elsewhere in the Principality the parties of the *turno político* maintained their positions. Not until the famous Solidaritat Catalana coalition of

[26] On the history of the Catalanist Movement before this moment see especially José Antonio González Casanova, *Federalismo y autonomía: Cataluña y el estado español, 1868–1938* (Barcelona, 1979), 129–78.

republicans, traditionalists, and regionalists in 1907 was the stranglehold of the *turno* parties in the other three Catalan provinces finally broken.

After the success of the four presidents in the May elections of 1901, the forces which were responsible for this breakthrough reconstituted themselves as the Lliga Regionalista. As Borja de Riquer shows, the great majority of its original leaders were members or directors of the Fomento del Trabajo Nacional.[27] Throughout its history the Lliga remained tightly controlled by a closely knit group of politicians, lawyers, businessmen, and financiers. It was to be dubbed by the left 'el partido industrial'.[28]

Under the leadership of Prat de la Riba and Cambó, the long-term aim of the Lliga was not, as its detractors in Madrid maintained, to bring about the creation of an independent Catalan state. Rather, the industrial élite of Catalonia aimed to carry out a thoroughgoing reform of the Spanish state. Both men envisaged a decentralized, modern capitalist economy with Lliga luminaries holding the reins of power in Madrid. Although in its early years the party capitalized on anti-monarchist sentiments, under Cambó's influence this soon gave way to a studied accidentalism. Faced with revolutionary pressure on the left (the anarchist-inspired general strike in Barcelona of 1902, the electoral triumph of Lerrouxismo in 1903, the chaotic events of the Tragic Week in 1909), the leadership sought to transform the Lliga into a Catalan Conservative party. Mistrusted both by a large section of the political establishment in Madrid and by the party's rank-and-file, Cambó embarked on a high-risk strategy. This strategy was one of *pactismo* (doing deals), when the Lliga showed itself prepared to negotiate with the most reactionary elements in the Spanish capital. From 1907 to 1909, after the victory of the 'impossible' Solitaritat Catalana coalition, the Lliga broke ranks with its electoral allies and negotiated with Antonio Maura for a Local Government Act based on a corporate franchise. Once this was achieved, the next step was to take power in the municipalities and eventually gain control of all four provincial Deputations. Thus fortified, the new power brokers would be in a position to cajole a hostile Cortes into granting political and administrative autonomy. Encouraged by Maura, Cambó even harboured illusions of leading a regionalist reformist party which would

[27] Riquer, *Lliga Regionalista*, p. 204.
[28] See Joaquín Maurín, *Los hombres de la Dictadura: Sánchez Guerra, Cambó, Iglesias, Largo Caballero, Lerroux, Melquíades Álvarez* (Madrid, 1930), 101–50. For the history of the party see Isidre Molas, *Lliga Catalana: Un estudi de estasiologia* (2 vols. Barcelona, 1972).

take over from the Liberals as the second party of the *turno político*.[29] On the eve of the First World War, the main achievement of this collaborationist tactic was a limited form of autonomy in the shape of the Mancomunidad. Although the latter was a purely administrative body, with no political content, it nevertheless constituted the first official recognition by the Restoration regime of the personality of Catalonia.[30]

BUSINESS INITIATIVES AFTER THE LOSS OF CUBA

In the years which followed the loss of the lucrative Cuban market, Catalan business became all too aware of the lopsidedness of the regional economy. Cotton textiles accounted for about three-fifths of the output of the large companies and 70 per cent of fixed capital. Yet outside markets for cotton goods were dwindling. Cuba, Puerto Rico, and the Philippines, which between them took 22.2 per cent of Catalan textile production in 1896, bought only 6.2 per cent in 1902. In the short term, at least, a number of factors acted to the advantage of domestic manufacturers. A fall in the exchange rate, provoked by a drop in business confidence after the disastrous war with the United States, served to stimulate exports while at the same time staving off foreign competition in the home market. The exceptional harvest of 1898 and an above average crop in 1899 increased the spending power of the agricultural community. Meanwhile, the return to the peninsula of 200,000 troops from Cuba and the Philippines led to an extraordinary rise in the demand for clothing of all kinds.[31]

However, manufacturers were still hampered by the limited purchasing power of the Spanish market as well as by a sharp increase in the price of raw cotton. Attempts to drive down the costs of production by substituting female for male labour and wage-cutting resulted in

[29] Borja de Riquer, 'La Lliga Regionalista o els límits del catalanisme conservador', in Josep Termes *et al.* (eds.), *Catalanisme: Historia, Política i Cultura* (Barcelona, 1986), 122–3. Riquer cites a letter from Cambó to Prat dated 21 Oct. 1909 in the Prat de la Riba archive. Cambó's own intriguing memoirs are less specific. But see 'Què podria haver fet amb Maura', in Francesc Cambó, *Memòries, 1876–1936* (Barcelona, 1981), i. 177–80.

[30] See Balcells, *Historia*, p. 198.

[31] Eusebio Bertrand y Serra, 'Un estudio sobre la industria textil algodonera', *Boletín del Comité Regulador de la Industria Algodonera*, 4 (Mar. 1931); *El Trabajo Nacional*, 20 Sept. 1900 and 30 July 1901; *Parliamentary Papers, Diplomatic and Consular Reports on Trade and Finance*, 96 (1900), 265 (Barcelona).

costly strikes such as occurred in the manufacturing districts of the Ter and Freser Valleys in 1901 and the Barcelona general strike of 1902. To many, it seemed that the best way out of the dilemma, which was commonly viewed as a crisis of overproduction, was the conquest of new markets. At the turn of the century, considerable importance was attached to restoring trade links with the long-neglected nations of Spain's former empire in Latin America.[32] The Fomento, in particular, elaborated specific proposals aimed at building upon common links of race and language. Heading the organization's list of priorities was the demand of a free port or neutral zone for Barcelona. The construction of a vast dockland complex with factories and warehouses, it was contended, would have a considerable modernizing effect on the nation's leading seaport. Moreover, the waiving of import duties might encourage the Latin American republic to use the port as their European entrepôt.[33] In December 1900, a Commission of the Ministry of Agriculture, Industry, and Public Works was set up to study the question of neutral zones. Yet this concession to Catalan public opinion served only to excite considerable opposition to the proposal, not least from the cereal cultivators of Castile. A neutral zone, the latter claimed, would do nothing to protect the wheat farmers of the Meseta from ruinous imports. Besides, the planned free port of Barcelona would provide a haven for smugglers. Despite a number of attempts to get the project approved, the landed interests won the day.[34]

A further initiative to develop trading relations with Latin America centred around campaigns for commercial agreements with individual republics. In 1900 the Argentine government called for a treaty with Spain, while two years later the economic societies of Barcelona petitioned Madrid for a treaty of commerce with Cuba.[35] The thought of such negotiations once more provoked noisy reactions from Castilian farmers who considered the proposed treaties as prejudicial to their wheat and stock-rearing interests. The Catalans, moreover, were ridiculed for their volte-face on the tariff question.[36] Despite the sympathy

[32] See Angel Marvaud, 'La Plus Grande Espagne', *Questions Diplomatiques et Coloniales* (Nov. 1905), 531–9.

[33] See José Elías de Molins, *Puertos francos: Puertos de Marsella, Génova y Barcelona: Estudio económico* (Barcelona, 1901), *passim*.

[34] For the complaints of the Fomento see Guillermo Graell, *La cuestión de las zonas neutrales* (Barcelona, 1903), *passim*.

[35] *Revista de Economía y Hacienda*, 7 Apr. 1901 and 24 Aug. 1902.

[36] *Reunión extraordinaria celebrada en el Círculo de la Unión Mercantil e Industrial el día 30 de octubre de 1903 sobre tratados de comercio* (Madrid, 1903), 10–11.

of a number of Latin American governments, these negotiations came to nothing.[37]

From the autumn of 1903 the Fomento joined forces with the Liga Vizcaína de Productores to lobby for higher customs duties. After almost three years of negotiations the Catalans were rewarded with a doubling of duties on cheap cotton imports.[38] Nevertheless, large stockpiles of cotton goods continued to accumulate at the mills of the Principality. Accordingly, in June 1907 leading manufacturers gathered in Barcelona and established an association of cotton weavers known as the Mutua de Fabricantes de Tejidos de Algodón, whose purpose was to promote the export of those goods which could not be sold in the peninsula and to indemnify exporters for any losses incurred. Eighty-three per cent of manufacturers joined the scheme which, in its brief existence of eighteen months, sold $7.5 million of cloth to 176 separate markets, of which the most common destinations were Argentina and Turkey. During its short lifespan the association was racked by discontent, especially by subscribers required to under-write heavy losses. For these reasons, the Maura administration of 1907–9 resolutely refused to grant it financial support.[39]

The collapse of this well-intentioned initiative to find a modest niche in the external market as an antidote to the loss of the last colonies finally threw the textile sector fairly and squarely on the domestic market. Writing in 1908, the French commentator Edouard Escarrà clearly demonstrated that the great majority of Catalan manufactures were destined for the peninsula, while foreign sales played only a minor role. The bulk of cotton goods produced in Catalonia (325–50 million pesetas) was sent to Spain while Spaniards consumed three-quarters of all production of woollens, linen, hemp, jute, and silk. Domestic sales of woollen goods amounted to 65 million pesetas and silk to 30 millions. In addition, the Principality also sent substantial amounts of flour, chemicals, electrical, and metallurgical goods to Spain, bringing the value of Catalan sales to the rest of the country to 500 million pesetas. By comparison, the total value of exports from

---

[37] See J. Puigdollers y Maciá, *Las relaciones entre España y América: Manera de fomentarlas* (Barcelona, 1902), 5–7.

[38] Angel Marvaud, 'La Politique douanière de l'Espagne, 1816–1906', *Annales des Sciences Politiques*, May 1907. For the demands of the Fomento see Guillermo Graell, *El arancel, los tratados y la producción* (Barcelona, 1905), *passim*.

[39] Ralph M. Odell, US Dept. of Commerce and Labor, Bureau of Manufactures, Special Agents Series, no. 46, *Cotton Goods in Spain and Portugal* (Washington, 1911), 33–4.

Catalonia was only 125 million pesetas, of which cottons accounted for 45–50 millions.[40]

The paramount importance of the Spanish market was recognized by the Fomento del Trabajo Nacional throughout the early years of the twentieth century. In his study of the Catalan question published in 1902, Guillermo Graell, secretary of the organization, wrote that 'the market of Catalonia is the rest of Spain . . . to such a point that if they separate both will be ruined, commercially, economically and financially. . . . Every Catalan, therefore, who tends towards separatism is attacking the interests of his country and is a bad Catalan.'[41] Even so, spokesmen for the Fomento were helpless in the face of the weakness of the domestic market. Every year tens of thousands of Spaniards were forced to emigrate. In 1910, at a time of hostile press comments about the treatment of Spanish emigrants in Brazil, Manuel Pugés asked how the Principality could ever aspire to large industries when production and consumption in such areas as the *latifundio* belt of the South was so weak.[42]

THE IMPACT OF THE FIRST WORLD WAR

The decision by the Conservative administration of Eduardo Dato to declare Spain neutral during the European conflict inaugurated a period of unexpected prosperity for the Catalan economy. After a fleeting panic on the Barcelona stock exchange, Catalan industry entered a phase of feverish activity. Thanks to the disruption of the economies of the belligerent nations, Catalan manufacturers suddenly discovered seemingly boundless opportunities to export their products. In particular, the textile mills were inundated with orders from north of the Pyrenees.[43] Factories which had recently worked short-time now began to recruit skilled and unskilled workers from throughout Barcelona and further afield. In response to on-the-spot cash payments from a host of commercial agents and speculators, Catalan mills

[40] Edouard Escarrà, *Le Développement industriel de la Catalogne* (Paris, 1908), 98–113.

[41] Guillermo Graell, *La cuestión catalana* (Barcelona, 1902), 107. On the crucial importance of the Spanish market see also Fomento del Trabajo Nacional, *Memoria leída en la junta general ordinaria de socios celebrada el día 31 de enero de 1904* (Barcelona, 1904), 5.

[42] *El Trabajo Nacional*, 1 Aug. 1910.

[43] On the wartime bonanza see especially Joaquín Aguilera, 'La guerra europea y sus efectos en la industria de Cataluña', *Revista Nacional de Economía*, 1 (1916), 35–48, and Fidencio Kirchner, *La influencia de la guerra en las industrias catalanas* (Barcelona, 1919), *passim*.

worked round the clock to fulfil orders. According to one source, by March 1915 French buyers had placed orders worth 350 million pesetas in the Principality.[44] Although the avalanche of orders from France for cotton and woollen goods fell back after 1916, average annual sales remained above pre-war levels until 1920.[45] Towards the end of the war, the woollen sector began to capture new markets in Latin America, above all Argentina and Chile. During the years 1914–18 exports of woollen goods from Sabadell and Terrassa averaged twenty times to 1913 level. Over the same period, foreign sales of cotton goods rose by 150 per cent.[46]

In other sectors of Catalan industry, the disappearance almost overnight of British, German, and French rivalry in the Spanish market acted as a firm stimulus to import substitution. Electrical goods, engineering, metallurgy, and vehicle building all benefited from this development, while the region's economy lost some of its lopsidedness.[47]

To meet the new situation, representatives of the Catalan business community maintained a constant stream of demands and petitions to Madrid, where Lliga politicians forcefully advocated the virtues of advanced capitalism. In August 1914, Prat de la Riba, on behalf of the recently established Mancomunidad, summoned a gathering of all Catalan representatives in the Cortes together with the presidents of the main economic societies of the region, at which a junta was set up to assess the economic situation during the early months of the war. Prat circulated a questionnaire on the position of raw materials, transport, finance, the stock market, and other topics. The Lliga Regionalista undertook a study of how best Catalonia could approach the war in a spirit of efficiency, co-ordination, and patriotism. Throughout the conflict Catalan deputies including Cambó, Ventosa, Rahola, and Sedó intervened in Cortes debates on industrial policy, finance, and the cost of living.[48]

The first major initiative was taken in October 1914 when representatives of the Fomento del Trabajo Nacional, the Sociedad Económica

---

[44] Aguilera, 'La guerra europea', p. 39.   [45] Sudrià, 'La exportación', p. 381.

[46] Balcells, *Historia*, p. 157.

[47] By the end of the conflict 10,000 new jobs had been created in the mechanical engineering, vehicle, and associated industries in the province of Barcelona alone. See Instituto de Reformas Sociales, *Información sobre emigración española a los países de Europa durante la guerra* (Madrid, 1919), 76–7.

[48] *El Trabajo Nacional*, 1 Sept. 1915. But see especially the brilliant study of Jesús Pabón, *Cambó* (3 vols. Barcelona, 1952–72), 1. 429–32.

de Amigos del País, the Cámara Industrial, and the Casa de América among others reissued their demand for a free port for Barcelona. The subject received added impetus since, in a royal decree of September 1914, free port status was granted to Cádiz. Yet fourteen years and two enquiries had elapsed since the Catalans first tabled a Bill in the Congress. Barcelona, it was argued, dealt with one-fifth of Spain's foreign trade as well as being the country's main industrial centre. As such, it would benefit greatly from such a concession. Cádiz, by contrast, was a non-industrial town with a primarily agricultural hinterland.[49]

A second wartime demand made upon Madrid by Catalan business interests was for export subsidies (*bonos de exportación*). Above all, they sought official backing to capture and hold on to markets in Latin America which had been abandoned by the belligerent nations. In July 1915 representatives of the major economic organizations of Barcelona, led by the Fomento, visited the Spanish capital to make known their demands. The only effective result of their trip was a special commission set up by Finance Minister, Bugallal, charged with 'the study of national industry and means of stimulating exports'. To the Catalans, such a course constituted a prima facie case of evasion when the situation obviously required immediate action.[50]

Bugallal's delaying tactics, however, reflected profound disquiet within the rest of Spain towards the petition of the Catalans. In Saragossa, both agrarian and business groups campaigned vigorously against the establishment of free ports which, they maintained, would lead to the destruction of domestic industry and rural depopulation.[51] Further opposition to the Catalan plans came from the Castilian wheat lobby. Cambó's biographer tells how the Dato government was forced to ban a rally in Valladolid early in 1915 summoned to attack the plans of the Fomento.[52]

Even so, throughout the second half of 1915, all sections of business and political opinion in the Principality spoke in terms of 'an economic blockade' of the region by entrenched interests represented in the

[49] See Marcelino Graell, *Las zonas neutrales: Su importancia para Barcelona* (Barcelona, 1914), passim; El Trabajo Nacional, 15 Oct. 1914, 15 Nov. 1914, and 1 Dec. 1914, and *Boletín de la Cámara de Comercio y Navegación de Barcelona*, Jan. 1915.

[50] *El Trabajo Nacional*, 17 July 1915, 1 Sept. 1915.

[51] La Cámara Oficial de Comercio y de la Industria de Zaragoza, *Las zonas neutrales* (Saragossa, 1914), *passim*; A. Giménez Soler, *Las zonas francas* (Saragossa, 1915), *passim*, and J. Ruis y Casas and M. Trilla y Rostoll, *El plieto de las zonas francas* (Saragossa, 1915), *passim*.

[52] Pabón, *Cambó*, I. 431.

Spanish capital.[53] Never before, argued the Lliga Regionalista, had the divorce between the government and the governed been so crudely demonstrated. The former had displayed nothing but contempt for the patriotic initiatives of the Catalan community.[54] When the political oligarchy in Madrid did act, in the opinion of the Catalans they conceded too little too late. For example, it was not until October 1916 that Barcelona was granted a commercial depository, a concession which fell far short of their original demands. Moreover, it took another year before the original decree secured final approval, while not until 1921 did work start on the site.[55] In addition, Bugallal's commission to study government support for Spanish exports took eighteen months to report, while its financial provisions were deemed woefully inadequate by Lliga politicians.[56]

Yet the measure which put the Lliga and the Fomento in combative mood was an attempt by Santiago Alba, Finance Minister of Ramonones's Liberal administration to carry out a ten-year programme of public works, naval, military, and cultural expenditure. To pay for his plans Alba announced his intention of levying a tax on excess war profits earned by industry and trade. This move was clearly understood to be directed against Catalan business. Over the last six months of 1916 until the proposals were withdrawn, the Cortes was to witness a series of heated debates involving Alba and Cambó, the two great *vedettes* of the disintegrating Restoration system.[57] The Alba–Cambó confrontation was undoubtedly a clash of personalities; these men were the two most gifted members of the younger generation of politicians. They also embodied rival ideologies whose common purpose was the patriotic ideal of the economic regeneration of Spain. Alba, a disciple of the Aragonese reformer Joaquín Costa, was a believer in the regeneration of Spanish agriculture by the selective application of a series of infrastructural projects, particularly in the field of irrigation.

[53] *El Trabajo Nacional*, 15 Aug. 1915.

[54] For an expression of hurt pride see the short preface to Lliga Regionalista, *El pensament català davant el conflicte europeu* (Barcelona, 1915).

[55] *El Trabajo Nacional*, 1 Nov. 1916 and July 1921; *Boletín de la Cámara de Comercio y Navegación de Barcelona*, Oct. 1917 and July 1921, and *Economia i Finances*, 28 Feb. 1918, 10 Nov. 1918, and 25 July 1921.

[56.] See Francesc Cambó, *L'acció d'estat i l'acció privada en las industries que tienen sobre producció* (Terrassa, 1917), 15–21, and M. Viada y Viada, *La economía y las finanzas españolas en la postguerra* (Barcelona, 1924), 40.

[57] For Cambó's account of the two men's intense rivalry see his *Memòries*, 1. 231–49. His hatred of Alba, whom he saw as a 'public enemy', is discussed in Carlos Seco Serrano, 'Cambó en sus "Memòries" ', *Cuenta y Razón*, 4 (1981), 46.

Cambó was the great exponent of Spanish capitalism who favoured government intervention to encourage the development of a modern industrial economy. There was nothing at all original about taxing war profits. Similar measures had been enacted in most of the belligerent nations. Yet in Spain those business groups that had seen the authorities in Madrid turn a blind eye to their own schemes for fostering economic advance were now ill prepared to sacrifice their recent gains when the landed interests would be hardly touched.[58]

Shortly after the withdrawal of Alba's Bill, in July 1917, the Lliga Regionalista, angered by the decision of the minority Dato government amidst escalating social and political tensions to close the Cortes and rule by decree, called a 'seditious' assembly of parliamentarians to meet in Barcelona. As rebel army officers held the country to ransom, German submarines blockaded the Mediterranean coast, and the Socialists threatened a revolutionary general strike, Cambó, the Conde de Romanones recounts, believed that his hour had arrived.[59]

THE STATE, HOME RULE, AND THE CLASS STRUGGLE

The Assembly Movement, which dominated Spanish political life from July until October 1917, represented an attempt by the industrial bourgeoisie of Catalonia to cement an alliance with Basque and Asturian business interests, whose spokesman was Melquíades Álvarez, and the *petit bourgeois* Republicans of Lerroux. Others wooed in this audacious, if forlorn, attempt at a controlled revolution were the military juntas, arbiters of the current political situation, the Conservative politician Antonio Maura, who took upon himself the role of 'reformer from above', and the traditionally non-revolutionary Socialist Party. The expressed intention of yet another impossible coalition was to overthrow the wheat and finance oligarchy which had ruled Spain since 1875. In seeking to lead these disparate forces, Cambó, a profoundly Conservative politician, was again gambling for high stakes, in a situation reminiscent of the Solidaritat Catalana electoral alliance of 1907. When Maura, one of the few politicians Cambó admired,

[58] In his memoirs, the only criticisms which Cambó makes against Alba's proposals is that they were conceived in haste and lacked consistency, *Memòries*, 1. 236–7. For a wider discussion see my article 'The Failure of Economic Reconstitution in Spain, 1916–23', *European Studies Review*, 13 (1983), 63–88.
[59] Conde de Romanones, *Notas de una vida*, iii. *1912–31* (Madrid, 1947), 144.

chose to stand aloof, the juntas refused to sanction the movement. Meanwhile, the Socialists were provoked into declaring a general strike in August. Cambó retreated: he had no intention of playing the role of Spain's Kerensky.[60] Thus Catalan business' view of an *Espanya Catalana*, with a fully autonomous Catalonia in the forefront of a modern industrial Spanish economy, was not destined to come about as a result of a new bourgeois political grouping. The Lliga quickly decided that it would be expedient to do a U-turn and throw in its lot with the oligarchy.[61]

After a shaky coalition led by García Prieto, which included two Catalanists, Rodés and Ventosa, Cambó's adjutant, Cambó himself assumed office as Development Minister in Maura's National Government. Although Maura's administration, a coalition of many political factions, proved a ramshackle affair, Cambó, in only eight months in office, proved his own worth as a committed and dedicated reformer. With boundless enthusiasm and a capacity for hard work rarely experienced in Spanish government circles he embarked on a far-reaching programme for the modernization of the nation's economic infrastructure.[62] Cambó's proposals, which touched on road building, a mining code, irrigation, and afforestation, had as their focus Spain's notoriously incomplete and dilapidated railway network. His railway plans, set out in a detailed six-volume survey, called upon the state to nationalize and thereafter maintain and develop the Spanish system as well as to assume responsibility for subsidizing passenger fares and freight rates. He also envisaged that the Spanish network would utilize cheap electricity generated by newly constructed hydroelectric stations.[63]

[60] There is, of course, an extensive literature on this historic moment when a Catalan politician determined the fate of the Restoration system. For an account sympathetic to Cambó's dilemma see Eduardo Aunós, *España en crisis, 1874–1936* (Buenos Aires, 1942), 205–33. On his alarm that the Assembly Movement was turning into a left-wing affair see Maura's confidant, Joaquín M. de Nadal, *Memòries: Vuitanta anys de sinceritats i de silencis* (Barcelona, 1965), 267–8. Cambó's 'Girondin' stance is criticized in Manuel Burgos y Mazo, *Vida política española: Páginas históricas de 1917* (Madrid, 1918), 106 ff.

[61] In his memoirs, Cambó claims that, far from betraying its supporters by abandoning the Assembly Movement, the Lliga were successful in expelling the Dato government, thus finally putting an end to the *turno político; Memòries*, i. 269.

[62] Romanones refers to Cambó as the leading spirit of the Maura coalition, see *Notas*, iii. 153. Even Burgos y Mazo, no friend of the Lliga, viewed him as at home with high office, see *El verano de 1919 en Gobernación* (Cuenca, 1921), 35. Cambó's own thoughts are set out in *Vuit mesos al Ministeri de Fomento: Mi gestió ministerial* (Barcelona, 1919), *passim*.

[63] Francisco Cambó, *Elementos para el estudio del problema ferroviario en España* (6 vols. Madrid, 1918).

From the beginning, however, Cambó's prospect of a new post-war political economy was considerably at odds with his colleague at the Exchequer, the Liberal Augusto González Besada. Besada, preoccupied with the traditional tasks of early twentieth-century Finance Ministers, viz. balancing the budget and curbing inflation, vigorously opposed the issue of the large amount of public debt which Cambó's schemes would have entailed.[64] To the dismay of the Fomento del Trabajo Nacional and other business groups, in May 1918 Besada announced that his long-term ambition was to put Spain on the Gold Standard, a policy which was judged to have considerable deflationary implications for the real economy.[65] When Alba brought down the coalition government on the pretext of schoolmasters' wages, few of Cambó's proposals had become law. The Catalans' much-sought-after 'revolution from above' had become, as Carlos Seco Serrano informs us, 'a great hope frustrated'.[66]

The fall of the Maura government marked a crucial point in the fortunes of the Catalan business community. Its political wing, the Lliga Regionalista, no longer close to the reins of power, met with hostility and abuse from both the Spanish army and left Catalanist groups when it attempted to secure an autonomy statute for Catalonia. Within the Cortes the attack on their 'modest' aspirations was led by Niceto Alcalá Zamora. Years later as president of the Spanish Republic Alcalá Zamora would defend and sign the Statute of Catalonia. In December 1918 he stung the undisputed leader of the Catalan right with the accusation that he was attempting to be the Bolívar of Catalonia and the Bismarck of Spain, two roles which it was impossible to perform simultaneously.[67] As a sign of its good faith, the Romanones government set up an extra-parliamentary commission charged with drafting an autonomy Bill. Yet on 27 February 1919 Romanones was forced to close the Cortes following an outbreak of labour unrest in Catalonia. From that moment onwards, Catalan busi-

[64] On the possibility of harmonizing the policies of the two ministries see *El Economista*, 20 Apr. 1918. For the view that Cambó was frustrated from the start by Treasury orthodoxy see *España Económica y Financiera*, 14 Dec. 1918.

[65] *Revista de Economía y Hacienda*, 25 May 1918, 8 June 1918. The Fomento del Trabajo Nacional's annoyance at Besada's Gold Standard proposals is referred to in Emilio Ríu, 'La crisis económica actual', *Revista Nacional de Economía*, 26 (1921), 16.

[66] Seco Serrano, *Militarismo y civilismo*, p. 277. See also Pabón, *Cambó*, 1. 615–31.

[67] See Cambó, *Memòries*, 1. 303.

ness submerged its regionalist aspirations amidst an orgy of strikes, lock-outs, and assassinations. The new factor in the political equation was the region's industrial labour force.[68]

Over the second decade of the twentieth century working-class living standards throughout Spain were severely reduced. In Barcelona, food prices rose on average by more than one-fifth between 1914 and 1917. The annual budget of a working-class family in the region's capital was estimated to have doubled between 1910 and 1920, while wages increased by between 20 and 40 per cent.[69] One result of the escalating cost of living was a steep climb in the membership of the anarcho-syndicalist trade union movement, the Confederación Nacional del Trabajo. Founded in Barcelona in 1911, the CNT had only 15,000 members by 1915. In 1918 it had 73,860 members in Catalonia, and by the end of 1919 it claimed a national membership of 714,028, with Catalonia comprising by far the largest area of support.[70] In late June 1918 the regional federation of the CNT, meeting in Sants, Barcelona, decided to reorganize the structure of the workers' organizations in Catalonia so as to make them more effective in their struggles with the employers. In many branches of Catalan industry a single union (*sindicato único*) was adopted for all workers, both skilled and unskilled, in an attempt to heighten the revolutionary fervour of the proletariat.[71]

The prelude to the new era of industrial turmoil was an attempt in January 1919 by the Anglo-Canadian hydroelectric concern 'La Canadiense' of Barcelona to reduce the wages of clerical staff. The CNT, spoiling for a confrontation, declared a strike which soon became general throughout Catalonia and other parts of Spain. Within three weeks the strikers claimed victory as individual employers began to concede to their demands.[72] Moreover, on 3 April 1919, the

[68] For the view that big business' preoccupation with regionalism caused them to ignore the groundswell of unrest among the Catalan proletariat see E. G. Solano, *El sindicalismo en la teoría y en la práctica: Su actuación en España* (Barcelona, 1919), 68.

[69] See Instituto de Reformas Sociales, *Informes de los inspectores de trabajo sobre la influencia de la guerra europea en las industrias españolas* (Madrid, 1918), 146; Instituto de Estadística y Política Social, Barcelona, *Estadísticas sociales; monografía estadística de la clase obrera* (Barcelona, 1921), 127.

[70] Instituto de Estadística y Política Social, *Estadísticas sociales*, pp. 36–7; Manuel Buenacasa, *El movimiento obrero español, 1886–1926* (new edn., Paris, 1966), 81; Albert Balcells, *El sindicalismo en Barcelona, 1916–23* (Barcelona, 1966), *passim*.

[71] Confederación Regional del Trabajo, *Memoria del congreso celebrado en Barcelona los días 29 y 30 de junio y 1 de julio del año 1918* (Barcelona, 1918).

[72] On the Canadiense and general strikes see especially Francisco de Madrid, *Ocho meses y un día en el Gobierno Civil de Barcelona: Confesiones y testimonios* (Madrid and Barcelona, 1932), 13–23; R. Plá y Armengol, *Impresiones de la huelga general de Barcelona*

Romanones government, inclined towards conciliation, decreed an eight-hour day, the major historic demand of Spanish labour, to come into effect from the beginning of October. This declaration, hotly opposed by the employers, opened up a new and unbridgeable rift between Catalan business and the central authorities. On 9 April 1919, representatives of the employers established a new organization, the Federación Patronal de Barcelona, which spoke less in terms of con-ciliation and arbitration than of concerted action and a show of force.[73] Passing over all legal means, both the Federación Patronal and the Fomento went straight to the Captain General, Joaquín Miláns del Bosch, who imprisoned thousands of trade unionists.[74]

Romanones's replacement, Sánchez de Toca, dispatched Julio Amado to Barcelona as civil governor. Upon his arrival, Amado immediately set about the creation of arbitration committees (*com-isiones mixtas de trabajo*) composed of both employers' and syndicalists' leaders. However, the employers now allowed their politics to be determined by the extremists of the Federación Patronal. From the summer of 1919 they responded to working-class militancy by the systematic use of lock-outs, scab labour (*esquirols*), and bands of hired assassins (*pistoleros*). In December 1919, deprived of the terror squads led by the false Barón de Koening, expelled by the Conde de Salvatierra, the Federación offered their support to the anti-CNT yel-low unions, the *sindicatos libres*, founded by the ex-Carlist militiaman Ramón Sales.[75] For his part, Cambó, fearful of being outflanked by hard-liners within the business community, publicly offered his reluc-tant, though not theoretical, support for the tactics of the employers' federation. Such an attitude, he conceded, was essential at this vital moment in Spanish history.[76] Indeed, in an atmosphere of almost daily

del 24 Marzo–7 Abril 1919 (Barcelona, 1930), *passim*; Miguel Sastre y Sanna, *La esclavitud moderna: Martirología social* (Barcelona, 1921), 138–47, and E. G. Solano, *El sindicalismo*, pp. 70–130.

[73] See II Congreso de la Confederación Patronal Española, *Memoria General, Barcelona, 20–6 octubre de 1919* (Barcelona, 1919), 81–118. For the pressure which the Federación Patronal de Barcelona put on the Romanones government see Romanones, *Notas*, iii. 170–2, and Burgos y Mazo, *El verano de 1919*, pp. 553–4.

[74] For the famous episode when Miláns del Bosch placed two of Romanones's appointees, the chief of police Doval and civil governor Montañés, on the train back to Madrid see Seco Serrano, *Militarismo y civilismo*, pp. 281–6.

[75] On the self-styled Barón de Koening, former head of German espionage in Barcelona, who lived in Gaudí's La Pedrera building owned by Miró y Trepat, head of the construction employers, see Madrid, *Ocho meses y un día*, pp. 54–64. For the *sindi-catos libres* see the dispassionate study of Colin Winston, *Workers and the Right in Spain, 1901–36* (Princeton, 1985), 108–70.

[76] See Francesc Cambó, *La crisi social de Catalunya* (Santiago de Chile, 1920), 20.

strikes and public disturbances, when employers were gunned down in the street in regular tit-for-tat assassination attempts, Cambó seems to have played a more fateful role in influencing events than historians previously suspected. According to the little-consulted memoirs of socialite Piedad Iturbe, Princess Hohenlohe, recently unearthed by Carlos Seco Serrano, it was Cambó who in November 1920 suggested to Prime Minister Dato the name of General Severiano Martínez Anido as civil governor of Barcelona.[77] Martínez Anido, whose appointment was warmly applauded by the Federación Patronal, the Fomento, and the Lliga Regionalista, was to rule Barcelona until October 1922 as his personal satrap.[78] He quickly endeared himself to his industrial backers by his indiscriminate arrest and deportation of trade unionists, the outlawing of the CNT, official protection for a campaign of terror led by the *sindicatos libres*, and, most of all, his implementation of the notorious *ley de fugas* by which political undesirables were reported 'shot trying to escape'.[79]

POST-WAR ECONOMIC DEPRESSION

The main reason for the stiffening of support from all sections of the Catalan business community for repressive measures was clear to see. From the winter of 1920, the Principality was hit by a severe post-war economic depression caused by a fall in exports of manufactured goods together with a drop in domestic consumption. The first sign of recession was a spate of bank crashes, beginning with the Bank of Terrassa in November 1920. A month later the prestigious Bank of Barcelona suspended payments, and in the ensuing panic a number of less important financial houses were forced to close their doors to the public. Deprived of opportunities for profitable investment in Catalonia after the war, a number of individuals and financial institutions had unwisely dabbled in currency speculation.[80] By the beginning

[77] Piedad Iturbe, *Sucedió una vez . . .* (Madrid, 1954), 263–4, cited in Seco Serrano, *Cambó en sus Memòries*, p. 44. There is a fuller reference in *Militarismo y civilismo*, pp. 290–1.

[78] In May 1921 all the economic societies of Barcelona paid homage to Don Severiano, see *El Trabajo Nacional*, May 1921.

[79] On Martínez Anido's encouragement of the *libres* see Winston, *Workers and the Right*, pp. 141–63.

[80] On the Catalan banking crisis see especially Francesc Cabana, *Bancs i banquers a Catalunya* (Barcelona, 1972), 183–205, and his *Història del Banc de Barcelona* (Barcelona, 1978), 163–229. For a wider view of the problems of Catalan banking see Carles Sudrià, 'Desarrollo industrial y subdesarrollo bancario en Cataluña, 1844–1950', *Investigaciones Económicas*, 18 (1982), 137–76.

of 1921 the crisis was generalized. Especially hit was the textile sector. In April 1921, 140 mills were at a standstill, throwing 20,000 operatives out of work. A further 120 establishments worked at below full capacity, putting an additional 50,000 on short-time. In their submission to a government inquiry, the millowners blamed a number of factors for the downturn in trade, among them the depreciation of the leading European currencies against the peseta, which both discouraged overseas sales and led to the invasion of the Spanish market by foreign competition, as well as a slump in the fortunes of the nation's cereal growers and wine owners who together constituted an important section of the domestic market for textile goods.[81] In addition to the slump which affected the mill towns, half of the labour force in the Catalan metallurgical sector was laid off.[82]

Apart from holding down labour costs, through a frontal assault on the trade union movement, Catalan business also called for higher customs duties to defend those industries hit by the post-war recession, along with official support to resolve the Catalan banking crisis. They were to get one further opportunity to tackle Catalonia's (and Spain's) economic problems from the seat of power. After the routing of the Spanish army in Morocco in August 1921, Maura was again called upon to form a National Government. In a second phase of collaboration between the Catalan industrial élite and the political oligarchy in Madrid, which it had so vehemently assailed over the previous three years, Cambó accepted office as Minister of Finance. In another short-lived term of eight months in the Calle Alcalá, Cambó succeeded in introducing a more protectionist tariff and a new banking law (*Ley de Ordenación Bancaria*) which malicious tongues claimed was designed purely to aid the reconstitution of the Bank of Barcelona.[83]

Nevertheless, the golden days of Lliga representation in the highest offices of state were soon to be over. Already, Catalan business' aspiration of spear-heading the modernization of the Spanish economy to meet the post-war challenge had given way, under the threat of proletarian militancy, to a backs-to-the-wall defence at all costs. After La

[81] Comisión Protectora de la Producción Nacional, *Crisis de la producción y del trabajo* (Madrid, 1921), *passim; El Trabajo Nacional*, May 1921, and Joaquín Aguilera, 'Informe sobre la crisis industrial de Cataluña', *Revista Nacional de Economía*, 49–50 (1923), 29–48.

[82] *Boletín de la Cámara de Comercio y Navegación de Barcelona*, Apr. 1921; *El Trabajo Nacional*, Apr. 192.

[83] In his memoirs Cambó dismissed this suggestion, attributed to La Cierva, as fantastic, see *Memòries*, 1. 352–3.

Cierva brought down the Maura government in March 1922, the new administration presided over by Sánchez Guerra again preached class collaboration. CNT leaders were released from gaol. To loud protests from the Fomento del Trabajo Nacional, Martínez Anido, the butcher of Barcelona, was sacked.[84] During the first half of 1923 the Lliga faced a critical challenge from the newly founded Acció Catalana, which had inherited the business party's mantle of accidentalism. In the provincial elections of 10 June 1923 the Lliga found itself defeated in Barcelona. Cambó resigned from the Cortes and retreated into silence. Meanwhile, his *bête noire*, Santiago Alba, minister of state in García Prieto's government of Liberal Concentration, set about undoing Cambó's achievements in his last spell in office by negotiating commercial treaties with Britain and France.[85] Moreover, the general transport strike of May–June 1923 showed signs that the CNT was recovering from the days of repression.[86]

Disenchantment with the politicians once more, as in 1898, caused Catalan business to court a general. Miguel Primo de Rivera, Captain General of Catalonia, had already built up good relations with Puig i Cadafalch, president of the *Mancomunitat*, and the Marqués de Alella, mayor of Barcelona.[87] When he staged his *coup d'état* in Barcelona on 23 September 1923 the Fomento del Trabajo Nacional pledged its unqualified support.[88] They were to be rewarded by the Primo de Rivera dictatorship's commitment to infrastructural reforms, including road and railway building and irrigation schemes, which the Fomento and its sister organizations in the Principality saw as the most effective way of raising the real disposable income of the Spanish population.[89] Yet events did not prove so propitious for the politicians of the Lliga. Despite previous assurances to the contrary, in 1924 the dictator abolished the *Mancomunitat* of which they were so proud. Cambó went into exile from where he waged a hostile campaign against the politics of the dictatorship.

In sum, the period 1898–1923 represented a remarkable phase in the history of the Catalan business community. Spain's military defeat in the Spanish–American War, followed by the loss of her lucrative

[84] *El Trabajo Nacional*, Aug. 1922.

[85] For this low point in Cambó's political career see *Memòries*, 1. 366–9.

[86] *Producción: Publicación de la Federación Patronal de Cataluña*, June 1923.

[87] Cambó, *Memòries*, 1. 375.

[88] See 'La adhesión del Fomento', *El Trabajo Nacional*, Sept. 1923.

[89] See especially Guillermo Graell, *La crisis algodonera: Su relación con la general en España: Obras públicas como remedio* (Barcelona, 1923), 5–30.

colonial markets, pushed the Fomento and other industrial organizations into seeking a new *modus vivendi* with the political oligarchy in Madrid. The first tentative steps taken by the industrial élite of the Principality in supporting Polavieja in his quest for 'reforms from above' soon gave way to an overtly regionalist stance, largely due to Silvela's insensitivity towards the Catalans' modest demands for purely administrative decentralization. Frustrated in their endeavours to capture alternative overseas outlets for their products, Catalan business was forced to fall back on securing a larger slice of the domestic market. Fortunately, they were not the only regional pressure group to lobby for greater tariff protection. To pursue their growing demands in Madrid, the Catalan industrial élite could count on its own party, the Lliga Regionalista which, along with Lerroux's Radicals, was to dominate Catalan political life during the last two decades of the Restoration. Under the leadership of Cambó, whose ambitions seemingly knew no bounds, the Lliga embarked on a breathtaking course of impossible political coalitions, daring U-turns, collaboration with selected oligarchs, attacks on conciliators in government, flirtations with the military juntas, some civil governors, Captain Generals, etc. In the end, their opportunism brought about their demise within Catalan politics. During the Second Republic (1931–9), it was the less cynical Esquerra Republicana which secured an autonomy statute for Catalonia. Republican politicians, moreover, preoccupied with the problems of the Spanish countryside, were less inclined to lend an ear to the schemes and protestations of the Fomento and its business friends.

5. THE CRISIS OF THE DYNASTIC ÉLITE IN THE TRANSITION FROM MONARCHY TO REPUBLIC, 1929–1931

Shlomo Ben-Ami

A leading role played by élites characterizes transitions from traditional politics to a modern political system. Spain's transition to the Second Republic was preceded by years of social and political change that undermined the position of the traditional élites—bourgeois politicians, landowners, army, and church—as real power élites. Moreover, social and political development brought these traditional élites into conflict with each other over the proper role of government in a changing society. Consequently, they failed to respond in a united and coherent way to the challenge of modernization.

Extreme and revolutionary solutions generally occur during regime transition when the rigidity of élites produces an unbridgeable polarization within society. In the present case, however, a democratic republic emerged precisely because of the ability of important elements in the élites, notably the army and the politicians, to contemplate change, thus complying with the insistent pressure of a growing number of politically motivated Spaniards.

A distinction must be drawn however between the harsher, even fanatic, reaction of the social, non-governing élite and that of the governing élite.[1] The latter responded to the crisis with a curious attempt to absorb important elements of both the ideology and the patterns of political organization of their republican rivals. It was in their democratic credentials rather than in an authoritarian monarchist philosophy that important elements in the dynastic political élite claimed to look for legitimacy; a posture conspicuously reminiscent of Franco's political élite during the recent transition to democracy in Spain.

However, the governing élite was hardly immune from tensions

---

[1] The terms are used by the Italian sociologist of élites Vilfredo Pareto, *The Mind in Society* (New York, 1935). Gaetano Mosca made a similar distinction within the ruling class between the political class and the political élite: *The Ruling Class* (New York, 1939).

between modernism and *politique à l'ancienne*. Moreover, these tensions exposed the incoherence and weaknesses of its essay in political modernization. Rather than a positive enterprise, this experiment was the reflection of the élite's weakening of resolve and of its fragmentation and conceptual disorientation while its republican opponents reached their highest stage of organization. Gaetano Mosca rightly described such a disintegration of the ruling minority as an avenue to its perdition. For years it had failed to absorb into its ranks new and youthful elements; hence it now faced the crisis of transition in a state of numerical and qualitative decay. Indeed, the Republic can be seen as the result of a peaceful 'circulation of élites' that originated in the decline of the monarchist ethos and the emergence of a more powerful democratic one.

The immediate source of the crisis of Spain's political élite did not lie, however, in the emergence of the republican movement; it stemmed from the policies of a royal dictator, Primo de Rivera (1923–30). The dynastic parties had been virtually disbanded by his consistent policy of ostracism and persecution. The systematic harassment of politicans initiated by the dictator, the closure of their centres, and the suspension of their press, succeeded in depriving them of their political strongholds. Especially detrimental to the *políticos* were the royal decree dismissing any state functionary suspected of being 'in contact with politicans'[2] and another barring ex-ministers from positions in public companies. Thirty-four prominent figures of the old governing élite, among them Romanones, Sánchez Guerra, and Sánchez de Toca, were affected by this measure which denied them the indispensable prerequisite of power: the position of dispensers of benefits and largess.[3]

Deprived of official favour, the old political clienteles simply disbanded. 'This is a period of desertions', wrote one of Antonio Maura's followers.[4] No less adversely affected was the Liberal Party. Eleven ex-ministers considered themselves as Romanones's personal clientele,[5] yet he had no party to lead. He could see his 'friends' only at funerals, where they looked to him 'as if they have just emerged from some attic, where they had been put by the landlord as useless items'.[6] His colleague Villanueva, who claimed to be followed only by his own shadow,

[2] Archivo Historico Nacional, serie A, Gobernación, Leg. 45, no. 33, 2 Nov. 1923.

[3] *The Times*, 15 Oct. 1923.

[4] Maura Archive, Leg. 322: Blas Aguilar to Antonio Maura, 10 Apr. 1924.

[5] Romanones Archive (henceforth RA), Leg. 33, no. 1: 'Ex-ministros'.

[6] A. Hurtado, *Quaranta anys d'advocat* (Barcelona, 1964), ii. 220.

had to cancel more than one meeting because of lack of participants.[7] Many Liberal figures, especially among the Albistas—sixty-three ex-deputies considered themselves as such—started now their estrangement from the 'perfidious' king who had allowed the dictatorship and the maltreatment of their political patron, Santiago Alba.[8] By the end of the dictatorship, even Romanones—perhaps the most typical embodiment of old politics—was ready to question the prerogatives of the crown.[9]

The major impact of the dictatorship on the dynastic political élite was that it demolished its power bases. Moreover, as is usually the case with one-party regimes, the dictatorship accelerated the *political* decline of the traditional élites, and created the channels for the emergence of a new political élite. The old one either kept aloof or was barred from the institutions of the new regime. 'New men', mostly agrarian bourgeois and officials of Catholic corporations untarnished by old political connections and alliances with the so-called 'traditional oligarchy', moved to key positions in Primo's institutions and administrative apparatus.[10]

The 'circulation of élites' under Primo de Rivera was mostly confined to the governing sphere; the dictator was not a revolutionary bent on dislocating the traditional social and economic élites, that is, Mosca's political class and Pareto's non-governing élite. However, his regime did bring about important changes in the social structure of Spain that were to have far-reaching consequences.

Indeed, the whole process leading to the rise of the Second Republic points to the association between changes in the social structure and the rise and fall of élites. Spanish society reached a turning point during the 1920s. The economic 'boom' of the dictatorship increased wealth, technological potentialities, and urbanization. In 1932, 42 per cent of Spain's population lived in towns of more than 10,000 inhabitants; the population of Madrid and the provincial capital cities increased during the 1920 by 30 per cent.[11] It was precisely in urban Spain that the Republic was to achieve its greatest electoral gains in 1931. In other words, the flight from the Spanish countryside

---

[7] RA, Leg. 28, no. 35: Belmonte to Romanones, 13 June 1925.

[8] Alba Archive, Emilio Gómez to Alba, 30 Mar. 1925; M. García Venero, *Santiago Alba* (Madrid, 1963), 219–22.

[9] RA, Leg. 63, no. 31: Romanones to the king, n.d.

[10] S. Ben-Ami, *Fascism from Above* (Oxford, 1983), 143–7.

[11] *Anuario Estadístico de España*, 20–1 (1929); J. Diez Nicolás, *Tamaño, densidad y crecimiento de la población en España, 1900–1960* (Madrid, 1971), 19.

had seriously undermined the grip of the old political élite on the electorate; the once almost legendary omnipotence of the Ministry of the Interior was eroded by the sheer weight of the structural social changes.[12] Thus, if the dynastic political élite were to return and remain in power after the dictatorship it would have to articulate an alternative way to electoral *caciquismo* and to the politics of immobilism.

The challenge to old politics lay in the substantial de-archaization of Spain's social structure. The proportion of the work-force employed in agriculture decreased by about 12 per cent in the 1920s, while that employed in industry and in the service sector increased by about 5 per cent and 6 per cent respectively.[13]

People seemed to be more curious and to travel more than ever before as the number of commuters using the rail system increased by about four million, and the spectacular development of the road system brought about an increase of 400 per cent in the number of cars in the country. Private consumption of electricity showed a sharp increase; the number of telephones tripled; the radio and the movies completely changed the patterns of domestic life.[14] An increasingly urban society was now attracted by the material and political temptations of 'Europeanization'. For the middle classes, republicanism became in 1931 a vehicle through which they could express their political dignity and independence. They 'threw themselves', to use the expression of a contemporary, into the Republic as an outlet for their expectations for change.[15] With the fall of Primo de Rivera in 1930 'nothing would be the same. . . . He had launched great schemes of modernization', and there was bound to be 'much political fruit in addition to economic changes'.[16]

The democratization of society undermined the validity of the political culture of the old dynastic oligarchy. The traditional ways of vying for power by means of sinister manoeuvres in the corridors of the Palacio de Oriente rapidly lost their legitimacy once the collapse of the dictatorship triggered an explosion of political passions throughout urban Spain.[17] But the *políticos* were ill equipped both mentally and

[12] Cf. G. Maura, *Bosquejo histórico de la Dictadura* (Madrid, 1930), 9.

[13] *Estadísticas Básicas de España 1900–1970* (Madrid, 1975), 369.

[14] Ibid. 290; *Boletín de la Camara de Transportes Mecánicos*, Apr. 1928; *la Nación*, 20 Dec. 1928; *Radio y Luz*, Mar. 1931.

[15] *La República*—el sentido de una evolución social, *La Voz de Galicia*, 25 Apr. 1931; Gil Robles, *No fue posible la paz* (Barcelona, 1968), 33.

[16] H. Buckley, *Life and Death of the Spanish Republic* (London, 1940), 26.

[17] S. Ben-Ami, *The Origins of the Second Republic in Spain* (Oxford, 1978), 30–67.

organizationally for mass politics. Long used to an intimate distribution of the spoils of power, they were never disposed to absorb new and vigorous social segments. Now, moreover, they exhibited a weakening of resolve, which as both Pareto and Mosca observed, is the avenue to the political perdition of élites. They possessed neither the mental residues necessary for keeping them in power nor the confidence necessary for using force against the rising challenge from the left.

It is precisely in a period of modernization, when ideals long accepted as the foundation of society appear antiquated and useless,[18] and when a political effervescence is apparent even among sectors that have always been disgusted by politics,[19] that the importance of élites capable of inspiring effective action is greatly enhanced. The dynastic political élite was in no position to provide the necessary leadership and security to a society in transition. Its world-view was in a state of advanced decay, a new and more vigorous one was now asserting itself.

With no new political notions to advance, the old governing élite capitulated to the superior values of its republican enemies. A growing number of politically motivated Spaniards clamoured for a political shift, and the élite had no choice but to comply. Republicanism was further legitimized by the desertion of members of the élite and their adoption of the new republican gospel. Republicans appeared where they were least expected: in royal academies, convents, among the clergy, and 'even under the stones'.[20] In Ossorio y Gallardo's house 'even the cat' had become republican.[21] Romero Otazo, a professor of canon law, made a republican confession,[22] monarchist councillors in Madrid converted to republicanism,[23] and a spokesman for the upper-middle class and monarchist Lliga, Vallés i Pujal, shocked his hearers when he declared that 90 per cent of the members of his party were actually republicans.[24]

But the most spectacular defections of élite members in favour of republicanism were that of the grand Andalusian cacique and ex-Minister of War, Niceto Alcalá Zamora, and that of Miguel Maura, the son of *the* conservative statesman of modern Spain. Their desertion underlined the crisis of confidence in the old order experienced by

---

[18] A. Ossorio y Gallardo, *Incompatibilidad* (Madrid, 1930), 6.
[19] *La Ciencia Tomista*, Mar.–Apr. 1931.
[20] *El Progreso*, 25 June 1930.
[21] J. A. Balbontín, *La España de mi experiencia* (Mexico, 1952), 206–7.
[22] *El Sol* (henceforth *ES*), 22 May 1930.
[23] *El Progreso*, 25 June 1930.
[24] *El Imparcial* (henceforth *EI*), 27 Mar. 1930.

many in the 'respectable' classes. As in France where the Thiers and the MacMahons had made possible the advent of the Third Republic, so the desertion of Alcalá Zamora and Maura came to mean for many in the upper classes of Spanish society the institutionalization of an orderly democracy as a barrier against the 'red menace'.[25] The notion seemed to be permeating the Spanish élites that security might perhaps be achieved through change.

As Mosca observed, élites rule because of their cohesion. The Spanish élites faced the crisis of Alfonso's throne in a state of disintegration. To begin with, the desertion of prestigious members of the élite dealt a serious blow to the solidity of traditional monarchism.[26] Secondly, neither in their halfhearted adoption of a strategy of change nor in their entrenchment in old-style monarchist positions did the remaining leaders of the dynastic parties shed the appearance of a coherent class. Furthermore, a rift between the governing and the non-governing élite developed because of what appeared to be their different response to the challenge of modern politics posed by the republican offensive. The *políticos* seemed better disposed to flirt with the values of their enemies.

As early as 1929, in the midst of an impressive revival of Spanish republicanism, conservatives started to coin slogans of modernization. In a daring book, the Marqués de Carvajal spoke of the need to transform his party into a 'Conservative party of opinion in the English style'.[27] This modern notion of 'open democracy', and of conservatism in close contact with the 'street', that was also endorsed by the party's organ *La Epoca*, was expected to attract wide segments of society such as the working class, small businessmen, and property owners.[28]

Yet this novel line did not really reflect the attitude of the leadership of the Conservative Party. The formation of the Berenguer government, following Primo de Rivera's departure in late January 1930, with a majority of Conservative ministers, virtually removed from the agenda of Spanish Conservatism the issue of modernization. Once they were established in power, 'renovation' simply became unnecessary.[29] The Conservative leader Bugallal even cynically dismissed the dictatorship as a minor episode which in no way reflected upon the

---

[25] Alcalá Zamora in *ES*, 15 Apr. 1930; *Nueva España*, 1 Sept., 18 Oct. 1930.
[26] *ABC*, 1 June 1930; *EI*, 4 May 1930.
[27] Marqués de Carvajal, *¿Cuál es el horizonte político de España?* (Madrid, 1929).
[28] *La Epoca* (henceforth *LE*), 20, 23 Feb., 25 Mar., 1 July, 8, 13 Aug. 1929.
[29] *LE*, 30 Jan. 3–27 Feb., 7 July 1930.

validity of the Constitution, and hence made superfluous any call for constitutional reform.[30]

Without any 'new definition' in a period of high expectations, the Conservative Party was inevitably condemned to fall back on the politics of *caciquismo*. But even the reviving of old Conservative circles ran into difficulties as the party hierarchy was deeply split into personalistic factions. The political barons who supported Sánchez Guerra's flirtation with democratic politics—Bergamín, Hernández Lázaro, Abilio Calderón—questioned Bugallal's leadership;[31] in Alicante, Salvador Canals resigned altogether from the party.[32] In Córdoba and Seville party discipline collapsed; and in the wheat growing area of Valladolid, Conde de Gamazo's fief, no mood of accommodation with 'modernism' could be detected.[33] 'Reorganization' in other places was a simple caciquista revival. Bugallalista strongholds in Galicia and elsewhere, those of La Cierva in Murcia, and the Vizconde de Eza in Soria showed some signs of life after long years of complete lethargy.[34]

Yet, tactically at least, tribute was still paid to the current fashion of 'modernization'. Youth sections were being set up in the provinces, meetings were held to discuss central issues, contacts were initiated with the British Conservative Party, the demand to 'imitate' its organization was again put forward, and an ultra-modern secretariat was organized under the auspices of the Conservative minister Sr. Weiss.[35]

Probably the most dynamic offspring of Spanish conservatism's essay in modern politics during the crisis of Alfonso's monarchy was the Constitutionalist movement. Its original founders—prominent caciques like the Conservative Burgos y Mazo and the Liberal Villanueva—were joined after the dictatorship by prestigious politicians like Bergamín, Melquíades Alvarez, and the ex-Prime Minister Sánchez Guerra, whose devastating criticism of the authoritarian Spanish monarchy as early as 1925[36] had been encouraging Conservatives to 'a rapprochement with the left'. It was indeed in this 'crisis of the con-

[30] *LE*, 11 Feb. 1930.

[31] *ABC*, 12–15 Feb., 5 Mar. 1930.

[32] *El Agrario* (Alicante), 25 Oct. 1930.

[33] *La Vanguardia* (henceforth *LV*), 19 Feb. 1930; *ABC*, 13 Mar. 1930; *Unión Monárquica*, 15 Jan. 1930.

[34] Vicente Risco, *El problema político de Galicia* (Madrid, 1930), *passim*. J. de La Cierva, *Notas de mi vida* (Madrid, 1955), 336; *ABC*, 18 Sept. 1930.

[35] *ABC*, 21 May, 5–27 June, 5 July, 6 Sept., 1 Oct., 6–19 Nov. 1930; *LE*, 20 Sept. 1930.

[36] *ES*, 28 Feb. 1925.

servative feeling'[37] that the origins of the Constitutionalist group, officially launched in 1927, should be looked for. The Constitutionalists consistently demolished the politics of immobilism by lending their prestige to the growing call for constitutional reform.[38] Constitutionalism, however, was seen by these political barons and their respective clienteles as a way to safeguard the hegemony of Spain's traditional élites by dissociating them from the personal fate of a doomed 'perjurer' king who had trampled upon the Constitution by sanctioning the dictatorship. Essentially, Constitutionalism was proposed as a conservative solution to the crisis of the monarchy. Should the left not get its constituent parliament peaceably, the Constitutionalists warned, it would resort to 'Soviet-style means'.[39]

The tragedy of the Conservative élite was compounded by its inability to respond to the challenge of Constitutionalism on the one hand, and by its incapacity to present a coherent reactionary response to the crisis of the monarchy on the other hand. True, once the possibility emerged in the summer of 1930 that a renovated Liberal Party might assume power, the recent Conservative rhetoric of modernism was replaced by one of resistance to change; a new coalition was sought that could be 'the strongest bastion of social conservatism, the most impregnable wall against revolutionary tumults'. Moreover, the same *La Epoca* which had previously toyed with modernist slogans lent now its support to this new attempt to rally 'the defenders and saviours of western civilization'. But rhetoric was never matched by reality. The coalition formed in the summer of 1930 by Bugallal with the aristocratic Acción Nobiliaria, agrarian conservative groups, and Catholic syndicates never got off the ground.[40] This failure clearly underlined the rupture between the old political élite and its natural social base. The rejection by large peasant and landowner organizations of Bugallal's *démarche* was indicative of the very low credibility of 'old politics' among conscious agrarians, who had been consistently drifting away in recent years from mere conservatism towards prefascist postures.[41]

The failure to create a strong conservative bloc behind Spain's uncertain crown was also due to the diffusion and isolation of other

[37] A. Ossorio y Gallardo, *La crisis del sentido conservador* (Madrid, 1925).
[38] M. de Burgos y Mazo, *La Dictadura y los Constitucionalistas* (4 vols. Madrid 1935), *passim*.
[39] See the manifesto in *EI*, 19 Dec. 1930, and Bergamín in *ABC*, 13 Féb. 1931.
[40] *LE*, 15, 21, 29 Oct. 1930.
[41] *El Campesino*; *España Agraria* (1929–31).

conservative parties and groups. They were 'anaemic remnants . . . exhausted by the years'.[42] The noble ambitions of Gabriel Maura to integrate 'the healthy elements of the right' into his newly formed Derecha Nacional ended in complete failure.[43] Primo de Rivera's ex-ministers converted indeed their Unión Monárquica—a party of ex-functionaries, businessmen, and engineers who looked back with longing to the 'boom and law and order' years of the dictatorship—into a highly motivated party. However, rather than constituting an all-out effort to save the conservative constitutional monarchy, it pointed towards the Falange and Franco's Spain. Hence the Alfonsist political élite ostracized the UM both because of its ideological radicalism and its belligerent model of action; it preferred its own spiritless brand of conservative politics.[44]

A severe blow at the chance of creating a socially solid base for Spanish conservatism in this crucial hour for the fate of the Spanish monarchy was also delivered by the upper-middle-class Catalan Lliga Regionalista. Resentful at the role played by the king in Primo de Rivera's vendetta against Catalonia, Lliga leaders started to espouse a quasi-accidentalist theory, claiming that Catalonia would fare no worse under a republic.[45] It was only in the last weeks before the fall of the monarchy that Lliga leader Cambó managed to patch up a conservative coalition of Mauristas, Regionalists, and personal friends across the country. But, though paying tribute to the current fashion in politics and underlining the élite's wavering search for a way to cope with modernism without abandoning the most vital interests of socially conservative Spain,[46] the new Partido del Centro Constitucional did not really get off the ground, and in any case came too late to save the monarchy. The liberal *El Sol* welcomed the new party as 'a modern and European right of which Spain would not have to be ashamed',[47] but the masses did not rally behind the by now negativistic perception of politics by the élite: the new party promised to fight the anti-religious, the anti-monarchists, the Separatists, and the Communists.[48]

[42] *LV*, 15 Feb., 1, 3, Mar., 4 June, 5 Sept., 8, 12 Nov. 1930.

[43] D. Berenguer, *De la Dictadura a la República* (Madrid, 1946), 112.

[44] S. Ben-Ami, 'The Forerunners of Spanish Fascism: Unión Patriótica and Unión Monárquica', *European Studies Review*, 9 (1979).

[45] *EI*, 27 Mar. 1930; *LV*, 28 Sept. 1930; Ventosa y Calvell to Alba, 27 May 1930, in Alba Archive.

[46] Baldomero Argente in *LV*, 3, 10, Mar. 1931.

[47] *ES*, 5 Mar. 1931.

[48] *La Veu de Catalunya*, 4 Mar. 1931; Maura Archive: Gabriel Maura to Indalecio Abril, n.d.

The extent of the Liberal élite's flirtation with modernism was perhaps larger than that of the Conservatives, but hardly more convincing. As early as 1928, Liberals spoke of the need to absorb socialist ideas;[49] and a year later, Baldomero Argente, a prominent spokesman of the party on agrarian affairs, called for the creation of a 'modern Liberal Party' open to both proletarians and bourgeois.[50] With the fall of the dictatorship, the semblance of accommodation with modernism gained strength. The major party baron, the Conde de Romanones, voiced his view that the king should become the 'hereditary president' of a republicanized monarchy.[51] The party's organ, *El Imparcial*, and grand Liberal caciques—such as ex-premier Garciá Prieto—endorsed that view, along with the lofty expectation that a renovated Spanish Liberalism would 'radically transform Spanish society'.[52]

But when it came to real life Liberals fell back on the good old caciquista practices. Romanones and his political friends were too deeply embedded in their political culture for them to lead Spanish liberalism to a bold encounter with a changing society. The party's reorganization was essentially a revival of lethargic circles of political friends.[53] Even Romanones's novel attempt to win over the peasants of the province of Alicante through a programme of agrarian reform soon fizzled out.[54] That a Liberal politician with a dignified past like Santiago Alba should have failed in his attempt to create a broad Liberal coalition that would curb republicanism by preventing 'a sterile return to old politics', was highly indicative of the inertia of caciquista residues in the Liberal élite.[55] Alba's plan for democratizing the monarchy on the model of Belgium and England, a plan accepted by the king in the summer of 1930 in a reflection of the strains under which the crown was living,[56] was frustrated by the pettiness and lust for power of Romanones.[57] Thus, when the Liberals helped to bring down Berenguer's government in February 1931, it was not because

[49] *El Socialista*, 19 Jan., 15 Feb., 3 Mar. 1928.
[50] *LV*, 21 Apr. 1929.
[51] *ABC*, 6, 12, 13 Feb. 1930.
[52] *EI*, 5–12 Feb., 4–12 Apr. 1930.
[53] Ben-Ami, *The Origins*, pp. 196–7.
[54] RA, Leg. 49, no. 24: *Problemas Agrarios-Ante una Cruzada*, Nov. 1930; *ABC*, 9 Nov. 1930.
[55] Hurtado, *Quaranta anys*, ii. 280; *ABC*, 23 Apr. 1930.
[56] *El Socialista*, 25 May 1930; Alba Archive: Alba to Duque de Almodovar del Valle, 25 June 1930.
[57] García Venero, *Alba*, pp. 307–8; *ABC*, 7 July 1930; Romanones, *Notas de una vida* (Madrid, 1947), 231–2.

they had any novel solutions to the crisis of the Spanish monarchy. They rather acted as an impatient club of political friends eager to distribute favours to their anxious clientele. They wanted to rule not because they possessed any new solutions, but because it was their 'turn' to do so.

Compared with the waverings and internal squabbles within the politically inept governing élite, the response of the social élite to the republican offensive was as determined as it could be. Sánchez Guerra's devastating Philippic against King Alfonso in February 1930 moved scores of voluntary organizations to a staunch defence of the monarchy. Middle-class 'patriotic' ladies,[58] members of the nobility,[59] Catholic lay organizations, non-Marxist syndicates, and sections of monarchist youth spread throughout the country to propagate 'the monarchist ideal'. Huge files of signatures for the monarchy were organized, mass meetings and demonstrations were staged, aeroplanes scattered propaganda sheets over provincial capitals,[60] and, when necessary, monarchist youth even defended the king's honour in physical clashes with his enemies.[61] 'Non-political' associations, such as the Casa de la Democracia Monárquica, the Partido Socialista Monárquico Obrero Alfonso XIII, which coined socialist slogans in a pathetic attempt to dissuade urban workers from joining the swelling trend to the left, the Instituto Alfonso-Victoria, and the Centro Cultural Monárquico laboured vainly against the 'corrupting' influence of republicanism.[62]

Moreover, whereas the *políticos'* response to the challenge of republicanism was essentially pragmatic, even cynical, that of the non-governing élite was ideological; it reflected a commitment of the conservative social base of the monarchy to articulate an ideological answer to republicanism. This was best exemplified by the activities of the Campaña de Orientación Social founded to propagate the 'four basic principles of society' as Catholic intellectuals like Severino Aznar, Ramiro de Maeztu, Pío Zabala, and Angel Herrera perceived them. These were religion, family, order, and monarchy. The assumption of the organizers of the campaign was that the Spanish monarchy would not be saved by petty political manoeuvres, but rather through a

[58] *Mujeres Españolas*, 1930–1; *La Unión, Revista de las Damas Españolas*, 1930–1.
[59] *ABC*, 5–14 Mar., 4, 22 Apr. 1930.
[60] *ABC*, 14–28 Mar., 5–16 Apr., 7–20 May 1930; *Estampa*, 22 Apr. 1930.
[61] *ABC*, 25 Apr., 9 May, 16 July, 26 Sept. 1930; *EI*, 7 Mar., 4 Apr. 1930.
[62] *ABC*, 7 May, 3, 10 June 1930; *LV*, 15 Feb., 5–12 Mar., 22 July, 20 Aug. 1930.

crusade against the culture of unlimited freedom from which republicanism drew its strength, the alarming symptoms of sexual permissiveness, the upsurge of pornographic literature, and the new 'dissolvent'
tendencies in family life. In huge gatherings throughout the country,
social stability, a return to religious certainty, and family cohesiveness
were repeatedly advanced as the pre-condition for the salvation of
Spain.[63].

The ecclesiastical establishment lent its unconditional support to
this 'non-political' campaign. It did so through its pastorals and educational institutions, through the indoctrination conducted by parish
priests,[64] through its large network of lay organizations—such as
Acción Católica, the Asociación de Estudiantes Católicos, and the
Confederación Nacional Católico-Agraria with its 5,000 syndicates.[65]
The hierarchy also sponsored the energetic Asociación de Mujeres
Españolas and the Unión de Damas Españolas del Sagrado Corazón in
their campaign against the 'immoral and unpractical ideology of feminism', and in their 'crusade on behalf of religion, the fatherland and the
king'.[66] To preserve society from 'emancipatory and revolutionary'
ideas, such was the unyielding endeavour of the ecclesiastical
establishment;[67] meanwhile the dynastic political élite, engaged in the
self-same battle, displayed a mixture of ineptitude and defeatism. The
primate, cardinal Segura, was relentless in his encouragement of
Catholics to defend 'our august king'. In December 1930, he even
succeeded where politicians failed, in the test of unity. He unified the
Catholic and the free (that is, non-confessional but anti-socialist)
syndicates and launched them in a campaign against the wave of political and revolutionary strikes of that fateful winter.[68] Segura did not
shrink from urging the Catholic masses to vote in the next elections for
those who supported the Church's vision of right and wrong. Bishops
across the country seconded his initiatives. Indeed, Acción Católica's
main effort centered on encouraging those who believed in 'Catholicism and its civilization' to actively engage in monarchist politics.[69]
Contrary to some self-righteous claims about the Church's neutrality

---

[63] For the campaign see *El Debate*, 15, 29 Apr., 6 May, 11 Nov., 9 Dec. 1930; *ABC*,
11 Apr., 21, 28 Oct., 25, 27 Nov. 1930.
[64] Cf. *La Cruz de la Parroquia*, Alcalá de Henares, 28 Dec. 1930.
[65] *EI*, 8 Nov. 1930.   [66] *Mujeres Españolas*, 1930–1; *La Unión*, 1930–1.
[67] *Acción Católica de la Mujer*, Jan.–May 1930.
[68] *La Ciencia Tomista*, Mar.–Apr. 1931; *ABC*, 16, 20 Nov., 17 Dec. 1930.
[69] *Boletín de Acción Católica*, Jan.–Sept. 1929; Segura in *ABC*, 9 Mar. 1930;
J. Requejo, *El Cardenal Segura* (Toledo, 1932), 101–12, 128–9.

in political contests,[70] the ecclesiastical establishment was a bastion of monarchism. Its spokesmen justified any strong measure that the Berenguer government took against the excesses of republican propaganda.[71] In response to the question posed by Canon Hilario Yaben's book *¿Monarquía o República?* the Church definitely opted for the 'absolute monarchy'.

However, as in the case of the dynastic political élite, the monarchist social reaction remained divided among its various components. As *ABC* pointed out, it was 'a prolix movement without any organic coherence'.[72] Interestingly, it was Acción Nobliliaria, an aristocratic entity, which, motivated by an instinct of self-preservation, acted as the main agent of monarchist unity. This venture, too, failed once it reached the operative stage. The Duque de Almenara Alta reminded his peers that 'the Russian Tsar was overthrown because his aristocracy did not rally behind him'.[73] Acción Nobiliaria and its offspring, Acción Monárquica and Reacción Ciudadana, were indeed instrumental in mobilizing the Spanish nobility against the 'Soviet hurricane', but hardly successful in forging a common strategy for Spanish monarchism.[74]

The last cabinet of the Spanish monarchy, formed in February 1931, was not exactly imbued with the fighting spirit exhibited by its social base; it started by bowing to the insistent call of the opposition for municipal elections. It was a fatalistic team of ministers reluctantly forced to serve in a national unity government under the colourless leadership of an admiral, Aznar. A minister for the first time in his life, Gabriel Maura had the feeling of 'escorting the crown to the cemetery', while García Prieto waited anxiously for the elections to relieve him of his ministerial burden.[75] Moreover, whereas the republicans were said to be running in the spring of 1931 'one of the most skilful electoral campaigns in world history',[76] the government, 'a heterogeneous mixture of egoism and colourless neutrality',[77] failed to overcome caciquista and personalistic considerations in favour of a nationwide strategy.[78]

[70] *La Ciencia Tomista*, Mar.–Apr. 1931.
[71] Ibid., Feb.–Apr. 1931.   [72] *ABC*, 9 Dec. 1930.
[73] *ABC*, 3 Apr. 1930, 25 Jan., 3 Feb. 1931.
[74] *ABC*, 23 Mar., 2 Apr., 1 May, 22, 25 June, 11, 20 July.
[75] G. Maura, *Recuerdos de mi vida* (Madrid, n.d.), 198–9; García Prieto to Romanones in *RA*, Leg. 63, no. 18.
[76] García Venero, *Alba*, p. 328.   [77] *ABC*, 24 Mar. 1931.
[78] J. M. Hoyos y Vinent, *Mi testimonio* (Madrid, 1962), 53–4.

It was again mainly up to the non-governing, social élite to lead the counter-offensive against republicanism. For the first time in their history monarchists ran a modern electoral campaign—which they had not felt the need to do so long as their rule did not depend on public opinion. Advertising companies were contracted;[79] aeroplanes were used to drop leaflets; electoral meetings were held all over the country;[80] bishops warned that voting for the left 'would be judged by Jesus Christ on the Day of Judgement',[81] parish priests crudely threatened their flock with 'whips and scorpions' should they vote against religion,[82] aristocratic balls were cancelled to allow the nobility to join the general effort—some aristocrats even rushed home from abroad especially for the elections;[83] and a women's organization was so overwhelmed by volunteers as to claim that 'never before have women been so motivated by political sentiments'.[84] The manifestations of the monarchist reaction were so intense in Madrid, and their electoral centres were so crowded, that their opening hours had to be extended, and thousands of volunteers enlisted.[85]

The stagnant and unimaginative governing élite was outdone by its social base in the electoral campaign of 1931. This accounts in part for both the intensity of monarchist propaganda and, more importantly, the novelty of its message. The monarchy had been so seriously undermined in recent years that the social élite preferred to concentrate upon the defence of its social position and of 'traditional Hispanic values' rather than that of the monarchy as such. The radical right in the Second Republic, which relegated the monarchy to a secondary position in order to adopt a fascist oratory, had its immediate origins in this erosion of the monarchy's inviolable position. Suddenly, it was no longer indispensable to the defence of vested interests and of Spain's traditional values.

Furthermore, a panic-stricken conservative élite overtaken by a sense of approaching disaster now laid the foundations of a civil war mentality by rejecting in advance any unfavourable verdict at the polls. The Republic was portrayed as an illegitimate communist take-over

[79] RA, Leg. 9, no. 12: Estudio de Publicidad.
[80] *El Debate*, 7, 12 Apr. 1931; *ABC*, 27 Mar., 12 Apr. 1931.
[81] The Bishop of Tuy in *La Voz de Galicia*, 7 Apr. 1931; the bishop of Orense in *Boletín Oficial Eclesiástico del Obispado de Orense*, 10 Apr. 1931.
[82] *La Cruz de la Parroquia*, 22 Mar. 1931; *El Socialista*, Apr. 1931.
[83] Marqués de Valdeiglesias, *la sociedad española* (Madrid, 1957), 239–40.
[84] *Mujeres Españolas*, 5 Apr. 1931.
[85] *ABC*, 26 Mar. 1931; *El Debate*, 8–12 Apr. 1931.

that would destroy business, undermine Christian values by a policy of crude materialism and sensuality—a future founder of Acción Nacional, Marín Lazaro, even warned of the sharing of women by the republicans, land confiscations, and cathedrals being turned into garages. In short, the Republic was a barbarian invasion that would exterminate hispanic civilization, enthrone 'the darkest instincts of men', and allow 'the bolshevik jews to take over our beloved Spain and sow it with prostitution and wretchedness'. Democracy was now frequently dismissed as a 'foreign idea', as the Duque de Canalejas put it. In what was seen by some as an inevitable war between 'historic Spain' and 'anti-Spain', the right was urged to muster its forces and meet the left 'in the streets'. It was high time 'to organize a crusade that would show whether there still remain Catholics in Spain, brave men in our fatherland, and gentlemen in Castile' that could respond to any 'violent steps' taken by the republicans. 'Violence' could well mean the conquest of power by democratic means.[86]

The Republic was built upon the ruins of the elements of a Spanish democratic right within the Restoration's political élite. But, under the strains of the crisis of the monarchy, the traditional sociological base of that right accelerated its departure from parliamentary monarchism in order to embrace extremist notions of politics. The ideological provisions of the Republic's extreme right, its determination to undermine the foundations of the liberal state and to erode compromising tactics, together with its apocalyptic approach to social and political issues—all these were already in an advanced stage of crystallization while the *políticos* were still indulging in 'undignified abandonism'.

Unlike the highly motivated non-governing élite, the *políticos* embarked upon the electoral contest in a defeatist mood. A significant reflection of their defeatism was their grudging acceptance of the republican emphasis on the plebiscitary character of what were after all municipal elections. They were forced to admit that what was at stake was the very fate of the monarchy.[87] Thus under consistent pressure from the left, the *políticos* virtually abandoned the 1876 constitution according to which the monarchy was an inviolable institution which should, under no circumstances, become an electoral issue.

---

[86] *El Debate*, 7–12 Apr. 1931; *ABC*, 10–12 Apr. 1931; *LE*, 25, 26 Mar. 1931; Electoral Propaganda, file in Hemeroteca Municipal de Madrid, A/1681, 1685, 1691, 1700.
[87] Electoral Propaganda, file, A/1691, 1700; Conde de Romanones, *Las últimas horas de una monarquía* (Madrid, 1931), 129–31.

The philosophical capitulation of the monarchy's governing élite, reflected so far in its halfhearted adoption of 'modernist' politics, was brought to its ultimate conclusion by its prompt admission of electoral defeat once the news came in, on the evening of 12 April, that the republicans had won in most of the provincial capitals. This total absorption of the enemy's political logic was reflected in the recognition by most of the ministers that the numerical monarchist victory in rural districts was, as Gabriel Maura put it, nothing but the expression of a caciquista 'sheep-like obedience and routine', while the Republic's victory in the big cities was 'a clear verdict of the national will'.[88] Romanones even admitted the monarchy's 'absolute' defeat;[89] and Minister of War Berenguer did not lose time in exhorting his generals to abide by 'the logical course imposed by the supreme national will'.

King Alfonso's crown was sunk into oblivion by a group of confused and leaderless politicians overtaken by a mixture of weariness and defeatism. At a cabinet meeting on 13 April, most of the ministers acknowledged the monarchy's defeat and the inevitability of the government's resignation. Only La Cierva and Bugallal among the ministers attempted to resist the modern notion of the primacy of national sovereignty over that of the king. La Cierva's call to defend the monarchy 'under all circumstances' was entirely out of tune with the mood of the government. He was isolated in his now archaic attachment to the Canovite conception of the king as the sole source of power. The admission of defeat did not mean, however, that the government had a clear policy on how to handle the crisis. The ministers, caught off balance, engaged in a confusing series of individual initiatives, allowing the shrewd Romanones to emerge as the architect of 'the peaceful transmission of power' to those who now represented the 'national will'.[90]

However ready to abide by the imperatives of modernity, the ministers did not really grasp the full meaning of mass politics. The possibility that a lasting republic might be established and abolish the monarchy *for ever* did not cross their minds. Their sanguine attitude to the Republic is otherwise hardly explicable, an attitude reminiscent of that of Giolitti, the master of Italian 'old politics', towards the

[88] Romanones, *Las últimas horas*, pp. 131–2; G. Maura and M. Fernández Almagro, *¿Porqué cayó Alfonso XIII?* (Madrid, 1948), 387–9.
[89] *ABC*, 14 Apr. 1931.
[90] Ben-Ami, *The Origins*, pp. 239–44.

emergence of fascism as 'a temporary crisis'.[91] The Spanish ministers strove to solve the present 'crisis' in a gentleman-like manner as they had done with so many others in the past. They acted on the assumption that the monarchy would be restored during the next 'crisis' within a few months or even weeks. The more democratic elements within the governing élite, politicians like the Constitutionalists Villanueva, Melquíades Alvarez, and Alba, had a clearer vision of reality. They turned down the king's offer that they should lead a Constitutionalist government as a highly inadequate solution to the crisis. Melquíades Alvarez called upon the king to 'give free access to the republican ideas of the nation',[92] while Alba urged him to 'give way to the new generation'.[93] The monarch was definitely left with no alternative but that of capitulation.

This was further brought home to him when he realized that not only had his court politicians deserted him, but the army, by its 'abstentionist' attitude, had shaken an essential foundation of the regime—the personal bond between the king and his army. Thus, whereas a gap did open between the more determined social élite and the helpless governing élite, the two central élites of the monarchy—the army and the *políticos* in charge of government—were united in their attitude to the crisis and indeed to the proper role of government in a changing society. They both realized the futility of resistance. A fragmentation of the political and military élites was thus avoided, and a peaceful transmission of power was made possible. Neither the army nor the political élite exhibited the kind of rigidity that might have resulted in an extreme and revolutionary solution. The prime mover in the fall of the monarchy, Romanones, rejected out of hand the notion of the use of force. 'The Mauser gun', he said, 'is an inadequate answer to the manifestation of suffrage'.[94]

Resistance had never been part of the political tradition of Spanish politicians. Theirs was a culture of compromise and accommodation. But for La Cierva, all the members of the government bowed to the profound changes in the political mood of the country. They realized that the rapturous republican jubilation in the streets of the cities of Spain was not a problem of public order to be settled by the Civil Guard as the hard-line La Cierva maintained. The Civil Guard was

[91e] A. Lyttleton, *The Seizure of Power* (London, 1973), 94–102, 124.
[92] Burgos y Mazo, *Dictadura*, ii. 123–4.
[93] *ABC*, 14 Apr. 1931.
[94] Ben-Ami, *The Origins*, pp. 239–44.

there to fight a disorderly public, not a politically mobilized nation. This was perfectly understood by the commander of the Civil Guard, General Sanjurjo, when he warned the ministers, on 12 April, that he could not guarantee the availability of the Civil Guard for a policy of resistance.[95]

Above all, the Republic was made possible by the posture of the army's hierarchy. The experience of the dictatorship had shaken the 'monarchist cohesion' of the army[96] and made important sections of it renew the old nineteenth-century alliance between liberalism and the military; Minister of War Berenguer noted that an attitude of 'pessimism' and disorientation predominated in military circles in the months that preceded the Republic.[97] Romanones referred to this erosion in the army's loyalty to the crown as the reason why the king had to go and give way to the Republic.[98] Sanjurjo's attitude was highly discouraging for the king. Nor was General Mola's recognition of the elections as the 'indisputable expression of the national will'[99] likely to encourage policemen to fight the jubilant people. Berenguer's telegram urging his generals to abide by 'the national will' did not 'paralyse' the military, as La Cierva alleged. It is unlikely that it would have deterred any general from staging a last-ditch defence of the monarchy. Not even a personal telephone call from the Minister of War had prevented Primo de Rivera from carrying out his coup in 1923. General Cavalcanti assured the king of the loyalty of the cavalry, but none came to speak on behalf of the infantry, the artillery, or the air force.[100] Not even on the level of a local garrison were army units eager to come out against the people; they preferred to remain confined to barracks or to join the festive crowds in the streets.[101] As a whole, the military in 1931 looked upon their recent authoritarian model, Primo de Rivera's dictatorship, as a highly discredited affair that did not deserve nostalgic sighs, let alone a bid for revival. Azaña had every reason to congratulate the army, when he took over the Ministry of War on behalf of the Republic, for its 'patriotism and discipline'.[102]

[95] Ben-Ami, *The Origins*, pp. 239–44.
[96] Maura and Fernández Almagro, *¿Porqué cayó?*, p. 395.
[97] Berenguer, *De la Dictadura*, pp. 350–3.
[98] *ES*, 4 June 1931; Romanones, *Las últimas horas*, pp. 79–80.
[99] E. Mola, *Obras completas* (Valladolid, 1940), 849, 858–9.
[100] La Cierva, *Notas*, pp. 375, 378.
[101] *ABC, LV*, 15 Apr. 1931.
[102] *ABC*, 15 Apr. 1931.

Oppositions frequently win power thanks to the loss of nerve of those in government. In the present case, the prospects of republicanism were dramatically enhanced by the abandonism of the monarchy's political élite. Romanones started to prepare King Alfonso's departure, under the conviction that 'everything was lost', even before he knew about the Civil Guard's abstentionist attitude; and when he met Alcalá Zamora, the head of the Republican Revolutionary Committee, to discuss the transmission of power, he did it, as he said, with a white flag in his hand.[103] It was only after that capitulation that Sanjurjo rushed to put himself at the disposition of the Republican Committee.[104] The symbolic defender of the monarchy, the Civil Guard, had now definitely crossed the lines. If anyone could guarantee order in the streets, it was no longer the official government but its opponents. Furthermore, had it not been for the government's concession of defeat, it is hard to see how the republicans could have turned a municipal election into a political plebiscite. On the morrow of the elections the republican leaders were as disorientated as the government. Most of them still looked forward to the general elections rather than to an immediate republican take-over.[105] It was the defeatism exhibited by the government which encouraged the Republican Committee to exhort the monarchy publicly 'to submit itself to the national will', and to warn that should it fail to do so under the excuse of its numerical victory in its 'rural fiefs', the republicans would not be responsible 'for what might happen'.[106] Yet, up to the last moment before the king's departure, Alcalá Zamora was still disturbed by the possibility of a military reaction sponsored by the government.[107]

The future president of the Republic worried in vain, for the monarchist regime disintegrated without resistance. Nothing reflected better its collapse than the spontaneous declaration of the Republic throughout the cities of Spain, while the agents of the government stood by. The proclamation of the Republic in Barcelona with its separatist connotations was an especially severe blow to the authority of the dissolving government.[108] The Ministry of the Interior—the tradi-

[103] Romanones, *Las últimas horas*; and in *ES*, 23 May, 4 June 1931.
[104] Sanjurjo in *ES*, 7, 9 June 1931.
[105] Josep Pla, *L'adveniment de la República* (Barcelona, 1933), 19; M. Maura, *Así cayó Alfonso XIII* (Barcelona, 1962), 152–3; Conde de Romanones, . . . *Y sucedió así* (Madrid, 1947), 38.
[106] *ES*, 14 Apr. 1931.
[107] F. Solá Cañizares, *El moviment revolucionari a Catalunya* (Barcelona, 1932), 117.
[108] José Gaya Picón, *La jornada histórica de Barcelona* (Madrid, n.d.,), 5–58; *LV*, 15 Apr. 1931.

tional nerve-centre of the country—lost control of events. The minister was not available during most of the day; an eyewitness at the ministry observed telephones ringing with no one to answer them. He watched 'the regime dropping like a juicy, over-ripe plum from the tree'.[109] The republicans simply picked up the fruit. They drew enough strength from the weakness of the government to demand, on 14 April, that power be transmitted to them 'before sunset'.[110] However, sunset approached and the government was not even in a position to co-ordinate an orderly transmission of power. The republican emissaries arriving early in the evening at the Ministry of the Interior to make the necessary arrangements found a deserted building. By 8.00 p.m. the monarchist government had not yet appeared, and so the Republican Committee simply stepped into the ministry and unilaterally assumed a power which was 'lying in the streets'.[111] 'Public authority', as *El Crisol* put it, 'existed no more'.[112]

The smoothness of the transition to a republic was so remarkable because there was none to oppose it. A governing élite that had never conceived the people as a legitimate source of power was politically castrated the moment the only source of power it saw as legitimate, the king, abandoned it and left the country. Dynastic politicians did not even bother to present the semblance of a dignified acceptance of the national will; some probably because they were already laying the groundwork for the myth of the Republic as the product of an illegal *coup d'état*.

[109] Buckley, *Life and Death*, p. 44.
[110] Maura, *Así cayó*, 168–9; Alcalá Zamora in *ES*, 17 May 1931.
[111] R. Sánchez Guerra, *Proceso de un cambio de régimen* (Madrid, 1932), 165–9; Maura, *Así cayó*, pp. 169–72.
[112] *El Crisol*, 16 Apr. 1931.

6. THE POLITICAL MOBILIZATION OF LANDOWNERS IN THE PROVINCE OF BADAJOZ, 1931–1933

Timothy Rees

The proclamation of the Republic found landowners socially isolated and politically vulnerable in the countryside of Badajoz. Their position in rural society was based on the control of a system of great estates (*latifundios*) which had been consolidated by the purchase of lands, beginning with the ecclesiastical and civil disentailments of the 1830s and 1850s. Concentration of ownership led to some 26.6 per cent of the total area of the province, 32.5 per cent of the cultivated area, accumulating in the hands of only 400 persons. The families they came from, mainly of bourgeois origins but also including some powerful nobles, were at the heart of a pattern of provincial landownership in which just 1.74 per cent of all those owning rural property had control over the use of 61.94 per cent of available land.[1] These large land-owners (*latifundistas*) relied on the labour of the majority of rural society to work the estates, some 80,000 families in 1930, who were either landless or held insufficient property to support themselves. This rural work-force was divided into a majority of *jornaleros* (day labourers), who lived a precarious and dependent existence working the *latifundios*, and a less numerous group of *yunteros* (labourers with teams of ploughing mules or oxen), perhaps 30 per cent of the total, some of whom sharecropped the parcels of land allocated to them by landowners. Within the province there was also an important 'middle-stratum' of around 12,000 families who supported themselves on their own smallholdings (*minifundios*), or rented land in agreement with landowners (*aparcería*).[2] Despite the variety and complexity of social divisions, *latifundistas* were clearly identified as the most important

[1] Pascual Carrión, *Los latifundios en España* (Madrid, 1932), 160–80; E. Cerro, 'Algunos datos sobre la vida en la provincia', *Revista del Centro de Estudios Extremeños* (1927); E. E. Malefakis, *Agrarian Reform and Peasant Revolution in Spain* (New Haven, 1970), 75–6.

[2] *Censo de la población de España: Región de Extremadura 1930*; N. Ortega, 'Política hidráulica y reforma agraria', in M. Gaviría (ed.), *Extremadura saqueada* (Paris, 1978), 120–5.

élite of the province, controlling the destinies of the 70 per cent of the population who worked on the land. In comparison, the urban professionals (mainly doctors, lawyers, teachers, and engineers), artisans, shopkeepers, and businessmen, although often having great social status, lacked the power and influence of the agrarians.

Entrepreneurial landowners used latifundism as the basis for the commericalization of agriculture in Badajoz, incorporating the province into the national food market. As a consequence the pattern of economic life, especially in the favoured Vegas and Barros regions, shifted away from a mix of agriculture based on pastures towards the intensive production of wheat on commercial farms. By the 1930s Badajoz had become the third largest wheat producing province in Spain, but at the same time it also had some of the most marginal agriculture in the country. Landowners who were able to take advantage of these opportunities also sponsored 'scientific agriculture' and the growth of professional bodies and the use of technical experts, which had led to the formation of the Cámara Agrícola in 1908. However, within the élite these changes had a divisive effect, pitting the traditional landowner against the modernizer.[3] Further down the social scale, tenants and share-croppers faced the loss of their lands and independence, as landowners adapted to wheat by forcing those dependent on them into growing for the fluctuating market and by changing the terms of agreements. With a growing population, landlessness and pressure on the land increased enormously in the period between the Great War (a time of agricultural boom in Spain) and the arrival of the Republic. Consequently, landowners found their privileged position in the province coming under attack.

Landowners exercised their authority through the mechanisms of *caciquismo*, a system of corrupt local bossism, whose effectiveness relied on a lack of organized opposition. Caciques vied for influence through the appointment of their nominees for town councils and as parliamentary deputies for Badajoz, largely unaffected by the occasional attacks on property and short-lived strikes that occurred, usually spontaneously, before 1917. However, between 1917 and 1920, a wave of organized social and political protest by *jornaleros* swept across the province. Any complacency amongst the landed élite, used as they

    [3] José Luis Martin Galindo, *La dehesa extremeño como tipo de explotación agraria* (Valladolid, 1965); Consejo Provincial de Fomento, *Estadística social agraria* (Badajoz, 1921); *Anuario de las producciones agrícolas* (Madrid, 1925–33); Antonio Cruz Valero, *Para los agricultores extremeños* (Madrid, 1936).

were to virtually unquestioned control through deference and *caciquismo*, was shattered. Landowners were forced to use their permanent workers, the Civil Guard, and troops sent by sympathetic monarchist governments, to break the *sociedades obreras* (workers' societies) that developed. However, once the immediate threat had passed, the years of the dictatorship saw a temporary respite from further protest. Landowners failed to give their support to plans by the Cámara Agrícola to create permanent landowners' organizations to protect their interests and to develop support for monarchism in the countryside.[4] In 1931 landowners faced the challenge of the Republic divided, and largely alienated from the rest of rural society.

The vulnerability of *latifundistas* became obvious during the final confusions of the dictatorship, as social and political protest gathered momentum. *Sociedades obreras* began reforming and affiliating themselves to the socialist Federación Nacional de Trabajadores de la Tierra (FNTT). By the summer of 1931 virtually every village in Badajoz had its *casa del pueblo* where union and political campaigns were organized. Meanwhile, alienation from the social and political forms of the monarchy grew as socialist and republican organization and ideas gained a firm hold, politicizing the province and breaking the monopoly of landowners' nominees in local and provincial administration in the process. The monarchist paper *El Correo Extremeño*, owned by the Prensa Católica, contrasted the strengthening organization of the socialists with the lack of unity and purpose in the monarchist camp.[5] In the absence of a state that could be relied upon to act as final guarantor for them, all landowners were awakening to the fact that they could not now mobilize and organize sufficient resources within Badajoz or elsewhere to defend themselves or the social order that they favoured.

El Correo Extremeño, reacting to the attacks by the socialists and republicans on the corruption and oligarchism of the established order, warned the landed élite that they had sacrificed support and that the vestiges of the old *caciquismo*, far from being a force to preserve the established rural order, were now the focus of discontent that could

---

[4] J. Polo Benito, *El problema social del campo en Extremadura* (Salamanca, 1919); A. Merino de Torres, *El obrero del campo* (Badajoz, 1919); J. C. Molano Gragera, *Introducción a la historia del movimiento obrero en Montijo* (Montijo, 1982), 33–45; Unión Patriótica, *Barógrafo de un lustro: Badajoz 1923–1929* (Madrid, 1929).

[5] *El Correo Extremeño*, 4 Jan. 1931. Archivo Histórico Nacional, Gobernación, serie A, Leg. 45, reports to minister. J. Simeón Vidarte, *No queríamos al Rey* (Barcelona, 1977), 367–70.

sweep it away. A characteristic plea for renovation to meet the evident crisis of conservatism stated that,

... perhaps in no other [province] has there been so lively a longing for liberating oneself from the ancient practices of the old *caciquismo*, that is trying to revive today. It is urgent here, more than in other provinces, to form a great regional party, that has as the basis of its programme the study and solution of the great economic and social problems of *Extremadura*. ... The time of the old castes and the despotic empire of the feudal lords is passed. There are in the people of *Extremadura* yearnings for liberation, a vague opinion, but widespread, that abominates the old practices and that shall lend great force to persons that have the valiance to undertake this saving task.[6]

Such frankness was obviously a recognition of the immediate urgency of the crisis for conservative landowners, who saw the fall of the cacique and the monarchist system as the beginnings of disaster.

In the face of this threat, landowners were divided as to how best to defend their interests. During the contest for council seats on 12 April 1931, *caciquismo* proved largely powerless in the expanding towns and pueblos. Only in the remoter corners of the province where the cacique still wielded power, could voters be persuaded and coerced to vote the right way, or article 29 of the 1876 Constitution used to prevent a competition. In most areas old established local rivalries hampered any united response by landowners, leading to a variety of competing monarchist candidates being put forward, representing different factions of the two old oligarchical parties. Socialist and republican candidates took control of *ayuntamientos* (local councils) across the province, and were able to use them to begin a campaign of local reforms and as bases to pursue further political gain.[7] Landowners reacted with fear and bewilderment to the changes that were sweeping over them. The Marqués de Valderrey, an old-style cacique from Almendralejo who was opposed by rival monarchists in the elections, voiced the feelings of many in lamenting the apparently sudden disaster that was occurring and the 'spirit of rebellion and anarchy' that seemed to have gripped the populace.[8] With the proclamation of the Republic in Madrid, the caciquista image of Badajoz was broken, its erstwhile practitioners and beneficiaries thrown into disarray.

Moreover, from the winter of 1930 latifundism was caught in a

[6] *El Correo Extremeño*, 'Los partidos regionales', 10 Mar. 1931.

[7] See *La Vanguardia de Badajoz*, 14 Apr. 1931. On the elections see *El Correo Extremeño*, 8–14 Apr. 1931; *La Libertad*, 10–14 Apr. 1931.

[8] Manuel Pidal, *El nuevo regímen en el campo* (Madrid, 1934), 21, and *El Correo Extremeño*, 15 Apr. 1931.

social and economic crisis that fuelled what to landowners appeared to be a growing revolutionary threat to landownership itself. *Jornaleros* and *yunteros* rushed to join *sociedades obreras* and renewed demands for recognition of their rights to bargain over wages, conditions, and availability of work. The presence of the *yunteros* was especially important as it ensured that the main weapons of the *sociedades*, control of the labour market and the use of the strike, were more effective. They had become the most radicalized section of the rural work-force, having suffered a decisive loss of independence and seen their animal power replaced by an increased use of machinery. Sporadic strikes followed as rural workers resisted the decisions of landowners to alter the availability and conditions of work according to their needs. Landowners were also affected by falling animal and cereal prices caused by world depression and over-production. In particular, world wheat prices fell from a base of 100 in 1929 to a level of 43 in 1933. The vulnerability of latifundism, and hence the whole rural economy, to commercial fluctuations led landowners to put marginal land out of production and to accelerate the substitution of direct labour for share-cropping. This combined with wage cuts finally eroded any remaining reality to the 'partnership' that landowners still proclaimed with rural labour.[9]

When Socialist *alcaldes* (mayors) raised local taxes to subsidize public works and bread prices, intervened to support striking workers, prevented the Civil Guard from punishing those who gleaned firewood or acorns, and set up commissions to adjudicate conditions of pay and employment, the landowners saw themselves as facing 'the proletarian dictatorship' and 'socialist tyranny'.[10] Such feelings were reinforced by the symbolic destruction of the old order that took place, with Republican flags unfurled over the town halls, Socialist demonstrators carrying red banners welcoming the new regime, and street names changed to those of the new heroes of the Republic. Landowners' attitudes hardened, so that by the summer of 1931 a pattern of confrontations was set that was to recur in much the same form as every new period of agricultural tasks approached. As demand for labour rose, and was especially high during the crucial harvest season, *sociedades* used their advantage to press for the signing of collective contracts covering the work to come.[11]

[9] Manuel Pidal, *La farsa del llamado problema de yunteros en Extremadura* (Madrid, 1934), *passim*. On agriculture and the crisis see *El Correo Extremeño*, 'Cuestiones agrarias', 28 Feb. 1931, and J. Hernández Andreu, *España y la crisis de 29* (Madrid, 1986), 31, 69–90, for figs.

[10] *El Correo Extremeño*, editoral, 29 Apr. 1931.

[11] FNTT, *Memoria: II congreso* (Madrid, 1932), 53–5, 115, on activities in Badajoz.

Most landowners were determined to resist this combination of municipal and workers' demands, which they saw as threatening the rights
of landownership and the economic and social basis of its profitability.

However, their ability to utilize sanctions that had previously been
available to them was now limited by decrees from the Ministry of
Labour that were designed to alleviate the rural crisis in provinces like
Badajoz, and to offer reinforcement for the actions of *sociedades*. These
measures were far-reaching in their effects, completely reshaping the
balance of influence in the countryside. The first of the decrees,
laboreo forzoso, prevented landowners from taking land out of cultiva-
tion and enforcing a lock-out. *Términos municipales* was aimed at
preventing the use of labour from outside of pueblo boundaries before
all that was locally available was employed. It prevented the long-used
practice of bringing in workers from Portugal, and other parts of the
province, to undercut local wages and to break disputes, making control of the local labour market easier for the *sociedades*. However, the
most important of the decrees was that which established the *jurados
mixtos* (arbitration committees) in Badajoz. These extended state intervention in collective bargaining and applied social legislation to the
land for the first time. *Sociedades obreras* were able to appeal to these
bodies to have their claims on landowners adjudicated and enforced.
Likewise tenants were able to have fair rent agreements fixed.[12]

The extension of a corporatist framework to buttress the rights of
non-landowners was fiercely resented by the landowners, who saw it as
an unjust intervention when an already frightening assault on them,
spearheaded by the *sociedades obreras* and provincial socialism, was taking place. This view was reinforced by the operation of the *jurados
mixtos* which began to produce a stream of judgements favouring workers and tenants. As far as was possible *latifundistas* tried to boycott the
new laws and decrees, or ignored judgements made against them.
Certainly they had some success in this individual resistance, often
with the connivance of local officials who were consequently
denounced by the Socialists and Republicans. By October 1933 the
Institute of Agrarian Reform reported that the *jurados mixtos* in
Badajoz had granted the largest number of 'intensification of cultiva-

---

[12] See *El Correo Extremeño*, 8 May 1931; *La Voz Extremeña*, 8, 9 May 1931; *Anuario
Español de Política–Social* (Madrid, 1935), 186–99, 419–22; *El Socialista*, 10 Oct. 1932;
FNTT, *Memoria*, pp. 40–6; José Estadella, *El fracaso de los jurados mixtos* (Madrid, 1936),
on their problems.

tion' decrees in Spain, to try to force landowners to work the land. However, landowners recognized reluctantly that if they didn't organize representation for themselves on unwelcome bodies like the *jurados mixtos* and agrarian reform commissions they would eventually be dealt with anyway. Indeed, in cases where landowners failed to provide representation on the *jurados mixtos* in Badajoz, Largo Caballero as Socialist Minister of Labour appointed his own nominees from Madrid to fill the positions and dismissed a delegation of landowners from the province who complained.[13] Existing organizations in Badajoz had proved totally unprepared for the tasks of providing united defence and representation for landowners in the transformed social and political environment that was becoming established.

Immediate responses from landowners varied from the signing of harvest agreements with *sociedades obreras*, in order to get the crops in, to attempts to abandon collection and enforce a lock-out. Direct actions and violence followed, with reports of invasions of fields, attacks on machinery by desperate workers, armed retainers patrolling the estates, and clashes between demonstrators and the Civil Guard filling the provincial newspapers and bulletins. Some *latifundistas* saw themselves as fighting for their very survival, virtually a war against socialism and the Republic. Politically they clung intransigently to the monarchy, eventually in 1934 forming themselves into a minority party, Renovación Española de Badajoz, under the leadership of the Marqués de Solana, who had been the provincial governor during the dictatorship. A few gave support to Derecha Republicana, the party of former monarchists like Miguel Maura. Rather more, at least to judge from the complaints of cacique infiltration that followed, chose to join temporarily the Radical Party as the most conservative and anti-socialist force in the republican camp.[14] The Radicals had established themselves after the 1917–20 disturbances as the best organized republican force in Badajoz, with a core of support amongst urban professionals and small businessmen, especially those linked to the Cámara de Comércio y Propiedad Urbana. Radical leaders in Badajoz, like Salazar Alonso, welcomed these landowners as a reinforcement to the party's campaign to widen its appeal.[15] Although conservative in one

---

[13] *El Correo Extremeño*, 16 June 1931. See also Manuel Sardiña, 'Las exigencias del momento', *El Correo Extremeño*, 25 Apr. 1931.

[14] A charge frequently made by Diego Hidalgo (Radical deputy) via his paper *la Voz Extremeña*.

[15] R. Salazar Alonso, *Bajo el signo de la revolución* (Madrid, 1935), 23.

form or another, none of these organizations was specifically the creation or vehicle of the majority of landowners.

The need to provide a political platform for landowners was made all the more urgent by the Constitution Cortes elections in June 1931. With no previous experience of well-organized direct representation for landowners in the province, leadership was taken by organizations which had provided spokesmen in the past. The Cámara Agrícola, in particular, had been thrust to the forefront by its negotiations with the provincial FNTT over the *bases de trabajo*, in resolving strikes, and providing representation to the *jurados* and commissions. It was also in close contact with individual landowners' social clubs in the pueblos, where the message was clear that landowners' organization had fossilized and now needed revitalization to lead and organize the 'landed middle classes'. It was equally evident that any defence had to be within the existing legal framework, which made the announcement of the formation of Acción Nacional in Madrid a rallying point for landed interests in Badajoz.[16] On 31 May 1931 *El Correo Extremeño* published the national manifesto on its front page, proclaiming the need to guarantee private property, the Church and a Catholic social order, and attacking Marxism and separatism. The regional party was announced on the same day, with a leadership of prominent landowners from the Asamblea de Proprietarios de Badajoz (an organization of predominantly wheat growing landowners formed in 1919) and members of the Cámara Agrícola and Federación Católica Agraria. In the short period before the elections the party presented a vitriolic and doomladen propaganda campaign that condemned 'the revolutionaries' and forecast the ruin of the province.[17]

However, the *ad hoc* formation and close identification of the party with old monarchist corruption during the republican euphoria meant that it was denied a serious following in the electoral battle. Francisco Asís y Sánchez Miranda, a Badajoz lawyer sent by Acción Nacional from Madrid to organize the province, later made the position clear: 'I arrived on the 11th of May. I found the forces of the right in disorder, filled with panic by the recent events. . . . The failure (of Acción Nacional) convinced me that propaganda was needed to gain hold of rightwing opinion in the province.'[18] Even in centres such as Mérida and

[16] See the remarks of Francisco Diaz Gimenez and Baldomero Argente, *El Correo Extremeño*, 12 June 1931.

[17] *El Correo Extremeño*, 10–26 June 1931, on campaign. Also *La Voz Extremeña, La Libertad*, 1–25 June 1931.   [18] *Hoy*, 30 May 1933.

Almendralejo with relatively large numbers of smallholders and strong Catholic agrarian syndicates, the rightist cause failed to attract a following. Republican–Socialist coalition candidates swept the board, with two Radicals, one Radical–Socialist, and eight Socialists taking up parliamentary seats, alongside one Independent. The banner of conservatism in the province was grasped by the Radicals, who had benefited from the floating conservative, but anti-monarchist, vote that *El Correo Extremeño* had predicted. This led to a complete break in the provincial republican coalition, to the satisfaction of landowners who noted with approval the enhanced anti-Socialist rhetoric of the Radicals and the overtures by Salazar Alonso to appease landed interests.[19] In the aftermath of the elections Acción Nacional was dissolved in the province, followed by the closure of *El Correo Extremeño* in August 1931 with the promise that it would return as an 'anti-revolutionary' voice as soon as conditions were more propitious. However, despite the scale of the rejection of the right in Badajoz, initial groundwork towards renovating landowners' organizations began virtually straight away.

The need to resist the demands of the *sociedades obreras* and Socialist councils seemed ever more pressing, now that a Republican–Socialist government was preparing to apply its own legislation to support their cause. An agrarian reform to redistribute land in the south was promised and in August 1931 the commission to investigate its application in Badajoz began work. At the same time the Ministry of Labour announced the creation of an 'electoral register of rural organizations' that would serve as the basis for the corporate structure of labour relations that Largo Caballero was extending to the countryside. Despite their distaste for this process, if landowners were to ensure that they would be fully represented they needed to act swiftly. A setback had already been suffered when the authorities refused to accept the *sindicatos católicos agrarios* as representatives for the workers' side on the *jurados mixtos* or on the *comisiones mixtas* (municipal council arbitration committees), on the grounds that they were not true workers' organization because they also had employers in their ranks. On 6 July 1931 a meeting in the provincial capital created the Federación de Propietarios de Fincas Rústicas de Badajoz as an umbrella organization of landowners. It brought together delegates from all over the province from individual *centros agrarios* and representatives from the agrarian and patronal organizations that already existed. The meeting

---

[19] *La Libertad*, 7 July 1931, and *El Correo Extremeño*, 9 July 1931.

was chaired by Pedro Navarette, head of the Cámara Agrícola which
was to co-ordinate the activities of the other organizations now linked
in the Federación de Propietarios. An interlocking network of
spokesmen and representatives was finally being created. In turn, the
provincial organization was associated with the national Agrupación de
Propietarios de Fincas Rústicas, which co-operated with other
patronal organizations.[20]

The Federación de Propietarios provided *latifundistas* with an organization that not only brought the divergent interests of the élite together
for defensive reasons but also had a leadership with clear positive
purposes. Of first importance for them was to confront the *sociedades
obreras* and new legislation by every means possible. The tactics open to
them were to use the withdrawal of work to boycott the decrees and
labour agreements, and to offer co-operation only in so far as it allowed
delaying tactics and objections to be deployed. To support landowners
in their individual battles with workers the Federación de Propietarios
offered the services of its lawyers and members on the *jurados mixtos*.
During disputes and clashes in the countryside the Federación de Propietarios, under its president Muñoz Casillas, co-ordinated the propaganda and responses of other agrarian organizations. As a lobby in the
name of all landowners in Badajoz, the Federación de Proprietarios
was active from the very start. From the autumn of 1931 to the summer of 1933 delegations were sent to Madrid to meet ministers, to seek
links to other patronal organizations, and to represent landowners on
any new government body concerned with social or agrarian reform.
Landowners' organizations from the province presented numerous
petitions and objections on all aspects of rural affairs, ranging from the
actions of the *jurados mixtos*, condemnation of the unions, criticisms of
the agrarian reform being prepared in the Cortes, and appeals to be
allowed to use machinery for harvesting.[21] Such activities, vital as they
were to defend landowners in this period, were only part of the actions
of the Federación de Propietarios and its affiliates. In the longer term
the leadership sought to restore fully the position and power of landownership in Badajoz, which ultimately could only be achieved
through political organization and action.

---

[20] *La Libertad*, *El Correo Extremeño*, 6 July 1931. The Federación de Propietarios
included the Asamblea de Propietarios, Asociación de Ganaderos, and Federación
Católica Agraria. On the national organization see, M. Cabrera, *La patronal ante la II
República* (Madrid, 1983), 66–71.
[21] See *El Correo Extremeño*, 10 July 1931, for example of petition.

An alternative was needed to the corporate system that had been erected in the countryside, which had institutionalized the position of the *sociedades obreras* and permanently placed constraints on the exercise of landownership and on the profitability of the estates. Landowners faced the problem of counteracting organized protest from below, whilst lacking social support. It was made clear in statement after statement from the Asamblea de Propietarios de Badajoz that large landowners regarded the ownership and use of rural property as a fundamental right, which along with religion should not be undermined.[22] Such a commitment made frequent declarations of sympathy for the plight of the *jornaleros* and *yunteros* seem very hollow indeed, especially when the provincial FNTT and Socialist deputies were continually denouncing the effects of boycotts and lock-outs on rural workers. In practice landowners sought the disciplining and regimentation of the rural work-force in order to reassert their control. Simultaneously the idea of the political mobilization of a propertied bloc was resurrected as the basis for a Catholic agrarian party. The first such attempt had followed the 1917–20 disturbances and was inspired by the existing Acción Social Católica and projects sponsored by local notables and the Church. Landowners had hoped to use the handful of *sindicatos católicas* and *cajas rurales* (rural savings banks) — which had developed to aid smallholders and tenants and foster the idea of the mutual interest of all property owners — to protect latifundism against the spread of protest. However, such efforts were almost completely abandoned when the dictatorship arrived.[23]

The campaign to create such a force in Badajoz drew aid and inspiration from links, personified by Sánchez Miranda, with *El Debate* and the formation of a national Catholic Conservative Party around Gil Robles. First steps to find a popular following for the principles of social order, religion, and property ownership were made early on by the Federación de Propietarios. In July of 1931 the Asamblea de Propietarios de Badajoz called an assembly to propose the creation of *sindicatos de propietarios*, which aimed to bring all the tenants and smallholders of the province into a tightly knit federation under the control of large landowners. Francisco López de Ayala, a notable from Mérida involved in the Cámara Agrícola and Catholic syndicates, made the

---

[22] *El Correo Extremeño*, 29, 31 July 1931, and *Ara y Canta*, 18 Jan. 1932, 12 Feb. 1932, on agrarian reform.

[23] E. Fernández Santana, *La cuestión social en Extremadura* (Los Santos, 1935); 'Constitución y misión de los patronatos locales', *Ara y Canta*, 31 Aug. 1927.

problems of creating such a coalition clear in a key address. He pointed out that for this organization to be successful *latifundistas* would
have to make concessions to the 'small men' to benefit them economically and to convince them that their security could best be defended in
such an alliance.[24] This approach was eventually approved by the
assembly, which added condemnations of absenteeism, unfair renting,
and usury to its statement of aims. Concentration on issues such as
agrarian reform, the *jurados*, and the threat from the *sociedades obreras*,
that could be represented as a danger to all property holders, provided
the basis of this appeal for support.

The ideological cement that was to bind together this propertied
alliance was the defence of religion and a Catholic social order. Landowners could appeal not only to the general notion of the Church
under attack by the Republic, but also to specific grievances that affected Catholics in Badajoz. These involved actions by some Socialist and
Republican councils to ban bell-ringing, to prevent church services,
and, most unpopular of all, to prevent burials by priests.[25] Despite the
strength of feeling that the landowners' organizations could tap of a
Catholic community under siege, this was not sufficient to bring
instant success. Smallholders and tenants, especially those involved in
their own organizations, the *comunidades de labradores*, did not come
flocking into the *sindicatos* designed for them. In areas like Mérida and
Almendralejo, where far-sighted local landowners had been cultivating
the support of their neighbours, the basis for a relatively strong rightist
movement was laid down and these became the most important centres
of support. However, landowners' leaders lamented the general distance that was shown to persist between landowners and the rest of
rural society.

During 1932, obstacles to the emergence of an agrarian party led by
landowning interests did break down to some extent, because of a
general anti-socialist current gaining ground in the province. As social
conflicts and violence deepened in the countryside, with land invasions, strikes, and clashes with guards reaching new high points in the
summer and winter of 1932, polarization in Badajoz became more
acute. Landowners contributed to this process by their continued
stubborn resistance to change, which fed the misery and frustration
felt by rural workers who saw their expectations being denied. Conse-

---

[24] *El Correo Extremeño*, 30 July 1931.
[25] See frequent reports in *El Correo Extremeño*, *Hoy*, and *La Voz Extremeña*. E. Santos,
El secretario (Badajoz, 1984), 20.

quently the *sociedades obreras* turned increasingly to the Socialist councils and *jurados mixtos* to try to enforce agreements and reforms, drawing less and less distinction between property holders in the process. Tenants and smallholders were affected by this, in that they also began to face hard-line bargaining and strikes over the employment of the few labourers they hired, became the objects of land invasions, and of thefts of acorns, olives, and wood. Conflict also grew between tenants and their sub-tenants over rent agreements and the division of crops.[26] Condemnations of Socialism by the Federación de Propietarios joined those of the Radicals, led by Salazar Alonso who called for the 'dismantling of the Socialists and the tyranny and caciquismo they have brought'.[27] Throughout the year Catholic and patronal organizations followed a similar line, stressing the grievances felt and dismissing any wariness on the part of the *latifundistas*. To hammer home the message of solidarity landowners began to make highly publicized grants of land to *sindicatos católicos* for settlement, at the same time proclaiming the unnecessary and disruptive effect of any agrarian reform.[28]

This did not translate into direct recruitment into *sindicatos de propietarios* as had been hoped. Tenants and smallholders remained largely resistant to joining bodies directly under the control of landowners, preferring to keep contact through their own local organizations, the *comunidades de labradores*, and within Catholic social action. Even so, the Federación de Propietarios claimed in February 1933 that 105 *cajas rurales* and *comunidades* were behind their policies.[29] They remained a volatile and diffuse force, benefiting the Radicals' growing organization as well as the Catholic right, and in some instances keeping ties with the Socialists as well. Whatever the limitations of the landowners' campaign, the extent of the social and political polarization of the countryside by the final months of 1932 allowed the formations of an agrarian Catholic political party to begin in Badajoz.

The cornerstone of this provincial organization was laid with the appearance of *Hoy* in January 1933 as the new newspaper of the Catholic right, replacing *El Correo Extremeño* and published by

---

[26] See J. S. Vidarte, *Las Cortes Constituyentes* (Barcelona, 1976), 504–6; Margarita Nelken, *Porqué hicimos la revolución* (Barcelona, 1936); 45–7; Molano Gragera, *Introducción*, pp. 57–60. Also the articles in *El Obrero de la Tierra*, 'La lucha del capital y el trabajo' (26 Nov. 1932), 'Para los propietarios de la provincia' (3 Dec. 1932).

[27] R. Salazar Alonso, *La Libertad*, 5 Jan. 1933.

[28] Frequent denunciations in *Hoy* and *Ara y Canta*, *passim*.

[29] *Hoy*, 11 Feb. 1933.

the Prensa Católica. This was followed by the announcement in Madrid
that the formation of Acción Popular in Badajoz had been approved.
The provincial leadership was drawn from the ranks of the landed élite
and their representatives, who quickly changed the name of the party
to Acción Popular Agraria (APA) in order to emphasize its agrarian
basis. Immediately the APA began a furious recruitment and propaganda campaign throughout the province, broadly based on the
previously developed lines of defence of the Catholic social order and
property. A 'peasantist' ideology was proclaimed, with the small farmer
as the backbone of the family and fatherland, which was specifically
aimed at consolidating the hold that the party had already in the
regions of Mérida, Don Benito, and Almendralejo.[30] It was here that
the constituent organizations of APA, divided into separate women's,
men's, and youth groups under a political committee, had begun to
spring up with eager landowner support even before the formal proclamation of the party. The social struggles of spring and summer 1933
erupted at a time when agricultural prices hit a new low and the
Instituto de Reforma Agraria was preparing to implement the reform
laws in the province, giving a great spur to the landowners' party. By
the end of May, APA claimed to have established organizations in
fifty-two pueblos, was awaiting registration with the authorities in
twenty-three others, and was trying to form branches in thirty more.[31]

The party and *Hoy* were uncritical supporters of the aims of the
Federación de Propietarios—unsurprisingly, given that they were led
by the same people. In its propaganda APA expressed the militancy of
landowners towards the Republic in general, and the Socialists in particular. However, the leadership realized that there were severe limits
to any success that APA could achieve under the electoral system of
the Republic, given the strength of the *sociedades obreras* in Badajoz, the
uncertainties and weaknesses of the constituency of a provincial right
so closely identified with large landowners, and the existence of Radical competition for the anti-Socialist and Conservative vote. It would
have been suicide for APA to stand alone in the elections, so the party
negotiated, with some difficulty and distrust, an 'anti-Marxist front'
with the Radicals and Conservative Republicans.[32] Although necessary

---

[30] *Hoy*, 14, 17 Jan. 1933, 9 Mar. 1933; *La Libertad*, 9 Mar. 1933; J. R. Montero, *La CEDA* (Madrid, 1977), i. 394–5, 436.

[31] *Hoy*, 30 May 1933, gives details of the provincial organization.

[32] Announced *Hoy*, 19 Apr. 1933; *La Libertad*, 20 Apr. 1933. See also Salazar Alonso, *Bajo el signo*, pp. 24–5, J. Simeón Vidarte, *El bienio negro* (Barcelona, 1978), 30–3.

as a means to oust the Socialists from power in the province, this uneasy coalition placed limitations on the opportunity of landowners to rule directly. APA had to offer the local Radicals the chance to run the provincial administration and the councils as the price of their support. In return landowners expected that there would be aid for their plans, which they hoped would alter the whole basis of social power in the countryside once more to their advantage.

Having survived the first two years of the Republic, created a new unity amongst themselves, and forged links with national agrarian organizations, landowners in Badajoz began to make their first concerted efforts to exploit the social divisions and misery of the province to go beyond just a haphazard defence of their interests. *Hoy* had denounced the 'red dictatorship in the countryside' and attacked the *jurados mixtos* and rural decrees from its earliest issue. In February 1933 the Federación de Propietarios announced that landowners could not afford another summer like the previous two, that labour costs must fall, that it was determined to use more machinery and to bring down local taxes.[33] Landowners began systematically to ignore the intensification decrees and the rulings of the *jurados mixtos* on pay, conditions, and rents. In Barcarrota, the president of the Federación de Propietarios led other local landowners in a drive to raise rents to *yunteros*, locking out any that did not comply.[34] *Paro forzoso* rose rapidly as the summer approached and landowners continued to withhold work. By the harvest season *sociedades obreras* complained of a 'landowners' offensive', with agreements broken in a campaign to bring down wages and split workers away from the FNTT by giving work only to loyal labourers. In May the Federación de Propietarios went a stage further by withdrawing all its members on the *jurados mixtos*, to protest at their bias towards workers and tenants.[35] Meanwhile the administration of the agrarian reform laws, which had been held up so successfully by the agrarian deputies in the Cortes, was easily undermined by every landowner affected applying for exemption on a variety of spurious grounds. As a consequence the Junta Provincial of the reform, short of officials, ground to a halt.[36]

With new elections to the Cortes approaching, landowners had effectively paralysed the province and deepened social and political

---

[33] *Hoy*, 16 Feb. 1933. [34] *El Obrero de la Tierra*, 11 Feb. 1933.

[35] See *El Obrero de la Tierra*, 3 June 1933; *Boletín del Instituto de Reforma Agraria*, May 1933, July 1933; *El Socialista*, 1, 2 July 1933.

[36] See Pablo Campos, 'El intento de reforma agraria', in Gaviría (ed.), *Extremadura squeada*, pp. 135–57; A López López, *El boicot de la derecha a las reformas de la Segunda República* (Madrid, 1984).

divisions, preparing the way for APA to condemn the situation as the product of Socialist fanaticism and the failure of the Republic. As an alternative APA proposed a campaign to make 'permanent and lasting changes in the province' that would restore 'traditional values'.[37] Order and harmony would be restored, from the point of view of the élite, if 'political unions' were replaced by Catholic unions 'opposed to the war of the classes', which landowners would support by granting them work. The control enjoyed by the *jurados mixtos, casas del pueblo*, and Socialist councillors would be ended, and a 'just Catholic order' encouraged. A further distribution of lands, under the control of landowners, to suitable tenants and workers, would strengthen a social barrier of smallholders. The authoritarian implications of these promises were clear. The promise implicit in cartoons in *Hoy* showing a chick labelled 'fascism' in a nest inscribed 'spring 1933',[38] and the confrontations taking place in the countryside, offered chilling evidence of the determination of landowners to complete their resurgence. Their ability to create this new order, restoring the position of landownership to the same as under the discredited older order, would only be achieved by overcoming the resistance of rural workers to regimentation and the dismembering of their organizations. Likewise the rural institutions and social legislation of the Republic would be emasculated, to be replaced by Catholic alternatives that the élite would be more comfortable with.

In the elections of November and December the conservative coalition gained a narrow victory, which put three APA deputies, in comparison with five Radicals, into the Cortes. Landowners had gone from a position where they had been reeling, unprepared, from the blows inflicted on them, to one where they were now ready to fight back decisively. However, the lack of widespread appeal for APA had forced them to compromise with uncertain allies, in the form of the Radicals. Furthermore, the restoration of their position in the countryside required the virtual destruction of all the changes that the Republic had brought in Badajoz. Such actions could only lead to direct confrontation with organized rural workers, who were not prepared to relinquish the gains of the two previous years.

[37] See *Hoy*, editorial, 19 Oct. 1933, on choices facing province.
[38] *Hoy*, Mar. 1933. The electoral campaign of APA clearly illustrated these aims. *Hoy*, 20 Oct.–19 Nov. 1933; also *La Libertad*, 2–19 Nov. 1933.

7. THE POLITICIZATION OF CATHOLIC WOMEN IN SALAMANCA, 1931–1936

Mary Vincent

The enfranchisement of Spanish women under the Second Republic was heralded by the extraordinary spectacle of a woman parliamentary deputy arguing against female suffrage. Victoria Kent, the Radical–Socialist representative for Madrid and one of three female deputies voted into the Cortes in 1931 by an all-male electorate, argued that extending the franchise to women would endanger the Republic as so many of them followed 'the inspiration of priests and friars'. Fortunately for the defenders of women's rights, Kent was vehemently opposed by the Radical deputy Clara Campoamor in a parliamentary confrontation described by the Republic's future president Manuel Azaña as 'very amusing'. Despite the entertainment value, however, Azaña did appreciate the seriousness of the point at issue, agreeing with Campoamor that: 'it is an atrocity to deny women the vote out of suspicion that they would not vote in favour of the Republic'.[1]

For all Azaña's sentiments, the fear of undue clerical pressure being brought to bear at election times through the female vote remained widespread. Indeed, Azaña's closest collaborator throughout the Second Republic, the Socialist leader Indalecio Prieto, expressed his concern in August 1933 that conceding the vote to women would threaten the electoral chances of both Socialists and Republicans.[2] It is an argument which has since found some favour among historians and the participation of female voters is frequently listed among the reasons for the right's electoral victory in November 1933. Middle- and upper-class women are thought to have voted overwhelmingly for the confessional interest, being especially attracted to the CEDA (Spanish Confederation of Autonomous Right-Wing Groups), the first mass political party to have appeared on the Spanish right. It is generally agreed, however, that working-class women had no reason to

---

[1] Manuel Azaña, *Memorias políticas y de la guerra* (2 vols. Madrid, 1978), i. 199.
[2] Indalecio Prieto, *Del Momento: Posiciones socialistas* (Madrid, 1935), 35.

vote for the right and, like their husbands, either supported the Socialists or failed to vote at all, often because of anarchist sympathies.[3]
Women's influence on the outcome of the election is, in fact, difficult
to assess as, owing to the lack of reliable statistics, the relative numbers
of those voting right and those voting left cannot be determined.

The assumption that women were natural defenders of traditional
values was made by the right itself. Angel Herrera Oria, then editor of
the Madrid Catholic paper *El Debate*, told an assembly in Valencia in
December 1931 that 'certain political parties' had good reason to fear
the female vote. 'Women', he said, 'will give us victory in the next
elections.'[4] Both the Church and its political champions devoted much
time and energy to mobilizing women in defence of their faith. Conscious of the fact that levels of religious practice were higher among
women than men, Catholic leaders, both clerical and lay, did much
campaigning in the name of the Spanish woman: she who is, above all
else, 'Christian, wife, and mother'.[5] Such propaganda deliberately
conveyed the impression that the priorities of all women were the
same. There was no acknowledgement that members of the same sex
could have different political or class interests. This belief in a single,
feminine, community of interest was both widespread and easily
accepted, especially when the idea was propagated by women themselves. Indeed, the readiness with which the 1933 results have been, at
least partly, explained in terms of women's entry into the electorate
may stem from the belief evident amongst those on the right that they
had a 'natural' appeal to women.

Despite this faith in the inherently conservative character of Spanish
women, however, Catholic leaders were acutely aware that they could
not simply rely on nature to bring newly enfranchised women into the
polling booths. Rather, once the 1931 Republican constitution had

[3] Gerald Brenan, *The Spanish Labyrinth* (Cambridge, 2nd edn., 1960), 266; Stanley
Payne, *The Spanish Revolution* (London, 1970), 111; Paul Preston, *The Coming of the
Spanish Civil War* (London, 1978), 90–1.

[4] Angel Herrera Oria, *Obras selectas* (Madrid, 1963), 39.

[5] Asociación Femenina de Educación Ciudadana propaganda, *La Gaceta Regional*
(henceforth *GR*), 8 Feb. 1936. While it is undoubtedly true that women went to church
more than men, little work has been done on the nature or the effect of this gender
difference on Spanish religious practice. Some rather scanty figures are given by Rogelio
Duocastella, 'Geografía de la práctica religiosa española', in Duocastella (ed.), *Análisis
sociológico del catolicismo español* (Barcelona, 1967), 63. These indicate, albeit tentatively,
that the greatest difference between the sexes was found in areas of high Catholic
practice, e.g. rural Vitoria where 73.7% of men but 91.3% of women attended Mass
regularly in 1962. In contrast the gender gap narrowed in Aliá (Toledo) to a mere 2%
but here only 4.3% of men and 6.3% of women were Sunday church-goers.

been passed and female suffrage was a certainty, the right began to woo women voters, making a direct and concerted appeal to them on both moral and practical grounds. The politicians looked to enlist the support of church-going, middle-class women, rather than to convert anticlerical female workers and, away from Madrid, their campaigns were launched in the Catholic and conservative cities of Old Castile, places where much of the groundwork for mobilizing women had already been done by the Church.

The Church in Spain had not found it easy to accommodate itself to the social and constitutional changes experienced since the end of the eighteenth century. Its institutional strength had been curtailed by the expropriation of ecclesiastical lands, most of which were sold under the state orders of 1836 and 1855. Further restrictions placed on the religious orders in 1837 led to all but a handful of male religious communities being dissolved and, although the orders returned to Spain following a loophole in the concordat of 1851, the memory of this attack remained. Catholicism's spiritual monopoly was then challenged in the Liberal Constitution of 1876 which, while recognizing the 'Apostolic, Roman, Catholic religion' as the religion of the state, also allowed the private practice of other cults. Such an explicit declaration of religious toleration flew in the face of the teachings of a church which held that, just as there was only one God, so there was only one way to achieve salvation and anything which deviated from this path was false, erroneous, even evil. The holders of the revealed truth could not be expected to compete with the followers of false gods.

By the turn of the twentieth century, a lay apostolate had been brought into being 'as a reaction to the dechristianization of the modern world and the work of liberal governments'.[6] This apostolate was like an auxiliary priesthood, free to take the Christian message into all areas of life, preaching by example as well as by word. This mission for lay people was commonly known as Catholic Action, defined by Pius XI as 'the participation and collaboration of the laity with the Apostolic Hierarchy'.[7] By the 1930s women were seen to have a key role in this secular mission, as Angel Herrera, who became the

---

[6] Cipriano Montserrat, *Enciclopedia del Católico* (3 vols. Barcelona, 1951; 1st publ. Milan, n.d.), 'Acción Católica', ii. 18. The movement was officially launched in Spain by Cardinal Moreno in 1881, Frances Lannon, *Privilege, Persecution, and Prophecy: The Catholic Church in Spain 1875–1975* (Oxford, 1987), 147.

[7] *Non Abbiamo Bisogno* (1931). In practice Catholic Action tended to be a diocesan umbrella committee, co-ordinating separate pious and charitable associations.

national director of Catholic Action in spring 1933, pointed out. Women, he argued, now had to be able to educate their children in a way unknown to their mothers and grandmothers, for the times had changed and more serious responsibilities now fell upon them.[8]

Catholic Action had separate sections for men and women, boys and girls, assigning to each the roles appropriate to their sex and age. Unsurprisingly, women's work was seen as essentially domestic: they were the 'guardians of the hearth', the 'angels of the home'.[9] Indeed, women's emancipation was condemned in Pius XI's 1931 encyclical on Christian marriage as: 'a degradation of the spirit of woman and of the dignity of a mother'.[10] The tasks of home-making and child-raising, however, brought no authority with them. *Casti Conubii* spoke of the primacy of the husband as the 'order of love' and gave wives to understand that their uxorial duties were those of 'honourable obedience' and humble, though dignified, submission. Wifely sub-servience was, however, supposedly compensated for by maternal affection. 'If the husband is the head of the domestic body', wrote the pontiff, 'then the wife is the heart.'[11]

This 'order of love' was brought outside the family, being reiterated in all Church associations and confirmed in the structure of Catholic Action. Even when he was informing women of their electoral power, Angel Herrera urged them to be a 'model of discipline and of submis-sion' while their political work was spoken of in terms of 'sacrifice'.[12] Self-abnegation was another recurrent theme in Catholic discussions of women's place in society. Abilia Arroyo, foundress of the Asociación Femenina de Educación Ciudadana (AFEC) wrote in Salamanca's Catholic paper, the *Gaceta Regional*, that the virtues needed by a woman were those of 'patience, sweetness and renunciation'. In a similar vein, an article in the same paper the following month stated that Christian mothers were: 'tears, heart, forgetfulness of self, joyful sacrifice, willing acceptance of sorrow, divine humility'.[13] Motherhood was exalted

[8] Herrera Oria, 'Derechos y deberes de los padres', *Obras selectas*, p. 108.

[9] Lannon, *Privilege, Persecution, and Prophecy*, pp. 53–8, for these and other examples of Catholic images of women.

[10] *Casti Conubii* (1931). Emancipation was defined as control over reproduction ('an abomination'), economic independence, and social emancipation. The second of these was specifically condemned as enabling women to run their own affairs without the consent or knowledge of their husbands.

[11] *Casti Conubii*.

[12] Herrera Oria, 'El voto femenino', *Obras selectas*, p. 39.

[13] Abilia Arroyo, 'Las virtudes del hogar', *GR*, 27 Jan. 1931; Mânuel Siurot, 'Superioridad femenina', *GR*, 5 Feb. 1931.

and romanticized at the same time as the status of women was subtly degraded. A married woman not only submitted to her husband through duty, she also sacrificed herself to her children and this she did through love.

Church directives to women, however, were not all laudatory. In a confusing and contradictory double image of the female sex, women, and in particular women's bodies, were consistently seen as sexually dangerous, even while their moral stature and selflessness were being extolled. As traditional Church teaching maintained that 'passions of the flesh' could only be overcome by 'fleeing occasions of sin', segregation by gender was normal practice and coeducation was unthinkable.[14] The female body was seen as a source of extreme provocation and the teaching on the imperative need to avoid Satan's snares was translated by a celibate, male hierarchy into an overriding preoccupation with the incompatibility of fashion and female modesty.

The Spanish bishops demonstrated the strength of such ideas in their 1926 pastoral letter which roundly said that: 'immodesties contribute to the apotheosis of the flesh and are the lure and the attraction, the seducer of the most vile passions'.[15] The apocalyptic language used in the collective pastoral set the tone for the following decade. When Enrique Plá y Deniel took possession of the Salamanca bishopric in 1935, his first pastoral letter contained a warning of the need to be vigilant of female modesty. A year later, in his famous wartime pastoral *Las dos ciudades*, he spoke of the need of all to win God's favour and work for Franco's crusade, specifically addressing those Catholic women who received the sacraments but were 'occasion of sin with your provocative fashions, your liberties'. Not even schoolchildren were exempt from the rules of modesty. From their very first year, girls in confessional schools had to wear skirts down to their knees and, after the age of 12, they could not go bare-legged.[16] The habits of purity had to be taught young.

Liturgical practice in the Catholic Church also reinforced the sus-

---

[14] This doctrine was spelt out in the collective pastoral *Sobre la inmodestia en las costumbres públicas* (1926), in Jesús Iribarren (ed.), *Documentos colectivos del episcopado español 1870–1974* (Madrid, 1974), 119. Coeducation was condemned in the 1929 encyclical *Divini Illius Magistri*. In 1935, there was a directive that the dramatic evenings produced as fund-raising events by Catholic associations were never to contain sketches involving male and female actors together, *Boletín Eclesiástico del Obispado de Salamanca* (1935, henceforth *BEOS*), 199.

[15] Iribarren, *Documentos colectivos*, p. 120.

[16] *BEOS* (1935), 178; (1936), 301; (1937), 205.

picion with which women were viewed and confirmed their secondary status. Separate seating for the two sexes during church services was encouraged, although not insisted upon, by the clergy. Mixed choirs were absolutely prohibited and women were permitted to form a choir only if there were insufficient men or children to do so. When the bishop of Salamanca visited the parishes of his diocese to confirm children he administered the sacrament first to all the boys and only then to the girls. Girls whose skirts did not reach their knees were refused confirmation, as were those whose female sponsors were not dressed 'decorously'.[17] Catholic women were to be kept quiet and covered, devout in church and demure outside it.

Ironically, the first allies to whom the Church looked in its crusade to keep women in their place were women themselves. The 1926 collective pastoral, having unhesitatingly identified women as sources of temptation, even ended with the words: 'In extirpating this libidinous plague we expect the collaboration of all, but principally that of Spanish and Catholic 'women'.[18] The bishops' letter had previously named Catholic Action as providing the lieutenants of its new moral army and, indeed, the main aim of Acción Católica de la Mujer was the moralization of contemporary society.[19] The identification of this as a specifically female task was not simply because it was seen as somehow suitable for the weaker sex but because, as a 1934 Catholic Action manual written by an Italian churchman, Luis Civardi, put it, 'certain moral misfortunes of women, frighteningly contagious, can only be cured by loving and patient female surgery'.[20] This was a direct reference to the biblical models of Eve and Mary. Just as Eve, the first woman and the first sinner, was responsible for the Fall through disobedience, so Mary atoned for the sin of her sex by submitting to God's will and thus brought about the redemption of the world.

Eve's sin, however, was far from forgotten. Women remained weak, prone to temptation and seduction. As Monsignor Civardi's manual succinctly stated: 'It has been said that "woman outside her home is like a sacred vessel outside the temple that is in danger of being profaned". Unfortunately this is true. How many dangers to faith and

---

[17] *BEOS* (1934), 186–7; (1935), 198; (1936), 197–8.

[18] Iribarren, *Documentos colectivos*, p. 123.

[19] The *Boletín de la Confederación de Mujeres Católicas de España*, established in 1936, gives details of the secretariats for morality and the family run by the national junta of women's Catholic Action.

[20] Monsignor Luis Civardi, *Manual de Acción Católica* (Barcelona, 1934), 223.

morals are found by women in the social environment!'[21] In coming through these moral dangers unscathed, woman's most powerful shield was purity, her greatest example the Virgin Mary. The Virgin herself, convent schoolgirls were taught, protected and defended her purity, shielding herself from 'her enemies' by modesty and 'prudent discretion in fleeing occasions of sin'. The occasions of sin encountered by the Queen of Heaven were not specified.[22]

The Church festival which women were most encouraged to make their own was that of the Immaculate Conception, a laudatory celebration of Mary, the only human being born free of the stain of original sin, the only woman freed of the legacy of Eve. A favourite theme for the sermons and novenas to Maria Purissima on her feast day was the origin of good and evil and the redemption of the world through the woman who crushed the head of the snake, the cause of the Fall. Christianity had remedied the miserable condition of pagan woman, dignifying her through the 'angelic virtue of purity'. The beauty of Mary, congregations were told, came only from the purity of her heart.[23]

The example of Mary was continually held up to Catholic women, most frequently in the advocation of the Immaculate Conception but also as the sorrowing mother at the foot of the cross. The cult of the Sorrowful Mother centred on the elaborate Holy Week processions and was immensely popular. Our Lady of the Sorrows, of Solitude, of Anguish, and of Pity were all separate devotions and greatly venerated. Yet they all symbolized one thing: the ultimate sacrifice of Christian motherhood. Mary, prostrate at the foot of the cross, accepting of the divine will in decreeing the death of her son, was the model for Catholic mothers everywhere.[24]

Such passive images of Mary were those chosen by a Church whose veneration of God's mother was 'the exaltation of the principle of sub-

[21] Civardi, *Manual*, p. 222. For the theological significance and origins of Mary as the Second Eve see Hilda Graef, *Mary: A History of Doctrine and Devotion* (London, 1985; first publ. as 2 separate vol. 1963 and 1965), 1–3, 37–8, 59–62, 246–7. The theologians Mary Daly, *Beyond God the Father* (London, 1973), 44–69, 81–92, and Rosemary Radford Ruether, *Mary: The Feminine Face of the Church* (London, 1979), 41–57, offer respectively a feminist critique and a feminist reinterpretation of the dogma.

[22] *Ecos de Mi Colegio* (Hijas de Jesús, Salamanca), 57 (1932), 239.

[23] 'Novenas a la Purísima', *GR*, 4 Dec. 1931, 5 Dec. 1931, 8 Dec. 1931. The Immaculate Conception was an immensely popular feast; in 1931 an estimated 8,000 people took communion in the city of Salamanca and the churches were full from the early morning.

[24] Sermon to the Hermandad de la Soledad, *GR*, 17 Mar. 1931.

mission and receptivity'.[25] As Virgin, Mary was depicted as a pure young girl, not as the representative of humanity in its original goodness; as Mother, she was the pitiful figure grieving over the battered body of Jesus but never one of her son's disciples, praying with them in an upper room.[26] This selective depiction of women in passive roles was maintained even when directed at women actively involved in the Church, for instance those in Catholic Action, a movement which deliberately looked to mobilize the élites of society, to win the hearts and souls of the nation's natural leaders. This nucleus of 'lay apostles' was said to follow in the footsteps of Christ's disciples. Their work in winning over the élites of society was of paramount importance as Catholic Action was both a mass and a select task. As Christ chose the disciples before evangelizing the masses, so 'the modern apostles of Catholic Action [must] ... Christianize those above and ... the Christianization of those below is given to us easily'.[27] In their task of evangelization, however, the female apostles of Catholic Action were encouraged to emulate, not Mary Magdalen who first told the good news of the resurrection to the disciples or the woman of Samaria who became the first apostle to the Gentiles, but Mary of Bethany and her sister Martha who were shown by Jesus that 'spiritual suggestions are perfectly compatible with domestic duties'.[28]

In the face of such determined efforts to keep Catholic women in a domestic role it is perhaps remarkable that they ever entered the political arena at all. That they should have done so with the full blessing of the Church and often of their husbands seems even more extraordinary, but such blessings were not given lightly. The arguments for female political activity were carefully justified. Women had entered the world of parliamentary politics and public oratory in order to defend their husbands and children: they had come out of the home in defence of the home. Their duties as wives and mothers now included the public protection of their loved ones. They were to fight like 'a hen defending her chicks' against a regime which threatened to tear from

---

[25] Ruether, *Mary*, p. 4.

[26] Ibid. pp. 56–7; Acts 1: 14.

[27] 'Seamos menos paganos', *GR*, 26 Feb. 1936.

[28] 'La mujer en la Acción Católica', talk given in Béjar (Salamanca) by the Propagandist José María de la Torre, *El Adelanto*, 15 Feb. 1930; Elisabeth Moltmann-Wendel, *The Women around Jesus* (London, 1982), recuperates Mary and Martha from their traditional roles as dreamer and housewife in an analysis of the dominance of certain biblical images of women to the exclusion of others.

them 'faith, love, and family'.[29] The spectres of divorce, free love, and the end of religious teaching in schools were used to convince Catholic women that their help was urgently needed. As soon as female suffrage was certain, women were reminded of their duties both as citizens and as mothers by those mobilizing support for the Catholic right. It was a well-timed appeal and the response came quickly.

Ironically, the Catholic political party, Acción Popular, later the CEDA, launched its appeal to women at a rally for the revision of the very constitution which had introduced female suffrage. This was held in Ledesma (Salamanca) on 18 October 1931 where the local deputy Cándido Casanueva lauded the Spanish and Castilian woman who, unlike her menfolk, rejected political compromise.[30] Three days later, an article addressed to Castilian women appeared in Salamanca's *Gaceta Regional* calling on them to respond to the invitation issued by the orators in Ledesma. The article was signed in the name of all Castilian women by 'Teresa of Castile', the sobriquet used by Abilia Arroyo for her occasional religious columns, and declared that: 'We will support all that is [for] Catholicism, Hispanicism, order, the family, and all that is great, honourable and suitable for Spain.'[31] Women were now not only defending the natural values of the home but also the traditional values of Spain. The fate of the *patria* depended on its daughters.

The following week, nearly a month before the national women's committee was established in Madrid, the Asociación Femenina de Educación Ciudadana became the first ever female branch of the recently formed Catholic party, Acción Popular.[32] After approaches to Abilia Arroyo and a series of private meetings arranged by Manuel Torres López, professor of law at the University, and José María Gil Robles, Salamancan leader of Acción Popular, the AFEC held its inaugural meeting in the Catholic Workers' Circle in the city of Sala-

[29] Enriqueta Albarrán de García, 'Salamanca, en defensa del hogar', *GR*, 2 Oct. 1931.

[30] *GR*, 19 Oct. 1931; *El Debate*, 20 Oct. 1931.

[31] *GR*, 21 Oct. 1931.

[32] The Asociación Femenina de Acción Popular (AFAP) was established in Madrid on 5 Nov. 1931; although theoretically the AFAP was the national women's co-ordinating committee, in practice it was little more than the female branch of the Madrid AP. Similar women's sections were soon set up all over Spain and, although statistics are lacking, among the most important groups were those in Málaga, Córdoba, Seville, Murcia, Valencia, Saragossa, Cuenca, Soria, Palencia, León, Zamora, Orense, Lugo, and Vizcaya. José Ramón Montero, *La CEDA: El catolicismo social y político en la II República* (2 vols. Madrid, 1977), i. 665, 681–2.

manca. Despite the call to all women published earlier in the *Gaceta*, this assembly, attended by over 600 ladies, was by invitation only. The AFEC's first public meeting retained an air of exclusivity, even of a social occasion: 3,000 requests for invitations were reported to have been turned down. The foundation of the new organization was, however, far from being a spontaneous or frivolous affair. The AFEC was the first women's organization to be set up by Acción Popular and its success was vital. In order to keep its appeal as wide as possible it began with no fixed programme and defined itself as 'a civic association ... above political parties'. Such a definition was also part of a recognizable tactic to convince women that their political involvement was inspired only by the highest of motives. The female electorate of Salamanca was being assured that it was enlisting in a moral crusade, not falling prey to some grubby exercise in vote-catching.[33]

Unsurprisingly, this high moral tone was set in the very first assembly by orators who, nevertheless, insisted on reminding women where they really belonged. Gil Robles, the leader of Acción Popular, spoke first saying that while women had 'a greater sensibility and a greater sacrifice' than men they were inferior in intellect. It was, therefore, dangerous for women to be given authority which required fortitude or the dispensing of justice. Female suffrage and participation in public life were, however, not unnatural provided that such activities did not take women away from their families where Christ himself had put them on the 'Throne of the Queen of the Home'. Belittling as this speech may appear, it paled into insignificance beside that given by the local Traditionalist deputy, José María Lamamié de Clairac who began by explaining to the meeting why he had voted against extending the franchise to women. He had, however, overcome his fear that female suffrage endangered the home, believing that support for the AFEC was necessary if the field of female voters was not to be left free for extremists, but he failed to give any more positive reasons for the political emancipation of Catholic women.[34]

This picture of woman being forced out of her home in order to do God's work was repeated again and again by the male orators visiting the association. In an address given in November 1931, José Cimas Leal, director of the *Gaceta Regional* and legal advisor to the AFEC, echoed Gil Robles's words by saying that the throne of the home had

[33] First meeting of AFEC, *GR*, 26 Oct. 1931; interview with Arroyo, *GR*, 16 Mar. 1931.
[34] *GR*, 26 Oct. 1931.

been won for women on Calvary. He talked of the pressing need to improve the conditions and wages of women workers which were often 'inexplicably' lower than men's but made no secret of his views on the evil of female labour, claiming that medical statistics showed the premature exhaustion of working mothers, which was one of the main reasons for the depopulation of France. Both Cimas Leal and another local speaker, José Durán y Sanz, a member of Angel Herrera Oria's National Catholic Association of Propagandists (ACNdeP), dwelt on the modern crisis of the family and the tragedy of homes where children scarcely saw their mothers, either because they were out working or because they were too involved in 'frivolous occupations'. Responsible women, therefore, had to fight for the family, firm in the knowledge that the fate of the fatherland depended on their success.[35]

This call to arms must have struck a chord in the hearts of many women for, by the beginning of 1932, members of the AFEC were not merely listening to roll-calls of their duties, they were out converting other women to the cause.[36] These female orators, several of whom were extremely skilled, stressed women's moral superiority to men but made no mention of their supposed intellectual inferiority. The phrase 'queen of the home' was, however, a popular one and the role was claimed as a 'supernatural duty' by Abilia Arroyo. All were agreed that women's first duties were domestic, although the definition of domestic was often expanded to include religion. One speaker at a rally in Ciudad Rodrigo, the faded cathedral city near the Portuguese border, said that women's role in society was to look after their homes, carry out their religious duties, and sustain the faith of their menfolk, thereby ensuring that their children were brought up in the Church. The moral guardianship of the family was entrusted to the woman and she was the one who had to ensure that religious and moral standards were maintained. On one occasion women were even told that they had to educate their husbands as well as their children, hardly the respectful attitude normally expected from a dutiful wife.[37]

AFEC orators frequently spoke of women's moral strength and firmness. Occasionally they talked of women as the saviours of Spain, struggling to straighten out the ethical and legal mess created by weak-willed men. Such words should not, however, be taken as feminist

[35] *GR*, 17 Nov. 1931; 22 Dec. 1931.
[36] Women speakers were a common and popular feature of Acción Popular rallies in many different parts of Spain, e.g. Luis Miguel Moreno Fernández, *Acción Popular Murciana: La derecha confesional en Murcia durante la II República* (Murcia, 1987), 111.
[37] *GR*, 13 Mar. 1931, 26 May 1932, 12 May 1932.

subversion, or even sabotage, of family and social structures. On the contrary, the AFEC exhorted women to come out in defence of 'what is ours, just ours: our husbands, our children, our religion'.[38] These they saw as being threatened by the Republican laws on divorce, the secularization of education, and other anticlerical measures, and they were acutely aware of the need to make other women accept this analysis of government-inspired social change if they were to mount an effective campaign against it. But, as they also knew, they were wielding powerful weapons. In a society where women worked outside the home only if absolutely necessary, their first and overriding concern was for the family. Middle-class women's lives revolved around their husbands and children and they valued and judged themselves as mothers and housekeepers, not as managers or wage-earners. Their working lives were spent caring and catering for their families and homes.

This battle for the home, women's undisputed sphere of interest, assumed such importance that, during the run-up to the general elections in November 1933, 'La Mujer Charra', the women's page the AFEC had been running in the *Gaceta Regional* since the previous April, printed a piece which instructed women to vote according to their consciences, if necessary against the will of their husbands. Such an instruction could be justified in terms of the divine will: duty to God came before duty to men, even husbands. The tone of the article, however, implied more traditional feminine wiles. Readers were asked if they had never disobeyed their husbands in other matters, attending Mass, for instance, or dressing their daughters more expensively than their fathers would like.[39] The inference was that they would be able to bring their husbands round, persuade them to change their minds without directly flouting their authority, a skill recognized by women in many societies.

However, advocating such ethically dubious practices was unusual, at least in print. Generally, AFEC members claimed the high moral ground and defended it against all comers. In the election campaigns of both 1933 and 1936 the AFEC worked tirelessly for the CEDA candidature, making far more use of religious imagery and language than did male Acción Popular speakers. In November 1933 the AFEC held an electoral meeting in a shrine to the Mother of God with the

---

[38] *GR*, 14 Mar. 1932.
[39] *GR*, 10 Nov. 1933.

speakers being introduced by the local priest. On another occasion during the 1936 campaign the election progaganda of a group of AFEC members included a christening. On discovering the presence of three unbaptized children at a rally in an outlying village the speakers immediately, and successfully, undertook the 'pious task' of persuading their parents to comply with their Christian duties and promptly had the children baptized in the parish church, the AFEC members acting as godmothers.[40]

The insistency with which the AFEC presented their political propaganda as a religious cause gave greater weight to their claims that women, by their very nature, were above party politics. Following Acción Popular's accidentalist line that forms of government were unimportant, the AFEC campaigned on policies, looking to mobilize as wide a support as possible against Republican legislation. Constitutional issues were presented as particularly irrelevant to women who were only concerned with the welfare of their families. As Abilia Arroyo put it: 'Republic? Monarchy? What does it matter! What we want . . . is that our children are brought up Christian.'[41] Arguments over the nature of the regime were also represented as petty and insignificant. Arroyo was greeted with great applause at an Acción Popular assembly in Madrid later in the year when she said that she had never been either republican or monarchist. Having brought twelve children into the world she had not had time to bother with such questions.[42]

To take these comments about female disinterest in politics at their face value, however, would be to underestimate the efficiency and the sophistication of the party machine established by these same women in Salamanca. The AFEC was the first political organization in the area to mobilize a mass following among women and, although its political creed clearly had considerable appeal for some, it would not have attracted great numbers of women, still less have kept their support, if it had not offered more than mere rhetoric to its many sympathizers and adherents.[43] The organizational structure of the association was erected remarkably quickly, largely because of the support given by the Catholic political parties and the *Gaceta Regional*. The

---

[40] *GR*, 2 Nov. 1933; 8 Feb. 1936.

[41] *GR*, 23 Apr. 1932.

[42] Montero, *La CEDA*, i. 686.

[43] Membership figures issued by the AFEC (published *GR*) are unreliable. These claimed 1,000 members in Nov. 1931, 3,000 in Salamanca city alone in Dec. 1931, 4,000 in Jan. 1932, nearly 7,000 with over 3,000 in the provincial capital in Mar. 1932, and, finally, 25,000 throughout the province in Feb. 1936.

speed with which the new association was constructed was also helped by the fact that there were no elective posts: all officers were appointed, at first by Arroyo and her advisers, later by the directive committee.[44]

The *junta directiva* was announced at the first public meeting in October 1931. By mid-December two *juntas de propaganda* had also been named, one with responsibility for the city of Salamanca, the other to co-ordinate work in the province. These juntas were, in turn, followed by local committees, established in all the main market towns of the province by March 1932, which made up the backbone of provincial recruitment to the AFEC.[45] They would send out teams of speakers to the neighbouring villages, hold a public meeting, and then form a branch of the AFEC, appointing women volunteers from the *pueblo* as officers. Such activity was at its most intensive during election time, when rallies in the villages would invariably be followed by the founding of another local caucus. In the week leading up to the February 1936 elections, for instance, members of the AFEC in Vitigudino established no fewer than thirteen branches in the surrounding villages.[46] Such intense activity was helped by the fact that, during election campaigns, speakers from the provincial capital also travelled around the province; but they tended to join teams from the local town as guest speaker rather than set out on separate missions.

The achievements of the heady weeks of non-stop campaigning may have seemed spectacular, but they were hardly likely to give lasting results. AFEC groups in the smaller villages only ever became centres of attention during election campaigns and many branches had only a nominal existence. Members from Ciudad Rodrigo, for instance, campaigning in the area during November 1933 dutifully ensured that they left AFEC juntas behind them in every *pueblo* they visited, printing the names of the new *directivas* in the *Gaceta Regional*. However, at the last village they had so little time left that they were not able to write down the names of the newly formed committee. A new branch of the

---

[44] In similar fashion, the AFAP's first committee was appointed by the male AP executive and was approved by acclamation at the inaugural assembly, Montero, *La CEDA*, i. 665.

[45] The same organizational pattern of a provincial executive and local committees was followed in other areas: by mid-1933, the Madrid AFAP had established 40 committees in the surrounding districts while Badajoz's Acción Popular Agraria had founded 36 female associations around the province, 9 of which were in *pueblos* which had no corresponding male committees, Montero, *La CEDA*, i. 680; *Hoy*, 30 May 1933.

[46] *GR*, 13 Feb. 1936.

AFEC thus came into existence even though the provincial association did not even know the name of their contact in the village.[47] The devolution of responsibility for recruitment to the AFEC groups in the towns also made for some unevenness in establishing new branches. In contrast to the very active groups working from Ciudad Rodrigo, Vitigudino, and Béjar, the AFEC in Alba de Tormes, a town of considerable importance in the province, was a complete disaster. Founded in the first flush of enthusiasm in the autumn of 1931 it had still not organized a single rally by the time of the critical election of November 1933. The directive committee had met only once and, although it claimed 300 members, there was no list of names and no dues were collected.[48] Relying on this group to evangelize the surrounding countryside was obviously a waste of time.

If this method of intensive propaganda and instant creation of party branches was unlikely to have a lasting impact in terms of organizational structure it was still effective electioneering. The AFEC groups in the villages may have had little chance of survival but at least they would be remembered until polling day. The AFEC were, understandably, concerned that as many women as possible reached the polling stations and they made considerable efforts to ensure that all women were registered to vote. In 1932, a *sección del censo* was established to address this problem directly. In July they opened an office in the city of Salamanca to give advice to those wishing to put their names on the electoral roll. The section also used the association's membership files to ensure that all the women who had joined or expressed an interest in the AFEC were eligible to vote.[49]

At first, such tactics may seem surprising, even absurd. Belonging to a party usually indicates a considerable degree of political commitment and paid-up and enlisted members are not generally found among the ranks of the disenfranchised. Aware of the fact that poorly educated, working women were less likely to register as voters, the AFEC made concerted efforts to win their allegiance and offered considerable material benefits to those that joined. By March 1932 the Association had established a mutual benefit section. Dues paid to the AFEC by

---

[47] *GR*, 1 Nov. 1933.
[48] *GR*, 10 Nov. 1933.
[49] *GR*, 25 July 1932; 28 Nov. 1932. The women's section of the Murcia branch of Acción Popular was involved in similar work of drawing up electoral rolls and encouraging the registration of those entitled to vote, Móreno Fernández, *Acción Popular Murciana*, p. 111.

working women automatically went to this section.[50] Regular payments entitled those on the scheme to sickness benefit as well as to maternity insurance which paid 125 pesetas at the birth of a child and provided baby clothes. The section also planned to give dowries to girls hoping to enter religious orders.[51] The practical rewards to be gained by enrolling in the AFEC could, therefore, be considerable. Certainly, the maternity scheme offered working women an essential, and often overlooked, service.

Female workers were encouraged to join the Association in order to avail themselves of these facilities. AFEC members went into the city's factories and sweatshops to ensure that the dressmakers, milliners, and factory-hands employed there were fully aware of the material and spiritual benefits to be gained from joining their organization. Despite their conviction that women found true fulfilment as 'queens of the home', the AFEC showed an awareness of the problems faced by working women, especially those with children. Their orators frequently spoke of the need to improve the conditions of female labourers, both in the towns and in the countryside. At the beginning of 1936, plans for a separate section for peasant women were announced.[52] This aimed to encourage the regeneration of country life by establishing cottage industries for peasant women whose products would then be sold through a retail outlet in the city. This scheme had the secondary aim of helping country women find practical employment for their leisure time. The AFEC were organizing introductory lectures throughout the province on how to run a small business and on poultry, rabbit, and bee-keeping. The implementation of these extremely ambitious plans was prevented by the outbreak of Civil War, but their very existence indicates that the condition of working women was treated with some care and even imagination by the ladies of the AFEC.[53]

The Association was also concerned to provide for its better-off members who used it as a source of entertainment and respectable employment rather than practical help. For the actively minded the

[50] AFEC funds were divided between dues paid by workers and those paid by ladies. The latter went towards running costs and campaigning while the *mutualidad* was supposedly entirely funded by workers' contributions which began in Nov. 1931. Finance does not seem to have been a problem for the AFEC as it benefited both from its close links with CEDA and from wealthy patrons of its own.

[51] Special report on the AFEC, *GR*, 16 Mar. 1932.

[52] A national organization, the Liga de Mujeres Campesinas, had been established at the beginning of 1935, Montero, *La CEDA*, i. 705.

[53] *El Adelanto*, 16 Jan. 1936; *GR*, 5 Mar. 1936.

work the AFEC offered was plentiful and varied. Office-work, administration, public speaking, canvassing, and campaigning were just some of the tasks undertaken by the stalwarts of the organization. Outside the frenetic activity of election times, however, members were encouraged to attend the women's study circle which had been started in the provincial capital. At the circle's inaugural meeting, the vice-chairwoman's introductory speech said that such groups were badly needed because of the prevailing view of women in Spain which saw them as having hearts, but no brains. After this trenchant start, however, the circle confined itself to the study of Catholic apologetics and papal encyclicals. The same strongly Catholic image was given by the Association's youth section, established in January 1933. This had its own study circle, as well as weekly meetings to make baby clothes for the workers belonging to the mutual benefit scheme. Significantly, the youth section saw charitable work and catechetics as being as important a part of its work as electioneering.[54]

The similarities between the AFEC and other non-political Catholic women's organizations are striking. Events arranged by the Association frequently had an air of sentimental piety to them. An evening held for working women in January 1932, for instance, gave prizes of babies' layettes to those women who had given birth nearest to midnight on Christmas Eve, the hour when Jesus was born.[55] This kind of sentimental religious imagery was immensely popular among Catholic women's groups, as were charitable activities such as the making of baby clothes for the deserving poor and Sunday school teaching, both of which were duplicated by the AFEC and by the only other Catholic women's political association in the district, the Traditionalist Margaritas. On the feast of the Epiphany in 1936, the Margaritas met to distribute clothes made by their members to 200 poor children from the outer suburbs of Salamanca where the Traditionalist ladies also worked as catechists.[56] The strongly confessional images fostered by both the AFEC and the Margaritas undoubtedly gave the political organizations respectability, as well as a considerable air of familiarity. The matrons and married ladies of Salamanca had long occupied themselves with good works, religious philanthropy, and church-going. By creating the AFEC in the image of more established women's

---

[54] *GR*, 21 Apr. 1932, 10 Jan. 1933. Women's branches of AP commonly established charitable sub-committees (Sección de Asitencia Social), e.g. Montero, *La CEDA*, i. 693; Moreno Fernández, *Acción Popular Murciana*, p. 111.
[55] *GR*, 9 Jan. 1932.   [56] *El Adelanto*, 7 Jan. 1936.

associations, its founders were able to draw on a considerable fund of organizational experience among women, at the same time as reassuring potential members that politics was far from being a strange and frightening occupation.

The women who made up the AFEC's directive committee demonstrated a wide range of administrative expertise, all of it gained from work with Catholic societies and sodalities. Abilia Arroyo was a long-standing member of the pious group known as the Marías of the Sanctuaries and a regular contributor to its monthly bulletin. Agrapina Carrasco, vice-secretary to the AFEC, also belonged to the Marías and was vice-treasurer to the Workers' Catechetical Centre which gave religious instruction and elementary schooling to workers, 300 of whom were registered there in 1930. She was also secretary to the Old Girls' Association of the school run by the Daughters of Jesus, an organization of over 400 members with its own magazine. Eusebia González Cobos, the AFEC's secretary, was vice-president of the Workers' Catechetical Centre and president of the Children of Mary, the most popular women's devotional association in the city of Salamanca, with around 1,200 members during the Republic, 250 of whom were regular attenders at meetings.[57]

José Montero, the historian of the CEDA, has stressed the lack of a ready-made female political élite able to lead and co-ordinate Madrid's Asociación Femenina de Acción Popular. To illustrate this, he points to the preponderance of wives and relatives of leading members of Acción Popular on the AFAP's first *junta directiva*.[58] Unsurprisingly, leading Catholic families were also represented on the *directiva* of the AFEC. Abilia Arroyo's husband, Emilio Román, was on the board of the local rural savings bank and was involved in such Church initiatives as the Catholic Parents' Association and the Federation of Catholic Students. Another AFEC office-holder, Paz Durán was sister to José Durán y Sanz, secretary to the Castilian–Leonese region of Angel Herrera's Propagandists and a leading light in the local Acción Popular. The dowager Marchioness of Llén, widow of one of the most influential of local notables, also had a place on the directive committee.

[57] Information on the Marías and the old girls of the Daughters of Jesus from their respective bulletins: *Crónica de las Marías* and *Ecos de mi Colegio*. For the Workers' Centre see *El Adelanto*, 1 Mar. 1930. Figures for the Children of Mary are given in 'Memoria de la Residencia de Salamanca durante estos 25 años', *Bodas de Plata de la Provincia de León: 1918–1943* (private publication for the Society of Jesus), 20.

[58] Montero, *La CEDA*, i. 666.

Montero's interpretation, however, takes insufficient account of the nature of the power wielded by women in contemporary Spanish society. Women of influence and position were the wives and daughters of wealthy and important men. Few women had economic power and those who were powerful in their own right were usually widows or, on occasion, heiresses. The lack of outright economic influence, however, did not mean that bourgeois and aristocratic women had no experience of administration or management. Many were used to running large establishments, organizing the household economy, hiring and firing servants, and being generally responsible for the smooth operation of domestic life. Work with voluntary and religious societies had then given these women valuable experience in bringing these domestic skills into the public sphere. There was thus a considerable fund of experienced female labour to draw upon, something capitalized on to great effect by the AFEC.

The willingness with which organizations like the AFEC galvanized Catholic women into political action, or encouraged and developed female administrative expertise, did not, however, mean that they were looking to cast their members in a different social role. In Salamanca, Arroyo was the only female political figure to achieve anything other than parochial stature. She was the only AFEC member to address Acción Popular rallies, the only one to speak outside the province, or to hold office in the national party.[59] Representing the AFEC, she was also the only woman to serve on the first junta of the Autonomous Right grouping founded in Salamanca in February 1932. A year later, however, when the definitive list of junta members was issued, there were no women on it at all.[60] Even Arroyo did not escape the female subservience she expounded in her oratory. Catholic women were not expected to take public office except in women's organizations. There were no right-wing female deputies in the Cortes and scant admiration was shown for those women who had managed to win seats in Parliament. In January 1932, the AFEC even sent a telegram to the President asking that the Socialist deputy for Badajoz, Margarita Nelken, be expelled from the Cortes and from Spain as a disgrace both to her country and her sex.[61]

The situation was no different at a regional level. Despite the effi-

---

[59] Arroyo's appointment to national party office was ratified at the first CEDA assembly in Mar. 1933, Montero, *la CEDA*, i. 292. However, she continued to live and work in Salamanca.

[60] *GR*, 2 Feb. 1932; 27 Feb. 1933.   [61] *GR*, 9 Jan. 1932.

cient political work of the AFEC there was a conspicuous absence of
women in local government in Salamanca, even during the 1934–5
Radical–CEDA ascendancy. It was not until March 1936, after the
right-wing coalition had lost power to the Popular Front in the February elections, that the AFEC encouraged women to stand as candidates themselves. Until then female political activity had been
severely limited. They were exhorted to work for Catholic candidates,
vote for right-wing slates, pray for victory, but not to usurp male authority or win power for themselves. Yet now 'Teresa de Castilla' was
urging 'true women' to stand in the forthcoming municipal elections.
The picture she gave of the work they would do there, however, was
far from radical or exciting. The new female councillors, 'so
enamoured of order and of cleanliness', would be able to defend the
rights of the needy, protect workers' families, care for the old, and
reward exemplary mothers.[62]

The women of the AFEC were, however, to be denied even this
small foray into public life. The municipal elections were postponed
and all democratic procedure was brought to an abrupt end by the
outbreak of Civil War in July. Salamanca immediately declared for the
insurgents and became Franco's first wartime capital. The AFEC
exchanged electioneering for war work and prayed for a Nationalist
victory just as they had once implored God for a CEDA triumph in the
elections. As true Catholic and Spanish women they could do nothing
less. Nor could they do anything more.

[62] *GR*, 5 Mar. 1936.

8. THE ECLIPSE OF THE SOCIALIST LEFT: 1934–1937

Helen Graham

On 17 May 1937 the veteran socialist trade union leader, Francisco Largo Caballero, resigned as prime minister of the Spanish Republican government. His 'fall' has been interpreted as symbolizing the death of the popular revolution which had swept through much of the Republic's territory in the first months of the Civil War. Even more crudely, the collapse of Largo's government has been viewed purely as the result of the machinations of the Spanish Communist Party (PCE) and its allies on the national executive of the PSOE (Spanish Socialist Party). However, in order fully to appreciate the underlying reasons for a political failure which heralded the beginning of the end for the party left, a much wider perspective must be taken.

The eclipse of the Socialist left and the resignation of Largo Caballero in particular, far from being sudden, were the culmination of a lengthy government crisis. This crisis sprang from the basic ideological and organizational incoherence of the *caballeristas*. It was, in part, the product of a process of erosion initiated by the abortive Asturian revolution of October 1934 which had led some of the Socialist Party hierarchy to question the revolutionary credentials of the *caballerista* leadership. This article seeks to analyse the contradictions and consequent passivity of the Socialist left as the root causes of its failure to take real control of the party, or even the government, in spite of appearances to the contrary. These same contradictions would ultimately be responsible for the defeat of the party left by the end of 1937 at the hands of the parliamentary Socialists linked to the PSOE's national executive.

The enduring and ultimately fatal division in the PSOE pre-dates the Second Republic (1931–6). Nevertheless, the division was to develop a truly destructive potential as a result of the Socialists' experience of government between 1931 and 1933. In this period of coalition, the PSOE's immense will to carry out reform was matched only by the enormity of the need for a programme of social and economic modernization. The will to reform at that stage united the entire party. However, as a result of the intransigence of the clerical-Conservative right, determined to protect the privileges of oligarchy and to preserve the pre-republican social and economic status quo, both by filibuster in the Cortes and by conniving at the non-implementation of new legislation at a local level, there occurred two very different reactions within the PSOE.

For many of the party left, the experience of government was an entirely negative one. This attitude often reflected their close links with the Socialist-led trade union federation (UGT), whose general secretary Largo Caballero, as Minister of Labour in the Republican--Socialist coalition, had been the target of particularly violent Conservative attack. The experience of 1931–3 was taken as proof that substantial reform was impossible within the context of a bourgeois democracy. Hence the left deduced that the party had to prepare to seize political power in order to implement a fully Socialist programme. However, the inveterate reformism of the Socialist left prevented the translation of this resolution from the theoretical sphere to that of practical action. The enormous inconsistency between rhetoric and political practice where the party left was concerned would form the basis of the parliamentary Socialists' case against it. The reformists in the PSOE had reacted to the Conservative intransigence of 1931–3 in quite the opposite way. They had simply become more determined to ensure the enactment of thoroughgoing reform. Initial failure had only convinced them of the absolute necessity of persevering with the Republican–Socialist pact, in order to support to the hilt the numerically weak Republicans.

The Socialist who epitomized this intense commitment to reform was Indalecio Prieto and he defended a collaborationist tactic on the basis of his assessment of the balance of class forces in Spain in the 1930s.[1] Prieto believed that the weakness of the republican parties — reflecting that of the middle classes in Spain — made it necessary for the Socialists to take on the historic task of the bourgeois democratic revolution. The modernization of Spain would be accomplished by means of a programme of social and economic reforms which, whilst not integrally socialist, would be immensely radical in the context of Spain's economic backwardness.[2] Thus, in a sense, Prieto's critics   on

---

[1] I. Prieto, *Discursos fundamentales* (Madrid, 1975), 169–70.

[2] 'In our country, which is politically so backward, we socialists must *replace* the progressive bourgeoisie': I. Prieto, interview in *Le Populaire* (Paris), 17 Jan. 1931; 'The greatest tragedy for the Spanish Republic is that there are really no republican parties in Spain': I. Prieto, 'Discurso en el cine Pardiñas', *El Socialista*, 6 Feb. 1934; Prieto, *Discursos fundamentales*, pp. 185, 279.

the left were correct to charge him with 'thinking as a republican' ('pensar en republicano'). However, the logical concomitant of such a criticism would have been the elaboration of a revolutionary alternative tactic to that of collaboration. But the Socialist left made no attempt to provide such an option, beyond mouthing a hollow revolutionary rhetoric. This became doubly damaging in the circumstances. It meant antagonizing right-wing politicians when the Socialist left had no strategy for meeting their catastrophism. Moreover, it also deepened the divide in the PSOE by alienating the parliamentary wing which was, very early on, aware that the left's maximalism amounted to nothing more than empty posturing.

The bankruptcy of the Socialist left was made abundantly clear to the rest of the party by its lack of initiative when faced with the revolutionary rising of October 1934 in Asturias. In so far as the revolt of the Asturian miners against the abrogation of republican reforms by a succession of conservative governments had a 'general staff', it was the Socialists, Anarchists, and Communists of the Workers' Alliance *in situ*. In the aftermath of October, the left Socialists and most stridently the Socialist youth organization (FJS), began a vitriolic campaign to purge the party of the 'centrists' to whom the failure of the October revolution was being attributed. It did not deceive the PSOE's parliamentary leadership. The subsequent FJS-led campaign to 'bolshevize' the party was seen for what it was, a smokescreen, a device to deflect attention from the real lesson of October, namely that the left Socialist leadership had been tried and found wanting.[3]

By the time of the Popular Front elections in February 1936, two parallel developments can be discerned which were to be central to the erosion of the Socialist left and thus, ultimately, to the crisis of May 1937. In the first place, the Comintern's policy volte-face, its espousal of inter-class collaboration in the form of Popular Front, heralded a

---

[3] See letter from Amador Fernández to Juan Pablo García, Brussels, 29 Aug. 1935, in I. Prieto *et al.*, *Documentos socialistas* (Madrid, 1935), 217–21; cf. Rafael Henche, during discussion of the youth report at the PSOE national committee meeting, 17–21 July, Valencia. Stenographic record (AH-24-2), in the Archivo Histórico de Moscú (hereafter AHM), Fundación Pablo Iglesias (FPI), Madrid, 'I marvel at the degree of personal loyalty which comrade Caballero is able to command. When one views it all in the cold light of day, Caballero has far from measured up to the standards of our party, either before October, during October or after October ...'. See also Asturian representative Antonio Llaneza's criticisms of the party left and his exhortations to Lamoneda to break the *caballeristas*, as 'elements without moral solvency, without history, without merit', and to do it 'in the name of Asturias', ibid. 81; P. Preston, *The Coming of the Spanish Civil War* (hereafter *CSCW*), (London, 1978), 127, 132.

realignment which would eventually lead to the wartime collaboration between the Spanish Communist Party (PCE) and the parliamentary wing of the PSOE. The basic philosophies of both over the constitution and aim of Popular Front were the same. Before the Civil War, Prieto was anxious to avoid linking up with the PCE. However, his conviction that the need to re-establish the Republican–Socialist government coalition was paramount eventually came to be echoed by the Communist leadership, which was similarly seeking the election of a coalition of Republicans and moderate Socialists, or even of an entirely Republican cabinet.[4]

Secondly, whilst the political attitudes and objectives of parliamentary Socialists and Communists in Spain were converging, left Socialist relations with both the Anarchists (CNT) and left Communist groups were in a state of crisis. This was largely due to the general suspicion on the left of the absorptionist intentions of the *caballeristas*. The left Communist initiative of Workers' Alliance was conceived in 1933 as a means of achieving real rank-and-file unity and co-operation across the organizational divide. Its failure had much to do with the *caballeristas*' bureaucratic and limiting conception of the Alliance's function as merely a liaison committee between existing organizations.[5] This reflected the *caballeristas*' fear that by participating in the Alliance, rather than furthering their hegemonic designs, they would actively risk losing control of their own base. The left Socialists were severely traumatized by the extent of the political repression which followed the October events in Asturias. Fearful of the effect on the Socialist rank and file, they observed, almost passively, as the mainstream Communists (PCE) not only assumed the political responsibility and therefore the kudos for October, but also adopted and thence totally transformed the structure, political significance, and objective of the Workers' Alliance.[6] Implemented at the local level, it was to become an expres-

---

[4] Cf. the PCE leadership's reluctance to accept Largo's designation of Communist ministers in Sept. 1936. This reluctance was only vanquished by pressure from the Comintern. Burnett Bolloten, *The Spanish Revolution: The Left and the Struggle for Power during the Civil War* (Chapel Hill, 1979), 122.

[5] For the genesis and development of the Workers' Alliance, Preston, *CSCW*, pp. 117–20; Marta Bizcarrondo, 'De las Alianzas Obreras al Frente Popular', *Estudios de Historia Social*, 16–17 (1981), 83–104, also M. Bizcarrondo (ed.), *Octubre del 34: Reflexiones sobre una revolución* (Madrid, 1977), *passim*; Santos Juliá, *La Izquierda del PSOE (1935–1936)* (Madrid, 1977), 202–16.

[6] For a justification of Largo's public court-room denial of Socialist 'responsibility' for October, L. Araquistain, 'Largo Caballero ante los jueces', in P. Preston (ed.), *Leviatán (Antologia)* (Madrid, 1976), 266–77; for the PCE's exalted possession of

sion of embryonic popular frontism.[7] The PCE's determination to woo the Socialist base, combined with the vast wave of grass-roots support for electoral unity on the left to secure a political amnesty for the prisoners of October, would end by clinching Largo's own support for the Popular Front by November 1935.[8]

Throughout 1935 and 1936 relations between left Socialists and Anarchists were fraught with difficulty. The *caballerista* leadership's dealings wth its Anarchist counterpart were always characteristically high-handed. Yet the hegemony of the Socialist left in the 1930s could not have been achieved except by means of an agreement with the CNT. That this was never realized had much to do with the intense and increasing rivalry between the two union leaderships and their respective rank and files.

Contrary to what has often been suggested, however, there is no evidence that the radicalization of the Socialist left's leadership between 1934 and 1936 occurred as a direct response to Anarchist pressure. By 1933 the Socialist landworkers' federation (FNTT) had become the giant of the UGT. The radicalization of the left Socialist leadership owed much to that of the FNTT base of landless labourers who were demanding immediate and thoroughgoing agrarian reform. This occurred precisely at a time when the CNT appeared weak as a result of various abortive attempts at insurrection and when the organization was beset by internal divisions. The return of the UGT leadership to its traditional reformist positions came as the Anarchist organization emerged once again as a revolutionary force in the spring of 1936.[9]

'responsibility', J. Díaz, 'Discurso en el cine Monumental, Madrid, 2 June 1935', in J. Díaz, *Tres años de lucha* (Barcelona, 1978), i. 42–3; see also B. Bayerlein, 'El significado internacional de Octubre de 1934 en Asturias: La Comuna asturiana y el Komintern', in Jackson *et al.*, *Octubre 1934* (Madrid, 1985), especially pp. 25, 29, 39.

[7] PCE report, 9 Dec. 1935, Archive of the Spanish Communist Party, microfilm XIII (170), for a list of Workers' Alliances in existence by late 1935 and for rivalry over the alliances and Socialist complaints about the PCE's manipulation of the strategy, see correspondence involving Socialist organizations in both Seville and Córdoba; also Bizcarrondo, 'De las Alianzas', p. 92; see also S. Juliá, 'Las alianzas obreras y campesinas eran, pues, una pieza . . . de la política global comunista de Frente Popular', *Izquierda*, pp. 212, 214.

[8] For left Socialist fears for PSOE/UGT control, Bizcarrondo, 'De las Alianzas', p. 91.

[9] For analyses of left Socialist radicalization, see Juliá, *Izquierda*; Preston, *CSCW*; M. Bizcarrondo, *Araquistain y la Crisis Socialista de la II República/Leviatán (1934–1936)* (Madrid, 1975); A Blas Guerrero, *El Socialismo Radical en la II República* (Madrid, 1978); A. and I. Aviv, 'Ideology and Political Patronage: Workers and Working Class Movements in Republican Madrid 1931–4', *European Studies Review*, 2 (1981), and 'The

The interpretative difficulties facing the historian attempting either a definition of left Socialism or a coherent explanation of its behaviour are the inevitable product of the fragmentary nature and the inconsistencies of the Socialist left itself. Any valid analysis of *caballerismo* needs to distinguish, first and foremost, between the phenomenon of rank-and-file political radicalization in the later period of the Second Republic (1934–6) and the quite separate factors that shaped the political behaviour of the left Socialist leadership which apparently espoused the radical cause. There remained an insoluble contradiction between the radical aspirations of the *caballerista* power base and the innate conservatism and political caution of the veteran trade union leaders who constituted the nucleus of the left Socialist leadership. Their trade union roots entirely determined their political behaviour. The fundamental objective remained the aggrandizement of the Socialist organization in Spain.[10] Since the UGT's leaders remained acutely aware of Anarchist competition, it is hardly surprising that no common ground could be found for political co-operation with the CNT.

By November 1935, the Socialist left and even Largo himself had accepted the idea of a Popular Front electoral pact, if not a repeat of coalition government. This left the Anarchists isolated once again, the sole defenders of a homogenous worker front, and proletarian revolutionary action as the only real protection against Fascism. The 'revolutionary pact' which the CNT proposed to the UGT leadership was effectively a way of channelling its fundamental 'apoliticism' at a time when the massive appeal of Popular Front had closed off the possibility of a thoroughgoing critique of political and parliamentary tactics.

By the end of May 1936, against the background of the increasingly tense and polarized political life of the Republic, there was evidence of a serious decline in relations between the two union leaderships. Inter-union rivalry was particularly evident in Madrid where the CNT had begun to mobilize workers in a city which had traditionally been a UGT stronghold. Increased confrontation between capital and labour and the tangibility of class conflict gave the Anarchist organization its chance to agitate in order to conquer a significant segment of the

Madrid Working Class, the Spanish Socialist Party and the Collapse of the Second Republic (1934–36)', *Journal of Contemporary History*, 16 (1981); J. M. Macarro Vera, 'Causas de la Radicalización Socialista en la Segunda República', *Revista de Historia Contemporánea* (Seville), 1 (Dec. 1982).

[10] For the phenomenon of bureaucratic reformism, J. Andrade, *La burocracia reformista en el movimiento obrero* (Madrid, 1935), *passim*; Juliá, *Izquierda*, pp. 289–304.

UGT. In April 1936, on the fifth anniversary of the Republic, many individual *ugetistas* joined the general strike declared by the CNT in the face of the official hostility of both Socialists and Communists. No sector of the Socialist party or union leadership was able to prevent the massive indiscipline of the UGT rank and file on that occasion, or, indeed, to prevent it from joining subsequent strikes in the capital.

The defensiveness of the Socialist left leadership—its refusal to meet the Anarchist challenge to declare itself unequivocally for or against the revolutionary syndical pact or the Popular Front strategy as logically mutually exclusive policies—provides the clearest indication that, in the last analysis, it was the trade union leadership which dictated the practical policy of the Socialist left. Just as its real strength lay in the union, so too its preoccupations were essentially syndical.

The only possible way of making sense of the apparently schizophrenic nature of the Socialist left is to employ the distinction posited by recent scholarship.[11] This places the formulators of its revolutionary language (intellectuals such as Carlos de Baraibar and Luis Araquistain) on the outside looking in, as far as the workings and policies of the UGT are concerned. They had no impact on the daily action of the union and thus their theory was reduced to a mere tactical weapon in the hands of veteran union leaders. Ultimately, this revolutionary language only served to isolate the Socialist left from the parties of the Popular Front, while the very real predominance of reformists in the trade union leadership equally precluded any alternative strategy involving the CNT. The Socialist union bureaucracy was condemned to isolation and impotence precisely because its overriding concern was to maintain its organization intact. This precluded the leadership from tapping the vast potential of the radicalized sectors of the Socialist base; the phenonemon defined as *caballerismo*.[12] The Socialist left's verbal maximalism, its exalted proclamations of the imminence of a new revolutionary order, must not be taken as evidence of the genuine assumption of leadership of a radicalized working class. For all the noise generated by the Socialist youth and the bolshevizers of the Madrid Socialist section (ASM), the single most important component of *caballerismo*—without which the others combined amounted to little—was the FNTT's radicalized rural base. It could not have

[11] See Juliá, *Izquierda*, and *Madrid 1931–1934: De la fiesta popular a la lucha de clases* (Madrid, 1984)—to which this section owes a considerable debt.

[12] For a definition, F. Claudín, *The Communist Movement* (Harmondsworth, 1975), 218.

been otherwise in a country whose economy turned on an agrarian axis.

By the spring of 1936 the left Socialists were badly isolated in the Republic's political arena. With the wreckage of the Workers' Alliance behind them and relations with the CNT increasingly tense, disaster struck much closer to home. At the beginning of April 1936, the radicalized, pro-Caballero leadership of the Socialist youth federation (FJS) initiated a process of unification with its Communist counterpart (UJC) which would eventually deprive the socialist movement of its youth organization. The united group gravitated out of the *caballerista* orbit directly into that of the PCE.[13]

As the strike in the Madrid construction industry dragged on into July 1936, a considerable hardening of attitudes towards the PSOE left occurred in the rest of the party. Already held morally responsible for the youth débâcle, the left was also criticized for having lost control of the UGT base in Madrid. What is more, the reformist Socialists were also beginning a series of tactical manoeuvres within the party organization aimed at undermining the left's strength. The *caballeristas'* failure to consolidate an alternative power base on the left, as a bulwark against what would turn into a concerted attack by both the parliamentary Socialists and the PCE in 1937, emerges as crucial to their eclipse.

THE BATTLE FOR CONTROL OF THE PARTY ORGANIZATION 1936–1937

After the experience of October 1934 and the subsequent bolshevization campaign of the party left, Indalecio Prieto had adopted, on behalf of the reformists, a tactical approach to the internal division which amounted to seeking to draw the sting of the left by revealing the fatuity of its revolutionary claims. His initial plan had been to call for a general congress of the party—but in Asturias instead of Madrid as was customary. There, in the heartland of October, which was also, ironically, *prietista* territory, he hoped to debunk the purely verbal max-

---

[13] For the origins and process of the youth unification, Ricard Viñas, *La formación de las Juventudes Socialistas Unificadas (1934–1936)* (Madrid, 1978); for the effect on the Socialist left, the author's article, 'The Socialist Youth in the JSU: The Experience of Organisational Unity 1936–1938' in M. Blinkhorn (ed.), *Spain in Conflict* (London, 1986), 3, 9–11; F. Largo Caballero, 'Notas históricas de la Guerra de España (1917–1940)', MS Fundación Pablo Iglesias, i. 254–5, for Largo's disapproval of the youth unification.

imalism of the Socialist left and to defuse what he saw as the threat which it posed to the discipline and integrity of the party.[14] However, after a long and complicated struggle in which both sides attempted to mobilize the support of the party base, the *prietistas* gave way to the left's insistence that the congress should be held in Madrid at the end of June 1936. The reformists were motivated in all this by the desire to establish an unambiguous line on party policy in order not to waste the opportunity afforded by the Popular Front electoral victory of February 1936.

However, by the end of May 1936 the situation had changed once again. The resolutions passed by the *prietista*-dominated PSOE national committee, which met at the end of the month, indicate a fundamental change in the tactics of the reformist wing. The origins of this tactical shift can be traced back to Indalecio Prieto's bitter defeat at the hands of the party left. At the beginning of May the *caballeristas* had successfully opposed his bid to lead a resurrected coalition government of Republicans and Socialists. When Manuel Azaña, as the new Republican president, called upon Prieto to form a government, he refused, arguing that he would not be able to count on the support of the left-controlled Socialist parliamentary minority in the chamber. However, it is difficult to avoid concluding that Prieto gave up the struggle rather too easily. He had the backing of the PSOE national executive which urged Prieto to call the left's bluff, arguing that, in the end, Largo Caballero would not use his control of the Socialist minority against him in the Cortes. In choosing to decline the power being offered to the PSOE without resorting to the full range of inner party mechanisms to support his case, Prieto seems to have lacked the courage of his convictions. The consequence of Prieto's refusal was government by the weak and ineffectual Republican, Casares Quiroga. He was entirely unequal to the task of countering the growing military conspiracy which threatened the Republic's very existence. As a result, Prieto himself must bear some part of the responsibility for the fatal undermining of the government in the spring of 1936.

In May 1936 the reformist executive effectively abandoned the idea of precipitating a direct confrontation with the party left such as would have occurred at a congress. The national committee opted to suspend

---

[14] *El Socialista*, 26 Feb., 9 Mar. 1936; G. M. de Coca, *Anti-Caballero* (Madrid, 1975), 194–7.

this until October 1936.[15] It was also unanimously agreed that the
party executive should be given the power to dissolve and reorganize
those Socialist sections which refused to recognize the authority of the
elected party leadership.[16] This laid the foundations for the purge of
the left from the party organization. As a result of civil war and popular
revolution, this concerted attack on *caballerista* nuclei in the party was
perforce delayed, in the event, for a whole year.[17] Nevertheless,
throughout the second half of 1937 it was to be this resolution on party
discipline which served as the chief weapon against any manifestation
of what the PSOE executive interpreted as left factionalism.

Such an onslaught on the left could be properly directed only by a
strong 'general staff'. Accordingly, the *prietista* executive announced
partial elections to fill the vacant seats on the executive committee.
These vacancies were created when the national committee finally and
formally accepted the resignations which had been submitted by Largo
Caballero's three supporters in December 1935.[18] The list of replacement candidates drawn up by the national committee consisted entirely
of moderates. Ramón González Pena stood for the presidency, to
replace Largo Caballero. Luis Jiménez de Asúa ran as vice-president
to replace the moderate Remigio Cabello who had died in April 1936.
Ramón Lamoneda stood as general secretary—a post previously
occupied by the fervent *caballerista*, Enrique de Francisco. Francisco
Cruz Salido stood as administrative secretary to replace the *Caballerista* Pascual Tomás and the list also included Jerónimo Bugeda and
Manuel Albar as new ordinary members.[19]

On sending out its list to the party base, the national committee
added a warning that votes must be cast only for candidates to replace
those who had resigned. Any votes cast for an entirely new executive
committee would be considered as evidence of blatant indiscipline and

[15] Stenographic record of discussion, AH-24-2, AHM; the left's criticism of the
proceedings in *Claridad*, 27 May 1936.

[16] See the resolution on party discipline, stenographic record, AH-24-2.

[17] Felix Morrow, *Revolution and Counter-Revolution in Spain* (London, 1976), 38;
Gabriel Morón, *Política de ayer y política de mañana* (Mexico, 1942), 61–2.

[18] According to PSOE statute, the *comisión ejecutiva*, elected by party congress,
formed part of the larger *comité nacional* and was answerable, between congresses, only to
the full *comité nacional* in session. The *comisión ejecutiva* was, in short, invested with the
full executive authority of the party between (bi-annual) congresses.

[19] J. S. Vidarte, *Todos Fuimos Culpables* (2 vols. Barcelona, 1977), 193–6; Juliá,
Izquierda, p. 116. This was the same list which had lost out to the *caballerista* candidacy
the previous March in the elections for the ASM executive. The left Socialist resignations had been as follows: Largo Caballero, Enrique de Francisco, Wenceslao Carrillo,
and Pascual Tomás.

therefore counted null and void.[20] However, since the left, and more specifically the left-controlled Madrid Socialist group (ASM), chose to ignore this and to offer the Socialist rank and file not only alternative candidates but a list comprising an entirely new executive committee, then a clash was inevitable.[21]

The left Socialists were desperate to ensure that the elections in the party did not take place before the party congress for which they were still petitioning.[22] The ASM elaborated an extremely ambitious congress agenda which ran the gamut of the issues dividing the party.[23] But, most importantly, the left wanted the congress as a forum in which to elect the new party executive. It doubted very much that a poll of local party sections would favour its candidates, as the reformists would be controlling the procedure as returning officers.

In the event, the *caballeristas* found themselves faced with a *fait accompli*. On 1 July, the victory of the national committee's list in the executive elections was announced. The results as published in *El Socialista*, the newspaper of the Socialist executive, were in stark contrast to those which appeared in the left's mouthpiece *Claridad*. According to the latter the *caballeristas* had taken the new executive by a substantial majority. The acrimonious debate which followed hinged upon the validity of the exclusion of a significant percentage of the ASM vote by the returning officers, the reformist Socialists, Ramón Lamoneda and Juan Simeón Vidarte.[24] It has been calculated that powerful though the party left was in certain areas, such as the South, the Levante, and Madrid itself, in terms of the total number of party militants throughout Spain, it would have been unlikely to have achieved, as a maximum, more than a third of the total party vote. Even had the disqualified votes been allowed, this would not have reversed the reformist victory.[25] However, in terms of the real significance of this victory for the internal life of the party, the arithmetic of the defeat

[20] Cf. the behaviour of the left at the time of the elections for party president in Jan. 1936, Coca, *Anti-Caballero*, p. 132, Preston, *CSCW*, pp. 145–6.

[21] The left Socialists had taken control of the ASM executive in the Mar. 1936 elections, see Preston, *CSCW*, p. 191; Vidarte, *Todos*, i. 66. For the ASM candidacy in the June elections, see A. Pastor Ugena, *La Agrupación Socialista Madrileña durante la Segunda República* (Madrid, 1985), 612–13.

[22] For a 'chronology' of the June dispute over the issue of the party congress, Juliá, *Izquierda*, pp. 132–3.

[23] The agenda included the events of Oct. 1934, Socialist–Communist unification and PSOE participation in government.

[24] The voting returns in (AH-22-1) AHM, also in Pastor Ugena, *Agrupación*, pp. 555–635; Vidarte, *Todos*, i. 206–8; Juliá, *Izquierda*, pp. 119, 306–8; Preston, *CSCW*, 198–9. [25] Juliá, *Izquierda*, pp. 134–6, 306–8; Pastor Ugena, *Agrupación*, pp. 612–13.

was secondary to the effect which the event had upon the perceptions of the left. The *caballeristas* convinced themselves that they had been defrauded and so strong was this conviction that henceforward they held that the PSOE had no legitimate or representative executive beyond the ASM.

It was at the beginning of June 1936 that the reformists first openly accused the ASM of placing itself in 'a position of open rebellion' by usurping the executive's own functions in corresponding directly with an increasing number of sympathetic Socialist groups all over Spain.[26] The complaints made by the new Lamoneda executive had no effect and the ASM continued to act as a second factional executive throughout the autumn and winter of 1936.[27] The reformists' strategy of purging the left was manifestly inoperative and would remain so until the middle of 1937 when Lamoneda, as general secretary, felt able to tackle the dissident provincial federations, the most prominent of which was in Valencia. The genesis of the policy of controlling, containing, or replacing hostile federations (used by Lamoneda during the war) lies in this serious organizational dislocation of the party in 1936.

Nevertheless, from mid-1936 it was clear to the *caballeristas* that the reformists were awaiting an opportunity to turn the party machine against them. In respect both of this strategy and the forthcoming congress, the reformist Socialists had but one aim, to win a mandate from the party base which would reopen the door to Socialist collaboration in government—a door which the party left, according to its rhetoric, wished definitively to close. With the outbreak of civil war, a party congress naturally came to be entirely out of the question. However, the legitimacy of Lamoneda's purge of the Socialist base during the war rested upon the moral conviction that, had the October

---

[26] E. de Francisco's letter to the party executive, complaining about the accusation, 17 June 1936 (AH-17-1), AHM. W. Carrillo, in his report to the II International, 23 May 1939, justified the behaviour of the ASM, maintaining that the national executive was not functioning properly and that many federations and Socialist groups had approached the ASM for guidance, Correspondencia de Luis Araquistain (hereafter CLA), Archivo Histórico Nacional, Madrid, Leg. 42, no. 76, p. 17. ASM correspondence with national executive of PSOE 1935–6, AHM; see also correspondence of *caballerista* Socialist groups with the national executive, spring and summer 1936, e.g. Almería, 7 Mar., 27 May (AH-13-43), and Alcira (Valencia) (AH-0-12), AHM, FPI.

[27] 'It was simply not permissible that such a spectacle be allowed to continue—that a *local* committee should take it upon itself to establish a kind of second national executive . . .'. Lamoneda's political report to the National Committee of the PSOE, July 1937, stenographic record, AH-24-2, AHM.

congress taken place, then the reformist option would have emerged victorious.

The popular revolution precipitated in Republican Spain by the military coup of 17 and 18 July made the left Socialists the titular masters of the political scene in Madrid and thus postponed the day of reckoning within the party. On the strength of his revolutionary image, Largo Caballero was appointed prime minister on 4 September 1936, thereby eclipsing the reformist wing of the party and its leader Indalecio Prieto in particular. The latter had been acting as chief advisor to the Republican administration of Prime Minister José Giral since its formation on 20 July. When Giral resigned, Largo, with a keen sense of the strength of the left's position, given the reality of grass-roots revolution, refused to consider anything less than left Socialist control of the cabinet. A bitterly disappointed Prieto had no choice but to withdraw as, for a second time, the chance of forming a government slipped away. Indeed, his chagrin must have doubled as he noted that the left was about to assume the very function it had for so long denied the reformists, namely collaboration in a coalition government of the Popular Front.[28]

By September 1936, the extent of agrarian and industrial collectivization and the fervour of the militia made inevitable a government of a more radical complexion than that envisaged by Prieto. It was clearly a case of the very singular political good fortune of the Socialist left. The *caballerista* leadership had not initiated the popular revolution, nor did it ever attempt to harness its force, as might have been expected, given its revolutionary rhetoric during the republican period. Yet it was to this revolution that Largo Caballero owed his government mandate.

However, the advantage which control of the government gave the *caballeristas* was, in terms of the struggle for the party organization, far more apparent than real. The structure of Largo's governments demonstrates the weakness of the left Socialist position in the cabinet. Furthermore, the manner in which Largo accepted the premiership only served to aggravate the bitterness of the party divide. He did not seek the permission of the national executive, headed by Ramón Lamoneda as general secretary, before accepting government office. Thus Largo's acceptance technically contravened a central aspect of

---

[28] Bolloten, *Spanish Revolution*, p. 121; L. Araquistain's government blueprint in letter to Largo Caballero, 24 Aug. 1936 (CLA), Leg. 32, no. 30a.

party discipline. The left's behaviour was entirely consistent with its view that the victory of Lamoneda's executive in the June party elections had been the result of fraud. However, the gravity of the situation lay in the fact that the internal Socialist division was about to become a major destabilizing factor in the political life of the Republic. The party divide was about to become a schism at the vital heart of a wartime coalition government.

THE FORMATION OF THE LARGO CABALLERO GOVERNMENTS

To all appearances, the left Socialists were in firm control of the first Republican cabinet to reflect the constitution of the Popular Front electoral pact. Largo held both the premiership and the defence portfolio, leaving his rival, Prieto, with only the naval and air forces. However, in view of the nature of the other left Socialist appointments, this concentration of power in Largo's hands, far from indicating the strength of his position, was, ironically, the source of his future political isolation.

The choice of the ardently fellow-travelling Socialist Alvarez del Vayo as Foreign Minister had in fact been imposed on the left as a result of Soviet pressure.[29] It had originally been intended that Luis Araquistain should serve in this capacity. By August 1936, Alvarez del Vayo was already considered to be a political outsider by the party left. His appointment effectively destroyed from the outset any semblance of a left Socialist nucleus in the cabinet. Luis Araquistain, Largo's chief support and the man who had drafted the original cabinet proposal in August, would be far away in Paris as Republican ambassador. The third left Socialist nominee, Angel Galarza, an ex-Radical Socialist who had only recently joined the PSOE, would prove to be a far from competent Interior Minister.

The news of Galarza's ministerial appointment was greeted with considerable dismay by the PSOE executive. As with General Asensio, the undersecretary of war, and another of Largo's personal appointments, the Socialist leadership felt that the background of the individual concerned was somewhat dubious and that the charge of political opportunism might justifiably be levelled, to the general detri-

---

[29] Bolloten, *Spanish Revolution*, p. 189; José María Aguirre to Luis Araquistain, 4 Sept. 1936, leg. 71, no. 22, p. 2 (CLA); Américo Vélez (pseud. J. M. Aguirre), *Informaciones*, 8, 9, 10 Nov. 1977.

ment of the PSOE's prestige.[30] Galarza was subjected to vehement attacks by the Socialist executive. They considered him, with some justification, to be unequal to the task of dealing with the extremely vicious political infighting and organizational rivalries which characterized the early months of the war. By the beginning of 1937, editorials in *El Socialista* were, by implication, criticizing the actions, or rather the inaction, of Galarza.[31] Gabriel Morón, veteran Socialist and civil governor of Almería at the time of the fall of Málaga in February 1937, was also vehement in his criticism of Galarza's ineffectualness and what he saw as downright negligence in the face of chaos and civil disorder. By the time of the cabinet crisis in May 1937, the Socialist executive had made its continued support of Largo as prime minister conditional upon Galarza's removal from the Interior Ministry.[32] Indeed, Largo was the first to admit his minister's inadequacy. However, with characteristic stubbornness, the more savagely Galarza was attacked, not only by the reformist Socialists, but also by the PCE and the CNT, the more determinedly Largo supported him.[33] As with the campaign against Asensio, not only was the prime minister piqued by criticism of his chosen collaborators, but he also knew it to be an oblique political attack upon his own position.

Galarza's appointment had also put an enormous strain on the relationship between the UGT executive and Largo, its general secretary, and thus was responsible for increasing the prime minister's political isolation still further. Galarza's Radical Socialist antecedents did not inspire the union leadership with confidence. His failure to deal firmly with the numerous Communist and Anarchist assaults on party and union militants, and upon the property of the UGT, only confirmed them in their hostility.[34]

At every level, the assumption that the *caballerista* power base constituted a coherent whole has to be challenged. The left had lost control of the Socialist youth. A further fragmentation was produced by the intensely pro-Communist stance of certain members of the UGT executive, namely Amaro del Rosal and Felipe Pretel, who were constantly pressing for a resolution in favour of the campaign to unite the

---

[30] Ibid., 9 Nov. 1977; Vidarte, *Todos*, ii. 673.
[31] Ibid. 655; minutes of the UGT executive committee, 23 Oct. 1936.
[32] Morón, *Política*, p. 77; Vidarte, *Todos*, ii. 661–2.
[33] J. M. Aguirre to Luis Araquistain, 28 Feb. 1937 (CLA), Leg. 23, no. A 28a, p. 3.
[34] Minutes of the UGT executive, 1, 23 Oct., 24 Dec. 1936; R. Lamoneda's report on the unification of the parties to the National Committee of the PSOE, July 1937, stenographic record (AH-24-2).

PSOE and the PCE. In addition, there was the increasing alienation of the *caballerista* 'old guard' on the union executive from Largo and his cabinet. Indeed, the UGT executive, that supposed bastion of the Socialist left, had never been consulted about the form of Largo's cabinet.[35] The fact that Largo had chosen not to consult the PSOE executive on forming his government in September 1936 had angered it. The members were convinced that they had been supplanted by the UGT executive, believing that this had been consulted not as well as but *instead of* the party executive. It is thus interesting to note that the union leadership was equally unclear about its own status in relation to the 'left Socialist' ministers in Largo's cabinet.[36]

Largo's second cabinet, formed in November 1936, was a massive and unwieldy affair, totalling some eighteen ministers including Largo himself. If such a formation was to operate with even minimum unity and efficiency, the essential pre-condition had to be a dynamic and coherent nucleus. This ought naturally to have been provided by the PSOE. However, not only was left Socialism entirely atomized, but the aloofness of the reformist ministers associated with the Lamoneda executive—Prieto, Negrín, and Anastasio de Gracia—compounded PSOE fragmentation.[37] Indeed the three tended to exercise their ministerial functions in isolation even from each other. The lack of co-operation and solidarity between them, as the executive's appointees, reflected the precarious state of the Socialist leadership during the latter half of 1936. The reformist Socialist ministers, cut off from the support of the Socialist movement as a whole—which could only have been channelled through a strong and confident executive—had little choice but to cope as best they could on an *ad hoc* basis. Reformist remoteness from Largo himself can be explained at the subjective level, given the way in which *prietista* policies had been appropriated by an ideologically bankrupt socialist left. The net result, though, was the weakening of the PSOE as a whole, and not just of its left wing. During

---

[35] Minutes of the UGT executive, 17 Dec., 15 Sept. 1936. From Largo's memoirs, 'Notas históricas', p. 258, it is clear that the UGT executive was consulted about the *principle* of Largo's leadership of a national government, but *not* over its constitution. 'I immediately reported the situation to the union executive, whereupon it unanimously approved my forming a government.'

[36] Minutes of the UGT executive, 22 Nov. 1936; Amaro del Rosal, *Historia de la UGT* (2 vols. Barcelona, 1976), ii. 603; J. M. Aguirre to Luis Araquistain (CLA), 28 Feb. 1937, p. 2.

[37] See R. Lamoneda's comments in the 'Posición Política' report, at the PSOE national committee meeting, July 1937, stenographic record, AH-24-2, also Morón, *Política*, p. 72.

the first year of the war Prieto adopted a tactic which in essence consisted of waiting upon the political exhaustion of the left. Yet by so doing he fell into the very trap against which he had warned the *caballeristas*—undermining the stability of the Republic in the pursuit of a partisan political vendetta.[38]

THE PERMANENT CRISIS

The cabinet crisis which finally erupted in May 1937 was well in evidence by the beginning of the year. Within the government, Largo Caballero was almost entirely isolated. The reformist Socialists and the Republicans were siding with the Communist Party (PCE) against him during cabinet sessions. In addition, the Socialist executive was itself negotiating with the PCE to establish a national network of joint party committees throughout the Republican zone.[39] For Lamoneda, this was the spearhead of his drive to end the dislocation of 1936 and to reconquer the party base in its entirety for the reformists.[40] The party left was absolutely opposed to the formation of any joint body, whereupon the PSOE leadership was immediately able to accuse it of hypocrisy and of performing a political U-turn in order to be able to continue opposing the executive committee.[41] In fact the *caballeristas's* hostility to the Communist Party had another more obvious source. Keenly aware of the fact that the PCE coveted the Socialist base, the left's sudden manifestation of violent anti-Communism in the war period sprang from its appalled discovery that aggressive Communist proselytism, coupled with Socialist fragmentation, was causing a serious erosion of the PSOE rank and file. It was the issue of Socialist–Communist unification which revealed the internal fragmentation of the *caballerista* power base in the UGT. The personal allegiance to Largo Caballero of veteran *ugetista* leaders such as Carlos Hernández Zancajo was strengthened by the fact that they too were battling

[38] Prieto's speech at Egea de los Caballeros (Aragón), May 1936, in *Discursos fundamentales*, p. 282; for the 'desgaste del poder' and its effects on the socialist left, A. Ramos Oliveira, *Historia de España*, 3 vols. (Mexico D.F., n.d.), iii. 312.

[39] J. M. Aguirre to L. Araquistain, 28 Feb. 1937; for the Socialist executive's circular announcing the joint committee initiative, *El Socialista*, 7 Jan. 1937.

[40] Lamoneda's explanation at the meeting of the national committee, July 1937, stenographic record, pp. 60, 83–103; see also Manuel Cordero to Felipe Garcia, AHM Correspondencia de M. Cordero (n.d., but post-war).

[41] *Guerra y revolución en España 1936–1939*, iii (Moscow, 1967). 55; *El Socialista*, 7 Mar. 1937; for Lamoneda's view of the left's anti-Communism, see the discussion over the unification report, national committee meeting, July 1937, stenographic record.

against the PCE in order to retain control of their own union organizations. In contrast, those like Amaro del Rosal, who had been attracted
by Largo's apparent commitment to unity with the Communist Party,
withdrew their support once his underlying hostility to the PCE was
made overt by the intense organizational rivalry of Socialists and Communists during the war.

As prime minister, considerable and increasing pressure was
brought to bear on Largo to oversee the unification of the PSOE and
the PCE. This was exerted via the good offices of both the Comin-
tern's representative, Vittorio Codovila and the Soviet ambassador,
Marcel Rosenberg, the latter assiduously accompanied by Alvarez del
Vayo as a somewhat superfluous 'interpreter'. At the same time the
PCE was attacking the prestige and credibility of General Asensio,
Largo's undersecretary of war.[42]

The crisis of Largo's government was latent both in the cabinet and
in the streets by the beginning of February 1937. On the 14th, just
after the fall of Málaga, a demonstration organized by the provincial
secretariat of the UGT in Valencia in support of Largo was effectively
neutralized by a PCE-inspired swamping action. This shifted the
emphasis of the event to that of a general display of support for the
government's war effort.[43] In Valencia, the seat of Republican government, relations between left Socialists and Communists were
extremely difficult. There had occurred a very rapid distancing process
after 18 July 1936, once the aggressiveness of the PCE's drive towards
Socialist–Communist unification became apparent. One immediate
casualty of the deterioration in relations was Valencia's 'unity'
newspaper, *Verdad*, produced jointly by Socialist and Communist
editorial staff. By the beginning of February 1937 *Adelante* and *Frente
Rojo*, respectively the Socialist and Communist newspapers in the
province, were being produced separately.[44]

From the outbreak of the Civil War the distance between the UGT
and the CNT had also been increasing. This might at first appear
paradoxical. There was an abundant basis for at least a defensive pact

[42] Bolloten, *Spanish Revolution*, pp. 331–3; Largo Caballero, 'La UGT y la guerra',
speech in the Teatro Pardiñas, Madrid (Valencia, 1937); Largo Caballero, *Mis recuerdos*
(Mexico, 1976), 211–12; Luis Araquistain, 'El comunismo y la guerra de España'
(1939), in *Sobre la guerra civil y en la emigración* (Madrid, 1983), 216; J. Martínez Amutio,
Chantaje a un pueblo (Madrid, 1974), 215.
[43] *El Socialista*, 14 Feb. 1937; R. Llopis, *Spartacus*, 1 Oct. 1937; Bolloten, *Spanish
Revolution*, p. 341.
[44] *El Socialista*, 1 Feb. 1937.

between the two since the representatives of the political parties were going on to the attack in an attempt to reappropriate the economic power won by the unions as a result of the revolution.[45] The poor state of relations between the UGT and the CNT reflected not only the friction between segments of the union bases, but also the very evident ideological bankruptcy of the Socialist left. The *caballeristas* were superfluous. There was no political space for them to occupy between the Popular Front, as defended by both the PCE and the reformists in the PSOE, and the revolution, as symbolized by the Anarchists. In this sense, the reformist Socialists were correct in the substance of their accusation that, ideologically, the *Caballeristas* could not be differentiated from the rest of the party.[46]

The entire range of Largo's policy options was that of the reformist Socialists. His international strategy was based on securing the material support of the Western democracies for the Spanish Republic. His domestic policies were equally reformist—the reconstruction of central state power, the building of the 'popular' army, nationalization and centralization of industry, and the curbing of collectivization by decree. In short, his objective, like Juan Negrín after him, was a monopoly of political, military, and economic power for the central government.

On 1 February 1937, Largo emphatically set his face against Anarchist experiments. Yet the collectivization initiatives, especially in that area of the South still controlled by the Loyalists, were as much Socialist inspired and run as they were Anarchist.[47] Largo's unequivocally and unalterably reformist leadership, between September 1936 and the cabinet crisis of May 1937, was responsible for severely undermining the FNTT's projects for the thoroughgoing consolidation of agrarian collectivization in the Civil War. Largo never seriously took issue with the Communist Agriculture Minister, Vicente Uribe, whose agrarian policies harmed socialist collectives as much as Anarchist ones. Throughout some 1,500 pages of his political memoirs there is

---

[45] For the party vs. union conflict in the Civil War, see Santos Juliá, 'The Origins and Nature of the Spanish Popular Front', paper given at Southampton conference on comparative perspectives of the French and Spanish Popular Fronts, 15–17 Apr. 1986.

[46] 'A reasonable *modus vivendi* has to exist within the party, and particularly as no serious difference of doctrine or tactics has yet manifested itself, in such a way as to justify the stance adopted by the left ...': Lamoneda to the national committee, July 1937, stenographic record, p. 82.

[47] Luis Garrido González, *Colectividades agrarias en Andalucía: Jaen (1931–1939)* (Madrid, 1979), *passim*; Grandizo Munis, *Jalones de derrota, promesa de victoria* (Madrid, 1977), 423, 428–31.

scant reference to the issue of land reform and none to the FNTT's battle to preserve its collectives.[48]

Yet in December 1937, when the left Socialists were a spent force in every respect, it would be the FNTT which still sought to defend their cause by calling, ironically, for the reconstitution of the Workers' Alliance.[49] The landworkers' federation was certainly no stranger to the fray: it had long sustained its own battle both with the Agriculture Ministry and with the PCE's provincial peasant federations which had been turned into a haven for every disgruntled smallholder with a grievance. Nevertheless, by the end of 1937, an exhortation to resurrect the Workers' Alliance could have been nothing more than a reflex of desperation tinged with political nostalgia.

The May 1937 cabinet crisis forced the left Socialists out of power. Largo Caballero was replaced as prime minister by the reformist Socialist, Juan Negrín. These events marked the beginning of a concerted attack on the *caballeristas's* remaining power bases. The assault, although supported to the hilt by the PCE, was mounted by the executive of the PSOE. Its resolve to purge the left was significantly strengthened by the vote of confidence it received from the PSOE's national committee. This met in Valencia from 17–21 July 1937, against a background of strident calls for its resignation from left dissidents. They brought the familiar charge that it was unrepresentative of the party base. Yet it was the mandate, voted by the national committee, to restore internal discipline in the Socialist Party which was seen as setting the seal of legitimacy on the drive against the *caballeristas*.[50]

The most sustained and bitter part of the ensuing purge was certainly that which occurred between May and October 1937 in the UGT. The thoroughness of reformist Socialist efforts to remove Largo and his supporters from the political life of the Republic at war was quite remarkable. Not only was the left ousted by force from the provincial federation of the PSOE in Valencia—which was seen by Ramón Lamoneda as having assumed the ASM's function as the 'visible head' of faction—but the *caballeristas* were also deprived of virtually all their major newspapers. By the end of 1937, *Claridad* (UGT, Madrid), *Las Noticias* (UGT, Barcelona), *Adelante* (PSOE,

[48] F. Largo Caballero, 'Notas Históricas'.
[49] *Adelante* (Valencia), 21 Dec. 1937.
[50] *Memoria de la actuación de las federaciones provinciales* (Editorial Meabe, Valencia, 1937), AHM.

Valencia), and *La Correspondencia de Valencia* (UGT) were all under the control of the reformist leadership.[51] In the case of the Valencian press, Republican security forces were used to enforce the repossession of both premises, this tactic having already been employed to permit the reformists to take control of the provincial Socialist Party headquarters in Valencia on 26 July 1937.[52] By the end of September Largo and other leading left Socialists had also been removed from the executive committee of the Socialist parliamentary minority in which, prior to the war, they had enjoyed majority control.[53]

This swingeing series of moves against the left was clearly designed to reduce the likelihood of Largo making an embarrassing speech at the session of the Cortes scheduled for 1 October. Indeed, early in August 1937 Negrín himself informed Azaña that Largo's opposition to the government dictated his removal as general secretary of the UGT in order to defuse the impact of any statement or speech which he might seek to make.[54] In the event, and in spite of the entreaties of his supporters, Largo chose not to make the Spanish Parliament the forum for his exposé of what he saw as the political treason of others.[55] Instead, Largo addressed a public meeting and on 17 October he made his famous speech 'The UGT and the War' in Madrid's Teatro Pardiñas. The building was packed to overflowing and the speech was relayed to several other cinemas. But it was already too late. The most important battle, that waged by the *caballeristas* to retain control of the UGT executive, had already been lost, and with it the Socialist left had lost its own war within the war.

The division in the UGT had become overt on 17 May 1937, after the resolution of the cabinet crisis. The fact that the union executive

[51] For the fate of the left Socialist press and the *Claridad* dispute in particular, see Bizcarrondo, *Araquistain*, pp. 419–21.

[52] Lamoneda's letter of 25 July 1937, informing the *caballerista* incumbents of the provincial federation of their imminent replacement, ibid. 34–5; the order of dispossession, issued by the Interior Minister, reformist Socialist, Julián Zugazagoitia on 26 July, ibid. 35; Largo Caballero's vehemence at the abuse of public power involved, in 'La UGT y la guerra'.

[53] Minutes for 29, 30 Sept. 1937, from the minutes of the Socialist parliamentary minority 1936–1939 (AH-18-7), AHM, pp. 86–91.

[54] M. Azaña, *Memorias políticas y de guerra* (Barcelona, 1978), ii. 231. Largo was not present at the Cortes meeting which coincided with the battle for control of the UGT's HQ, see M. Koltsov, *Diario de la Guerra Española* (Madrid, 1978), 509.

[55] See also Largo Caballero, 'Notas históricas', pp. 1245ff., for an account of the meeting of *caballerista* deputies prior to the October Cortes meeting, in order to discuss the possibility of forming a separate left Socialist minority in the Chamber. Largo was one of those opposed.

did not issue a public declaration of support for Negrín's new government was taken as proof of the *caballeristas's* intention to boycott the new administration. The Socialist party press had immediately begun to gather declarations of support for Negrín from *prietista* sections of the UGT in Vizcaya, Guipuzcoa, and Santander. All in all, there was much criticism of what was termed Largo's 'política personalista', the overwhelming consensus being that not even a veteran leader such as he was irreplaceable ('insustituible').[56] This, by implication, was a criticism of the stance of the *caballerista* 'old guard' on the UGT executive which, during the May cabinet crisis, had taken the line that it would not be able to support a government in which Largo was not both premier and head of a unified national defence ministry. On 28 May the anti-*caballerista* attack was launched when the UGT's national committee, on which the left was no longer dominant, met without its executive committee and censured the latter by 24 votes to 14 for its conduct during the cabinet crisis and for its lack of solidarity with the Negrín government.[57]

The national committee meeting had been arranged by the two pro-Communist members of Largo's own executive, Amaro del Rosal and Felipe Pretel, in collaboration with like-minded national committee member Antonio Génova.[58] This blew wide open what had previously been a latent division on the UGT executive. It also highlighted the fact that the left Socialists' opponents in the UGT comprised two separate groups whose ultimate political objectives were quite distinct but which converged in their determination to neutralize the *caballerista* power base in the union.

One focus of opposition was the reformist wing of the PSOE associated with Prieto and with the Lamoneda executive's struggle to regain control of the party base throughout the loyalist zone. For this group, the erosion of the Socialist left in its union stronghold—for all that it was consistently denied in the party press—was an extension of the dispute in the PSOE. The reformists were clearly determined to put an end to what was seen as Largo's fomenting of opposition to fellow Socialists who were discharging extremely weighty responsibilities in government office.

The second source of opposition to the Socialist left in the UGT

[56] *El Socialista*, 19 May 1937.
[57] *Claridad*, 29 May 1937; M. Tunón de Lara, *Historia de Espana*, ix (Barcelona, 1981), 366.
[58] For Amaro del Rosal's 'forced' resignation from the UGT executive, *Claridad*, 26 June 1937; minutes of the UGT executive 17, 24 June, 1 July 1937.

was constituted by the unitarists; those *ugetistas* with either Communist affiliation or at least general fellow-travelling sympathies. They favoured the reorganization of the leadership to achieve a much higher level of Communist presence. It was, in essence, hardly a new line, and, as before, the debate centred around a form of positive discrimination which would, first and foremost, raise representatives of the PCE to membership of the UGT's national executive committee. It should hardly need emphasizing that the essential pre-condition of this was the removal of Largo Caballero as general secretary.

Neither the reformist Socialist leadership nor its supporters in the UGT were particularly keen to discriminate in favour of the PCE. Indeed, in Asturias, as an example of a *prietista* stronghold, the provincial congress of the UGT in April 1937 had, by a resounding majority, voted in an integrally Socialist candidacy, leaving the unitarist list out in the cold by a margin of some 75,000 votes.[59] However, such was the determination of the reformists to destroy the left's major power base that they effectively ended by aiding the unitarists in their task. Thus the PCE was able to gain entry to the UGT at the highest level. The ultimate prize of Communist representation on the union's national executive was finally, if relatively fleetingly, obtained by virtue of the tactics employed by the reformist Socialist leadership in its own struggle to purge the left.

After an extremely byzantine dispute during August and September 1937 in which the chief weapon wielded was the minutiae of party and union statute, the majority on the UGT's national committee, which was hostile to Largo and the old guard on the national executive, took matters into its own hands and called a full national committee meeting. This fell just about within the bounds of the technically permissible. The same could be said of most of the manoeuvres on both sides in the union dispute. As a result, on 1 October 1937, a new union executive was elected to replace Largo's. Its president was Ramón González Pena, veteran Socialist, long-standing *prietista*, and leader of the Asturian miners' federation (SMA). It was on this executive that the PCE was directly represented for the first time ever.

It was of some significance that González Pena was an Asturian. The single most effective weapon used against the left in the union dispute had undoubtedly been the exploitation in the press of the fact

---

[59] Voting was 87,000 to 12,000, see Antonio Llaneza's intervention during the discussion of the report on party unification at the national committee meeting, July 1937, stenographic record; Vidarte, *Todos*, p. 616.

that the Largo executive had, in its campaign against the unitarist opposition, expelled the Asturian miners' union (SMA) from the UGT as one of nine expulsions of industrial federations at the beginning of September 1937. It is extremely difficult to see what the *caballeristas* hoped to gain by expelling the SMA, especially at the height of the war in the North. Indeed, by September it was reaching its bloody climax and the Asturian miners, the heroes of 1934, were once again in the front line of the struggle against Fascism in Spain. Both the Socialist and Communist party press and the union newspapers, almost all controlled by those opposed to the Largo executive, made full use of this tactical blunder of epic proportions. The *Claridad* editorial of 9 September 1937 captures the force of the propaganda which did so much damage to Largo and the cause of the left: 'as Fascism bayonets its way into Asturias, ravaging its legendary people, the national executive of the union, as its only gesture of encouragement to the Asturians to continue the struggle, has offered to the miners ... expulsion from the UGT, isolation from the community of their class brothers'. Largo insisted that it was not the rank and file which had been expelled but only the federation's insubordinate hierarchy, the former reverting to the status of direct affiliates of the UGT's national executive. But this convinced very few, nor did his explanation do much to repair the damage done by hostile press propaganda. Largo was acutely aware of the way in which the historic stature of Asturias, its immense symbolic power, was being used against the left, but he could do little to counter what was an enormously successful reformist tactic.[60]

Throughout the union dispute the *caballeristas* has been characterized very singularly by their feet of clay. The old guard on the executive had showed itself to be virtually incapable of seizing the initiative from its unitarist opponents. Once again, the fatal passivity, the negativity, of the left was manifest. The executive's tactics, such as they were, consisted mainly of attempts to manipulate union regulations in order to gain time: beyond that, *it had no strategy*. There could be no clearer indication of the fundamental bankruptcy of the Socialist left.

In the final analysis, it was the other face of the legend of October 1934, working-class unity rather than revolution, which had defeated the left in its last stronghold, the UGT. Asturias was *prietista* territory, and since October 1934 the image of Asturias, and particularly the prestige of the Asturian miners' leaders, had been used consistently

---

[60] Largo Caballero, 'La UGT y la guerra', pp. 26–7.

and to consistent good effect against the party left. In the national executive elections of June 1936, Prieto had consciously pitted Ramón González Pena against Largo Caballero in the battle for the party presidency.[61] González Pena's assumption of the presidency of the new UGT executive on 1 October 1937 symbolized the defeat of the left. For the duration of the Civil War at least, it had lost the battle for control of the Spanish Socialist movement.

[61] Vidarte, *Todos*, p. 23.

9. ANARCHISTS IN GOVERNMENT: A PARADOX OF THE SPANISH CIVIL WAR, 1936–1939

Burnett Bolloten and George Esenwein

Of all the European upheavals of the twentieth century, the Spanish Civil War and Revolution stands out as a milestone in the history of the European left. This is because it was the first time that so many diverse ideological movements were simultaneously engaged in a common struggle against the forces of the right. This joint effort was beset with problems, since the various leftist groups held fundamentally divergent views, not only with regard to their respective interpretations of the war but also in their overall aims. For the Stalinist Partido Comunista de España (PCE), the war was a contest between Fascism and democracy, whereas for the Marxists of the Partido Obrero de Unificación Marxista (POUM), and the anarcho-syndicalists of the Confederación Nacional del Trabajo (CNT) and the Federación Anarquista Ibérica (FAI), Spain's classic revolutionaries, the war was a revolutionary struggle of the working classes against the bourgeoisie.

Notwithstanding these profound differences, the Spanish left managed for a short while to share political power. Perhaps the most striking feature of this brief experiment in left-wing rule was the participation of the anarcho-syndicalists in government. Rootedly opposed to the State, which they regarded as the 'supreme expression of authority of man over man, the most powerful instrument for enslavement of the people', the anarcho-syndicalists were clearly the strangest of bedfellows in this alliance. Why, given their impressive background of hostility to all governments, did they feel impelled to take such a fateful step?

It must be borne in mind that although members of the FAI were dedicated anarchist militants, this was not true for the CNT, which served as an umbrella organization for leftist workers who were, generally speaking, sympathetic to libertarian beliefs but not necessarily committed anarchists. The CNT had experienced a spectacular growth, mushrooming from approximately 15,000 members in 1910 to a staggering 700,000 by the end of the First World War. After CNT was forced underground in 1923, the anarchist movement underwent another metamorphosis. Because the socialists were exploiting the government-controlled arbitration boards (*comités paritarios*), anarchists like Ángel Pestaña began to argue for a 'possiblist' line towards unionism in the belief that it was better to collaborate with these government bodies than to lose ground to the socialists or the right-wing unions, *sindicatos libres*. The fear that the anarchist movement might jettison its anti-political creed brought about a polarization of the membership, driving a small but significant group of anarchists to form the FAI in 1927.[1] Its role was to give the CNT a revolutionary orientation.

The FAI's loosely federated network of 'affinity groups' (the FAI was organized along confederal lines in much the same way as the CNT) as well as its secretive nature helped the organization to survive the hard years of government repression. Then, with the change of political climate at the foundation of the Second Republic in April 1931, the FAI finally emerged from its clandestinity. At first it appeared as though the CNT was still firmly in the hands of the syndicalist leaders who had been at the helm during its meteoric growth in previous decades. But the FAI soon presented a formidable challenge to these moderate elements.

The FAI quickly achieved notoriety by relentlessly pursuing an ultra-revolutionary strategy that stood in bold contrast to the pragmatic trade-union agenda advocated by the syndicalists. After they announced their intention of controlling the CNT, the *faístas* exploited every opportunity to undermine the influence of their syndicalist rivals. Strike movements were heralded as examples of what the workers needed to build their revolutionary strength in preparation for the final struggle with the bourgeoisie. In the workers' cultural centres (*ateneos* and *centros obreros*), the *faístas* energetically worked to win the minds of the workers through an intensive propaganda programme.[2]

---

[1] On the historical background of Spanish anarchism during the 20th century, the following sources are recommended: Diego Abad de Santillán, *Contribución a la historia del movimiento obrero español*, i–iii (Mexico, 1962–71); Antonio Bar, *La CNT en los años rojos* (Barcelona, 1981); John S. Brademas, *Anarcosindicalismo y revolución en España, 1930–1937* (Barcelona, 1974); Gerald Brenan, *The Spanish Labyrinth* (Cambridge, 1971); Juan Gómez Casas, *La historia de la FAI* (Madrid, 1977); José Peirats, *La CNT en le revolución Española*, i–iii (Toulouse, 1951–3); and John Sefton, 'The Confederación Nacional del Trabajo, 1927–1938' (MA thesis, Univ. of California, Santa Barbara, 1978).

[2] See comments of Francisco Ascaso in Abel Paz, *The People Armed* (Montreal, 1977), 127.

Faístas won over *sindicatos* of the CNT by working as teams, using well-disciplined members of their groups to vote as a bloc on radical measures. Once they had won a union to their position it was but a short step to controlling the union paper or local meeting hall. By 1933 the *faístas* had in fact eclipsed the influence of their syndicalist rivals. Meanwhile, thousands of their opponents under Pestaña and Juan Peiró, known since the summer of 1931 as *treintistas*, were leaving the CNT. Most were expelled, but some abandoned the CNT in order to set up their own trade union movement. It was not until the Saragossa Congress of May 1936 that the *faísta/treintista* rift was smoothed over and the dissident factions were readmitted to the official anarcho-syndicalist movement.

The revolutionary training that the anarchists received under the FAI's direction proved during the first moments of the Civil War to be a critical factor in determining the outcome of events. The *faísta* tactic of staging social revolts, known as 'revolutionary gymnastics', had led to a cycle of popular risings in Catalonia (January 1932 and December 1933), Casas Viejas (January 1933), and elsewhere. By the time the Civil War and revolution broke out, the identification of the FAI as the vanguard of the anarchist movement was complete. The moving spirits of the July popular rebellion were all *faístas*: Abad de Santillán, Juan García Oliver, Francisco Ascaso, and Buenaventura Durruti.

When the Spanish generals rose on 17 July 1936, they hoped for an early victory. But within a few days it was apparent that their insurrection had backfired. Instead of achieving military control of Spain, the insurgent generals provoked a massive popular revolution which spread rapidly throughout much of the country. In its initial stages, the revolution distinguished itself from all others of the twentieth century by both its depth and range. Caught up in the whirlwind of change, Republican institutions either collapsed or were supplanted by revolutionary committees dominated in varying degrees by anarcho-syndicalists, socialists, and communists. Revolutionary changes varied in degree from place to place, depending on which group or groups exerted the greatest influence. In Catalonia, Aragón, and the Levante, where anarcho-syndicalist strength and influence predominated, the revolution went deeper than elsewhere.

In the wake of the street fighting in Barcelona, the largest and most industrially advanced city in Spain, the majority of civilians allied themselves with the revolutionaries, who besides seizing strategic military posts, immediately set about reorganizing society in accordance with their beliefs. This meant destroying or at the very least qualitatively altering the underlying supports of bourgeois society. Churches were gutted and burnt, businesses and factories were taken over or collectivized, and on the streets the symbols of the 'old' bourgeois social order vanished, for no one dared to wear a necktie, hat, or other apparel that typified the middle classes.[3] Many clerics and prominent members of the bourgeoisie were victims of extremist violence.

That the anarchists found themselves in the forefront of the popular revolt against the army in much of the Republican zone is understandable. Of all the doctrines in the anti-Franco camp, anarchism appeared eminently suited to the circumstances, primarily because its adherents had been conditioned through years of indoctrination and revolutionary practice to act directly and spontaneously.

It cannot be over-emphasized that in spite of their recourse to violence —including over-zealous attempts at collectivization—the anarchists were animated by a profound belief in the justice of their mission. 'Our revolution', they affirmed, 'will banish hate, envy, and egoism', and thereby will open the way for 'mutual respect and solidarity'. In the early weeks of the revolution the diversity and the scope of such attempts at moral regeneration were striking: brothels were emptied, and waiters, taxi-drivers, and barbers defiantly and with infinite pride refused tips as a degrading bourgeois practice. The anarchists' moral philosophy was integral to their overall revolutionary programme.[4]

The rapidity with which the anarcho-syndicalists set about restructuring society suggests that they had more than a vague notion of how to proceed towards their goal of *communismo libertario*. At the Saragossa Congress held on the eve of the Civil War the blueprint of the future society had been much debated. Not only were the needs of special interest groups considered—devoted vegetarians and nudists, for example—but also the forms of economic organization that would have to be developed in order for the anarchists to survive in an increasingly complex industrialized world. Abad de Santillán, one of the principal theorists of the FAI tendency, outlined in detail in his widely distributed tract, *El organismo económico de la revolución* (1936), the kind of economic structures that would characterize a functioning

---

[3] See e.g. the colourful descriptions found in: John Langdon Davies, *Behind the Spanish Barricades* (New York, 1936), and George Orwell, *Homage to Catalonia* (London, 1938).

[4] For cultural aspects see Jon Amsden, 'Industrial collectivization Under Workers' Control: Catalonia, 1936–1939', *Antipode*, 10/3–11/1 (1979), 106.

libertarian society. But these elaborately laid plans took place on the eve of the Civil War in the relatively tranquil atmosphere of Saragossa—the citadel of anarchist strength in Aragón—and such speculative thinking rapidly faded into the background once the revolution was set in motion.

One reason for this was that the revolution itself proceeded with such velocity that there was little time to reflect, let alone implement any complex plans. Despite their radical tradition, the anarchists were none the less confused as to the political role they were to play in the revolution. In the words of one anarchist purist: 'The CNT was utterly devoid of revolutionary theory. We did not have a concrete programme. We had no idea where we were going. We had lyricism aplenty; but when all is said and done, we did not know what to do with our masses of workers or how to give substance to the popular effusion which erupted inside our organizations.'[5]

When, after the defeat of the military insurrection, a small group of *faístas* entered the government offices of the *Generalitat*—physically exhausted from fighting, unshaven, and armed with their mausers— they confronted President Luis Companys as the undisputed victors of the hour. 'Today you are the masters of the city and of Catalonia', he told them. According to the Catalan left-republican politician Jaume Miravitlles, power lay in the streets and it was manifest that the anarchists were the only ones in a position to seize it. But because they lacked a programme for exercising political power, the anarchists faced a major dilemma. For the first time in their seventy-year history, they had the opportunity to abolish the state. Yet, surprisingly, the *faístas* accepted Luis Company's plan to allow the *Generalitat* to remain standing and to create a parallel body in which the CNT and FAI would share power not only with proletarian but also with middle-class organizations. Thus, on 23 July, four days after the military insurrection, there came into existence the Central Antifascist Militia Committee (CAMC), the first government body ever established in which anarcho-syndicalists were represented. The main work of the militia committee, attests Abad de Santillán, himself a member, included the creation of militia units for the front, the organization of the economy, and legislative and judicial action. 'The Central Antifascist Militia Committee', he wrote on another occasion, 'became the real and only power, the absolute revolutionary power.'[6]

[5] Jaime Balius, *Hacia la nueva revolución* (?Barcelona, ?1938), 15.
[6] *Tiempos Nuevos*, May–June 1937.

But since the CAMC was a government in essence, if not in name, why did the anarchist leaders violate hallowed principles by joining it? The FAI leaders Abad de Santillán and García Oliver justified their decision on the grounds that their only alternative would have been to establish a libertarian dictatorship, which, although popularly based, would have been tantamount to repudiating the most sacroscanct principles of their anti-authoritarian creed. Only a few weeks later, yielding to pressure from parties intent on reconstructing the state apparatus, the anarcho-syndicalists agreed to dissolve the CAMC and enter the *Generalitat*.

In order to understand how challenging it was for the anarchists to participate in the government, one must realize that in their eyes the unity of theory and practice had always been paramount. Before the revolution, governmental collaboration was unthinkable—except for the moderates grouped around Angel Pestaña. 'All governments', declared one libertarian in 1930, 'are detestable, and it is our mission to destroy them.'[7] Furthermore, the anarchists made it clear throughout the pre-war Second Republic that they made no distinction between governments of the left and of the right.[8]

The only significant shift in the anarcho-syndicalists' attitude towards politics and government occurred on the eve of the Popular Front victory in the February 1936 elections. Although they regarded the Popular Front programme as 'a profoundly conservative document', they decided not to urge the workers to abstain from voting, not only because the left coalition promised a broad amnesty for thousands of political prisoners in the event of victory but because a repetition of the abstentionist policy of 1933 would have undoubtedly meant as great a defeat for the libertarian movement as for the parties that adhered to the Popular Front alliance. This change of posture may have been opportunistic but did not necessarily imply any fundamental recantation of doctrine.

On the other hand, the participation of the anarcho-syndicalists in the CAMC represented a radical departure from their antistatist heritage. Hence, despite the fact that they regarded the CAMC as a 'revolutionary government'—which could be used as a vehicle for promoting purely working-class interests—and that its composition reflected the predominance of the workers, their collaboration did not diminish the cleavage between doctrine and practice.

[7] *Tierra y Libertad* (Barcelona), 15 Sept. 1933.
[8] See e.g. José Bonet in *Tierra y Libertad* (Barcelona), 22 Sept. 1933.

Whilst it is true that the military uprising of July had been contained by the hastily improvised peoples' militias, these columns suffered from numerous defects. The anarchist militias were organized according to their ideals of equality and individual liberty, ideals which stood in diametric opposition to the kind of obligatory discipline characteristic of the traditional army: there was no saluting, no regimentation, and no military titles or badges.

However, the exigencies of war soon forced the anarcho-syndicalists to question their methods of fighting. Mounting pressure from the enemy's relentless advance towards Madrid caused many anarcho-syndicalist militia leaders to reject their traditional attitude towards militarization. 'All my ideas regarding discipline and militarization were shattered,' confessed Cipriano Mera, the anarchist military figure, 'I understood that if we were not to be defeated, we had to construct our own army, a disciplined and capable army, organized for the defence of the workers.'[9]

Nevertheless, the anarcho-syndicalists insisted on maintaining control over their own units. This control, they felt, was essential not only because of their deep-seated opposition to a permanent army of the state, but also because of their conception of the nature of the war as a revolutionary struggle against capitalist bourgeois institutions.

In September 1936, the reorganization of the central government in Madrid under the premiership of the popular veteran socialist trade union leader, Francisco Largo Caballero, represented the first serious challenge to the power of the anarcho-syndicalists. Shortly after he entered the War Ministry, Largo promulgated—partly under pressure from the Communist Party, which had been the first to call for 'Discipline, Hierarchy, and Organization' in its own militia—a series of measures aimed at the militarization of the militias and the creation of a state-controlled army. Perhaps more than any other step taken by the newly reconstituted Republican government, this measure created considerable anxiety among the anarchists, an anxiety that spread quickly throughout the libertarian movement. From an ideological standpoint, the anarchists were convinced antimilitarists, and therefore to put themselves under a strict, hierarchical, military discipline was a supreme sacrifice. Furthermore, on a political level, militarization

---

[9] *CNT* (Madrid), 20 Sept. 1937. See also his proclamation to the anarcho-syndicalist militia in the Madrid front, published in *Castilla Libre*, 17 Feb. 1937, and his book, *Guerra, exilio y cárcel de un anarcosindicalista* (Paris, 1976).

threatened to destroy the enormous power that the anarchists wielded by maintaining control over their own forces.

The CNT and FAI were under no illusion with respect to the nature of the threat posed by their political adversaries. They therefore sought at all costs to prevent military power from slipping through their hands. They also knew that the Communists represented part of this threat and it was for this reason that the CNT proposed in September 1936 that a 'war militia' be created on the basis of compulsory service and under the joint management of the CNT and Socialist Unión General de Trabajadores (UGT).[10] However, none of their efforts to reorganize the military command outside the official channels met with success. As a result, some anarcho-syndicalist leaders concluded that, notwithstanding their revulsion to the state, it was necessary to compromise their principles and solicit representation in the cabinet. From their perspective, this unprecedented departure from anarchist tradition was the only way to ensure the libertarian movement some measure of influence in the military machine.

Republican government institutions virtually crumbled under the weight of the July revolution. Although the work of reconstructing state power began soon afterwards, it was apparent that this could not be easily achieved without anarcho-syndicalist participation in the government. Not surprisingly, the idea of inviting the libertarians to participate provoked controversy within the Caballero cabinet, although the advantages of having them share responsibility for its measures were indubitable. As early as October, *Claridad*, the chief organ of the UGT and the principal mouthpiece of Largo Caballero, intimated that the presence of the CNT in the Council of Ministers 'would certainly endow the directive organ of the nation with fresh energy and authority'. But would the anarcho-syndicalists wish to become ministers in the central government and be a party to the reconstruction of the state? This was questionable, even though quite recently they had joined the Catalan regional government.

By mid-September the CNT and FAI had come to a crossroads on the critical question of government. At a plenary assembly held on the 15th they decided that the newly constituted central government should be replaced by a national council of defence composed of five members of their organization, five of the UGT, and four members of

---

[10] Resolution approved at a plenary meeting of the regional committees of the CNT, as given in *CNT* (Madrid), 17 Sept. 1936.

the Republican parties.[11] In the hope of avoiding any resistance to the proposed council on the part of other political parties, the delegates of the CNT regional committee proposed that Manuel Azaña continue as president of the Republic. 'Our position abroad', explained the CNT daily *Solidaridad Obrera*, 'cannot deteriorate as a result of the new structure we propose; for it must be borne in mind that the decorative figures that characterize a *petit bourgeois* regime would be retained so as not to frighten foreign capitalists.'[12]

The CNT's campaign in favour of a national council elicited no support from any of the parties in the government. For this reason, at the next plenary assembly held on 28 September, Horacio Prieto, the national secretary of the CNT, condemned the project as a waste of time. Instead, he energetically promoted the idea of CNT participation in the government 'pure and simple'.

Although struck by Prieto's arguments, the delegates tenaciously clung to their proposal for a national council of defence. But Largo Caballero was adamant in his opposition. 'Look, if we were to agree to what you propose', he allegedly told a group of CNT leaders, 'we would, in effect, be putting ourselves on the same level as the Junta de Burgos [the Nationalist junta].' Faced by Largo Caballero's unbending attitude and by opposition from other quarters, Horacio Prieto decided to 'put an end to the last remnants of opposition' within the CNT and convoked a plenary session of the regional federations for 18 October. This time his arguments prevailed, and the plenum accorded him full powers to negotiate on the CNT's behalf for entry into the central government.

Reflecting the libertarians' new line, CNT declared:

We are taking into consideration the scruples that the members of the government may have concerning the international situation, . . . and for this reason the CNT is ready to make the maximum concession compatible with its anti-authoritarian spirit: that of entering the government. This does not imply renouncing its intention of fully realizing its ideals in the future; it simply means that . . . in order to win the war and to save our people and the world, it is ready to collaborate with anyone in a directive organ, whether this organ be called a council or a government.[13]

In their negotiations with Caballero, the CNT representatives asked for five ministries, including war and finance. Rejecting this demand,

---

[11] Ibid.
[12] 25 Sept. 1936.
[13] 23 Oct. 1936.

Caballero offered them only four, which they accepted on 3 November: justice, industry, commerce, and health. Significantly, none of these could be regarded as a vital post; moreover, the portfolios of industry and commerce had previously been held by a single minister.

We must pause here to note the rapid evolution of political viewpoints once the war and revolution had been set in motion. Given their pre-war attitudes as members of the *treintista* tendency, it was hardly surprising that anarcho-syndicalists like Juan López, Juan Peiró, and Horacio Prieto should have endorsed a policy of collaboration. As Horacio Prieto remarked, the CNT had 'to put an end to . . . so many moral and political prejudices, so many denials of reality, and so much semantic fuss'. 'I was convinced', Prieto continued, 'of the necessity of collaboration, and I smothered my own ideological and conscientious scruples.'[14]

What was surprising was the rapid evolution of a large segment of the *faísta* tendency from a pre-war position of implacable hatred towards the state to one of collaboration. Without doubt, García Oliver's decision to take a portfolio in Caballero's government was significant in this regard. As a member of the celebrated 'Los solidarios' and 'Nosotros' action groups, he had earned during the 1920s and 1930s the reputation as an uncompromising critic of the reformist wing of the libertarian movement. Although there is no way of knowing for certain, it is most likely that his participation in the government influenced other radicals of the FAI to accept collaboration as the only practical solution to the problem of prosecuting the war and revolution at the same time.[15]

Irrespective of their previous ideological orientations, the CNT–FAI representatives crossed the unfamiliar threshold of ministerial responsibility with trepidation. Not only did this step signify a complete negation of the basic tenets of Anarchism, shaking the whole structure of libertarian theory to the core, but, in flagrant violation of democratic principle, it had been taken without consulting the rank and file.

From the day the cabinet was reorganized the official publications of the CNT and FAI sought to justify the decision by minimizing the divergence between theory and practice. 'The entry of the CNT into the central government', echoed *Solidaridad Obrera*,

---

[14] *El anarquismo español en la lucha política* (Paris, 1946), 6–7.
[15] García Oliver discusses his role as a minister in *Eco de los pasos* (Paris, 1978).

is one of the most important events in the political history of our country. Both as a matter of principle and by conviction, the CNT has been antistatist and an enemy of every form of government. But circumstances . . . have transformed the nature of the Spanish government and the Spanish state.

At the present time, the government has ceased to be a force of oppression against the working class, just as the State no longer represents a body that divides society into classes. And both will oppress the people even less now that members of the CNT have intervened.[16]

Not everyone in the libertarian movement was prepared to accept this interpretation of events. For example, Federica Montseny, the Minister of Health and since late July a member of the Peninsular Committee of the FAI, gave unerring expression to the doubts and misgivings that had assailed a large segment of the anarcho-syndicalist movement when she declared some months later: 'As the descendant, I might say, of a whole dynasty of anti-authoritarians . . . I regarded my entry into the government, my acceptance of the post to which the CNT assigned me, as having more significance than the mere appointment of a minister. . . . What inhibitions, what doubts, what anguish I had personally to overcome in order to accept that post!'[17]

After taking office, though, Montseny quickly repressed her anti-political feelings and became a leading spokesperson for collaboration. Delivering a speech on 3 January 1937, she attempted to justify the course of action the leadership had recently adopted: 'The anarchists have come into the government to prevent the revolution from deviating from its course, to pursue it beyond the war, and also to oppose all possibility of dictatorial endeavours.'[18] Montseny was obviously suggesting here that collaboration was primarily a response to the growing threat posed by the political enemies of the libertarian movement. Only two days later she emphasized this point in another public address: 'We were compelled by circumstances to join the government in order to avoid the fate of anarchist movements in other countries. At the time we saw only one thing: the Communists in the government, and ourselves outside, and all our conquests endangered.'[19]

It is worth noting that the anarcho-syndicalists' decision to collaborate with the government gave rise to heated debates within the community of foreign radicals resident in Spain. Since the outbreak of civil

[16] *Solidaridad Obrera*, 4 Nov. 1936.
[17] *Fragua Social*, 8 June 1937.
[18] Camillo Berneri open letter to Federica Montseny in *Guerra de clases en España, 1936–1937* (Barcelona, 1977), 223.
[19] Letter to Burnett Bolloten, 7 Dec. 1950.

war in July, anarchist luminaries—notably, Emma Goldman, Helmut Ruediger, Agustín Souchy, and Camillo Berneri—had crossed the Spanish border in order to participate in the revolutionary movement. Some, like Berneri and Goldman, became outspoken critics of the collaborationist line adopted by the CNT and FAI. In an open letter to Federica Montseny published in the Italian anarchist paper *Guerra di classe* of Barcelona, Berneri indicted the anarchist ministers for defending their role in the government.[20]

While the anarcho-syndicalist leaders believed that their participation in the cabinet would enable them to defend more successfully the revolutionary conquests of their movement, the communists, socialists, and republicans hoped that this participation, by enhancing the government's authority among the rank and file of the CNT and FAI, would facilitate the reconstruction of the shattered machinery of the state and would, moreover, help them to gather into their hands all the elements of state power appropriated by the revolutionary committees at the outbreak of the Civil War. They further hoped that the CNT's entry into the government would hasten the supplanting of these committees by regular organs of administration. For their part, the anarcho-syndicalists contended that these revoutionary bodies, instead of being abolished, should become the foundation stones of the new society. 'The committees', declared the Madrid daily *CNT*, 'are organs created by the people to oppose the fascist insurrection. . . . We want the reconstruction of Spanish society . . . to be based on the organs that have sprung up from the people.'[21]

Inside the cabinet, the CNT–FAI ministers proved to be an unequal match for their political opponents, who applied constant pressure to end the power of the committees on the grounds of placating foreign opinion and enhancing the government's prospects of securing arms from the Western powers. Federica Montseny was well aware of how untenable the position of the anarcho-syndicalists was within the cabinet, but she did what she could to resist their adversaries: 'I can state positively that, although we lost in the end, we defended our ground inch by inch and never voted for anything that curbed the conquests of the revolution without first being authorized by the national committee of the CNT, on which there was a permanent representative of the FAI.'[22]

[20] 20 Dec. 1936.
[21] Berneri, *Guerra*, p. 226.
[22] Letter to B. Bolloten.

On the other hand, Juan Peiró, the former *treintista* and now Minister of Industry, supported the position taken by the more conservative members of the government that Britain and France would reverse their stand on the matter of supplying arms only 'on condition that we prosecute the war and not the revolution'. This, he added, did not imply renouncing the revolution.

The road to follow is this: We must wage the war, and, while waging it, limit ourselves to preparing for the Revolution by means of a conscientious and discreet control of the factories, for this is equivalent to taking up revolutionary positions and equipping ourselves in a practical way for the final assault on capitalist society after the end of the war.[23]

Whether they felt helpless to oppose the government's policies or whether, as in the case of Peiró, they supported them, the anarcho-syndicalist ministers acquiesced in the plan to dissolve the revolutionary committees and replace them with regular provincial and municipal councils, in which all the parties adhering to the Popular Front as well as the trade union organizations were to be represented. Thus, far from realizing their hope of giving legitimacy to the committees, entering the cabinet actually undermined the anarcho-syndicalists' predominant position in countless towns and villages and even resulted in their exclusion from village councils in certain instances.

One of the major reasons why the anarcho-syndicalists entered the government was that they hoped to exercise greater control over the war effort. But the role the CNT–FAI ministers were able to play in the counsels of the cabinet in regard to military matters also fell far short of their expectations. They found, in the words of Juan Peiró, that they had no rights and responsibilities regarding the direction of the war.[24] Once in government, the anarchists believed that it would be possible to redress the situation if they were allowed to participate in an inner cabinet which would be responsible for overseeing military affairs. This cabinet, called the Higher War Council, was formed on 9 November, with Caballero at its head and García Oliver, the newly appointed Minister of Justice, representing the CNT.

In spite of its official aim, this new body was condemned to futility from the outset, primarily because of the bitter rivalry among its members. Lacking the unanimity vital for effective operation, the Higher War Council was soon rendered impotent. This fact reflected a harsh

[23] Article in *Política* (Madrid), 23 Feb. 1937.
[24] Speech at Valencia CNT Congress, Nov. 1936, as reported in *Fragua Social*, 17 Nov. 1936.

reality; for although the anarchists hoped that their participation in the government would consolidate and even further their revolutionary gains, particularly with regard to military matters, they were obliged in the end to circumscribe their efforts to maintaining control of their own militia units and securing arms from the War Ministry.

The policy of collaboration created profound problems for the libertarian movement, not least because it threw the more extreme spirits who clung passionately to unadulterated anarchist beliefs into conflict with the leadership. This ever-widening split is illustrated by the example of the famed *Columna de Hierro* or Iron Column.

No column was more thoroughly representative of the spirit of anarchism, no column dissented more vehemently from the libertarian movements' inconsistencies of theory and practice, or exhibited a more glowing enmity for the state than the Iron Column that occupied a sector of the Teruel front during the first seven months of the war. Although it was mainly recruited from among the more fiery elements of the anarchist movement in the region of Valencia, the column also included several hundred convicts from the San Miguel de los Reyes Penitentiary; a fact that soon brought opprobrium upon the column and led to the widespread notion that it was an army of criminals. Yet the overwhelming majority of its members were dedicated anarchists who attempted at all costs to defy the collaborationist agenda that had been set by the national leaders of the CNT and FAI. 'Our entire conduct must not aim at strengthening the state, we must gradually destroy it, and render the government absolutely useless', exhorted a delegate of the Iron Column attending the CNT congress in November 1936.

Uncompromising in its ideological beliefs, the Iron Column did not hesitate to adopt a militant attitude towards its opponents within the anarchist movement, and on occasion the threat of force was used to ensure that their policies on certain matters were adopted. Thus, the continued existence of the Iron Column posed a threat to the regional committee of the Valencia CNT as well as to the National Committee of the CNT.[25]

The anarcho-syndicalists had agreed to join the *Generalitat* government formed in September 1936. Despite this move towards political unification, the division of power in the region continued. The revolu-

[25] On the Iron Column see especially: Burnett Bolloten, *The Spanish Revolution* (North Carolina, 1979), ch. 23; *Linea de fuego* (Puebla de Valverde); and *Nosotros* (Valencia).

tionaries, for example, continued to maintain their own police units—
patrullas de control—as well as their own armed militia, whereas the
Generalitat exercised control of the assault and national republican
guards and the militia of the moderate republican parties.

To end this duality of power became a primary objective of both the
Catalan Communists—represented by the Partit Socialista Unificat de
Catalunya (PSUC)—and the liberal Republicans of the middle-class
Esquerra Republicana de Catalunya (ERC). The PSUC in particular
took the initiative in pressing for the incorporation of the militia units
into a regular army of the state and for the fusion of all police forces,
including the *patrullas de control*, into a single internal security corps
under the control of officers of the assault and national republican
guards (formerly the Civil Guard).

Since late December 1936, when a government crisis provoked by
the PSUC had led to the expulsion of Andrés Nin, the councillor of
justice and sole POUM representative, the CNT's position in the
government had been steadily deteriorating. The POUM, the CNT's
only possible ally, was alarmed at the passivity with which the anarcho-
syndicalists had accepted its ouster from the *Generalitat* and at their
failure to perceive that the victory of the PSUC represented an obvious
menace to themselves.

Meanwhile, other political forces within the *Generalitat* were
becoming bolder in their efforts to undermine the anarcho-syndicalist
position in the government. A notable example was the ERC. At
a public meeting of their party held on 28 December, their anti-
revolutionary rhetoric was so shrill that their leader Luis Companys,
who still believed that the collaboration of the CNT and FAI in the
cabinet was essential if the libertarian movement were to be 'domestic-
ated' and gradually divested of its armed power, felt impelled to inject
a note of caution. Despite his party's hostility to the anarcho-
syndicalists, he continued to impress upon the CNT and FAI that
his administration was committed to the July revolution.

For all his subtle statecraft, Companys could not prevent the antagonism between the pro- and anti-revolutionary forces in Catalonia
from coming to a head. Chief among the causes of this irreversible
trend was the conflict over the control of the independent militias and
the *patrullas de control*. In response to the PSUC's aggressive campaign
for a regular army and to the mounting pressure from the central
government, which had long opposed the military independence
acquired by Catalonia as a result of the revolution, a growing number

of anarcho-syndicalists were refusing to submit to the demands of militarization. Early in March, nearly 1,000 militia men stationed in Gelsa, on the Aragón front, left in protest against the militarization decrees, fearing that these measures would transform the militia into an instrument of the State. Returning to Barcelona, they set up the Friends of Durruti (*Los Amigos de Durruti*)—named after the heroic figure, Buenaventura Durruti, who was killed on the Madrid front in November 1936. The 'Friends' not only opposed the militarization of the militias, the dissolution of the defence committees and of the anarchist-dominated *patrullas de control*, but also the intervention of the CNT in the government. On 24 March, the aims of the group were announced in their mouthpiece *La Noche*:

This new organization has as its primary objective to preserve intact the postulates of the CNT and FAI, harking back to 19 July, with a view to ensuring that it is the trade-union organization that has the responsibility for managing the economy and society, with no place given to the political parties, which are deemed incapable of carrying out the work of the revolution.[26]

Whether the withdrawal of the CNT militia stationed in Gelsa had any effect on the anarcho-syndicalist leadership cannot be said with certainty, but it is noteworthy that only a day after the first conscripts were to present themselves at their induction centres, in compliance with the military decrees, the CNT councillors, led by Francisco Isgleas, the councillor of defence, walked out of the *Generalitat* government, provoking a cabinet crisis. The stage was now set for a direct confrontation. On the afternoon of 3 May, Rodríguez Salas, commissioner of public order and PSUC member, ordered three truckloads of assault guards to raid the central telephone exchange, the Telefónica, which the CNT had occupied since the defeat of the military in July and regarded as a 'key position in the Revolution'. The incident ignited a series of bloody street battles that were to drag on for several days.

The 'May Events', as this episode came to be called, marked a turning point in the war and revolution. This was true above all because its outcome ultimately determined the fate of the libertarian movement. For the anarcho-syndicalists it was the second (and as it happened the

---

[26] *La Noche*, 24 Mar. 1937 as cited in Frank Mintz and Miguel Pecina, *Los Amigos de Durruti, los trotsquistas y los sucesos de mayo* (Barcelona, 1977), 11–12. For further information on the Friends of Durruti see: George Esenwein, 'Barcelona, May 1937: George Orwell, "Los Amigos de Durruti", and the Assassination of Camillo Berneri', *The Alarm* (San Francisco, 1983); and Paul Sharkey, *The Friends of Durruti: A Chronology* (Tokyo, 1984).

last) time that they were in a position to assume maximum control of Barcelona.

Comprised largely of the ultraradicals of the CNT and FAI, including the Libertarian Youth (Juventud Libertarias, FIJL) and the Friends of Durruti, the revolutionary forces were also represented by the independent Marxists of the POUM. With lightning speed, armed workers under their command seized control of key positions in and around Barcelona, and by nightfall on 3 May the 'rebels' had become — to paraphrase Manual Azaña — 'masters of the city'. Had the CNT and FAI been interested in taking power, asserted Abad de Santillán, their victory would have been complete, 'but this did not interest us, for it would have been an act of folly contrary to our principles of unity and democracy'.[27]

The street fighting intensified the following morning, and by midday it had reached such a pitch that the leaders of the CNT–FAI began appealing for a cease-fire. In Valencia, that same morning, Largo Caballero had called for the CNT ministers, asking them to leave at once for Barcelona to try and end the hostilities. A meeting of the national committee of the CNT was then summoned, at which it was decided to send Mariano Vásquez, CNT secretary, and García Oliver, Minister of Justice, to Barcelona.

Upon arriving in Barcelona, the CNT representatives joined the Catalan leaders in the *Generalitat* palace in calling for a cessation of hostilities. García Oliver urged his embattled followers to 'Think of the pain, think of the anguish ... of those anti-fascist workers in that part of Spain dominated by the whip of Hitler and Mussolini when they learn ... that [in Catalonia] we are killing one another.'

To the ultraradicals of the CNT, Libertarian Youth, and the Friends of Durruti, the pleas of the CNT leaders heard over the radio came as a stinging blow. 'It should not surprise anyone', observed an eyewitness, 'that when our representatives ... gave the order "Cease Fire!" there were some comrades who felt ... that it was a form of treachery to allow those assassins a [reference to the PSUC guards firing near the Casa CNT–FAI] to escape without just punishment.'

On the evening of 6 May news was received in Casa CNT–FAI that 1,500 assault guards were advancing towards Barcelona. Both Federica Montseny, who had arrived on the 5th, and Mariano Vásquez hurried to the *Generalitat* to communicate with Valencia, hoping to prevent the guards en route from provoking every anarchist-controlled

[27] *Fragua Social*, 15 May 1937.

community in their path to insurrection. Montseny and Vásquez worked feverishly throughout the night to arrange a truce which would allow the troops to proceed without hindrance.

In the early morning hours of Friday 7 May, there were signs that the ardour of the anarcho-syndicalists had finally spent itself. A feeling that it would be futile to continue the struggle against the will of their leaders had overwhelmed them, and disillusionment was widespread. Many withdrew from the barricades and disappeared into the pre-dawn darkness.

Instead of achieving unity, the intervention of the CNT–FAI ministers actually drove a wedge into the ranks of the libertarian movement. Even among the leaders the seeds of dissension were rapidly spreading. Helmut Ruediger, vice-secretary of the AIT (International Working Men's Association, the anarcho-syndicalist International), who was active in Barcelona at the time of the May Events, summarized the dilemma facing the anarcho-syndicalists at this critical juncture:

In view of the fact that on 3 May the CNT, representing the majority of the Catalan industrial workers, was in open conflict with *all* organizations comprising the other social layers ... the question of 'power' meant *whether the CNT at that time should crush them all, concentrate the leadership of public affairs in its own hands, and create its own repressive apparatus necessary to prevent the 'crushed' from returning to public life.*[28]

As a result of the May Events, the fermenting dissensions and contradictions within the anarcho-syndicalist movement finally boiled over. The Local Federation of Anarchist Groups of Barcelona, as well as the Barcelona Local Federation and the Regional Committee of the Catalan Youth, refused to support the efforts of the Regional Committees of the CNT and FAI to expel the Friends of Durruti.[29] The Libertarian Youth in particular grew increasingly strident in its criticism of the leadership, whom it held responsible for betraying the revolutionary intentions of the rank and file. In a manifesto issued shortly after the May Events, the Libertarian Youth announced its resolve to continue the revolutionary struggle: 'For our part, we must point out that we can no longer remain in silence nor tolerate all the counter-revolutionary activities which are taking place; so much Governmental injustice and so much political unfaithfulness—all in the name of the war and anti-fascist unity.'[30]

[28] *Ensayo crítico sobre la revolución española* (Buenos Aires, 1940), 23–4.
[29] *Nosotros*, 28 May 1937.
[30] *Man!* (London), June 1937.

The May Events also had a profound impact on the anarcho-syndical-ists' position in both the *Generalitat* and the central government. Towards the end of June, the moderate leadership of the CNT suf-fered a humiliating rebuff by President Companys. On 29 June a pro-visional government formed during the May Events was replaced by a new cabinet without anarcho-syndicalist representation. During the negotiations, Companys—without conferring with the CNT—gave a seat to Pedro Bosch Gimpera, the rector of the University of Barcelona and member of the small middle-class party Acciò Catalana Republi-cana, increasing the relative strength of the left republicans. The CNT regarded this move by Companys as a manoeuvre and threatened to boycott the government if he did not withdraw the nomination. Under-estimating the degree to which the balance had tipped against them and believing that Companys could not govern without them, the anarcho-syndicalists had obviously expected him to be as amenable as he had been during the heyday of the revolution. They were mistaken and were left out in the cold.

Meanwhile, in Valencia, political power was rapidly being shifted under the direction of Juan Negrín, who had replaced Largo Caballero as premier. On 17 May a new cabinet was formed, comprising only nine members as opposed to eighteen in the previous administration, and—most significantly—divested of left-wing socialists and anarcho-syndicalists.

The reaction in libertarian circles was swift and belligerent. The CNT and FAI press not only condemned the government as 'counter-revolutionary', but also accused the communists of having plotted to exclude the anarcho-syndicalists from the cabinet. On 25 May, the national committee of the CNT characterized the PCE as a counter-revolutionary party which 'in close collaboration with the bourgeois republican parties and right-wing socialists', had brought to fruition the 'political manoeuvre' that had culminated in the 'provocation in Barcelona' and the formation of the new government.[31]

A few days later Mariano Vásquez issued a report on the CNT plenum of the regional committees, which proclaimed that the CNT would not collaborate 'either directly or indirectly' with the govern-ment and that it would spread propaganda among the armed forces against the new regime and seek alliance with the UGT in order to conduct a joint campaign of opposition.

This defiance was short-lived, for only two days later Vásquez,

[31] *Boletín de Información, CNT–AIT–FAI.*

representing the national committee of the CNT in an interview with Negrín, promised him that the government could 'count on the material and moral support of the CNT' to defend the Republic.[32] The reason for the volte-face was clear. The national committee of the UGT, controlled by moderate socialists and communists, had just repudiated the position maintained during the cabinet crisis by the left socialist executive, and supported by the CNT, namely, that it would not support any government in which both the premiership and War Ministry were not held by Largo Caballero. Fearing political isolation, the CNT decided to reverse its stand and solicited representation in the government. In a minimum programme, hastily drawn up, the national committee proposed equal representation for the Marxist, republican, and libertarian sectors in all matters relating to national defence, the economy, and public order. But, considering the CNT's weak bargaining position, it was no wonder that the proposal came to nothing.

Just how far the FAI had strayed from its pre-war commitment to antipoliticalism was clearly reflected in the dictums passed at a FAI plenum held in July 1937 on the tenth anniversary of the founding of the organization. At this historic meeting, it was announced that the FAI was to undergo a transformation, becoming what was called the 'new organic structure'. The nerve-centres of the FAI, the *grupos de afinidad*, were to be dissolved and in their place there was to be the Agrupación or large group consisting of some several hundred members. In this way, the FAI was to be converted into a mass organization open not just to the disciples of the militant form of anarchism but to all willing to abide by the resolutions of the FAI plenums. Echoing the enthusiasm that most FAI members in attendance had for the new structure, Federica Montseny proclaimed that 'If Bakunin were alive today he would be able to watch with great pleasure the position adopted by us in this transcendant hour.'[33]

Following the plenum, the purpose of restructuring the FAI was explained to the rank and file by Alejandro Gilabert, a leading *faísta* and secretary of the Local Federation of Anarchist Groups in Barcelona:

With the new structuring, the FAI finds itself in circumstances whereby it can both orient and direct the revolution. The old organic structure, based on *grupos de afinidad*, was very effective before the revolution, when organized

---

[32] *Solidaridad Obrera*, 2 June 1937.   [33] *Fragua Social*, 15 July 1937.

anarchism existed clandestinely, on the fringes of legality, and against the law, when at times it was obliged to systematize violence in the struggle against the bourgeoisie and the State. Now, at least until a new situation arises that offers us a better perspective, it would be absurd if the FAI were to maintain a position on the margin of present realities.[34]

Neither Montseny nor Gilabert acknowledged that in its new form the FAI had to all intents and purposes become a political party; an external force that was 'to propel the Revolution *from all the popularly based organs of power*'.[35]

The underlying significance of the reorganization did not escape the notice of anarcho-syndicalists who were strongly opposed to the politicalization of the libertarian movement. At a regional plenum of the FAI held a month after the Valencia conference, a number of delegates rose up in violent protest against the restructuring of their organization. Writing in the dissident paper *Esfuerzo*, Felipe Alaíz, a well-known *faísta* and spokesman for this group of dissenters, denounced it as a 'new government party'. To him the decisive step was tantamount to rejecting everything the anarcho-syndicalists stood for:

By constituting itself as a new political party [the FAI] is asserting that the people are incapable of directing their own destinies. These are the very people who made up the deficiencies of the State in the trenches and on the barricades in July. . . . [They are] the same people who cultivate the land, who transport the products, improve the soil and sacrifice themselves on the land, sea and air, but are now nothing more than a bunch of yokels who are not worth anything to the politicians in office.[36]

Just how deep the resistance to the reorganization of the FAI ran within the libertarian movement is hard to gauge. Judging from the testimony of Alejandro Gilabert, opposition was considerable in Catalonia; so much so that the differences reached the point where some groups threatened to provoke a split.[37]

By this time, there was little the dissidents could do to reorient the political trajectory of the CNT–FAI leadership. The fragmented nature of the opposition tendency posed a major obstacle to them. In the main, their resistance lacked focus in that there were no formal organizational links among the different locally based groups. Unable to act as one body, they were in no position to challenge forcefully the

---

[34] *Tierra y Liberdad* (Barcelona), 21 Aug. 1937; see also, *FAI estatutos generales de la Federación Anarquista Ibérica* (Valencia, 1937).
[35] *CNT*, 12 July 1937.   [36] No. 1 (1937).
[37] Vernon Richards, *Lessons of the Spanish Revolution* (London, 1983), 149.

upper echelons of the CNT–FAI bureaucracy. Moreover, the commonly held belief that unity was paramount in order to defeat Fascism undoubtedly inhibited many of those in opposition from waging an all out struggle against the official representatives of the anarcho-syndicalist movement.

Although already plagued by disputes within their own movement, the libertarians faced an even greater threat from their opponents within the central and regional governments. After the power of the CNT and FAI had been broken in Catalonia, and the government of Largo Caballero had been replaced by that of Juan Negrín, the offensive against the revolutionary conquests escalated rapidly. In August 1937, the Negrín administration dealt a powerful blow to the revolutionaries by officially dissolving the anarchist-dominated Council of Aragón, which had been set up early in the war to control the revolution in that part of the Republican camp that was preponderantly libertarian. Soon afterwards, the Communist-controlled Eleventh Division headed by Enrique Líster swept through the Aragón countryside, destroying the collective farms of the region — including those that had been formed voluntarily — and thus effectively smashing the framework of the revolutionary order that had been established there since the outbreak of the Civil War.[38]

During the period they were excluded from the cabinet, the leaders of the CNT grew ever more anxious to forge an alliance with the Caballero-wing of the UGT, which had also been deprived of a voice in the government. But in October 1937 the Communists had delivered a *coup de grâce* to the left Socialist leader. Acting in agreement with the former supporters of Caballero and with the moderate socialists, they formed a new executive on 1 October. Ignoring the fact that the Communists and their allies, the Negrínistas, now controlled the UGT, the CNT representatives — in defiance of some FAI leaders — responded favourably to the idea of an alliance. However, a formal pact between the two groups was not signed until 18 March, when, under pressure of a crushing enemy offensive on the Aragón Front, the CNT felt compelled to cast aside its reservations and join forces with its age-old rival. While the pact appeared to consolidate the power of the largest working-class organizations, in practice it subordinated them to the central government. This was made clear in the provisions of the alliance, which, among other things, recognized the authority of the government and the state in such matters as the nationalization of

[38] See José Silva, *La revolución popular en el campo* (Valencia, 1937).

industry and the regular army. Even the stipulation that the two organizations would defend the collectives and would pursue 'a firm political line in order to receive legal and juridical recognition' implied submission to governmental authority.

It was not until the formation of the second Negrín administration on 5 April 1938 that the CNT re-entered the central government. However, their request for representation in the cabinet was only partially satisfied by the appointment of a single anarcho-syndicalist, Segundo Blanco. Little known in libertarian circles, Blanco was not a man of firm doctrinal convictions and he was soon regarded by fellow anarchists as another Negrínista.[39] In the event, his presence in the cabinet had no impact on government policy: apart from his perfunctory opposition to the militarization of the war industries, of the ports, and courts of law, the voice of the CNT was silent.

The re-entry of the CNT into the government, far from improving the position of the anarcho-syndicalists *vis-à-vis* their political rivals, only served to stoke the smouldering dissensions within the libertarian movement.

By the summer of 1938, it was so riven with discord that it had neither the unity nor the power to influence the course of events. The mainstream of the movement, as represented by the national committee of the CNT and its supporters, was still decidedly collaborationist, although few had gone as far as Horacio Prieto, who was now convinced that *apoliticismo* was dead and libertarian communism only a distant goal. He and his followers had shed all their inhibitions about politics and began campaigning for the creation of a libertarian socialist party that would participate in every organ of the state. Challenging these tendencies were the various opposition factions mentioned earlier, as well as a sizeable section of the FAI.

The antagonisms between the rival factions finally erupted during the national Plenum of the Libertarian Movement held in Barcelona between 16 and 30 October 1938. According to the unpublished record of the debates, Horacio Prieto railed against his critics for being 'politically naïve', and for 'lacking a concrete plan of action'.[40]

Prieto's sentiments were mirrored in an iconoclastic speech delivered by CNT secretary Vásquez, who attacked the anarcho-syndicalists for having balked at accepting the militarization pro-

---

[39] José Peirats, *Los anarquistas en la crisis política española* (Buenos Aires, 1964), 338; see also, Diego Abad de Santillan, *Por que perdimos la guerra* (Buenos Aires, 1940), 205.
[40] Peirats, *La CNT*, iii. 304.

gramme of the communists and socialists, and who asserted that the collectives would have fared better if they had submitted to the tutelage of the central government. The part of Vásquez's speech that created the biggest stir was not his positive view of state intervention but rather his glowing defence of the Negrín government.[41] Unlike many of the anarcho-syndicalists whom he represented, Vásquez backed the resistance policy being pursued by Negrín and the communists. The hope was that the Civil War would continue until general war broke out in Europe, thus making it possible to merge the two conflicts.

Visibly incensed by what both Prieto and Vásquez had said, the Peninsular Committee of the FAI replied bitterly: '[I]t is necessary to leave behind those who deprecate our principles. Those who are devoid of ideas should not be in the vanguard of our movement. . . . We have to recover our vast strength by working within our Organization, and by considering the government to be, as it is, something temporary.' And, in response to the thesis presented at the plenum that the CNT should 'introduce itself into the government in order to destroy it', the Catalan delegation of the FAI riposted: 'It is as if to abolish prostitution we should subscribe to the theory that it is necessary to take our loved ones into the brothels.'[42]

Despite their vehement insistence that collaboration was a bankrupt policy, the dissidents had little impact on the outcome of the plenum. In the end, the resolutions approved reaffirmed the anarcho-syndicalists' commitment to government participation as the lesser evil.

No debate among the upper echelons of the CNT and FAI could have illustrated more dramatically the unbridgeable divisions that had developed within the libertarian movement during the Civil War. But, now, after twenty-eight months of conflict and the uninterrupted decline of anarcho-syndicalist strength and influence, such doctrinal disputes had become patently academic to the rank and file. 'The people, debilitated by hunger', writes Peirats, 'had grown morally weary of the war. In order to reanimate them it would have been necessary to bring about a fundamental change in the political base and substitute it for the politics of Negrín.'[43] This of course was impossible not only because of the dissensions within the libertarian movement, but also because of the emasculation of other key opposi-

---

[41] Peirats, *La CNT*, iii. 90; see also, Juan Gómez Casas, *Historia del anarcosindicalismo español* (Madrid, 1969), 255 n. 17.

[42] Peirats, *La CNT*, iii. 309.

[43] Ibid. 318.

tion groups, principally the Socialists whose party and trade union movement were also irrevocably split into warring factions.

By serving in government the anarcho-syndicalists failed to consolidate—let alone advance—the revolutionary drive begun in July 1936. At first, the policy of collaboration adopted by the CNT–FAI leaders appeared successful. The belief that participation in government was the only effective way of rallying the diverse elements engaged in the anti-Fascist struggle prevailed over much of the anarcho-syndicalist movement. Yet it cannot be said that the majority of anarcho-syndicalists were ever deeply committed to this idea. When it became apparent that the anarchists in government were helpless to promote even a minimal revolutionary programme, the movement grew increasingly vulnerable to internecine bickering.

The anarchist leaders who remained faithful to the strategy of using politics as a vehicle for resolving the problems arising from the war and revolution managed to direct the libertarian movement until the final months of the conflict. Inevitably, they incurred the wrath of the purists, who, like the AIT representative Alexander Schapiro, never forgave the 'collaborationists' for compromising anarchist principles.[44]

Only a handful of critics took a more charitable view of the CNT–FAI leadership, perhaps because they better understood the dilemmas that the Spanish anarchists were forced to confront in a protracted civil war. No one gave clearer expression to this perspective than the American anarchist, Emma Goldman. From her first-hand experiences in Spain and her intimate knowledge of prominent anarchist figures, she reached the following conclusion:

I hold no brief for the foolish belief that in entering ministries, Anarchists could hope to affect the course of the Spanish revolution. Or that by accepting the paralyzing conditions of Stalin our comrades would hasten the triumph of the anti-fascist cause. Much less do I defend the weak stand taken by the leaders of the CNT–FAI in the tragic battle of May . . .

However, we outside of Spain, we who do not face starvation and danger, should at least try to understand, if not excuse, the motivations of the concessions and compromises made by the leaders of the CNT–FAI.[45]

---

[44] Alexander Schapiro's trenchant analysis of anarchist participation in government is found in several issues of *Le Combat syndicaliste* (Paris) between May and Nov. 1937.

[45] 'Where I stand', *Spain and the World*, 2 July 1937.

10. ÉLITES IN SEARCH OF MASSES: THE TRADITIONALIST COMMUNION AND THE CARLIST PARTY, 1937–1982

Martin Blinkhorn

Nine months after the start of the Spanish Civil War, on 19 April 1937, General Franco announced the arbitrary creation of Nationalist Spain's single party. The principal components of the Falange Española Tradicionalista y de las JONS, later more generally known as the Movimiento, were the two main mass parties of the pre-war extreme right, the Fascist Falange and the Carlist Comunión Tradicionalista. In officially extinguishing Carlism as an independent force, Franco was dealing with no ordinary political party. Whereas the Falange and the other leading organizations of the pre-Unification Spanish right—the Catholic-conservative CEDA and the rival monarchist party, Renovación Española—were creations of the 1930s, the Traditionalist Communion was heir to a century of history.

It was a history, moreover, of extraordinary complexity. Since its emergence in the 1830s, Carlism had consistently opposed, in the name of its royal pretenders, the 'liberal' monarchy of Isabel II, Alfonso XII, and Alfonso XIII, together with the 'oligarchy' associated with it. In the process, however, it had passed through several phases of ideological development and exhibited a variety of faces. While successive party élites were responsible for developing its characteristic right-wing 'traditionalist' ideology and programme, its remarkable powers of survival were due rather to its enduring command of popular support based on localist resistance to centralization and intrusive capitalism. Carlism's popular base, strongest in Navarre, the Basque region, Catalonia, and Valencia, while periodically susceptible to mobilization by its leaders, possessed an identity of its own, sustained by dynastic loyalty, local and family tradition, and popular culture.

The Traditionalist Communion itself was formed in 1931–2 as a new framework for the mobilization and organization of this 'pueblo carlista'. It represented a fusion, in response to the fall of Alfonso XIII and the advent of the democratic Second Republic in April 1931, of

Carlism's mainstream with two schismatic groups: the Integrists, intransigent Catholics who had broken away in 1888, and the Traditionalists, followers of Vázquez de Mella, Carlism's leading ideologue, who had abandoned the pretender Don Jaime in 1919. Between 1931 and 1936, first under the flexible political leadership of a Navarrese aristocrat, the Conde de Rodezno, and then from 1934 that of a Sevillian ex-Integrist lawyer, Manuel Fal Conde, the Traditionalist Communion had played an important role on the extreme right of Spanish politics. Under Fal Conde it had also developed an extensive, tightly structured, highly authoritarian political and paramilitary organization; for all its populist undertones and stress upon its 'masses', pre-war Carlism was a rigidly hierarchical movement, dominated by a well-defined socio-political élite. Although there were odd exceptions, this 'popular' movement of peasants, artisans, and Catholic *petits bourgeois* was run and controlled during the 1930s by comfortably off members of the Catholic urban and rural bourgeoisie, together with elements of the lesser aristocracy and clergy.[1]

The pre-war Carlist élite was held together by its members' common interests, fears, enemies, and commitment to the 'Traditionalist' programme developed earlier by Mella.[2] Devout Catholicism inspired bitter hatred of the Republic's anticlericalism, while attachment to private property generated fear of its 'socialist' tendencies. In place of liberalism and democracy, politically conscious Carlists yearned for a 'traditional monarchy' in which the king would rule actively within an elaborate corporatist system. Inspired by Catholic social and political doctrine rather than by contemporary Fascist example, this would involve the decentralization of political power and the restriction of exploitative capitalism. However well-meaning and paternalistic, in the context of the 1930s this vision was essentially reactionary and inevitably threw the Communion into alliance with other rightist forces.

In other respects the Carlist élite was riven by what proved to be deep and lasting divisions. Two main 'factions' took shape during the 1930s. The first was led by Rodezno and other members of the Carlist 'establishment' of Navarre and elsewhere; while convinced traditionalists, its members regarded Carlism as an influence in Spanish public life rather than as a party, and traditionalism as not necessarily

---

[1] For detailed discussion of pre-Civil War Carlism, see Martin Blinkhorn, *Carlism and Crisis in Spain, 1931–1939* (Cambridge, 1975).

[2] Martin Blinkhorn, 'Ideology and Schism in Spanish Traditionalism', *Iberian Studies*, 1/1 (1972).

synonymous with or dependent upon the Communion. A contrasting view was held by Fal Conde, his appointee as head of the paramilitary Requeté, José Luis Zamanillo, and other members of the new ruling sectors promoted after 1934; for them, Carlism, and specifically the Traditionalist Communion, were the only true repositories of traditionalism; compromise with other right-wing movements was thus to be guarded against.

These differences were accentuated by an acute succession problem. In 1931 Don Alfonso Carlos of Bourbon, a childless octogenarian with no clear heir, became the Carlist claimant to the Spanish throne. Between 1931 and 1934, Rodezno and Carlist 'transactionists' attempted to resolve the urgent problem of his successor by means of an agreement with the deposed Alfonso XIII. If achieved, this would have committed Alfonso, his heirs, and his supporters to traditionalism, while the Carlists would have recognized the Alfonsine line as heirs to Alfonso Carlos. Thus, it was hoped, the dynastic conflict which had divided Spanish monarchists since 1833 would end. The attempt failed, 'transactionism' was discredited, and Rodezno lost the party leadership to Fal Conde. The 'transactionist' or 'collaborationist' impulse nevertheless remained vigorous.[3]

Carlist intransigents, and there were many, who found the notion of a pact with the *alfonsinos* repugnant sought other solutions. One small group, the self-styled 'Núcleo de la Lealtad', left the Communion altogether and floated the candidacy of Alfonso Carlos' great-nephew, Archduke Karl Pius of Habsburg.[4] In 1936, however, Alfonso Carlos, only a few months before his death, bequeathed responsibility over Carlism's affairs to another great-nephew, Prince Javier of Bourbon-Parma: not as pretender but as 'Regent'.[5] The solution was anything but a satisfactory one, and contained the seeds of further divisions in the future.

The extent of rivalries and dissension within the Carlist leadership was evident immediately before the Civil War and during the months which preceded Unification. The Carlists joined the rising of July 1936 when the Rodezno faction, characteristically willing to commit the movement more or less unconditionally, outmanoeuvred Fal Conde who, just as characteristically, had wished to impose conditions

---

[3] Francisco de Melgar, *El noble final de la escisión dinástica* (Madrid, 1964), 116–30.

[4] *El Cruzado Español* (Madrid), 25 Jan. 1935. *El Cruzado Español* was the newspaper of the Núcleo de la Lealtad.

[5] Melchor Ferrer (ed.), *Documentos de D. Alfonso Carlos de Borbón* (Madrid, 1950), 299. The true name of Don Javier, a Frenchman, was François Xavier.

for Carlism's participation on the rising's military leaders. As Franco's grip on Nationalist Spain tightened during late 1936 and early 1937, Rodezno and the collaborationists went along with the process, while Fal Conde and his followers tried vainly to defend Carlism's integrity.[6] The 1937 Unification brought dissension to a head, dividing Carlism's ruling élite among those who actively connived at it, those who passively accepted it, and those who, in vain, opposed it. While neither destroying Carlism nor, from the regime's point of view, satisfactorily channelling it, Uni fication severed the 'pueblo carlista' from its leaders and condemned the Carlist élites to half a century of incestuous and kaleidoscopic factionalism.

The creation of the FET and the emergence of Franco's dictatorship, sealed in 1939 with the Nationalist victory, presented Carlists with an unprecedented situation and, for the movement's former leaders, an unfamiliar set of problems. Devotees of a cause which throughout its history had opposed the ruling system, they now found themselves faced with a regime they had helped to usher in, and in some cases actually to mould. Yet although the commitment of the overwhelming majority of Carlists to the myths and values of '18 July' and the Nationalist *Cruzada* was from the very outset total, this did not automatically imply accepting all aspects of the emergent Franco regime. In the obvious and purely negative sense that it was neither liberal-democratic nor left-wing, the regime was acceptable to most Carlists. Some, indeed, asked little more of it. Others, however, saw every reason for feeling let down. The *franquista* new order was not a Carlist or in any sense a 'traditional' monarchy, and showed little sign of ever becoming one. With Falangist Fascism, however superficially, in the ascendant during and after the war, only in the religious sphere could the new Spain be said to conform at all closely with Carlist ideals. Within the framework of this regime, moreover, Carlists found their organization, the Traditionalist Communion, officially absorbed into a larger, non-Carlist, fascistoid political movement, and their cause deprived of legal existence, something experienced under neither Alfonso XIII nor the Republic.

Not surprisingly, the new situation provoked wide differences among pre-Unification Carlist office-holders as to what attitude to adopt towards the FET and, as it took shape, the Franco regime: differences coloured by pre-existing rivalries, the difficulty of open political activity, and their own isolation from much of the rank and

---

[6] Jaime del Burgo, *Conspiración y guerra civil* (Madrid and Barcelona, 1970), especially pp. 509–60; Blinkhorn, *Carlism and Crisis*, pp. 228 ff.

file. At its starkest, the issue was that of where an individual's first loyalty lay: to the wartime alliance, the FET, and the Francoist new order; or to a historic Carlist cause whose importance and interests might be held to transcend short-term alliances and imposed political structures. For some, the choice was truly as simple as that. Between the two extremes, however, lay a range of subtler positions.

In April 1937, the majority of those pre-war Carlist leaders who had favoured close collaboration with the rest of the Spanish right, had pursued dynastic reconciliation, and in July 1936 had desired more-or-less unconditional commitment to the rising, willingly accepted the forced merger with the Falange. Many thereafter also followed Rodezno's example in accepting state, governmental, or party office within the new order. Rodezno himself became Minister of Justice in Franco's first cabinet (1938), inaugurating a 'Carlist' tenure of that office which, in the persons of Rodezno himself, Esteban Bilbao, Antonio Iturmendi, and Antonio María Oriol, endured for all but eight years of the regime. Bilbao, perhaps the single most important col-laborationist, not only served six years as Justice Minister but also occupied the influential dual office of President of the Cortes and of the Council of the Realm throughout the central years of the regime. In addition, control of the FET and of provincial administration in Navarre and Alava was handed over to collaborationist Carlists in rec-ognition of the wartime commitment to the *Cruzada* displayed by those provinces, the most Carlist in pre-Civil War Spain; Rodezno, the 'boss' of pre-war Navarrese Carlism, became for the last decade of his life the effective viceroy of Navarre. Such offices held considerable attraction for Carlist leaders accustomed to exercising power and influence within their own movement, attuned to the realities of the political situation, and able to convince themselves that thanks to them the spirit of Carlism lived on within the Franco regime.

Nor were they entirely deluding themselves, for collaboration in the unambiguous form of office-holding did bring solid achievements. Given that the FET, like it or not, was a *fait accompli*, and that within it radical Falangists nursed totalitarian dreams uncongenial to most Car-lists, there is little question that Rodezno, Bilbao, Iturmendi, and other collaborationists played an important part in ensuring that dreams never became reality. As well as securing the religious basis of the new state, they helped dilute the Fascist element in the regime's labour policy, and squash successive attempts, by Ramón Serrano Suñer in the 1940s and José Luis Arrese in the 1950s, at the further 'fascistiza-tion' of the regime.[7] Those Carlist intransigents who based their non-collaboration on a bitter opposition to the regime's fascistic, 'totalitarian' aspects might thus have had even more to complain about had former colleagues not chosen a different strategy.

From Unification onward, the more zealously collaborationist Carl-ists effectively ceased to regard Carlism as a discrete movement or party, as distinct from a 'tendency' and 'influence' within the Spain of Franco, to whom their commitment was limited only by calculation as to his likely survival. To the regency of Don Javier their loyalty was never much more than nominal—and eventually not even that. During the second half of the Second World War, when Franco seemed likely to go down with his Axis patrons, Rodezno and others attempted to keep open an escape route in the form of a never-quite-consummated agreement with rival monarchist supporters of Don Juan, third son of Alfonso XIII. Considering Don Juan the legitimate inheritor of the Carlist claim, Rodezno and his supporters sought to end the century-old dynastic rift by binding him to a statement of 'traditionalist' principles. Once launched, the *juanista* tendency remained very much alive, with Rodezno, José María Oriol and others maintaining close contact with Don Juan himself.[8] After 1945, nevertheless, as it became obvious that Franco would survive after all, Carlist collaborationists effectively committed themselves to the regime for as long as it might endure.

The wholehearted collaborationism of Rodezno, Arellano, Bilbao, and other pre-war Carlist potentates was anathema to the rival group around Manuel Fal Conde and Don Javier. Hostile towards the cre-ation of a Fascist-style, potentially totalitarian, single party and, of course, to the absorption of the Traditionalist Communion within it, these intransigents sought to uphold the autonomy and purity of Carl-ism, and to plough an 'isolationist' furrow in relation to the regime. The symbolic leadership of Carlist survivalism rested with Don Javier, but between 1937 and 1955 its course was mostly steered by the tough and uncompromising Fal Conde. The anti-Fascism of Don Javier, a

[7] Laureano López Rodó, *La larga marcha hacia la Monarquía* (Barcelona, 1979), 33, 165–9, 172–3, 667–8, 737–41; Stanley Payne, *The Franco Regime 1936–1975* (Madison, 1987), 260, 446–9. Arrese's plans are discussed in detail in his *Una etapa constituyente* (Barcelona, 1982).

[8] López Rodó, *La larga marcha*, pp. 39, 78–9, 670–2; Melgar, *El noble final*, pp. 141–4; Burgo, *Conspiración*, pp. 450–62.

French citizen and resident, was demonstrated during the Second World War; having fought in the Belgian army until its defeat, he later assisted the French Resistance and in 1944 was arrested by the Germans and committed to Dachau.[9] Fal Conde also maintained his sincere opposition to both Spanish and foreign 'Fascism', resisting the enlistment of members of the Requeté in the Spanish Blue Division, while unsuccessfully attempting to obtain official approval for Carlist volunteers to fight for the Allies.[10]

Following his release in 1945, Don Javier, initially from exile but later through repeated visits to Spain, attempted to clinch his leadership of those Carlists who were determined to defend the 'separateness' of Carlism and to pursue from outside the structures of the *franquista* regime the establishment of a Carlist monarchy. In the interests of legitimacy and of his own regency, Don Javier accordingly opposed Franco's 1947 Law of Succession.[11] Although down to the early 1950s he and Fal Conde continued to insist that the regency was not only valid in purely Carlist terms, but also a solution to the question of how the Franco regime itself might peacefully be replaced,[12] as time passed the institution became more and more of a liability to its supporters. Not only did it offer neither a credible alternative to Franco nor a plausible mechanism of transition, but as an emotional focus for the Carlists themselves it utterly lacked the appeal of even the most unexciting royal pretender. Given the obvious material attractions of outright collaboration with the regime and the insidious appeal of *juanismo*, it is hardly surprising that by the early 1950s Don Javier's loyalists were becoming frustrated, both with his reluctance either to assert his own claim to the throne or designate a legitimate Carlist claimant, and with the generally meagre achievements of intransigence and isolationism.[13]

A serious problem for Don Javier and his followers was their rejection by a significant sector of non-*juanista* Carlist opinion. While office-holding collaborationists, in dismissing the regency as ineffec-

---

[9] Josep Carles Clemente, *Historia del carlismo contemporáneo 1935–1972* (Barcelona, 1977), 127–31.

[10] Clemente, *Historia*, p. 131; *Montejurra* (Pamplona), Apr. 1971.

[11] 'Declaración del Príncipe Regente don Javier de Borbón Parma al Generalísimo don Francisco Franco Bahamonde', 7 May 1947, in Clemente, *Historia*, pp. 294–5.

[12] Burgo, *Conspiración*, pp. 442–3, 446–50, 454–7, 464–5; Clemente, *Historia*, pp. 286–94.

[13] Burgo, *Conspiración*, pp. 462–4; 'Carta de 43 carlistas navarros al Príncipe Regente, 1946', in Clemente, *Historia*, pp. 282–6; Javier Lavardin, *El último pretendiente* (Paris, 1976), 11.

tive and intransigence as futile, viewed the regime in generally positive terms, other Carlists no less scornful of the regency were offended by Carlism's political marginalization, by what they considered the regime's effective betrayal of traditionalist principles, and by its nurturing of both Falangist ultraism and 'liberal' *juanismo*. Between 1943 and 1953 much of this tendency came to be channelled through the strange, and still not fully explained, phenomenon of *carloctavismo*.

In 1943, at a time when Franco's future was beginning to look unsure and the cause of Don Juan commensurately hopeful, the 34-year-old Archduke Karl Pius of Habsburg reasserted his claim to the Carlist succession and the Spanish throne. Embraced before the Civil War by the schismatic Núcleo de la Lealtad, the cause of 'Carlos VIII' had since been allowed to languish. Now, however, it assumed a certain momentum. Handsome, educated, and a Spanish citizen, 'Carlos VIII' was an attractive pretender. During the decade down to his premature death in 1953, and especially in the late 1940s and early 1950s, his cause attracted the support of a significant number of influential Carlists; these included not only the founder of the Núcleo de la Lealtad, Jesús Cora y Lira, former deputies such as Juan Granell, José María Lamamié de Clairac, and Ginés Martínez Rubio, and the former Navarrese Requeté leaders Antonio Lizarza and Jaime del Burgo, but even, albeit more passively, the collaborationists Bilbao and Iturmendi, interested in a possible Carlist succession to Franco.[14]

The recent history of Carlism, written mainly by *juanistas*, intransigents, and members of the Carlist 'left', has dealt harshly with *carloctavismo*. It was, they all claim, an artificial cause, manufactured in the 1940s by Falangists in order to divide and weaken the monarchist cause generally, and funded from government sources.[15] The accusations in themselves appear to be justified, to judge from Falangist testimonies and the authorities' complaisance towards the activities of 'Carlos VIII' and his 'Catholic-Monarchist Communion'.[16] Even so, *carloctavismo* played a more significant and perhaps more positive role

[14] On involvement of noted Carlists see *¡Volveré!* (Madrid), 10 Apr. 1949, 10 Mar. 1950, 25 Mar. 1950; *Boletín Carlista* (Madrid), 1 Dec. 1948, 25 July, 4 Nov. 1949, 25 Feb. 1950; *¡Volveré!* and *Boletín Carlista* were the two leading *carloctavista* periodicals. Also Burgo, *Conspiración*, pp. 444–6, 484–5; Clemente, *Historia*, p. 35.

[15] For a typical critique, see Clemente, *Historia*, pp. 35, 183–93.

[16] Arrese, *Etapa*, pp. 154–6, 173–4; Dionisio Ridruejo, quoted by Josep Carles Clemente in *Montejurra*, Dec. 1970. There can be little question that the *carloctavistas's* bitter attacks on both Don Juan and the regency suited Franco's interests admirably in the years following the promulgation of the Law of Succession.

in the history of contemporary Carlism than all this might indicate. At a time when many collaborationists were writing off Carlism as a separate cause, and supporters of the regency enjoying little success in reactivating it, *carloctavismo* went some way towards transcending its murky origins and rekindling a degree of popular enthusiasm behind a Carlist current which combined loyalty to the regime with a semi-independent political posture.[17] Critics accused its protagonists of deliberately or, more probably, misguidedly dividing the Carlist forces. Technically this may be true; in retrospect, however, it would probably be fairer to recognize that Carlism's revival from the late 1950s onward owed something both to the modest enthusiasms reawoken by the *carloctavista* adventure and to the attitude towards the regime which made this possible.

'Carlos VIII' died in 1953, a mere 44. With him, to all intents and purposes, died his family's claim and the hopes of his anti-regency, anti-*juanista* supporters. Attempts to transfer his claim to one of his less hispanicized brothers, notably Franz-Josef of Habsburg, failed utterly.[18] What would have been the subsequent history of Carlism had 'Carlos VIII' lived on to push his cause amid the changing circumstances of the late 1950s and the 1960s it is obviously impossible to say; given other developments, it seems likely that the divisions he was accused of fomenting would have persisted and deepened. In the event, the bitter antagonism of the *carloctavistas* towards Don Juan ensured that the beneficiary of the death of 'Carlos VIII', *faute de mieux*, would be Don Javier. The rallying of many *carloctavistas* to his cause was only made possible, however, by Don Javier's gradual abandonment of the regency from 1952 onwards, in favour of an outright claim to the throne.

In adopting this course, and implicitly recognizing the bankruptcy of the regency, Don Javier yielded to longstanding pleas from his sup-

---

[17] A conclusion drawn after a necessarily cautious reading of the *carloctavista* press; see also Burgo, *Conspiración*, p. 470.

[18] 'Carlos VIII' was actually the youngest of four brothers. For various reasons his elder brothers had all earlier renounced their claims to the Spanish throne (see *Boletín Carlista*, 25 Feb. 1950). Following his death the second eldest of the four, Anton, after briefly reasserting his claim, repeated his renunciation and effectively ordered the dissolution of the *carloctavista* forces (*Boina Roja* [Madrid], 7, 1954). On the vain attempts to stimulate the cause of 'Francisco-José Carlos I', see Burgo, *Conspiración*, p. 470; López Rodó, *La larga marcha*, pp. 400, 634. When 'Francisco-José Carlos I' died in 1974 he left behind a last testament declaring that the Carlist dynasty died with him.

porters.[19] He nevertheless was anything but decisive in doing this. Having in 1952 somewhat reluctantly accepted the principle of his kingship, Don Javier then vacillated for four years concerning how explicitly, publicly, and strenuously his claim should be pursued: or whether, indeed, it should be pursued at all. Conflicting pressures, from *juanistas* and Carlist ultras, were being brought to bear on the potential pretender. One victim of the turmoil was Fal Conde, sacked as *jefe-delegado* in August 1955; Don Javier appears to have been inclining at the time towards an agreement with Don Juan, while Fal Conde was toying with the notion of a pact, behind Don Javier's candidacy, with Falangists unhappy at their declining power.[20] Nevertheless, by 1957 Don Javier's claim was public and irreversible, and a *javierista* cause was clearly in existence.

As Don Javier himself was obviously well aware, a price would have to be paid for the adoption of this new course. However dismissive they might be of the regency and its standard-bearer, *franquista* and *juanista* Carlists were able to remain nominally within the Carlist fold as long as Don Javier refrained from actually claiming the throne; the regency, after all, allowed for the possibility of what most of them desired: the succession of a dutifully 'traditionalist' Don Juan. Don Javier's adoption of the pretender's role set the *juanista* Carlists free; in December 1957, forty-five prominent collaborationists, representing a total of sixty-five, formally visited Don Juan in Estoril and, in return for his promising to uphold traditionalist principles, at last recognized him as legitimate monarch; the document announcing the event made frequent reference to 'Tradition' and 'Traditionalism', but only once mentioned 'Carlism'—and that to declare the Carlist dynasty 'extinguished'.[21]

The defection of the *estorilos* in one sense represented a schism at least as serious as those suffered by Carlism in 1888 and 1919. The list of signatories to the document recognizing Don Juan contained several former deputies, regional *jefes*, and other office-holders from the pre-war era; also, significantly perhaps in a movement whose foothold in

---

[19] Lavardin, *El último pretendiente*, p. 11; Melgar, *El noble final*, pp. 147–8; López Rodó, *La larga marcha*, pp. 145–6.

[20] Tomás Echeverría, *Franco ¿No era normal? Uno de sus hechos injustificable: La persecución de los carlistas* (n.pl., n.d.), 181–8. Echeverría's curious book contains the signed testimony of José Luis Zamanillo, Fal Conde's close collaborator, concerning the sacking and the events surrounding it.

[21] Melgar, *El noble final*, pp. 150–7, 203–6; López Rodó, *La larga marcha*, pp. 192–6; Clemente, *Historia*, pp. 297–9.

the Spanish aristocracy had never been strong, a disproportionate number of titled Carlists.[22] In reality, however, the loss was less serious than it appeared and the compensating gains significant. Most of the *estorilos* had already ceased to believe in Carlism as an autonomous cause, had been inactive within the re-formed Traditionalist Communion which had grown up around Don Javier and Fal Conde since the late 1940s, and had remained 'loyal' only as long as doing so seemed compatible with the eventual succession of Don Juan. From the point of view of Don Javier's supporters, the 1957 schism simply purged Carlism of disloyal and inactive elements, thereby preparing the movement for a new phase of activity.

The factional strife which reached its climax between 1952 and 1957 was largely confined within a Carlist élite whose members, irrespective of their attitude to the Franco regime, evinced no reservations concerning their commitment to the 1936 rising or the ideological baggage of traditionalism which they had brought to it. Throughout this time the Carlist rank and file played little part in Carlist politics. Opportunities were of course limited. Down to the late 1940s, former Carlist *apparatchiks* might pursue their tortuous politicking in clubs and restaurants, but links with the rank and file of an officially non-existent movement were to say the least difficult to maintain. Even with the more or less open re-emergence of the still strictly illegal Traditionalist Communion (and the *carloctavista* Catholic-Monarchist Communion) in the late 1940s, genuinely popular political activity continued to be discouraged and sometimes risky. Factionalism itself probably inhibited any true reawakening of the Carlist masses. Collaborationists—many of them élitists *par excellence*—had little interest in seeing them reawakened outside of the Movimiento; *javierismo* and *carloctavismo* were capable of striking sporadic sparks of popular enthusiasm, usually through the exposure of Don Javier or 'Carlos VIII' to the public gaze; but the much-spoken-of 'Carlist masses' remained by the mid-1950s largely cut off from the doings and ambitions of their leaders.

This is not to say, however, that rank-and-file Carlists ceased to be Carlists. Unlike the collaborationists within the movement's élite, there is little evidence that the great majority of ordinary Carlists were seduced from their habitual loyalites by the attractions of the system.

[22] To be precise, ten of the signatories bore a title, mostly that of *conde* or *marqués*. Clemente, *Historia*, p. 299.

On the contrary, rank-and-file Carlist commitment to the Movimiento, never great, had diminished appreciably even before the end of the Civil War, and did so dramatically thereafter as its distinctive blend of Fascism and careerism became evident. On official festive occasions—18 July and the 'Day of Victory'—Requeté veterans clad in the Carlist red beret would dutifully turn out in celebration of the *Cruzada* and of their own sacrifices for it; but as the years passed their detachment from the machinery of the regime became almost total. By the mid-1950s the 'pueblo carlista' was therefore in political limbo, uninvolved in the affairs of the regime and largely unresponsive to those of its own nominal leaders. For tens of thousands of Carlists, the cause had by now reverted, as it had done during earlier fallow periods, to being a matter less of politics than of family tradition and popular culture.

In so far as Don Javier's re-formed Traditionalist Communion was failing to arouse and harness popular enthusiasm, more was involved than official discouragement of popular politics. The passivity, and perhaps even shrinking, of Carlism's base was directly related to a broader contradiction between the supposed aims of the *Cruzada* and its actual accomplishments. Carlists of all ranks had gone to war in 1936 to save Catholicism and to destroy both 'communism' and liberalism—aims which, to all appearances, had been fulfilled. At a deeper level, however, they had also fought to preserve traditional, predominantly rural, and small-town patterns of life against a conglomerate of evils which they had customarily associated with liberalism and socialism—evils such as urbanism and cosmopolitanism, centralization and bureaucracy, big industry, financial speculation, cultural modernism, and what others, then their enemies, would have called 'alienation'. The Franco regime, by crushing their common enemies, removing immediate fears, and restoring 'order' and 'religion', was able for a time to satisfy many Carlists. In the longer term, however, it could not or would not resist the advance of these other horrors. As the 1950s progressed it was becoming painfully obvious that, far from embodying Christian spirituality and thereby limiting the effects of capitalism and state authoritarianism, the Franco regime was nurturing a new capitalism and materialism, and imposing an unprecedented barrage of restrictions on those kinds of liberty most prized by many who fought in the Civil War as Carlists: essentially, the freedom of the small community, and that of the individual to go his own way as long as he refrained from oppressing others. The result, for those Carlists unhappy to settle for second best, was confusion and disillusionment. Such a popular mood was immediately discouraging for Carlism's leaders, yet also held promise—if only it could be successfully harnessed. As yet, however, the *javierista* élite had failed both to grasp its political potential, and to develop an analysis, a programme, and a strategy capable of turning it to Carlism's advantage.

Nor had the *javieristas* fully grasped the significance of another contemporary development: the emergence during the 1950s of a new generation of Spaniards who had no recollection of the Civil War or its origins, and whose political consciousness was thus formed wholly in the context of the Franco regime. This was, of course, a phenomenon affecting all Spanish political movements, legal and clandestine alike. Nevertheless the unique role of family heritage within Carlism made the movement peculiarly susceptible to the generational revolution of the 1950s and 1960s. Young members of Carlist families from the 1950s onward frequently embraced their heritage, but within a political atmosphere totally different from that of the 1930s. Now, instead of interpreting their Carlism in the context of a republic they had never known, or a liberalism and a socialism which were forcibly excluded from the Spain in which they were growing up, they did so in relation to a reactionary, oligarchic, corrupt, and repressive regime from which many felt utterly alienated. Especially given 'popular' Carlism's traditional, almost instinctive, antagonism towards the exercisers of power, in this looking-glass world former allies were to become enemies and, eventually, vice versa.

The Traditionalist Communion that emerged from the upheavals of the mid-1950s was a still-shadowy and skeletal organization, dominated at its highest levels by figures prominent in the 1930s. Fal Conde's removal as *jefe-delegado* in 1955 could not and did not destroy his influence, which remained considerable for a decade or more to come; in his place was appointed a five-man secretariat effectively dominated by José María Valiente, a law professor who had converted to Carlism from the CEDA in 1935, and the abrasive José Luis Zamanillo, former head of the Requeté and a close associate of Fal Conde. In 1960 Valiente became *jefe-delegado* with Zamanillo, as secretary-general, his second-in-command. Under their leadership the strategy and, more slowly, the theory and programme of Carlism began to undergo a shift. The policy of intransigence towards the regime, identified with Fal Conde, was replaced by what might be termed neo-collaborationism.

Rather than being prepared to countenance the absorption of Carlism into the regime, however, the movement's new leaders sought, in a political atmosphere of slowly increasing openness, to combine defence of Carlism's separateness with acceptability to Franco: a strategy resembling that once pursued by the *carloctavistas*. Their goals were the transmission and official acceptance of Carlist principles, the admission of non-*juanista* Carlists into the government, and ultimately the designation of Don Javier, rather than Don Juan or the latter's son Juan Carlos, as Franco's successor.[23]

Carlism's theoretical ground also began to shift during the late 1950s, albeit at first in a subtle and subterranean manner. The highest levels of the Carlist élite remained ideologically paralysed. The kind of political and social order for which Don Javier, Zamanillo, Valiente, the ever-watchful Fal Conde clan, and most of the incumbent Carlist hierarchy had fought was in general terms 'reactionary' in its stress upon 'Catholic unity' and a religiously inspired corporativism. Although such ideas were even more outdated and unrealistic now than they had been in the 1930s, the Carlist leadership defiantly refused to abandon them in favour either of liberal monarchy or the repressive one-party state, let alone re-evaluate the entire theoretical basis of Carlism. However eager they may have been, in the wake of Estoril, to assert Carlism's integrity and distinctiveness, they had no wish to open the gates to the twin evils of liberalism and communism.

It was therefore left to a younger generation of Carlists, benefiting from the increased official tolerance which the neo-collaborationism of Don Javier and Valiente won for the Communion, to assume the task of ideological revision. Within the Carlists' student organization, the AET, and in a number of provincial centres such as Bilbao, Saragossa, Logroño, and Santander, youthful Carlists launched during the late 1950s a re-examination of the movement's theory, strategy, and programme which was to have revolutionary consequences. In clandestine periodicals such as *Azada y Asta* (Santander) and *La Encina* (Saragossa), the rising generation, gradually boosted by recruits from outside the established Carlist ranks, sought to highlight those aspects of Carlism which most differentiated it from the more repugnant aspects of *franquismo*: its attachment to the community, to local and regional rights and self-government, and to the rights and potentialities of ordinary people as against power-wielding individuals and organizations:

[23] López Rodó, *La larga marcha*, 153, 178, 257; Lavardin, *El último pretendiente*, pp. 45–6, 67–8.

in short that popular character which generations earlier had allowed Carlism to function, as it was hoped it might do again, as a vehicle for anti-oligarchic protest.[24]

Don Javier, dignified and honourable but also cautious and indecisive, was hardly fitted to lead Carlism into a new era. Instead it was his son, Carlos Hugo of Bourbon-Parma[25] who was to preside over Carlism's transformation. During the late 1950s Carlos Hugo, at the time in his late twenties, was taken up by a group of mainly youthful advisors who successfully endeavoured to prepare the embarrassingly French prince politically and linguistically for his vocation. Between 1957 and 1966, when it was dissolved, Carlos Hugo's so-called 'secretariat' became something of a legend among Carlists: a kind of intellectual and political 'ginger group' which acquired great influence and in 1965–6 came close to taking over the party organization.[26] Well before this, however, Carlos Hugo had begun to emerge as a significant figure in his own right. With Don Javier providing symbolic leadership which also helped hold the movement together during turbulent times, Carlos Hugo assumed a more active role, energetically assisted by his three sisters, and, following his much publicized marriage in 1964, by his wife, Princess Irene of the Netherlands.

Collectively the Bourbon-Parmas provided the Carlist rank and file with a lively and attractive focus for its loyalties such as had been lacking since Aflonso Carlos's death in 1936. Under Carlos Hugo's intelligent and flexible leadership, Carlism during the early 1960s began to reassert itself as a significant autonomous force within the eccentric politics of Franco's Spain. In line with the neo-collaborationist strategy of Valiente, now Don Javier's *jefe-delegado*, no attempt was made to repudiate the *Cruzada* or to oppose Franco himself; on the contrary, his favour was quite deliberately courted. The young Bourbon-Parmas and the 'secretaries' emphasized Carlism's dynastic and, in a studiedly vague way, its popular aspects, while insisting that its contribution to the *Cruzada* had never been justly rewarded.[27] They

[24] Pedro José Zabala, 'Evolución Carlista', *Montejurra*, Apr. 1971. Zabala, an inhabitant of Logroño, was a leading figure of the 'generation of the 1950s'. See also Lavardin, *El último pretendiente*, pp. 15, 31, 45, 100–3.

[25] The prince's name was actually Hugues. It was hispanicized to Hugo as soon as he was introduced to Carlism's affairs; the 'Carlos' was added, informally at first and later, in the 1960s, legally according to French civil law.

[26] The central theme of Lavardin, *El último pretendiente*, is Carlos Hugo's role between the late 1950s and 1969.

[27] Lavardin, *El último pretendiente*, pp. 107–66.

hoped to rekindle rank-and-file enthusiasm for the Carlist cause while persuading Franco—and as many as possible of the country's political élite—that the Bourbon-Parmas were worthy of serious consideration as Spain's possible future ruling family.

The strategy brought some rewards. Although the Traditionalist Communion itself, as an organization independent of the Movimiento, remained strictly illegal, its *de facto* existence was now clearly recognized and tacitly permitted; in addition, two new Carlist organizations, the Círculos Vázquez de Mella and the Hermandad de Antiguos Combatientes de los Tercios de Requetés, received official approval.[28] The combination of quasi-legality, the Bourbon-Parmas' appeal, and the organizing and propagandizing efforts of the new Carlist generation succeeded where the Carlist élites had for twenty years failed: in rekindling popular enthusiasm and activism. By 1966 Carlism, as evidenced by attendances of over 100,000 at the Carlist festival of Montejurra, had entered one of its classic phases of popular revival.[29] Moreover, within sectors of the regime and the Movimiento which, while not necessarily anti-monarchist, were hostile to the cause of Don Juan and his son Juan Carlos, Carlos Hugo had begun by the mid-1960s to attract some interest. Success went no further, however. Valiente's hopes of government posts for himself and other *javieristas* remained unrewarded, as did dreams that the Bourbon-Parmas might be allowed to push aside the descendants of Alfonso XIII; as the 1960s wore on, although the prospects of Don Juan grew dimmer, it was Don Juan's son, Juan Carlos, who was clearly marked out to succeed Franco. Franco himself never took the Bourbon-Parmas seriously, consistently refusing to accept their claims to the throne and to grant them Spanish citizenship.[30]

By the mid-1960s acute tensions were apparent within Carlism's leading echelons. The Valiente–Don Javier strategy was essentially contradictory. Its success depended upon Carlism's being taken seriously as a popular cause, yet this could be, and was, only achieved by stimulating developments within the movement which were prob-

[28] López Rodó, *La larga marcha*, p. 259; Lavardin, *El último pretendiente*, pp. 120–1, 131.

[29] *Boina Roja*, June 1964; *Información Mensual* (Madrid), Apr.–May 1965; *Montejurra*, 23–30 May 1965 and 17 May 1966; *Boletín de Información de la Comunión Tradicionalista de Andalucía Occidental* (Seville), May 1965, May 1966.

[30] Francisco Franco Salgado-Araujo, *Mis conversaciones privadas con Franco* (Barcelona, 1976), 412–4, 420, 426–7, 465, 472; López Rodó, *La larga marcha*, pp. 282–3, 317, 352; Lavardin, *El último pretendiente*, pp. 207–16.

ably incompatible with collaboration in the long run. While the Carlist 'establishment' remained devoted to '18 July' and left to itself was never likely to challenge the regime outright, the new generation of Carlists was developing a very different outlook. The 'populism' which gradually emerged after 1958 involved stressing those popular, decentralizing, and, it was claimed, 'freedom-loving' aspects of Carlism which most differentiated it at first from selected aspects of the regime, but ultimately from the regime itself and the whole ideological apparatus of '18 July'. In moving from 'traditional monarchy' to a 'monarchy of the people', from 'Catholic unity' to an acceptance of the spirit of Vatican II, from obsessive anti-leftism to excited anti-authoritarianism, Carlism's aspirant élite was guiding the movement along lines which some, at least, of its elders—and, indeed, of its contemporaries too—were certain sooner or later to find unacceptable.[31]

Carlism's new course claimed its first prominent victims as early as 1962, when Zamanillo and the party treasurer, Sáenz Díez, were manoeuvred out of office. During the next few years Zamanillo, a passionate devotee of '18 July' whose speeches resounded with references to 'blood' and 'martyrs', increasingly distanced himself from Carlism's affairs and adopted a more or less unreservedly *franquista* position.[32] By the mid-1960s a semi-public tug-of-war was under way between conservatives and mainly youthful renovators whose populism was propelling them towards opposing the regime. A complex period of confrontation opened in 1966 with the break-up of Carlos Hugo's 'secretariat', several of its members being frustrated at the prince's apparent reluctance to press his cause further; some, like the Catalan Ramón Massó, soon abandoned Carlism altogether.[33] A retreat into unabashed collaborationism seemed to be signalled in 1967, when Don Javier warmly accepted Franco's Ley Orgánica del Estado and instructed Carlists to work within the system.[34]

The decisive events in Carlism's evolution, however, came in

---

[31] The strains are apparent from the columns of three important periodicals of this period: *Información Mensual*, the increasingly populist organ of Carlos Hugo's secretariat; *Boina Roja*, the property and mouthpiece of the rightist and neo-collaborationist Ramón Forcadell; and *Montejurra*, which broadly reflected the views of the Communion's official leadership. See e.g. 'Confidentes', *Información Mensual*, Dec. 1965; *Boina Roja*, 85 (1963), 96 and 98 (1963), 96 and 98 (1965); *Montejurra*, 21–8 Mar., 23–30 May 1965.

[32] Lavardin, *El último pretendiente*, pp. 143–9.

[33] Ibid. 263–5, 273–81.

[34] *Información Mensual*, Apr.–May 1967. The change of direction apparent in *Información Mensual* after the disintegration of the secretariat was sudden and dramatic.

1968–9, took a clearly incremental form, and resulted in decisive defeat for neo-collaborationism. In January 1968 the continued strength of the radicals within the Communion was demonstrated and reinforced by Valiente's resignation as *jefe-delegado*.[35] Carlist hostility towards recent extremes of collaborationism, and a sudden rise in oratorical outspokenness, were unquestionably nourished by anticipation of Juan Carlos's imminent proclamation as Franco's eventual successor. In December 1968 the authorities, irritated by Carlist activity and anxious to smooth the way for the proclamation, expelled the Bourbon-Parma family from Spain.[36] Carlists were outraged. In the Cortes, the protests of their four *procuradores* produced one of the few lively passages in the history of Franco's tame assembly,[37] and at the annual Montejurra rally in May 1969 inflamed oratory was followed by physical clashes between young Carlists and the police.[38] When, in July 1969, the proclamation of Juan Carlos finally took place,[39] the credit of neo-collaborationism was already exhausted. With restraint now pointless, Carlism stood ready to embark on the last, and perhaps the oddest, chapter in its long history.

The departure of Valiente and the traumatic events of 1968–9 released the brakes from the process of ideological renovation which had been gathering momentum, especially within the AET and younger sectors of the movement, for a decade. For some time, Carlists such as José María Zavala, by now the sole former member of the 'secretariat' to remain close to Carlos Hugo, Pérez de Lema, head of the Movimiento Obrero Carlista, Javier María Pascual, editor of *El Pensamiento Navarro* from 1966 to 1971, and Josep Carles Clemente, a Catalan journalist and historian, had been stressing the supposed 'social' and 'democratic' elements in Carlism, and in so doing implying links between Carlism and certain forms of socialism. Between 1969 and 1972 the renovationists effectively took over what now became officially the 'Carlist Party'—nomenclature that would have been repugnant to the Carlists of the 1930s with their utter rejection of

---

[35] *Montejurra*, Jan.–Feb. 1968; Lavardin, *El último pretendiente*, pp. 282–3; López Rodó, *La larga marcha*, p. 353. Rightists believed Valiente had been sacked, but most accounts suggest that his departure was voluntary, inspired by differences with Carlos Hugo.

[36] *Montejurra*, Dec. 1968.

[37] *Ibid.*, Mar. 1969.

[38] *Ibid.*, May 1969.

[39] In the Cortes, the 4 Carlist *procuradores* were among the mere 19 who voted against Juan Carlos' succession. López Rodó, *La larga marcha*, p. 492.

'party politics'. The programme of the party, worked out at a series of meetings and assemblies and formally adopted in 1972, was frankly labelled 'socialist' and described as 'revolutionary'.[40] In conformity with the prevailing fashion throughout much of the renascent Spanish left of the 1970s, and with a selective reading of Carlist history,[41] this Carlist socialism was 'autogestionario'. It involved an extensive amount of provincial, local, and community self-government—which, it was argued, stood in direct line of descent from nineteenth-century Carlist foralism and communitarianism; workers' control of all economic enterprise at plant level would be combined with syndical control of overall economic activity and planning; politics would be a matter of debate among competing 'mass parties'; and the monarchy, deemed to be valuable if not essential as the disinterested guarantor of both continuity and revolutionary dynamism, would rest upon a 'pact' between dynasty and people which only the latter could sever. There was, the Carlist Party argued (with occasional references to the 'pseudo-monarchies' of Mao, Castro, and Tito, all of whom Carlos Hugo visited during the 1970s), no reason why a dynastic monarchy stripped of pomp and ostentation should be incompatible with the pursuit and achievement of socialism; on the contrary it might prevent the erection of personal and party dictatorships such as had too often besmirched contemporary 'socialist' systems.

The Carlist Party was by this time firmly under Carlos Hugo's leadership. In 1972, the ageing and infirm Don Javier handed his son full responsibility for directing the Carlist cause; three years later in 1975, shortly before Franco's death, he finally abdicated in Carlos Hugo's favour, enjoying only a brief retirement before his death in 1977. As leader of a party espousing *socialismo autogestionario*, Carlos Hugo, still banned from entering Spain, was also now committed to the anti-Franco opposition as it emerged into the open during the 1970s. The party, its allies now squarely on the political left, suffered

[40] The evolution of Carlist socialism gave rise to a large body of theoretical literature. Examples are: Pedro José Zabala, *Carlismo 68: Esquema doctrinal* (Saragossa, 1968); José María Zavala, *Partido Carlista* (Madrid, 1976) and *Partido Carlista* (Bilbao, 1977); and Carlos Hugo de Borbón-Parma, *La via carlista al socialismo autogestionario* (Barcelona, 1977). For the socialist programme adopted at the 1972 Arbonne Congress, see Clemente, *Historia*, pp. 342–50.

[41] Martin Blinkhorn, 'History in the Service of Politics: The *Partido Carlista* and the Carlist Past', *Harvard University Center for European Studies Working Paper Series*, 13 (1988); also Martin Blinkhorn, interviewed by Javier Alfaya, 'El carlismo de nuestro tiempo', *Triunfo* (Madrid), 3 Sept. 1977.

considerable official harassment from 1971 onwards,[42] and was a
founder member both of the Junta Democrática (1974) and the Plata-
forma de Convergencia Democrática (1975).[43] Amid the reopening of
Spanish politics which followed Franco's death in November 1975, the
Carlist Party sought a legal status for which—unlike the Communist
Party—it was made to wait until after the June 1977 election.

The fifteen-year transformation of the Traditionalist Communion
into a Carlist Party advocating socialism, openly opposing Franco, and
consigning '18 July' to the scrap-heap of history inevitably incensed
and alienated many self-confessed and sincere Carlists. In truth, the
movement, prone to schism throughout its history, had since 1958
been suffering a continuing leakage of mainly right-wing malcontents.
In 1958 a group led by Mauricio de Sivatte and consisting mainly of
Catalonian Carlists abandoned Don Javier to form the so-called
'Regency of Estella'; though 'pure' Traditionalists, the *sivattistas* were
also bitterly anti-*franquista* and objected less to any as yet faint signs of
'populism' than to the pretender's refusal to oppose Franco.[44] During
the 1960s, as the internal strains within Carlism became more acute, it
was the conservative collaborationists—Zamanillo, Sáenz Díez,
Ramón Forcadell, Miguel Fagoaga, Valiente, and others—who left,
mostly to succumb belatedly to the embrace of *franquismo*. Zamanillo
eventually surfaced as a pillar of the *continuista* rightist organization
Unión Nacional Española.[45] Valiente was formally expelled from the
Carlist Party in 1970 for too great a show of collaboration.[46] In 1971 he
joined Forcadell, head of the breakaway veterans' body, the Hermandad del Maestrazgo, in attempting to set up, under the regime's
patronage, a rival Carlist organization.[47] Other previously active Carlists sought refuge in emergent far-right groups like the one-time
Integrist Blas Piñar's Fuerza·Nueva and the Guerrilleros de
Cristo-Rey.[48]

[42] *Mundo*, 29 May 1971, provides an account of the repressive measures taken following the Montejurra rally of 1971.
[43] Paul Preston, *The Triumph of Democracy in Spain* (London, 1986), 63–4; Clemente,
Historia, pp. 268–72.
[44] Clemente, *Historia*, pp. 227–34; *sivattismo* lingered on, its founder and leader now
dead, into the 1980s: see *Unión Carlista* (Madrid), 1–5 (1981).
[45] 'Todos juntos en unión', *Cambio 16* (Madrid), 16–22 Feb. 1976.
[46] *Mundo*, 29 May 1971.
[47] *Informaciones* (Madrid), 8 May 1971.
[48] Blas Piñar had been a frequent speaker at Carlist meetings during the heyday of
Valiente's leadership in the early to mid-1960s: e.g. at Montejurra 1964. See *Boina Roja*,
90 (June 1964), and 92 (Aug. 1964). On *Fuerza Nueva* and the far right in the 1970s, see

The appearance of Carlist socialism in the 1970s provoked a further split on the part of die-hard Traditionalists and some of the more intransigently rightist elements of the Carlist youth. Having in 1973 re-formed the Traditionalist Communion,[49] late in 1975 these neo-traditionalists found themselves a leader, or at least a figurehead: none other than Carlos Hugo's younger brother, Sixto of Bourbon-Parma, a maverick who, far from sharing in the rest of his family's activities, had for several years been moving in extreme right-wing circles in Europe and Latin America. This latest schism was baptized in blood at the Montejurra rally of 1976, when supporters of 'Sixto-Rey' fired on those of Carlos Hugo, causing two deaths and several injuries. The full story of 'Montejurra '76', of the involvement of Spanish and non-Spanish neo-Fascist organizations, and of the possible complicity of individuals in the then Spanish government of Arias Navarro, has yet to be told. Nothing, however, could have illustrated more graphically than this episode the bizarre condition of a cause torn between advocates of socialism and fellow-travellers of Fascism.[50]

The Spanish throne was now, of course, occupied once more. For the Carlist Party, Juan Carlos's accession proved even more damaging than might have been anticipated. However disappointing Franco's choice of successor had been at the time, the expectation during the early 1970s that Juan Carlos would preside meekly over the continuation of *franquismo* had given Carlos Hugo's dynastic claim a *raison d'être* and his party a semblance of plausibility. His credibility as a 'democratic alternative' to a neo-*franquista* monarchy, never remotely strong, was utterly destroyed by Juan Carlos's emergence as agent and defender of a new democracy. Democracy itself, so much desired by Carlos Hugo's loyalists, brutally exposed his party's electoral and political limitations. Having repudiated its own right-wing past and with it the possibility of dominating the extreme right within a

Paul Preston, *Las derechas españolas en el siglo XX: Autoritarismo, fascismo y golpismo* (Madrid, 1986), 135–41.

[49] 'El Requeté, representado por sus mandos naturales, ante la gravedad del momento presente, siguiendo el mandato de nuestros muertos en tres guerras por traición perdidas, asume la tarea de rehacer la Comunión Tradicionalista', Madrid, 8 Dec. 1983. (I am grateful to Professor Alexandra Wilhelmsen for providing me with a photocopy of this document.) See also interview with Orts Timoner, a leading figure in the re-formed Tradionalist Communion, in *España 21*, 1–15 Sept. 1976.

[50] Josep Carles Clemente and Carles S. Costa, *Montejurra 76* (Barcelona, 1976), 87–144, 167–202, provides an account of the Montejurra events and a wide selection of press comment.

democratic Spain, the Carlist Party found itself totally overshadowed on the left by the big battalions of the Socialist and Communist Parties. With his party's base disintegrating around him, Carlos Hugo met Juan Carlos in 1978 for a family reconciliation, and announced that he no longer intended to press his dynastic claim. At the end of 1979, during which year he had finally been granted Spanish citizenship and led his party to electoral failure, he resigned as president of the Carlist Party. The break-up in 1981 of Carlos Hugo's marriage to Irene of the Netherlands seemed to symbolize the end of the extraordinary adventure to which he had committed himself a quarter of a century before.[51]

To proclaim the demise of a movement as enduring and protean as Carlism is doubtless rash, but from the perspective of the 1990s the risk appears justified. Of course there persist in Spain Carlist and Traditionalist *grupúsculos*, from the pathetic relics of the Carlist Party on the left to a bewildering motley of organizations on the far right. Since there is little in a democracy to inhibit the political activities of the ideologically passionate, the naïvely sentimental, the self-indulgent, and the downright sinister, there is no reason to think that the further shores of Spanish politics will not for a long time to come harbour small groups claiming to keep alive the Carlist heritage. Nevertheless it is probably safe to suggest that as a significant phenomenon Carlism now belongs to the history rather than the politics of Spain.

The last half-century of Carlism's odyssey, dominated as it has been by conflicts among rival élite factions, offers interesting insights into the élites–masses relationship. From 1937 down to 1957, members of the Carlist élite, mostly those who had run the movement during its revival in the 1930s and had survived the Civil War, argued among themselves as to the relationship of Carlism with the Franco regime, the identity of its rightful standard-bearer, and the very essence and future of the cause. During much of this period the 'pueblo carlista' remained passive and isolated. Following the climactic events of the mid-1950s, the *javieristas*, left as the sole protagonists of a discrete Carlism, faced the need to revitalize their links with the masses, and to mobilize the latter in ways relevant to a changed and changing situation. In the years roughly bounded by the sacking of Fal Conde (1955) and the expulsion from Spain of the Carlist dynasty (1969), a newer,

[51] *The Times*, 27 May 1981.

younger directive élite emerged, comprised like its predecessors of both 'Carlists by descent' and 'infiltrators'. At first with the encouragement of the incumbent leadership, but later in conflict with it, the new generation reinterpreted Carlist history, ideology, and policy so as to maximize the movement's popular, and populist, appeal against the national and international background of the 1960s.

Despite all the talk of the 'pueblo carlista', this remained an overwhelmingly 'top downards' process, symbolized by the powerful role of Carlos Hugo. Impressionistic evidence nevertheless suggests that the approach was successful as long as it remained an essentially populist one, and as long as the Carlist leadership was able to play the double game of opposing aspects of the regime from within while hoping to divert Franco from designating Juan Carlos as his eventual successor. The failure of this strategy precipitated Carlism from 1969 onwards into a spiral of open opposition, victimization at the hands of the authorities, and headlong flight towards the 'Carlist socialism' finally proclaimed in 1972.

This last development was an intrinsically fascinating one, which it has been possible to examine only briefly here. While it is striking that an explicitly socialist party should have succeeded in attracting over a number of years the support of a significant proportion of Spain's Carlists, the fact remains that from 1969 this support did decline steadily, and by the late 1970s rapidly and terminally, from the levels achieved by the looser, populist approach of the 1960s. Carlist socialism itself unquestionably alienated many who had been able to see in mere populism whatever they wished to see. The death of Franco and the rapid transition to a democratic regime were nevertheless decisive. With Juan Carlos combining monarchy and democracy, and others offering more credible paths to socialism, it is not surprising that the limb along which the Carlist Party had been moving should eventually have fallen from the tree. It may well be true, as Carlist Party propagandists tirelessly asserted, that one way—for them the only way—of understanding the history of Carlism during its first hundred years is as that of a unique, autonomous, self-perpetuating popular constituency, the 'pueblo carlista', falling captive to a succession of intrusive, manipulative élites: *apostólicos*, neo-Catholics, Integrists, and Traditionalists. Perhaps, save in the ideological outlook of the élite concerned, Carlism's final phase as a socialist party was not so very different.

11. DECAY, DIVISION, AND THE DEFENCE OF DICTATORSHIP: THE MILITARY AND POLITICS, 1939–1975

Paul Preston

At the beginning of the Spanish Civil War, General Mola stated that 'the reconstruction of Spain on a new basis is the exclusive task of the military, a task which corresponds to us by right, because it is the desire of the nation and because we have an exact concept of our power to do so'.[1] Mola's brutal statement could not have more clearly revealed the arrogance typical of certain parts of the military establishment. The idea that the nation's political destiny lay in the hands of soldiers was a commonplace of military ideology. Moreover, it was a belief readily accepted by the beleaguered upper and middle classes. They turned to the army in 1936 precisely because of their confidence that the military conception of the national destiny was such as to guarantee the defence of oligarchical privileges and middle-class social, economic, and religious interests.

Mola would no doubt have been surprised had he been present thirty-three years later when General Narciso Ariza, director of the Escuela de Estado Mayor (General Staff College), made a speech on 4 May 1970 about the lamentable condition of the armed forces as regards equipment, resources, and salaries. Claiming that the rapid economic development of the 1960s had passed the military by, Ariza described the armed forces as the 'poor relation of the boom' (*pariente pobre del desarrollo*). He was dismissed from his post. However, the fact that Ariza had been prepared to take the risk was a clear indication of the resentment felt among the high command about the fortunes being made elsewhere in the Francoist élite during the boom.[2] Mola would have been even more surprised to discover that in the 1970s Spanish society would increasingly reject the political destiny mapped out for it in 1939. The journey from swaggering arrogance in the 1940s to

---

[1] Julio Gonzalo Soto, *Esbozo de una síntesis del ideario de Mola* (Burgos, 1937), 53 (quoted by Josep Fontana, 'Reflexiones sobre la naturaleza y las consecuencias del franquismo', in *España bajo el franquismo* (Barcelona, 1986), 13.

[2] *Le Monde*, 12 May 1970.

political isolation and technical decay in the 1970s reflected the use to which General Franco had put the army since the Civil War. The sense of near omnipotence discernible in Mola's remarks was born of the fact that the Spanish armed forces, which had not won a war against an external enemy from the War of Independence to the Battle of Alhucemas in 1925, were used to fighting, and winning, against the civilian population. The despair of General Ariza reflected a sense of impotence born of the fact that, under Franco, Spain effectively lacked any kind of defence policy. With colonial wars fresh in the memory, Spanish army officers had still been able to feel a degree of professional pride in 1936. However, at the end of the 1960s, having just lost Ifni and Guinea, the remnants of Spanish Africa, those elements of the military with a developed sense of professionalism were appalled at the state of the armed forces.

A similar, and more ironic, reversal was evident in the relationship between the military and the Falange. In 1936, convinced of their role as the arbiters of the national destiny, senior army officers looked down on the Falangists as an unpleasant necessity, a rabble who provided some of the cannon-fodder of the war effort. Forty years later, that situation had been dramatically reversed. The Falangist old guard, known as the bunker because of its readiness to defend the dictatorship from the rubble, were confident of the support of the generation of ultra hard-line Francoist generals who now dominated the high command. Many of them had joined the army as extreme rightist volunteers during the Civil War, and became acting second lieutenants or *alféreces provisionales*. They had stayed on and, by the late 1960s and early 1970s, held posts of crucial importance in the military hierarchy. This military bunker joined its civilian counterparts in vain efforts to use the army to thwart the national will by blocking popular demands for democracy.

The tension between professional disquiet and political arrogance was constant in the military during the period 1939–77. Reminders of victory in the Civil War, and of the army's role as the guardian of national destiny and as the bulwark against communism, freemasonry, and godlessness, were used to build an exaggerated sense of pride which in turn was used to compensate the army for its real professional decay. When divisions emerged, they usually had at their core unease at the political role assigned to the army by Franco. At one level, the military could hardly have been surprised by the turn of events. In 1936, important sectors of the officer corps had acquiesced in defending conservative interests rather than the nation as a whole. On the other hand, few officers could have foreseen the extent to which the army would be reduced to becoming an inert barrier against social and political progress. Other forces of the Francoist coalition evolved during the years of the dicatorship in response to social and economic change. The army in contrast simply became more alienated from society.

That was the inevitable consequence of its explicit political commitment to Franco. Moreover, it was conditioned by a military education system based on the inculcation of Civil War values, to the defence of what by the 1960s were increasingly anachronistic political structures. Divorced from civilian society by the fact of ruling over it through the system of military justice, the army became more like the foreign occupation force which its deployment around the major industrial towns inclined it to be. Military tribunals were responsible for the trial of offences committed by the regime's political and labour opponents, deemed to be 'military rebellion'. Effectively, from 1939 to 1975, Spain was under martial law, although the wartime emergency powers of the army were officially relinquished in 1948. For thirty-two-and-a-half of the thirty-six years of the regime, the Ministry of the Interior was in the hands of soldiers.[3]

The fact that Franco put his own immediate political requirements before Spain's need for coherent military plans or defence policy could be seen in the overall organizational structure which he adopted. On January 1938, he had created the Ministerio de Defensa Nacional which, had it been maintained, would have permitted the co-ordination of the armed forces, unity of command, combined purchasing, and economies of scale. However, by a law of 8 August 1939, the Ministry was redivided into three separate Army, Navy, and Air Force Ministries. The only co-ordination between them was henceforth provided by a joint General Staff and a National Defence Junta. Neither was much more than an advisory body to Franco himself. Lacking any military rationale, this was largely an exercise in divide and rule, which also significantly increased the preferment at Franco's disposal. It

---

[3] For a thorough account of a system in which the army was both protagonist and judge in public order cases, see Manuel Balbé, *Orden público y militarismo en la España constitucional 1812–1983* (Madrid, 1983), 402–49; Pierre Celhay, *Consejos de guerra en España* (Paris, 1976), 64–88; Dionisio Ridruejo, *Escrito en España* (2nd edn., Buenos Aires, 1964), 284; José Fortes and Restituto Valero, *Qué son las Fuerzas Armadas* (Barcelona, 1977), 13; Jesús Ynfante, *El Ejército de Franco y de Juan Carlos* (Paris, 1976), 95–9.

prevented the emergence of a powerful Minister of Defence capable of challenging Franco's own pre-eminence or even of merely being able to see and express the professional discontents of the three services. Franco himself was supreme commander, the *Generalísimo de los Ejércitos*, and the three military ministers were merely administrators. A similar divide-and-rule rationale may be perceived behind the decision to revive the eighteenth-century institution whereby the army was distributed geographically and administratively into nine *Capitanías Generales*, or military regions.[4] The historical origins and the operational irrelevance of the post of Captain General were indicated by the fact that three out of the nine were in Castile. The post provided another level of seniority to complicate lines of command. The same was true of the reintroduction of the rank of Lieutenant General which had been abolished by the Republic. It created a greater sense of hierarchy and increased competition for Franco's favour within the senior ranks. The consequent conflict of authorities did nothing for efficiency but, since they all ultimately depended on Franco, they enhanced the capacity of the Caudillo to play them off against each other.

The territorial deployment of the army's best-equipped units was not related to any possible international conflict but followed pre-Civil War dispositions. In consequence, it was dictated by the needs of controlling the industrial working class and to a lesser extent the North African colonies. Otherwise, the post-1939 armed forces in Spain were a ramshackle affair. They possessed large quantities of equipment acquired before and during the Civil War whose heterogeneity was an obstacle to efficiency. Moreover, already worn out by use in the war, it was soon rendered entirely obsolete by the vertiginous technological advances of the Second World War.[5] Captured Russian equipment was still in use in the Spanish army at the beginning of the 1950s. The decision to maintain a large force meant that an absurdly high proportion of the total military budget was absorbed by salary costs. Once normal administration and running costs were added, this left very little for manoeuvres, exercises, or new equipment, let alone for the thoroughgoing rearmament that was required. The basic infantry rifle was either the 1893 Mauser first issued during the Cuban War or

---

[4] Francisco Javier Mariñas, *General Varela: De soldado a general* (Barcelona, 1956), 237–9; Julio Busquets and Gabriel Cardona, 'Unas Fuerzas Armadas para el Movimiento', in Justino Sinova (ed.), *Historia del franquismo* (2 vols. Madrid, 1985), i. 168–9.

[5] Fortes and Valero, *Fuerzas Armadas*, pp. 42–3.

the 1916 Mauser or else one of eight different foreign rifles or carbines. There were ten different types of machine-gun in service and four types of hand-grenade. The mortars, cannons, and armoured cars were museum pieces. At the outbreak of the Second World War, the Spanish army moved on foot, wore second-hand uniforms and rope sandals (*alpargatas de esparto*), carried its equipment on the backs of mules or on horse-drawn carts and lived in poor conditions on execrable rations. Moreover, at a time when the techniques of war were changing dramatically, of 22,100 officers, only 94 were trained in the command of tank and armoured car units, only 377 had taken radio transmission courses, and only 104 were skilled in topography.[6]

Penury might have been expected to be the seedbed of future military discontent. However, despite the deficiencies of its equipment and the fact that salary levels were relatively low, the morale of the Spanish armed forces was extremely buoyant. Spirits were high because of the recent victory in a war in which their cause had been legitimized by the Church as being for the defence of Christian civilization. Moreover, the fact that the German and Italian allies in the Civil War were expecting a forthcoming war to redistribute the political geography of Europe contributed briefly to a sense of bellicose expectation. In any case, there were numerous economic supplements for low salaries, if hardly for deficient equipment. In a period of acute hunger for the civilian population, with diseases like tuberculosis, typhoid, and rickets rampant, special military foodstores (*economatos*) and pharmacies were well stocked with food and medicines at subsidized prices, and there was an exclusive medical service at the disposal of military personnel. Access to supplies provided obvious opportunities for participation in the black market which were taken by some officers. There were other additional benefits such as housing facilities and widespread educational provision for the children of officers. These paternalist measures had the side-effect of intensifying the isolation of the military from civilian society.[7] In addition, wartime salaries were increased considerably on 1 July 1940, albeit on an extremely low base.[8]

[6] Busquets and Cardona, 'Fuerzas Armadas', pp. 170–1; cf. a report by General Arsenio Martínez Campos written for the Alto Estado Mayor in May 1940, quoted by Javier Tusell and Genoveva García Queipo de Llano, *Franco y Mussolini: La política española durante la segunda guerra mundial* (Barcelona, 1985), 98.

[7] Julio Busquets, *El militar de carrera en España* (3rd edn. Barcelona, 1984), 214.

[8] The increase for colonels was by 15 per cent, for captains by 26 per cent, for first lieutenants by 40 per cent; Stanley G. Payne, *Politics and the Military in Modern Spain* (Stanford, 1967), 527; Coronel Jesús Pérez Salas, *Guerra en España (1936–1939)* (México D.F., 1947), 88–9.

Senior officers also had the additional reward of posts and sinecures in the civilian administration. Between 1936 and 1945, 31.3 per cent of senior posts in the civil service were held by army, navy, or air force officers. The posts of *subsecretarios* and director general in ministries, in local administrations, and in the military justice system abounded. Of the *procuradores* in the pseudo-parliament, the Cortes, 12.3 per cent were officers nominated by Franco; 34 per cent of senior posts in the Movimiento were held by military men. The biggest presence in any department other than the specifically military ministries was in the Presidencia del Gobierno, Franco's cabinet office, in which military men held twenty-six senior posts, 89.6 per cent of the total. In the Ministry of the Interior, officers held thirty-two senior posts, 49 per cent of the total. In the subsecretaría de Orden Pública within the Ministry of the Interior, 70 per cent of senior posts were held by officers. In the regime's first ten years of existence, 106 army officers held the job of civil governor of a province. Between 1938 and 1945, that constituted 38 per cent of the total of civil governors. From 1945 to 1960, officers made up a steady 22 per cent of the total.[9] There can be no doubt that such a prominent role in the civilian state apparatus not only handsomely supplemented the income of the officers concerned but also greatly augmented their self-esteem and professional pride.

However, if Franco still had any worries about military discontent, the spirit of unity and messianic anti-communism generated by the recent war and also the generational structure of the armed forces would have reassured him. The greatest source of dissent would be found among the Caudillo's peers, the high command. It was dominated by Africanista generals and senior colonels who had risen to prominence during the Moroccan wars, had been behind the 1936 military rising and had voted to make Franco supreme commander, generalísimo, and head of state on 28 September 1936. None had done so in order to make Franco *de facto* regent for life and most were anxious to see an early monarchical restoration. However, of those who had started out in the war, many were already dead—Sanjurjo, Mola, Fanjul, Goded, Cabanellas—some in suspicious circumstances.[10]

---

[9] Carlos Viver Pi Sunyer, *El personal político de Franco (1936–1945)* (Barcelona, 1978), 70–2; Miguel Jerez Mir, *Elites políticas y centros de extracción en España 1938–1957* (Madrid, 1982), 228–39.

[10] Paul Preston, 'Franco and the Hand of Providence', in John M. Merriman (ed.), *For Want of a Horse: Choice and Chance in History* (Lexington, Mass., 1985).

Others—Queipo de Llano, Yagüe, Kindelán, Aranda, Varela, Orgaz, García Valiño—would mount some timid opposition to Franco in the 1940s. Their dissidence consisted largely of muted attempts to oblige Franco to keep Spain out of the Second World War and, as it became clearer that an Axis defeat was likely, to make provision for a monarchist restoration. However, their remonstrations aside, Franco had relatively little to worry about. As a caste, the Africanistas had reached a level of seniority when the risks of conspiracy were no longer attractive. Moreover, they also had their ambitions and Franco was supremely skilful in maintaining their loyalty by the cunning distribution of post, promotions, decorations, pensions, and even titles of nobility.[11]

Below the most senior generals, the Caudillo had even less to worry about. The ranks which in many armies often produce dangerous machinations were, for different reasons, of proven loyalty to Franco. Many colonels, majors, and captains were of the generation educated at the Academia General Militar de Zaragoza in its so-called second epoch between 1927 and 1931, under the direction of General Franco himself.[12] In the period in which Franco had been able to impose his views on the Academy, the level of technical education had been lamentable and stress laid on anti-democratic indoctrination. The teaching body had been dominated by Africanista friends of Franco, noted more for their ideological rigidity than for their intellectual attainments and brutalized by their experiences in a minor but cruel colonial war. They included Franco's close friend Camilo Alonso Vega, later to be a dour Minister of the Interior, Bartolomé Barba Hernández, later to be leader of the conspiratorial organization Unión Militar Española and Emilio Esteban Infantes, later to be involved in the attempted Sanjurjo coup of 1932. Virtually without exception, the Academy's teachers were to be prominent in the military uprising of 1936. With such men on the teaching staff, the AGM had concentrated on inculcating the ruthless arrogance of the Foreign Legion, the idea that the army was the supreme arbiter of the nation's political destiny, and a sense of discipline and blind obedience. Franco's brother Ramón wrote to him to complain of the 'troglodytic education' imparted at the Academia

---

[11] Alfredo Kindelán, *La verdad de mis relaciones con Franco* (Barcelona, 1981), 118; José María Gil Robles, diary entry for 15 Jan. 1943, *La monarquía por la que yo luché (1941–1954)* (Madrid, 1976), 27.

[12] Mariano Aguilar Olivencia, *El ejército español durante la segunda República* (Madrid, 1986), 119–29.

General Militar. A high proportion of the officers who passed through the AGM were later to be involved in the Falange.[13]

The lieutenants and junior captains were dominated by the so-called *alféreces provisionales*. Largely Falangist, with some Carlist, volunteers, these 'acting second-lieutenants' had swelled the ranks of the army in the early days of the Civil War. Many stayed on after 1939. After a period of eight months study in the specially created Academias de Transformación, 10,709 were incorporated into the regular army as lieutenants between 1939 and 1946. That was the equivalent of fifty years of graduates from the military academies.[14] The glut of *alféreces provisionales*, in a system based on promotion only by strict seniority, would soon choke promotion channels. Even where preference was not given to *alféreces provisionales*, their mere presence blocked or slowed down the promotion of better-trained officers from the academies. This undermined morale and devalued initiative. The solution adopted, of occasional block promotions, did little to resolve the congestion and stagnation in the middle ranks.[15] However, from Franco's point of view, the political loyalty of the *alféreces provisionales* outweighed their military deficiences. Their ideological commitment ensured that they would be a loyal counter-balance to monarchist conspiracies against the victorious generalísimo, the *Jefe Nacional* of the Falange, and the man most likely to ensure that Spain would benefit from the forthcoming war for a new Fascist world order. As the years passed, that loyalty was consolidated by habit and by the 1970s the one-time *alféreces provisionales* were to be the fiercest defenders of the regime in its dying agony.

Problems with even younger generations would come later as they reached more senior ranks. In the 1950s and 1960s, it was to be officers produced by the revived AGM who would rankle at the inefficiency of an under-resourced army. Despite a transitory boost to military morale provided by the guerrilla war of 1945–7, the unchanging penury of the armed forces continued to take its toll in the early 1950s. There was the minimum of professional activity, extremely poor equipment, and limited career prospects.[16] Spain's lamentable

---

[13] Guillermo Cabanellas, *Cuatro generales* (Barcelona, 1977), 140, 142; Pérez Salas, *Guerra*, pp. 85–7; Antonio Cordón, *Trayectoria (recuerdos de un artillero)* (Paris, 1971), 192–4; Busquets, *El militar*, pp. 117–39.

[14] Carlos Iniesta Cano, *Memorias y recuerdos* (Barcelona, 1984), 141–2; Busquets, *El militar*, pp. 107–8, 263, gives slightly contradictory figures.

[15] Balbé, *Orden público*, p. 437; Busquets, *El militar*, pp. 109–14.

[16] Manuel Gutiérrez Mellado, *Un soldado de España* (Barcelona, 1983), 55–6.

economic situation did not permit any significant renovation of equipment. Nevertheless, the military budget itself remained high because of the still-inflated officer corps. Equipment was delapidated when not technologically obsolete and often out of use for lack of spare parts. There were insufficient funds for petrol and ammunition for exercises and manoeuvres other than drilling on open spaces near bases. The exceptions were the units based in Spanish Africa and the air force. Even the latter was humiliated by being equipped with German-designed aircraft of Second World War vintage, Messerschmidt 109, Heinkel He 111, and Junkers Ju 52, built under licence. To prevent discontent reaching boiling point, substantial pay rises of 40 per cent were decreed across the board in 1949,[17] the first since 1940.

Two other things helped keep dissent under control, the international situation and a slide into cynicism. The ongoing action against the communist guerrilla and the sense of beleaguerment drummed up by the regime in response to the international ostracism to which Spain was subject at this time helped unite the armed forces around the Caudillo. He was helped by the outbreak of the Korean War in June 1950. The generalized fear of world war had the effect within the Spanish forces of intensifying awareness of poor equipment but banishing any thoughts of dissent. Franco for his part made a major effort to rekindle the military spirit of anti-communism. At the same time, he made a successful bid to ingratiate himself with the Western Allies by an offer at the end of July to send Spanish troops to fight in Korea. Convinced also that, in the event of war with the Eastern bloc, if Europe fell, the USA would need a base on which to land men and material, Franco offered Spain as a last redoubt. This was to help dramatically in his quest for international recognition, despite being a meaningless offer, given the technological backwardness of his armed forces and the lamentably antiquated condition of Spain's road, rail, and port infrastructure. Franco himself admitted to the American Admiral Forrest P. Sherman that the Spanish armed forces had no radar and were short of aircraft, heavy tanks, anti-aircraft, and anti-tank equipment.[18]

In consequence, morale continued to plummet. As it reached its lowest ebb, the situation was saved by the signing on 26 September

[17] Payne, *Politics and the Military*, p. 532.

[18] Angel Viñas, *Los pactos secretos de Franco con Estados Unidos* (Barcelona, 1981), 88–9, 99; Ricardo de la Cierva, *Historia del franquismo*, ii, *Aislamiento, transformación, agonía (1945–1975)* (Barcelona, 1978), 92–3; Juan Antonio Ansaldo, *¿Para qué ..? De Alfonso XIII a Juan III* (Buenos Aires, 1951), 523–5.

1953 of the Defence Pacts with the USA and the arrival of massive economic, military, and technological assistance. In return, Franco permitted the establishment of American air bases at Torrejón near Madrid, Saragossa, and Morón and a naval base at Rota in Cádiz, as well as an enormous range of smaller installations. The benefits for the regime were the integration of Spain into the Western system, the transfer of the bulk of non-salary military expenses out of the general budget, and the neutralization of military discontent over resources. The acquisition of more modern equipment than hitherto available and training in its use had obvious attractions for most, if not all, officers. The newly arrived armoured cars and tanks were to be refused by certain cavalry regiments whose generals reaffirmed the values of horsemanship.[19] However, improved technical preparation was welcomed by the more professionally aware officers though it was weighed against the diminution of national sovereignty and the fact that the majority of the equipment was second-hand. The tanks and the destroyers acquired had seen service in the Second World War and the jet planes and the more powerful artillery in Korea.[20]

The replacement of equipment courtesy of the Americans did little to resolve the problem of pay levels drifting along behind inflation. Increasing numbers of officers began to take civilian jobs in addition to their commissions. The sense of professional shame engendered by this necessity was counter-balanced by an increased stress on the special mission of the army and its 'apartness' from civil society. An intensification of the rhetoric of the Civil War filled the gap in professional pride for the majority. However, it was not accepted by all officers.[21] A significant minority of officers were forced by the need for supplementary civilian employment to extend their studies. This brought them into contact with civilian society and gave them a higher technical awareness and in consequence a somewhat more critical perspective on military problems. A few joined a society for cadets with religious, social, and professional preoccupations, called Forja and run by Colonel Luis Pinilla and Fr. José María Llanos. It developed in the 1950s into a private college preparing students for the military academies. It was closed down by the authorities at the end of the

[19] Busquets, *El militar*, p. 253.
[20] Gutiérrez Mellado, *Un soldado*, p. 56.
[21] A sense of the lack of direction felt by many officers can be gleaned from one of the more fortunate generals, Franco's cousin, in command of a relatively well-equipped unit stationed just outside Madrid, Francisco Franco Salgado Araujo, *Mi vida junto a Franco* (Barcelona, 1977), 328–9.

decade, but some of its products were to be involved in the 1970s in efforts made by the Unión Militar Democrática to ensure that the *azules* would not block progress to democracy.[22] Although politically moderate, the officers associated with the UMD would constitute one extreme of military politics. The other was made up of the die-hard Francoists known as *azules* (blues/Falangists).

In the middle, there were a number of relatively liberal officers, liberal, that is, by comparison with the *azules*. Their central concern was to raise the professionalism of the armed forces. They did not endorse the determination of the extreme right in the mid-1970s to use the army as the praetorian guard of a regime increasingly rejected by the bulk of society. Indeed, by the late 1960s, there would emerge a visible conflict between some of the more technocratic graduates of the AGM and the one-time *alféreces provisionales*. The former, while still extremely conservative, were interested in improving training, equipment, and contacts with other Western armies. Their concerns were technical rather than political. They believed that the armed forces should be truly apolitical. That brought them into conflict with frenetically committed *generales azules* like Angel Campano, Jaime Milans del Bosch, and Jesús González del Yerro. The military bunker also used the rhetoric of apoliticism. However, for them, political neutrality meant unquestioning loyalty to Franco and a determination to perpetuate the dictatorship.

This became apparent in the aftermath of the vertiginous social and economic change of the 1960s in Spain. At precisely the time that Franco's own physical strength was waning, his regime was becoming ever more anachronistic. From the early 1960s to the Caudillo's death anxiety festered for those officers who gave thought to politics and to the future. Student and labour unrest were on the increase and they would soon be augmented by opposition to the regime from the Church and the regions. For some, a growing awareness of the army's inadequacy as a national defence force and of its social isolation were causes of deep disquiet. Others simply accepted that the job of the army was to protect the regime. This was reflected in the fact that the Ley Orgánica del Estado introduced in 1966 contained the explicit statement that the job of the armed forces was 'to guarantee the unity and independence of the fatherland, the integrity of its territories and national security and the defence of the institutional order'. The

[22] Julio Busquets, *Pronunciamientos y golpes de Estado en España* (Barcelona, 1982), 142–5.

repressive function of the military was stressed by Admiral Carrero Blanco in a speech to the Escuela de Estado Mayor on 24 April 1968. In it he underlined publicly what had hitherto been the unspoken premise of the Francoist army, that national defence took a back seat to political repression.[23]

Concerns about the political future were the divisive obsession of both civilian and military Francoists throughout the 1960s. Within the armed forces, the fault lines ran between those who were happy with a conception of the army as an instrument of political repression and therefore as the praetorian guard of an increasingly beleaguered regime and those who were not and were indeed disturbed by its technical and professional poverty. By the late 1960s, the *generales azules*, such as Alfonso Pérez Viñeta, Tomás García Rebull, Carlos Iniesta Cano, Angel Campano López—some, if not all, of whom had been *alféreces provisionales*—were reaching key operational positions. In collaboration with the civilian bunker, they would use their political influence to block reform from within the system and their repressive apparatus to smash opposition from outside. The military bunker was countered by those with a more professional view who were, by comparison, liberal. In the navy and the air force, the primacy of technocracy over politics was increasingly the norm. Within the army, however, the 'liberals', like Generals Manuel Diez Alegría, Manuel Gutiérrez Mellado, and Jesús Vega Rodríguez, were a minority within the high command albeit not throughout the officer corps as a whole.

Significantly perhaps, in the cabinet changes of 29 October 1969 which followed the internecine fighting between Falangists and members of Opus Dei after the Matesa affair, in which Opus Dei technocrats were accused of fraudulently diverting government funds into their own pockets, Franco chose as Minister of War, not an *azul* but a technocrat, General Juan Castañón de Mena.[24] The appointment of Castañón suggested that Franco did not share the wilder fantasies of the *azules*. However, his declining health and his reclusion in the Pardo surrounded by a clique of ultra-rightists made him increasingly susceptible to their view of the future. They were unconcerned about the effect of their views on public opinion. The more professional ele-

[23] Admiral Carrero Blanco, *Discursos y escritos 1943–1973* (Madrid, 1974), 212–15.

[24] *ABC*, 29 Oct. 1969. See the profile of Castañón in Equipo Mundo, *Los 90 Ministros de Franco* (Barcelona, 1970), 431–4; Rafael Calvo Serer, *La dictadura de los Franquistas* (Paris, 1973), 166, 168; Alfonso Armada, *Al servicio de la Corona* (Barcelona, 1983), pp. 68, 72, 78, 93–4, 100–1, 119, 121, 135; José Ignacio San Martín, *Servicio especial* (Barcelona, 1983), 198, 253; Laureano López Rodó, *La larga marcha hacia la monarquía* (Barcelona, 1977), 200.

ments, however, felt considerable disquiet at the distance opening up between the army and society. The repressive function of the army had already caused unease over the execution of the Communist Julián Grimau in April 1963. The army was losing what popular affection it might have enjoyed. In late 1967, press coverage of the personal use of official cars being made by senior officers had led to the vehicles of several generals being attacked by gangs of youths.[25] It is difficult to know precisely how much effect the Grimau affair had in producing popular opprobrium. However, there can be little doubt that the army's responsibility for the trial and punishment of political and labour infractions divorced it from civil society. Doubts about the wisdom of permitting the military to have the role of political oppressor were to deepen over the trials at Burgos in December 1970 of militants of the Basque revolutionary separatist organization ETA. On 1 December, the retired General Rafael García Valiño, who had been responsible for ratifying the execution of Grimau, wrote to General Tomás García Rebull, Captain General of the VI Military Region (Burgos) warning him not to let the army be used in a way which would estrange it from the people. He saw this danger in the use of military justice in the trial of actions for which a state should have its own proper instruments.[26]

However, with the gradual break-up of the regime discernible, the *azules* were willing accomplices in an operation to block change. There was festering resentment among the *azules* of the rising tide of student, ecclesiastical, regional, and labour discontent and of the failure of the civilian apparatus to stem it. They believed that the State was simply not doing its job and that politicians were too busy lining their pockets. The Burgos trials were taking place, after all, only seven months after General Narciso Ariza had been dismissed from the post of director of the Escuela de Estado Mayor for his complaints about the poverty of the armed forces. Throughout the 1970s, the *azules* would use their extreme version of the values of the Civil War in order to consolidate their influence within the immediate entourage of the Caudillo. They could then scupper attempts at reform from within the system, by mobilizing the Caudillo against them. Franco's progressive senility in the 1970s made it easier for them to manipulate him. In the mean

[25] Franco Salgado Araujo, diary entry for 4 Dec. 1967, *Mis conversaciones privadas con Franco* (Barcelona, 1976), 511–12.

[26] *Le Monde*, 11 Dec. 1970; Luis Suárez Fernández, *Franco y su tiempo* (8 vols Madrid, 1984), viii. 218–19; Edouard de Blaye, *Franco and the Politics of Spain* (Harmondsworth, 1976), 302–3.

time, however, some just got on with the job of repressing what they saw as subversion. In particular, General Pérez Viñeta, as Captain General of Barcelona, stimulated Franco's enthusiasm by the energy with which he acted against the left-wing and liberal activities of priests and university students.[27] On the last day of the Burgos trials, 9 December 1970, Pérez Viñeta declared at a military ceremony in Mérida, 'The army is not in the least disposed to permit a return to the disorder and indiscipline which have once already imperilled our country. If necessary, a new crusade will be launched to rid Spain of men who acknowledge neither god nor law'.[28]

Pérez Viñeta was not alone in his belief that civilian politicians were incapable of maintaining order. There were rumours of secret associations of over 5,000 junior officers, mostly captains and majors, who since August 1970 had been meeting to discuss what they discerned as a deterioration of the political situation. With their slow promotions and poor pay, they were resentful of the fortunes being made in the economic boom. They were especially outraged by the Matesa affair. The Burgos trials and the anti-military propaganda provoked by it were the most obvious symptom of a deteriorating order, although there were also minor incidents of officers being insulted in the streets.[29] In response to international and timid domestic criticism of the trials, a bilious resentment fermented among ultra officers and was expressed in terms of contempt for the technocrats. In the Madrid military region, officers from key units, including the División Acorazada and the BRIPAC, or parachute brigade, the two crucial operational units for the control of the capital, began to meet to voice their complaints.[30] On 14 December 1970, the Captain General of Madrid, General Joaquín Fernández de Córdoba, called a meeting of twenty-odd generals and colonels to discuss the implications of the Burgos trials. They concluded that the opposition had been allowed to go too far and produced a manifesto calling for more energetic government. A delegation consisting of Fernández de Córdoba, García Rebull, Pérez Viñeta, and the Captain General of Seville, Manuel Chamorro, visited Franco to inform him of their deliberations. The Caudillo called an emergency cabinet meeting at which the Minister of the Interior, General Tomás Garicano Goñi, and the three military

[27] *Le Monde*, 14 Mar. 1969; Franco Salgado Araujo, diary entries for 30 Jan., 1 Mar., and 14 Apr. 1969, *Mis conversaciones*, pp. 540, 541, 547.

[28] Blaye, *Franco* p. 304.

[29] *Le Monde*, 29 Dec. 1970.

[30] San Martín, *Servicio especial*, pp. 168–9.

ministers called for the suspension of habeas corpus. Franco went along with them.[31]

The atmosphere was screwed even tighter on 16 December by a demonstration outside military headquarters in Burgos by army officers and Falangists. They were addressed by García Rebull. Not a sophisticated man, he was devoted to the Francoism and was a willing collaborator of those Falangists who were seeking military support to prevent change after the death of Franco. On the following day, many army officers joined in the massive demonstration outside the Palacio de Oriente.[32] The army wanted the strongest sentences against those on trial. When García Rebull hesitated to confirm the death sentences for the reasons indicated to him in García Valiño's letter, he was subjected to pressure for a hard line by delegations of officers from all over Spain. Some called for the executions to be by garrotte instead of by firing squad. Pérez Viñeta called García Rebull a 'softie' (*blando*).[33]

Although the army was united in wanting to see the defendants given death sentences, the more liberal elements were open to the idea of a pardon. Castañón and the other two military ministers recommended mercy at the cabinet meeting called on 29 December 1970. However, despite the fact that Franco subsequently pardoned the defendants, the army was left feeling, as García Valiño had predicted, that it had somehow been besmirched.[34] There were liberals who drew the conclusion that the army should distance itself from a regime in decomposition. A substantial group, however, believed that, now more than ever, the army should be defending the regime. Pérez Viñeta addressed a demonstration outside the headquarters of the VI Military Region and spoke again of the need for another crusade.[35] His words were a barely veiled criticism of the Opus Dei technocrats who ruled Spain's political destinies. Given Pérez Viñeta's closeness to Franco and the fact that his retirement was imminent, his indiscretion went unpunished.

Nevertheless, the military bunker's vision of the future was severely at odds with that of Carrero Blanco and the Opus Dei who were planning a modified Francoism under Juan Carlos. Accordingly, when

---

[31] *Le Monde*, 16, 18 Dec. 1970.
[32] Blaye, *Franco*, pp. 304–10; Vicente Gil, *Cuarenta años junto a Franco* (Barcelona, 1981), 140.
[33] *Le Monde*, 29 Dec. 1970; *L'Express*, 4 Jan. 1971.
[34] Suárez Fernández, *Franco*, viii. 221; *Times*, 11 Oct. 1971.
[35] *Le Monde*, 30 Dec. 1970.

General Fernando Rodrigo Cifuentes, Captain General of Granada, emulated Pérez Viñeta, he was punished. An energetic opponent of left-wing and liberal priests, students, and workers, he was none the less sacked on 8 January 1971 and placed under house arrest as a result of a speech made on the occasion of the Pascua Militar (the formal military celebration of the Epiphany). His offence was not his call for a harder line but rather his criticism of Carrero Blanco and the technocrats. In the aftermath of the Matesa affair, the term technocrat had come to be synonymous in ultra-rightist circles with civilian weakness. Rodrigo's speech, with its remarks about 'white freemasons' struck a chord in the hearts of many soldiers who were unhappy about the conduct of the Burgos trials and their outcome. He was inundated with telegrams of support, although he did nothing to encourage hopes that he might lead a faction to reimpose 'authority'. Within a few weeks, a similar incident occurred when the Captain General of Saragossa, Gonzalo Fernández de Córdoba, made a similar speech and was transferred to the general staff.[36]

Less vocal hard-liners, however, were rewarded for their loyalty to the regime during the Burgos crisis. García Rebull, a close friend of the Falangist ultra, José Antonio Girón de Velasco was promoted to be Captain General of the I Military Region, Madrid. Another crony of Girón, Carlos Iniesta Cano, was made Director General of the Civil Guard. These promotions reflected the extent to which Franco himself, or those in his immediate entourage, realized that the resurgence of opposition increasingly placed upon the army the onus for the defence of the regime against change. One of the key tasks would be the control of Madrid. The military governor of the capital, General Angel Campano López, had nailed his colours firmly to the mast during the Burgos trials with the widely publicized remark that what was needed was to impose martial law for a week and to shoot a thousand leftists.[37]

Through the Hermandad de Alféreces Provisionales and the ultra-rightist press, a major effort was being made to attract support within the army for the so-called *inmovilista* option. The same Falangists who had seen themselves defeated politically by the Opus Dei in the course of the 1960s were happy to generate military criticism of corrupt technocrats. Ultra officers effectively banned legally published journals and magazines from barracks and virtually imposed the reading of the

[36] Calvo Serer, *La dictadura*, p. 236; San Martín, *Servicio especial*, p. 268; Blaye, *Franco*, pp. 324–5.
[37] *Mundo Obrero*, 22 Jan.; *Le Monde Diplomatique*, Jan. 1971.

publications of the extreme right such as *Fuerza Nueva*.[38] The 'ultras' had two centres of power within the army. On the one hand, the generation of *azules* dominated the senior ranks and were consistently given the crucial posts in the key units in terms of the regime's political security—the armoured division at Brunete and the parachute brigade outside Madrid, as well as the Military Governorship of Madrid, the Captaincy General of the I Military Region, and the Directorship of the Civil Guard. On the other hand, less senior ultras held the important command positions within the intelligence services. Some, but not all, of the ultras were *alféreces provisionales*. In 1974, 328 full colonels, 956 lieutenant-colonels, and 792 majors had been *alféreces provisionales*.[39]

One of them, General Campano, who had been decorated twice with the Iron Cross during his service in the División Azul on the Russian front, held the key posts in quick succession. Having commanded the División Acorazada, the armoured division which dominated Madrid, in the late 1950s, by the end of the 1960s he was military governor of Madrid, by 1972 Captain General of Burgos, by February 1973 Captain General of Madrid, and Director General of the Civil Guard six weeks before the death of Franco. Others had been Africanistas, often Falangists, and had fought in the División Azul. García Rebull, who had joined the Falange in 1934, had also been decorated with the Iron Cross in Russia. Prior to being Captain General of Burgos, he had also commanded the División Acorazada and often tested his men in manoeuvres to seize Madrid. After his retirement in February 1973 when he passed command of the I Military Region to General Campano, García Rebull devoted himself to his role as Jefe Nacional del Servicio de Asociaciones de Antiguos Combatientes.[40]

Every bit as important as the dominance of the senior ranks and command of the most important posts, was the *azules*' control of the ever-proliferating military intelligence services. With parallel and often overlapping concerns in the universities, the labour movement, and the Church, there were a dozen intelligence services of which the most potent were Army Intelligence (SIBE or Servicio de Información del Ejército de Tierra, Segunda Bis), the special service for the General Staff, set up by Muñoz Grandes in 1968, and the Servicio de

[38] *Le Monde*, 197 Dec. 1970; José Fortes and Luis Otero, *Proceso a nueve militares demócratas: Las Fuerzas Armadas y la UMD* (Barcelona, 1983), 22.
[39] 'Reflexión crítica sobre el Cuerpo de Oficiales' (a clandestine document drawn up by young Academy-trained officers) in Ynfante, *Ejército*, pp. 69–74.
[40] Pierre Celhay, *Consejos de guerra en España* (Paris, 1976), 106, 109–10.

Documentación de la Presidencia de Gobierno set up by Carrero Blanco in the early 1970s under Colonel José Ignacio San Martín and Colonel Federico Quintero, both of whom were to be involved in the attempted military coup of 23 February 1981.[41]

The rhetoric of apoliticism used by the *azules* permitted them to describe the military as 'above politics', at the service of permanent or eternal national values, such as those of the 'crusade' and the Franco regime. The army was therefore free to intervene against anyone who opposed the survival of the dictatorship. In the final crisis-ridden years of Francoism, the *azules* made no secret of their partisanship. clearly riddled with an element of panic, their views were expressed in numerous public political statements. In late August 1972, General Carlos Iniesta Cano, Director General of the Civil Guard and a *procurador* in the Cortes, made a speech in El Ferrol. Using the rhetoric of the Falange, he declared that 'Francoism can never disappear, because God does not want it to come to an end in Spain and, after Franco, Francoism will continue and there will be Francoism for centuries because Spain which is eternal and which has an eternal destiny in the universal scheme needs Francoism'. Shortly afterwards, General José María Pérez de Luna, Captain General of the Canary Islands, affirmed, in a speech on 24 October 1972, that 'the mission of the army is political in so far as it is encharged with defending the fatherland against the exterior and against the internal enemy'.[42]

The 'liberal' generals, like the Chief of the General Staff, Manuel Díez Alegría, were committed to the army remaining neutral.[43] The difficulties which he faced were illustrated by the fact that when he tried to introduce a single Ministry of Defence, he was villified by the ultra press and eventually hounded out of his post.[44] Younger liberal officers were working actively to prevent the *inmovilistas* blocking change altogether. In 1973, a group of junior and middle-rank officers issued an appeal to the officer corps expressing their concern that, in the political disintegration of the dictatorship, one faction, the ultras, were working to use the army for their own purposes. The assassination by ETA of Prime Minister

---

[41] San Martín, *Servicio especial*, pp. 21–45; José Luis Morales and Juan Celada, *La alternativa militar* (Madrid, 1981), 67–78; Ynfante, *Ejército*, pp. 24–9; Balbé, *Orden público*, pp. 447–9; Colectivo Democracia, *Los Ejércitos ... más allá del golpe* (Barcelona, 1981), 52–3.

[42] Celhay, *Consejos de guerra*, pp. 112, 118.

[43] *L'Express*, 14 Dec. 1970.

[44] Ynfante, *Ejército*, p. 77.

Admiral Carrero Blanco on 20 December 1973 provided a brief glimpse of the tensions simmering within the officer corps. As Director General of the Civil Guard, Carlos Iniesta Cano issued an order for his men to repress subversives and demonstrators energetically 'without restricting in any way the use of firearms'. He explicitly ordered them to go beyond their rural jurisdiction and keep order in urban centres. It was a gross abuse of his authority. Cooler heads prevailed. After taking advice from the Chief of the General Staff, a triumvirate consisting of the Minister of the Interior Carlos Arias Navarro, the senior military minister Admiral Gabriel Pita da Veiga, and the interim prime minister Torcuato Fernández Miranda, acted to prevent a blood-bath. Within less than an hour, Iniesta was obliged to withdraw his telegram.[45]

Much more dramatic than the assassination of Carrero Blanco in intensifying divisions within the officer corps was the fall of the dictatorship in Portugal. Apart from disagreements over the wisdom of unleashing a night of the long knives against the left, the armed forces had been united in outrage at the murder of the prime minister. The Portuguese revolution of April 1974 polarized the ultras and liberals within the officer corps. Both events could only intensify fears for the future but the two major factions reacted differently, the liberals prepared to consider change and adjustment before it was too late, the ultras ready to batten down the hatches. Innumerable declarations were made dismissing the events in Portugal as irrelevant to the Spanish situation. General Jesús González del Yerro, an increasingly influential hard-liner and director of the Escuela del Estado Mayor del Ejército, told the press that 'the Spanish Army does not have rifles in order to decorate them with carnations and carnations do not bloom in the barrel of a gun'.[46] Despite such assertions, liberal junior officers were soon busy working to create the Unión Militar Democrática. In response to that disturbing development, the ultras resorted to their secret weapon, the intelligence services.

The military intelligence services responded with strenuous efforts to root out any Portuguese-style leftism within the armed forces. At the

---

[45] *Pueblo*, 22 Dec. 1973; Iniesta Cano, *Memorias* (Barcelona, 1984), pp. 218–22; San Martín, *Servicio especial*, pp. 90–114; Joaquín Bardavio, *La crisis: Historia de quince días* (Madrid, 1974), 111–16; *El País Equipo de Investigación, Golpe mortal: Asesinato de Carrero y agonía del franquismo* (Madrid, 1983), 184–7. The Communists claimed to have been in contact with Díez Alegría, but he denied this. Conversation of the author with Santiago Carrillo. See *Golpe mortal*, pp. 211–12.

[46] Morales and Celada, *Alternativa*, p. 26.

same time, the senior *azules*, both military and civilian, were distressed by the public, albeit intensely feeble, commitment to political reform of Prime Minister Carlos Arias Navarro. While José Antonio Girón launched the broadside against Arias known as the *Gironazo*, the military bunker set about blocking any slide to liberalism in the armed forces. A powerful group including the retired García Rebull, the Captain General of the VII Military Region, Valladolid, Pedro Merry Gordon, and of the I Military Region, Campano, and the Director General of the Civil Guard, Iniesta Cano, plotted to establish and maintain total control of the crucial sectors of the army. While Girón and other civilian ultras attacked the regime, García Rebull declared that he regarded political parties as 'the opium of the people' and politicians as 'vampires'. The parallel military scheme was for Iniesta to side-step his own imminent retirement and to replace the liberal Manuel Díez Alegría as Chief of the General Staff. Campano would take over as Director General of the Civil Guard and there was to be a purge of officers suspected of liberalism. The scheme enjoyed the support of Franco's personal entourage although the failing Caudillo was not kept informed. In fact, apart from that part of the plan concerning Iniesta, it was eventually, if not immediately, successful. The Minister for the Army, General Francisco Coloma Gallegos, was not sympathetic to Iniesta's plan to beat retirement and forced him to retire on schedule on 12 May 1974. However, Díez Alegría was removed from his post after a trip to Romania for medical treatment during which he met President Ceaucescu. He was replaced by the hard-line Captain General of the VIII Military Region, La Coruña, Carlos Fernández Vallespín. The removal of Díez Alegría was an enormous triumph for the ultras and greatly facilitated their efforts to put the army at the service of the civilian bunker. In parallel with the activities of Iniesta, the civilian extreme right was also mobilizing and Girón's Asociación Nacional de Ex-Combatientes changed its name to the Asociación Nacional de Combatientes.[47]

Just as the most senior ultras were closing ranks with the civilian bunker to prepare the last-ditch defence of the regime, liberal middle-rank and junior officers were meeting to discuss how to prevent the army blocking the increasing nationwide drive towards democracy. In Barcelona, a group of captains gathered around the seminal figure of

[47] *Le Monde*, 15 May 1974; *Financial Times*, 29 May 1974; Gutiérrez Mellado, *Un soldado*, pp. 47–9; Paul Preston, *The Triumph of Democracy in Spain* (London, 1976), 60–2.

Major Julio Busquets Bragulat, and in Madrid around Major Luis Otero. By the summer of 1974, the two groups were moving towards issuing the manifesto of what was to become in September 1974 the Unión Militar Democrática. The manifesto showed that the leaders of the UMD aspired to be truly apolitical, aiming only to prevent the army continuing to be the guardian of the system against the popular will. Accordingly, they called for all forces of the democratic opposition to unite while themselves refused steadfastly to be associated with any one group. Their model for how this should happen was the broad political front known as the Assemblea de Catalunya, although they were also influenced by the liberal Christian Democrat Joaquín Ruiz Giménez and, through Busquets, by the Catalan Socialist leader, Joan Raventós.[48]

The international and domestic press immediately began to speculate that the UMD was the Spanish equivalent of the Portuguese MFA. The leaders of the UMD denied the connection but it is difficult not to conclude that they were influenced by the events of the Portuguese April. Many of the most prominent figures, Julio Busquets, José Fortes, and Luis Otero, had contacts in the MFA. Moreover, not only did the UMD follow closely on the MFA, but one of their earliest and most important publications was entitled 'Where are the captains?' and began with the words 'In the aftermath of the military intervention in the Portuguese political scene, many Spaniards are asking themselves "what are our captains up to?" Why do they not rebel against the injustice of a regime which is repudiated by the great majority of the country?'[49] Nevertheless, there was an important difference. The officers of the UMD did not aim to make a revolution themselves, as their comrades in Portugal had done, but rather to persuade the Spanish army not to hinder the creation of a democratic Spain by civilian forces.

Almost from the first moment, the various military intelligence services were on the trail of those involved. The high command was outraged at the thought of the army being divided and appalled at the prospect of a significant number of officers joining the democratic cause. The wilder elements in the intelligence services, always given to exaggeration for their own political purposes, reckoned that as many as

[48] Unión Militar Democrática, *Los militares y la lucha por la democracia* (n.pl., n.d.), 1–15; Fortes and Otero, *Proceso*, pp. 28, 231–51; Francisco Caparrós, *La UMD: Militares y rebeldes* (Barcelona, 1983), 45–60.

[49] '¿Dónde estan los capitanes?', a pamphlet issued in Jan. 1975, reprinted in Fortes and Otero, *Proceso*, pp. 252–4. See also p. 27.

2,000 officers might have been contaminated by the UMD. The UMD itself never had more than 250 active militants, although eventually there were many more sympathizers. By the time that the UMD held its Second National Assembly in secret in Madrid in December 1974, contacts had been made with the Socialist Party through Raventós and Felipe González, with the Communist Party through Simón Sánchez Montero and Armando López Salinas, and with the left Christian Democrats through Joaquín Ruiz Giménez.[50]

The nervousness of the high command was revealed in February 1975 when Major Busquets and Captain José Julve were arrested in Barcelona.[51] The arrest of Busquets, who was famous as the author of a widely read book on the sociology of the Spanish officer corps, led to widespread speculation that the army was divided.[52] Throughout 1975, the UMD grew slowly but solidly, establishing a network of contacts across the major garrisons of the country. A decision was made to set up a 'tactical committee' which was devoted to identifying potential recruits and sympathizers and also to directing UMD members to seek transfer to units where they could best counter the political activities of the ultras. It was known that ultras were concentrating in key operational units. In particular, under the command of General Jaime Milans del Bosch, the armoured division was attracting transfer requests from hard-liners. By the same token, the UMD was anxious to prevent the preparation of a coup to forestall democratic reform and to hinder the use of the army against the civilian population in the event of strikes or demonstrations when Franco died.[53] By the summer of 1975, the intelligence services believed that 10 per cent of the officer corps was involved in one way or another. The prime minister and more liberal senior officers were prepared to keep a discreet eye on events without provoking an incident. However, the ultras were anxious both to smash the UMD as quickly as possible and to derive the greatest political benefit possible. They were aware of the growing debility of Franco and anxious lest the democratic neutrality advocated by the UMD should paralyse the armed forces at precisely the moment when they wanted them united to ensure the survival of the dictatorship beyond the dictator's death. Accordingly, they struck in such a way as to act as a deterrent against the spread of the UMD's political

---

[50] Fortes and Otero, *Proceso*, p. 35.
[51] Caparrós, *La UMD*, pp. 68–72; Fortes and Otero, *Proceso*, p. 36
[52] *Le Monde*, 18 Feb. 1975; *Mundo Obrero*, 4 Mar. 1975.
[53] Fortes and Otero, *UMD*, p. 37.

'neutralism' and at the time which they calculated would to the greatest damage to Prime Minister Arias Navarro's tentative drift towards political reform.

The clearly orchestrated sequence of events was set off by General Jaime Milans del Bosch, the hard-line commander of the División Acorazada who was also president of the board of directors of the extreme right-wing newspaper *El Alcázar*. Arias Navarro was away in Helsinki at the Congress on European Security and Co-operation, seeking to gain credibility among the Western democracies. On 23 July 1975, Milans sent a report to the Captain General of Madrid, the ultra Angel Campano, informing him that the intelligence services had uncovered the activities of the UMD which he denounced as a danger to the unity and the objectives of the armed forces. The report had been drawn up by the head of the army intelligence service, the SIBE, Colonel José María Sáenz de Tejada y Fernández Bobadilla, a close collaborator of Milans. It was not properly the province of Milans to forward the report to Campano, other than as a 'concerned' officer. However, with the Milans dossier on his desk, Campano had an excuse to move against the UMD.[54] Seven leaders of the UMD were arrested on 29 July 1975 and two more fell on subsequent days. Spectacular dawn raids were mounted which were more appropriate to the capture of terrorists. The arrests were carried out by large groups of policemen while the buildings where the officers lived were covered by snipers on neighbouring rooftops.[55]

The display of excessive force had the three-fold purpose of embarrassing Arias Navarro, busy in Helsinki masquerading as a democrat, of humiliating the officers arrested who were the lowest form of 'reds' as far as the ultras were concerned, and finally of mounting a deterrent to other officers sympathetic to the UMD.[56] The fears of the bunker with regard to the UMD could be discerned behind various public declarations about army unity made by senior hard-liners shortly after the arrests. On 8 August, the Chief of the General Staff, General Carlos Fernández Vallespín, tried to play down the importance of the UMD arrests when he claimed that 'the army is fundamentally healthy even if it has just had a slight cold'. However, he went on to talk of the danger of a repetition in the Spanish forces of what had happened in

[54] José Ignacio Domínguez, *Cuando yo era an un exiliado* (Madrid, 1977), 23–5, 104.

[55] Domínguez, *Un exiliado*, pp. 24, 31–2; Caparrós, *La UMD*, pp. 85–7.

[56] The official line subsequently was that Arias had authorized the arrests but it seems more likely that this was merely to cover the fact that he had been taken by surprise. Fortes and Otero, *Proceso*, pp. 41–3.

Portugal. Similarly, the Minister for the Army, Francisco Coloma Gallegos, the Director of the Academia General Militar, General Guillermo Quintana Lacaci, and other senior figures made declarations denying the existence of any divisions within the army.[57]

During the trial of ETA militants in the summer of 1975, the supreme judicial authority under whose jurisdiction the trial was taking place was the Captain General of the VI Military Region, Mateo Prada Canillas. He declared on 24 June that 'nowadays when so much is said about reconciliation, the forces of public order do not need to reconcile themselves with anyone'.[58] Coincidentally, Campano as Captain General of Madrid was to authorize the death sentences on militants of the extreme leftist FRAP being tried in the capital in mid-September. It was in such an ambience that the preparations were made for the trial of the arrested UMD officers who were accused of 'military rebellion'. They were refused permission to make use of civilian lawyers and subjected to frequent harassment during their pre-trial detention. Efforts to find a negotiated solution for their plight essayed by José María Gil Robles foundered on the fierce opposition of a newly appointed ultra Captain General of Madrid, Francisco Coloma Gallegos.[59] That was hardly surprising since the object of trying the officers concerned was to smash the UMD in the way that would have the greatest possible impact on members of the officer corps. There was an element of damage limitation in the entire process. The intelligence services had the names of hundreds of officers implicated to some degree in the UMD. To reveal them, and therefore expose the extent of sympathy within the armed forces for democracy, would shatter military unity. Accordingly, a brutal show trial of a few officers was preferred as a way of intimidating the liberals into silence and inertia.[60]

In the aftermath of the death of Franco, the military ultras worked hard on several fronts to maintain control of the armed forces. The trials of the UMD were held in March 1976 in the hostile atmosphere generated by the invited presence of an overwhelming number of ultra-conservative senior officers who made threatening comments throughout. The nine defendants received sentences ranging from

[57] *ABC* 8 Aug. 1975; Fortes and Otero, *Proceso*, pp. 88–9.

[58] Celhay, *Consejos de guerra*, p. 107.

[59] Campano had left the post of Captain-General of the I Military Region to become director general of the Civil Guard. He was replaced by General Félix Alvarez Arenas. On 8 Jan. 1976, Alvarez Arenas exchanged posts with Coloma Gallegos. Fortes and Otero, *Proceso*, p. 117; Domínguez, *Un exiliado*, pp. 134–5, 148–9.

[60] Fortes and Otero, *Proceso*, p. 126.

eight to two-and-a-half years and were expelled from the army.[61] The punishment received by the UMD officers was rather more severe than that to be imposed upon many of those involved in the attempted coup of 1981 and dramatically more so than for those guilty of the attempted 'Galaxia' coup of 1979. As a result of various amnesties, they were soon released but efforts to get reinstated into the army were unsuccesful. That this remained the case throughout the 1980s was a symptom of the continuing strength of right-wing feeling within the armed forces. After all, their crime had been to work by peaceful means for the establishment of democracy.[62]

The triumph of *azules* over the democrats of the UMD was to endure throughout the democratic transition. It was a symbol of their strength although an altogether more graphic illustration could be seen in the velvet glove treatment given to the army by successive governments.[63] Ultras continued to gather in key units like the División Acorazada and the BRIPAC. The Minister for Defence Affairs, General Gutiérrez Mellado was insulted and humiliated. *Golpismo* was permitted to flourish without punishment. There were serious attempts at coups in November 1978 and January 1980 before the fatal weaknesses of such a tolerant policy were brutally exposed by Colonel Tejero's seizure of the Parliament on 23 February 1981. In fact, the activities of the military bunker were almost always defensive. With the death of Franco, they had lost their trump card. Thereafter, they steadily lost ground with the appointment of Adolfo Suárez as prime minister and of Gutiérrez Mellado as vice-president of the cabinet with responsibility for Defence Affairs, with the success of Suárez's political reform, the legalization of the Communist Party, and the first democratic elections in June 1977. *Golpismo* was given a spurious relevance by the terrorism engendered by the failure of the government to resolve the Basque problem, by the post-1977 economic recession, and by political lethargy of Suárez's UCD after 1980. Ultimately, *golpismo* was the fruit of the way in which an army deprived by Franco of professional pride took refuge in the timeless notion that its main concern was Spain's political destiny. The most reactionary

[61] Domínguez, *Un exiliado*, pp. 182–92; Fortes and Otero, *Proceso*, pp. 155–79.

[62] Domínguez, *Un exiliado*, p. 161; Fortes and Otero, *Proceso*, pp. 10–11, 208–15; Caparrós, *La UMD*, pp. 169–70.

[63] Paul Preston, 'Fear of Freedom: The Spanish Army After Franco', in Christopher Abel and Nissa Torrents, *Spain: Conditional Democracy* (London, 1984). Domínguez, *Un exiliado*, p. 161; Fortes and Otero, *Proceso*, pp. 10–11, 208–15; Caparrós, *La UMD*, pp. 169–70.

group committed to that notion, the *alféreces provisionales*, held many key positions in the army when the moment came to dismantle the dictatorship.

Franco's defence policy was based on the calculated risk that nothing would happen in terms of external aggression. He permitted the Spanish armed forces to fall into a state of considerable professional and technical decay. The technological poverty of the Spanish army, the apathy of the many officers who gave top priority to their civilian jobs, its division along political lines, and the determination of its most influential sectors to thwart the national will were all part of the poisoned military legacy of General Franco. The army was used as an inert barrier against social change. This confirmed an existing tendency for it to be alienated from civil society and to function as if it were a foreign army of occupation. In the course of the forty years of Francoism, society evolved slowly and inexorably. The Spain which, in the eyes of the right, justified the military rising of 1936 and the violence of the Civil War, simply did not exist by 1975. However, the army was committed legally and institutionally to defending the basic premises of Francoism. It was also in technical terms not suited to any other more difficult task. Other elements associated with Francoism, the Church, the banks, political groups of monarchists and Catholics, managed to evolve and distance themselves from the regime. Only the Falange and the army failed to do so.

12. FROM WARRIORS TO FUNCTIONARIES: THE FALANGIST SYNDICAL ÉLITE, 1939–1976

Sebastian Balfour

One of the more obscure and fascinating corners of the Francoist state was that occupied by the Syndical Organization or OS. Set up at the end of the Civil War by the victorious regime, the OS was given formal control of industrial relations, social security, employment exchanges, and an extraordinary range of medical, welfare, housing, cultural, and recreational activities. By 1968, according to its head or national delegate, the OS had set up over 23,000 co-operatives and agricultural colonies whose members numbered two-and-a-half million, had constructed half-a-million buildings, including many working-class estates, was running 125 training schools for workers through which 40,000 trainees had passed, and had represented almost two-and-a-half million workers in the labour courts. Its income for the year 1972 amounted to over 12,000 million pesetas (about £72 million at the time).[1]

The OS's social influence, however, far exceeded its political power. As its wealth grew, from government grants, assets confiscated from the old unions, and obligatory contributions of employers and workers alike, so its political star declined. From the ideologues of the Franco regime, the OS leaders became its functionaries. One year after Franco's death, the OS had sunk without trace. Its 34,000 employées had been absorbed into the new state bureaucracy and many of its buildings lay derelict, awaiting allocation to ministries or unions.

The oblivion into which the OS fell is reflected in the almost complete dearth of studies of the organization.[2] Yet its history illuminates

[1] José Solís Ruiz, quoted in Jefatura Superior de Policia de Barcelona (JSPB), 'Informes Laborales', 1968 d. n. 1763 11, Civil Government archives (henceforth CG archives). The figure for the OS's income is from OS *Síntesis de actividades sindicales en el período 1968–1972* (Barcelona, 1973). For further details of the OS's assets see *Cambio 16*, 12 Feb. 1978.

[2] Among the few books on the subject are: Miguel A. Aparicio, *El sindicalismo vertical y la formación del estado franquista* (Barcelona, 1980), Manuel Ludevid, *Cuarenta años de sindicato vertical* (Barcelona, 1976), Carlos Iglesias Selgas, *Los sindicatos en España:*

the most important failure of the regime—its inability to banish the class struggle from Spain. The following account seeks to explain this failure through an outline of the history of its leaders, the Falangist syndical élite, between 1939 and 1977. Much of the material on which it is based is drawn from the archives of the civil government of Barcelona, in particular the extensive reports filed by Franco's secret police, the Social and Political Brigade. Other information was supplied to the author in interviews between 1982 and 1987. The account will focus on the central role played by the OS in the dictatorship's system of industrial relations. Four periods in the history of the syndical élite are delineated: the national-syndicalist period of 1939–41, a corporatist, bureaucratic period between 1941 and 1957, a populist phase from 1957 to 1969, and a period of retrenchment and reform between 1970 and 1976.

One of the main objectives of the Nationalist uprising of July 1936 was to restore control of the factories, mines, offices, and landed estates to the Spanish ruling class. The new system of industrial relations, enshrined in the Labour Charter of 1938, was intended to stamp out the class struggle for ever. Workers were denied the right to organize collectively in defence of their interests. The whole working population, now envisaged as a labour militia in the service of the new order, was enrolled into a corporatist structure modelled on the Fascist corporations of Mussolini's Italy. All units of production, from factories to industries, were incorporated into the new organization. Formal control of the productive process was handed over to the newly created single party of the victorious regime, the Falange. 'The nation has been given its orders,' announced Franco in 1942, 'civil life will be channelled through the organizations of the Falange, with its syndicates, its National Syndicalist Unions, and all the activities that it is empowered with organizing.'[3] The new syndical apparatus was envisaged not as a mass but as a cadre organization. The Falange, as its 1937 statutes stated,

will create and maintain the Syndical Organizations necessary to incorporate Labour and Production and the distribution of goods. In every case, the heads of these Organizations will proceed from the ranks of the Movement and will be controlled and guided by its leaders in order to guarantee that the Syndical

---

Origen, estructura y evolución (Madrid, 1966), Jon Amsden, *Collective Bargaining and Class Conflict in Spain* (London, 1972).

[3] Speech by Franco in Jan. 1942, quoted in Shelagh Ellwood, *Prietas las filas: Historia de Falange española 1933–1983* (Barcelona, 1984), 133.

Organization is subordinated to the national interest and imbued with the ideals of the State. The position of National Delegate of the Syndicates will be conferred on a single militant, whose subordinates will be organized on a graduated, vertical hierarchy, in the manner of a creative, just, and disciplined army.[4]

The origins of Falangist syndicalism lay in the tiny Fascist union, the Central Obrera Nacional Sindicalista (CONS), set up in 1933 by the Juntas de Ofensiva Nacional Sindicalista (JONS). The latter was an archetypal Fascist group made up of provincial public service employees, smallholders, agricultural labourers, and right-wing students. In 1934, the JONS merged with the more middle-class Fascist organization, the Falange Española Tradicionalista, founded by the former dictator Primo de Rivera's son, José Antonio. The national-syndicalist revolution that the new party called for envisaged the elimination of class divisions and the exaltation of Nation, Race, and Religion. The true Falangist was meant to be 'half-monk, half-soldier',[5] dedicating his life to the cause of a united, pious, and expansionist Spain whose prototype was a mixture of Nazi Germany and the Spanish Reconquest. The rhetorical image of the warrior-knight or soldier, in particular, would reappear in the discourse of Falangists throughout the dictatorship, though the cause would change to suit the circumstances.[6]

The Falange's sublimation of class interests for Nation and Race reflected the preoccupations of sections of the petit-bourgeoisie, the backbone of the early Fascist movements in Europe, whose very identity as a class was being threatened by the struggle between capital and labour. But the anti-capitalist tendencies within the Falange were expressed as a moral revulsion against economic liberalism and social injustice rather than a frontal assault against the bourgeoisie. The Spanish Fascists could by no means impose their revolution on the new order. The Francoist regime was based on a coalition of reactionary interests among which the Falange was neither a powerful nor an independent voice. Without any mass base before the Civil War and rent by internal disputes, the Falange was not in the same league as the other 'families' of Francoism, the army, the church, the landowning oligarchy, and the financial and industrial bourgeoisie. Indeed, the

[4] Estatutos de FET y de las JONS, articles 29 and 30, in Ellwood, *Prietas*, p. 116.
[5] Ellwood, *Prietas*, p. 38.
[6] e.g. the long-serving head of the Movement, José Solís Ruiz, said to an assembly of employers in 1965: 'In the struggle for progress and well-being we are all soldiers': quoted in *Acción Sindical*, Nov. 1965.

share it acquired of the spoils of victory were far greater than its strength merited. With key figures in government and state administration in the first years of the dictatorship, the Falange was second only to the military in the strength of political representation within the regime.[7] The reason for its relative influence was that it served a useful purpose for Franco. The Falange could be used as a counter-balance against the monarchists. It also provided a ready-made ideology that suited, for the time being, the pro-Axis alignment of the new regime.

After the Falange was merged by Franco's Unification decree of 1937 with the rest of the rank-and-file organizations supporting the uprising, its anti-capitalist rhetoric became even more muted. The revolutionary wing was then decisively crushed by Franco with the imprisonment of José Antonio's successor, Manuel Hedilla Larrey, for having balked at unification. The call for 'all power to the Falange', and aggressive anti-capitalist rhetoric could still be heard in speeches after 1937, but the freshly installed syndical hierarchy of 1939 under their first national delegate, Gerardo Salvador Merino, were too conscious of their dependence on the new regime to take the matter further.[8] The Falange had no mass base except that which the state would supply by decree. Its continued existence depended on accepting the limits set by Franco in his efforts to balance the different families that constituted the basis of the regime.

In any case, the Falange had been integrated into the power structure of the new order. The defeated working class lay before the syndical élite, ready, it seemed, to be moulded into a work militia or, in the jargon of the day, a community of producers. Nothing better illustrates the sense of omnipotence with which the new bureaucracy set about their task of reorganizing national production than the description by one of its national delegates, Fermín Sanz Orrio, of the brave new society they planned to create:

What is clear is that society is like an immense graph-paper. . . . The horizontal lines separate each class from the other; the vertical lines separate the professions. However, according to our observation point as we handle the graph-paper, the panorama varies fundamentally. We place it in a vertical position, while the Marxists do so in a horizontal position. The dominant perspectives are completely reversed in each case; but the pattern will always

---

[7] C. Viver Pi-Sunyer, *El personal político de Franco (1936–1945)* (Barcelona, 1978), 156.

[8] Aparicio, *El sindicalismo vertical*, pp. 110–11.

remain. In the trade unions of a liberal-Marxist society, there are classes divided into professions. According to our national-syndicalist conception there are professions within which exist class layers.[9]

The national-syndicalist project of 1939–41, therefore, was largely confined within the walls of the OS. The hierarchy was staffed by veteran Falangists named by Salvador Merino. Like most officials from the ranks of the Falange, the new élite sorely lacked experience.[10] Nor was this compensated by the incorporation of employers into the organization or old CONS militants who provided the personnel of the OS in some areas.[11] Teams of volunteer Falangist workers were sent to support the German war effort and courses in German were run in the headquarters of the OS. Processions of paramilitary work battalions filed through the streets. Any attempt to pursue a course independent of the regime, however, was further stifled by the Law of the Bases of the OS, promulgated in 1940, and the government reshuffle of May 1941, which brought the organization under the direct control of the state. The role of the syndical élite was reduced to that of a transmission belt, ensuring the execution of government policy within the field of production. The state determined the wage structure and the regulations for each industry and workplace, while the OS was responsible for carrying them out. The last act in the state take-over of the OS was Salvador Merino's dismissal in 1941, on the useful but dubious grounds that he had been a freemason. From then on, the dream of the 'incomplete revolution' or indeed the 'revolution betrayed' would haunt the minds of small numbers of purist Falangists, those who wished to see a neo-Fascist transformation of Spain.

The post-1941 leadership of the Movement and the OS completed the task of steering the organization into the political mainstream of the regime. The anti-capitalist tone of Salvador Merino's team gave way to the bland words of the new national delegate, Fermín Sanz Orrio, intent on reassuring the employers that the OS was their ally. 'It is said', wrote Sanz Orrio, 'that uniting workers and bosses into one immediate and total syndicate means bringing the authority of the employers to an end. In reality, the opposite is true since the employer,

---

[9] Quoted in Aparicio, *El sindicalismo vertical*, pp. 210–11.
[10] Miguel Jerez Mir, *Elites políticas y centros de extracción en España 1938–1957* (Madrid, 1982), 103–8.
[11] María Encarna Nicolás Marín, *Instituciones murcianas en el franquismo (1939–1962)* (Murcia, 1982), 471.

in the national-syndicalist regime is . . . the fundamental pivot of the whole system . . .'.[12] Merino's man in the all-important post of provincial delegate in Barcelona was replaced by an employer who used to be a member of the Lliga, the old (now disbanded) Catalan Conservative Party. The transformation of the OS was hastened by the victory of the Allies in 1945 that made the Fascist trappings of the earlier period inadvisable.

The new ideology of the OS represented a fusion of the pre-war Catholic corporatism favoured by many employers and the purely formal aspects of the now emasculated totalitarian project of the original Falangists.[13] Although incorporated into the OS, the employers were allowed to maintain their pre-war institutions, such as the Chambers of Commerce. Where there was a problem of legal status, the old organizations of industrialists changed themselves into limited companies or reproduced trade associations, or *gremios*, within the OS itself. Under Sanz Orrio, moreover, the employers were reorganized separately from the workers within the same trade or industry.

In their attempts to build the new organization, the syndical élite were faced by a far greater problem than integrating the employers. Neither the Fascist nor pre-war Catholic unions had any base among industrial workers. The OS had no experienced trade unionists nor any working-class leaders. The vast majority of organized workers throughout Spain owed their loyalty to the banned anarcho-syndicalist CNT and the socialist UGT. The new syndical bureaucracy could not hope to sustain its own interests within the regime without winning the participation of at least sections of workers.

Accordingly, two strategies were employed. With the active support of leading figures in the regime, Falangists made contact with CNT militants abroad and in Spanish gaols in an attempt to lure them into collaborating with the OS. The secretary-general of the Movement and OS national delegate, José Solís Ruiz, claimed that he had held talks with 800 CNT members in 1942 and had been on the point of reaching an agreement with a group of them whereby they would renounce the CNT and collaborate with the OS.[14] The Minister of Labour, José Antonio Girón, set up a collaborationist Labour Party in 1944 but attracted only a handful of ex-unionists. OS officials visited two CNT leaders in the Madrid gaol in 1947 with the extraordinary

[12] Quoted in Aparicio, *El sindicalismo vertical*, p. 208.
[13] Aparicio, *El sindicalismo vertical*, pp. 2˅0–11, 208.
[14] *Mundo*, 29 Jan. 1972.

proposal that in exchange for their co-operation and that of other members of the organization, the OS (whose other title was the CNS) would be renamed the CNT. They added that once the agreement had been signed, all political prisoners would be released. Franco, they claimed improbably, was ready to sign the agreement with them in his office.[15]

It was not merely expedience that prompted the syndical élite to look to the CNT movement for potential recruits to build their rank-and-file organization. There had been several informal contacts between anarcho-syndicalist moderates and the Falange before the Civil War.[16] The Falangists had been encouraged by the many superficial similarities that existed between the two organizations. In contrast to the socialist union whose reference-point was the 'evil empire' of Marxism, the CNT had deep ideological roots in Spanish soil. The Falange, at least in an earlier period, could identify with both the CNT's anti-capitalism and its refusal to take part in bourgeois liberal democracy. Moreover, the CNT's vision of a new society, based on the union and the commune, resembled some of the Falange's ideals. The language of the OS newspaper, *Solidaridad Nacional*, bore a certain resemblance to that of the old CNT daily, *Solidaridad Obrera*.[17] Indeed, it could be argued that the CNT exercised considerable influence on the Falange. Yet the syndical élite underestimated the political strength of anarcho-syndicalism. Only a handful of ex-CNT leaders seized the bait they offered, while many others paid with their lives for refusing to collaborate.

It was only after 1947, when it became clear that the Franco regime was going to survive the post-war period and when a new wave of repression had almost wiped out the clandestine opposition, that individual ex-unionists began to collaborate with the OS in any number. There was a compelling reason for doing so. The second means whereby the OS leaders hoped to strengthen their organization was through opening restricted channels of shop-floor and industrial representation for workers. A series of reforms from the mid-forties onwards introduced a system of election and representation designed both to increase participation in the OS and to give a formal veneer of

[15] César M. Lorenzo, *Les Anarchistes espagnols et le pouvoir* (Paris, 1969), 273–7.
[16] Francisco Candel, *Ser obrero no es ninguna ganga* (Barcelona, 1968), 121 and Ellwood, *Prietas*, p. 29.
[17] Ignasi Riera, *Pàries, sindicalistes, demagogs: Notes sobre sindicalisme i cultura obrera* (Barcelona, 1986), 17.

democracy for the benefit of the Allies. The new system offered some albeit limited opportunities to defend working conditions. It also gave status and backhanders to ambitious ex-unionists who could justify their collaboration on the grounds that workers had to be represented.[18] It was from this period, too, that Communist militants began to infiltrate the OS, the Party having abandoned its guerrilla strategy in 1948. The introduction of union representation was to prove a mixed blessing for the syndical élite. While it enabled them to create a clientele system among sections of workers, the representative structures of the OS would increasingly be taken over by militants whose aim was to destroy the syndicate itself.

Neither collaboration nor internal reform, however, could provide the syndical élite with a new role in industrial relations. Almost from its foundation, the OS had been deprived of any effective power in the production process. Control over wages and conditions lay in the hands of the Ministry of Labour and industrial disputes were dealt with by the Ministry's labour courts. The role of the syndical bureaucracy was at best consultative and conciliatory. Their more common function was as policeman of the government's industrial policies.

The economic transformation that swept through Spain from the mid-fifties, as the post-war autarky crumbled and US investment flowed in, made the regime's centralized and paternalistic system of industrial relations all the more irrelevant to the needs of industry. The introduction of new technology required productivity and piece-rate bargaining. Inflation led to increasing wage unrest among the more organized workers until the government's mechanism of wage determination by periodic decree gave way to a form of collective bargaining by riot. The political crisis generated by economic change came to a head in February 1957, when Franco appointed a new government in which the proponents of structural economic reform and integration into the economy of Western Europe, drawn from the ranks of the Opus Dei, would soon prevail over the supporters of autarky. Although they stood to gain little from eventual incorporation into the European political system, which would demand the dismantling of the OS as part of the price of membership, the OS élite never-

---

[18] e.g. a secret police report of 2 May 1972 noted tartly that the president of the Sabadell Textile Syndicate, an ex-CNT collaborator, lived in greater luxury than was compatible with his job as warehouse stock controller. JSPB report, CG archives, n. 1418.

theless gave their formal blessing to the new policy, bowing before the pressure of the government.[19] Moreover, the more prominent Falangists, such as José Luis Arrese, head of the OS, and José Antonio Girón, Minister of Labour, were dropped from the ministerial ranks.

This fundamental shift in the regime's policies, however, contained new opportunities for the syndical élite to build a power base. In 1958, a new decree, the Law of Collective Agreements, was passed that fundamentally altered the framework of industrial relations in Spain. The law devolved the all important mechanisms for determining wages and conditions to local or sectoral level. Though the government retained its right to intervene, in that all agreements had to be approved by the Ministry of Labour, collective bargaining between workers' and employers' representatives was now allowed within the framework of the OS. The new system presented the syndical bureaucracy with an enormous challenge. The importance of the OS officials and lawyers rose, as the number of disputes needing arbitration or legal representation grew. Although the larger firms developed their own plant agreements, the OS headquarters in each town and city became the centre of the negotiating process for local and provincial agreements covering every industry and trade. The representative structures of the OS, from the works councils to the provincial committees, became contested by militants, right-wingers, and moderates alike. Though there are no figures to prove it, there is no doubt that in the syndical elections after 1958, the number of spoilt ballot papers with Sara Montiel or Gina Lollobrigida written on them fell dramatically.

It was a time of optimism within the ranks of the regime. The sustained growth enjoyed by the Spanish economy from the late 1950s helped to shore up a dictatorship that had seemed to falter earlier in the decade. Bolstered by economic success, the government launched a campaign of 'liberalization', the so-called 'apertura', designed to consolidate the regime and lay the foundations for its continuation after Franco's death. The man Franco put in charge of 'opening up' the institutions of the regime, including the OS, was the secretary-general of the Movement and national delegate, José Solís Ruiz, nicknamed by some the 'smile of the regime' because of his easy charm and anodyne words. In an interview in 1966, Solís let it be understood that

---

[19] José Antonio Biescas, 'Estructura y coyunturas económicas', in José Antonio Biescas and Tuñon de Lara, *España bajo la dictadura franquista (1939–1975), Historia de España*, (Barcelona, 1980), 62.

the point of the operation was to prolong the regime beyond Franco's death:

I believe that though people are important ... for me, looking towards the future, what matters are institutions. If we get them right, if we manage to get the people to participate completely, if they feel involved and understand that the institutions need to be defended, then the problem of individuals, however important, is of secondary importance. For this reason, we are going all out to perfect the institutions and give them the necessary authenticity, since it is on them that we must base the future continuity . . .[20]

Under Solís's direction, the OS was remodelled. 'We are proposing', he said, 'to transform syndicalism, bringing up to date the law that governs it. The path of representation is now open to all.'[21] New electoral rules were drawn up that allowed secret ballots for all representative positions. New provincial councils representing workers and employers separately were set up. And in the Organic Law of 1967, the culmination of the regime's institutional shake-up, the OS was no longer defined as an instrument of the state, nor were its officials required to be Falangists. While the institutional changes were no more than cosmetic reforms meant to present a more democratic image at home and abroad, the changes in the electoral system opened up the representative structures of the OS even more to the opponents of the regime. Yet the OS élite exuded great confidence that they could control the internal affairs of the syndicates.

Their optimism was not entirely misplaced. Living standards had been rising rapidly since the mid-fifties. The economic boom gave workers increasing opportunities to move upwards socially. A new generation of workers in the factories and offices shared none of the political or union loyalties of their older fellow-workers. While the number of strikes had risen dramatically, labour protest was more fragmented in time and place and no longer took on the political dimension of the 1950s' unrest. The changing complexion of the working class seemed to present the OS bureaucracy with a new opportunity to build a social base. The head of the Catalan OS asserted in a newspaper interview, 'I have complete confidence in the common sense of workers. They know how to distinguish between those who speak with honour and those whose only aim is to create disunity.' He went on to refer to 'a new kind of worker who knows which side his bread is buttered on, who can tell what's fair and what

[20] *La Vanguardia Española*, 26 June 1966.
[21] *Solidaridad Nacional*, 21 June 1966.

isn't. The greatest achievement of our organization is in having created a change of mentality, a new union culture, a capacity to negotiate'.[22]

Solís himself was the main exponent of the new syndical populism. Speaking to a meeting of OS officials, he said, 'It is necessary to count on the rank and file at all times. Try to make contact with them as often as possible. Go straight to your man, wherever he is. Involve him in tasks and in responsibilities. In one word, we have to popularize our message.'[23] The culmination of the campaign to renew the OS base was the union elections of 1966. Solís launched the electoral period by addressing workers with the following bold words, 'Keep the best delegates, and get rid of the soft, the lukewarm, and the cowardly.'[24] The slogan adopted by the OS was 'Vote for the Best'.

The new populist tone was greeted with growing alarm by many within the ranks of the OS. The Falangist die-hards who had controlled the OS for two decades viewed, as the secret police reported, with 'uncertainty and demoralization the evident deviation of the Syndicates towards a path completely different to that laid down by the Principles of the Movement'.[25] The 'apertura' of Solís and his supporters brought shivers to many old Falangists who had grown accustomed to answering labour unrest with repression. Their horror at the new liberalization policies was echoed by the secret police: 'It should be pointed out that in the public sphere as much as in the syndicates themselves, the interpretation of labour indiscipline as a political attitude against the regime has been modified, and now it is accepted as a weapon used by the workers in defence of their interests and social demands . . .'.[26] In another report to the civil governor of Barcelona, the secret police gave voice to the apprehension of OS officials and pro-regime delegates that they might lose control of syndical branches to opposition militants: 'there is fear among supporters of the regime that these elements may get a high enough number of their people elected to begin eroding the policies of the syndicates, as a first step towards . . . converting them into a powerful and effective tool against the regime'.[27] Nor was their fear confined to the workers' structures of the OS, the so-called social sections. Falangists were being replaced in the employers' organizations of the

[22] *Tele-Expres*, 5 Sept. 1966.
[23] *Acción Sindicalista*, Jan. 1965.
[24] *Ibid.*, July 1966.
[25] JSPB, 16 Dec. 1965.
[26] JSPB, 5 Jan. 1967.
[27] JSPB, 15 Sept. 1966, CG archives, n. 1249.

OS by delegates indifferent if not hostile to the Movement, sympathizers, or members of the Opus Dei or the progressive Catholic Association of Employers (Asociación Católica de Dirigentes).[28]

The irreductible Falangists in the OS were not the only ones to fear the encroachment of militants. Before examining the results of the 1966 elections, a few words need to be said about the changing rank-and-file base of the syndical élite in Catalonia. The earliest collaborators of the OS had been drawn mainly from the scab unions of the 1930s, the *sindicatos libres*, and the Catholic and Falangist syndicates. By the 1960s, however, they had been replaced largely by a new generation of syndical delegates also sympathetic to the regime. Of these, the most important were groups of ex-anarcho-syndicalists who had climbed the ladder of representation in the OS through opportunism or co-optation by officials. Many now occupied important positions as presidents of local or provincial branches of the OS. It was they rather than the old-fashioned Falangists who enjoyed the support of top government officials in the Ministry of Labour. They were a useful though not entirely reliable source of support for the syndical élite, for the paradoxical reason that they claimed openly to be anarcho-syndicalists, while benefiting personally from the power and perks that high positions in the OS conferred. A secret police report of 1966 vividly conveyed the ambiguities of one of these presidents:

He is efficient in syndical matters, although a bit of an unscrupulous rogue. . . . Apart from personal qualities or defects, he is a typical syndicalist, quite a materialist, unwilling to make any personal sacrifices, but also a fighter. He will not oppose the regime unless he is forced to by his own interests; in fact he is caught in a highly compromising position. His avowal of CNT ideology is partly to win prestige among workers because of the strength of CNT traditions and partly because he genuinely believes in it.[29]

With the tacit collaboration of these ex-CNT demagogues, the local hierarchy of the OS had been able to orchestrate a clientele system that helped to ensure their control over syndical affairs in their area. If in the early 1960s they had lost influence in factories that had plant bargaining, they retained their grip on local and provincial agreements through the network of support in the small factories commanded by the collaborationists. In fact, so far had some of the OS bureaucracy travelled that they opposed the activities of a new generation of Falangist militants who believed that the national-syndicalist revolu-

[28] JSPB report, 19 Nov. 1965, n. 1249.
[29] JSPB, 26 Sept. 1966.

tion had been betrayed, while supporting people who claimed to be the heirs of anarchism. The ultimate irony was that, in the mid-1960s, the purist Falangists were making common cause with Communist militants, while the pro-regime Falangists were allied with ex-CNT unionists. The 1964 Madrid Comisiones Obreras, the semi-clandestine movement that was to dominate the labour movement in the last years of Francoism, was originally the result of an alliance between purist Falangists and Communists. Similar arrangements were made in Sabadell, during the 1966 elections, to oust the pro-regime leadership of local syndicates, while in the Barcelona transport syndicate pro-regime Falangists and Communists made a pact of mutual support.[30] Indeed, the workers' sections of the OS resembled nothing so much as a den of thieves.

The syndical elections of 1966 represented a crushing blow to the hopes of the populist leadership of the OS. In the major industries of the cities, over half the votes for the works councils and local committees went to candidates standing on the platform of demands drawn up by opposition militants. In some areas, militants penetrated as far as the provincial committees. The results suggested that, far from seeing the OS as an instrument of self-advancement, the new generation of organized workers wanted to replace it with a democratic and fighting union. A secret police report shortly after the elections, warning of the erosion of support for the OS, saw it as part of 'a process of decomposition that began with the loss of the deferential respect which workers once had towards the political and administrative leadership of the Syndical Organization'.[31]

The shock of the 1966 elections led the syndical élite to abandon their policy of liberalization. Solís's hope that the OS could ride on the back of the boom was effectively destroyed. The relatively relaxed attitude shown by the authorities and the OS bureaucracy during the electoral campaign gave way to a witch-hunt of militants. The repression was the combined work of the police and OS officials. Those militants who could not be put on trial were stripped of their representative credentials by the OS. By the end of the decade, a whole generation of shop-floor leaders had been wiped out. The crack-down on labour was part of a broader shift by the regime towards a more defensive economic and social policy. The economic growth on which the

---

[30] See Sebastian Balfour, 'The Remaking of the Spanish Labour Movement. Social Change, Urban Growth, and Working-Class Militancy: Barcelona 1939–1976' (Ph.D. thesis, London University, 1987), 156 n. 71.   [31] JSPB report, CG archives, n. 1249.

government's policy of institutional reform had depended was falter-
ing. The economy grew by less than 2 per cent in 1967, having averaged an annual growth rate of 8.6 per cent of GNP in the early 1960s.
The government declared an austerity package in November, including a year's wage freeze. The offensive against the opposition culminated in the three-month State of Emergency in 1969.

The Falangist élite had suffered a double blow. On the one hand,
their attempt to create a constituency among the new generation of
workers had failed and, on the other, their influence within the regime
was even further eroded. The Falangist top man in the regime,
General Agustin Muñoz Grandes, was replaced as Vice-President in
1967 by Admiral Luis Carrero Blanco. Solís Ruiz was dropped in
1969, along with another minister closely associated with liberalization, Manuel Fraga Iribarne. The new government was dominated by
the arch-rivals of the Falange within the regime, members of the Opus
Dei. The position of national delegate was subordinated to a new post,
that of Minister of Syndical Relations, whose incumbent, Enrique
García Ramal, was a businessman.

Indeed, the OS was fast becoming irrelevant both to workers and to
industrialists. It was well known that many large firms were making
secret pacts with their work-force to get around the ponderous
machinery of the OS, as well as government wage norms.[32] Many
employers were angry that the OS was unable to keep down militancy.
Despite the crack-down against militants that began in 1967, for every
one sacked by syndical officials two seemed to spring up in his or her
place in the early 1970s. The engineering employers of Barcelona
wrote to the provincial delegate of the OS complaining of the failure of
the syndicates to deal with subversion in the factories.[33]

Furthermore, collective bargaining was increasingly getting out of
control, as workers responded to rising inflation by strike action. A
secret circular from the Ministry of Labour to all the provincial delegates of the OS in 1971 revealed the extent of the crisis within the
organization. In it, they were urged to prohibit all mass meetings in
their headquarters, to suspend all negotiations if any industrial action
was staged, and to lean on the press not to report strikes that were

[32] Balfour, 'Remaking', p. 259.
[33] Gabinete Técnico Económico Sidero-Metalúrgico, 'Extremos de mayor con-
sideración expuestos al Delegado Provincial de Sindicatos por la presentación
empresarial del más alto nivel del Sindicato del Metal de Barcelona', 4 Feb. 1971
(Archivo Nacional de Cataluña).

occurring. They were also instructed to put pressure on employers not to make unofficial pacts with workers.[34] Increasingly the government was forced to intervene in industrial relations because of the failure of the bargaining machinery of the OS to cope with rising militancy. In 1974, for example, almost half the total workforce of Barcelona was bound by compulsory awards laid down by the government after negotiations in the OS had broken down.

In view of the increasing ineffectiveness of the OS, no amount of exhortation from government circles could restore its authority. The words of the new Minister of Syndical Relations to the National Council of Workers, the top rung of the OS's representative structures dominated by pro-regime people, had a ring of desperation: 'You have to be authentic leaders, be ahead of those who want to seize your banners from you, be more forceful, bolder, and more decisive than they, but with the difference that you are acting within the law and not outside it.'[35] Nor could any institutional tinkering, such as the Syndical Law of 1971 eliminating the notion of 'vertical' syndicates, narrow the gap between the OS and the growing unofficial movement led by Comisiones Obreras. The law of 1973 giving the OS a greater role in arbitrating collective disputes only served to deepen the contradiction that lay in its very origin; namely, that the OS was meant not only to represent workers and bosses but mediate between the two at the same time. The paternalist rationale of the OS as a fatherly representative of the state settling minor disputes within the family of production was always misconceived. But it was especially anachronistic in the industrial Spain of the 1970s.

The syndical élite was faced with a choice: to carry out a more radical reform of the organization or to retreat into the bunker. Most Falangists instinctively followed the latter path, which had been laid down, in any case, by the Carrero government in 1973 and by the Arias Navarro cabinet a year later. However, a section of the syndical bureaucracy, led by Rodolfo Martín Villa, the OS head between 1969 and 1973 and his protégé, José María Socías Humbert, provincial delegate in Barcelona, were indiscreetly orchestrating a campaign to change the style and the personnel of the organization. Martín Villa admitted later that any profound reform of the OS was not possible within the structures of the regime. To have given the OS greater

[34] Ministerio de Trabajo, 'Criterios ante una posible situación conflictiva', Madrid, 6 Dec. 1971, ANC archives.
[35] *Solidaridad Nacional*, 13 Dec. 1969.

autonomy, he argued, would have meant to create a state within a state.[36] In fact, the real purpose of this last reformist project was to preserve the life of the syndical élite beyond the death of the regime. In a newspaper interview in 1974, Socías Humbert called for the right to strike and greater free speech. He went on to say, in the cautious though pointed style characteristic of the day, 'Society is demanding things that were not on the agenda five years ago and there is a clear need to respond to the new social changes.'[37]

The heart of this campaign to modernize the OS was in Barcelona. Under Socías Humbert's leadership, the provincial syndical officials began to adopt a more professional style of intervention in industrial relations. Indeed, the secret police complained to the civil governor in 1973 that the OS was no longer acting as trouble-shooter but was displaying a 'dangerous' neutrality in labour disputes.[38] Socías Humbert began replacing die-hard Falangists with his own men. For example, a 23-year-old protégé of his, a labour lawyer from Badalona, was put in charge of the official Employment Exchange (Servicio de Colocaciones) of Barcelona (a service administered by the OS) to the dismay of the old veterans who had run it until then. In the gloomy corridors and offices of the OS headquarters in Barcelona, there were angry murmurs. Socías Humbert was accused of being a traitor and the fourth floor where his office was located was nicknamed the 'Red Floor'.[39]

But the most surprising activity of the new reformists lay in the contacts that they built with the underground opposition in Catalonia. By the early 1970s, the vast majority of organized workers supported the clandestine union movement, Comisiones Obreras, led overwhelmingly by Communists. Many branches of the OS's representative structures had been taken over by Comisiones Militants. Indeed, in some areas, like Baix Llobregat, the OS was used as the organizational centre of local general strikes. Under pressure from the rank and file, OS officials and hitherto pro-regime delegates were increasingly mouthing the militant demands of Comisiones Obreras. In some cases, long-serving bureaucrats were openly expressing dissatisfaction with

---

[36] Rudolfo Martín Villa, *Al Servicio del Estado* (Barcelona, 1984), 13–14.

[37] *Correo Catalan*, 15 Dec. 1974.

[38] JSPB, 'Nota Informativa sobre ausencia de intervención sindical en algunas alteraciones laborales', 4 Oct. 1973; and correspondence between Pelayo Ros and Socías Humbert, 23 Oct. and 7 Nov., CG archives, n. 1418 and 1425; also Villa, *Al Servicio*, pp. 21–1.

[39] Carlos Fanlo interview, 11 Nov. 1987.

the syndical organization.[40] Given the presence of opposition militants in representative posts in the local branches of the OS, it was inevitable that some accommodation had to be found between them and the local syndical officials over everyday union affairs.

More unexpected were the informal contacts maintained by Socías Humbert with people on the most wanted list of the secret police, the clandestine full-time leaders of Comisiones Obreras in Barcelona. During the huge strike in SEAT in 1974, for example, secret discussions took place between the managing director and Comisiones leaders in the syndical headquarters, at which Socías Humbert was reputedly present. In the course of one of these meetings, in an attempt to find a solution to the strike, a phone call was made to the Communist secretary-general in Paris.[41] These contacts between representatives of two organizations that were declared enemies served two useful purposes for the new reformists among the syndical élite. On the one hand, they were able to exercise some influence on the course of political and union affairs. With direct access to the full-time agitators of the Communist Party, they could act as secret mediators over strikes and demonstrations. On the eve of democracy, for example, on the occasion of the Atocha massacre when right-wing ultras in Madrid murdered five labour lawyers, Socías Humbert's successor secretly met Comisiones leaders in Barcelona to organize a two-hour protest stoppage, with the aim of forestalling a more virulent response that might, it was believed, jeopardize the transition.[42]

Contacts with opposition militants, on the other hand, gave the reformist wing of the OS the opportunity to influence the debate within their ranks about the future shape of the union movement in the democratic society that was clearly approaching. A small, influential section of the Catalan Comisiones Obreras, for example, was arguing that the OS structures could be used to build a united workers' union in the coming democracy, as the Portuguese Communists had done with the Intersindical in 1964.[43] Though the motives were different, their position was not dissimilar to that of Socías Humbert, who was attempting to organize a new Congress of the OS, or that of Martín Villa when he argued at the end of 1975 that the OS Council of Work-

---

[40] See e.g. *Can Oriach*, Oct.–Dec. 1974.

[41] Agencia Popular de Información (API), 18 Jan. 1975, and interview with Isidor Boix, 18 Feb. 1983.

[42] Fanlo interview.

[43] Isidor Boix and Manuel Pujades, *Conversaciones sindicales con dirigentes obreros* (Barcelona, 1975).

ers should be the future workers' Union, and the Council of Employers, the future Confederation of Industry.[44]

The new reformist project took shape in 1975 around the OS campaign for the syndical elections. It was Socías Humbert's idea to give it the portentous title of 'The New Frontier of Syndicalism'. The campaign had the backing of important sections of the establishment, including the perennial José Solís, back at the helm of the Movement and the Syndical Organization. Framed by a banner proclaiming the new motto, the Minister of Syndical Relations explained to a meeting of employers' representatives in Barcelona that the New Frontier meant the autonomy of workers' organizations from those of the employers and the independence of both from the government. The difficulty of reconciling such a radical change with the corporatist ideology that underpinned the regime was evident in his convoluted attempts to reassure his audience. 'We are going to reform syndicalism. This does not entail breaking with the past but recognizing the past—without renouncing it—as a platform for the future.'[45]

Outside Barcelona, the reformist project had little support. Madrid was the bastion of the OS bureaucracy. Ever since the brief flirtation of a handful of OS officials with the early Comisiones movement in 1964, the Madrid syndical leadership had played a virulently repressive role in labour relations. Indeed, the Atocha massacre was organized in the workers' section of the transport syndicate. In many other parts of Spain also, the syndical élite was largely made up of unswerving supporters of the dictator. Since the OS had traditionally been the preserve of post-Civil War Falangism, it was always less likely to be influenced by the ideological changes that had taken place in Spain from the early 1960s onwards. It is true that a new generation of more professional officials came to occupy some of the middle ranks of the organization and in some cases, such as that of Socías Humbert, its highest echelons. A post in the OS was a useful stepping-stone in the career of budding politicians and civil servants.[46] Yet as late as 1970, a quarter of the top officials of the OS central administration and a fifth of those in the OS's services (*Obras Sindicales*) were Falangists who had held positions during the first militant years of the dictatorship.[47] In the light of the demise of the regime's institutions in 1977, the New

[44] *Acción Sindicalista*, Jan. 1976.
[45] *Solidaridad Nacional*, 13 June 1975.
[46] Pi-Sunyer, *El personal político*, pp. 204–5.
[47] Ibid. 228–9.

Frontier of Syndicalism never stood a chance of succeeding. It was even less likely to do so because the OS was always the obedient servant of Francoist orthodoxy.

The history of the Falangist syndical élite is, therefore, one of failure. Their Fascist precursors in the 1930s, the JONS and the Falange, were easily absorbed into the ruling class coalition that overthrew the Republic in 1939. Like their much larger counterparts in Germany and Italy, the Spanish Fascists became subordinated to the needs of the bourgeoisie and its allies in Spain. They served a useful purpose to the conservative coalition on which the Franco state was based. Firstly, they provided a ready-made ideological framework that suited the pro-Axis alignment of the regime and justified the elimination of the independent organization of the working class on the altar of national unity. Secondly, they supplied the personnel for the bureaucracy of the Syndical Organization, whose main function was to ensure the continued suppression of the class struggle.

The early attempts by sections of the Falange to imprint their national-syndicalist conception of the state on the new order were given short shrift by the regime. The new orthodoxy imposed on the OS gave the employers the freedom to organize within and outside its structures while maintaining an iron grip on workers. At the same time, the OS was brought under the control of the government. The Falange had neither the power nor the will to challenge this emasculation of its political project. It was bound to the regime by a pact of blood and owed its continued survival to the favour of Franco. Besides, it was elevated into one of the regime's élites, endowed with a wide range of social functions that carried with them wealth and power. The privileges enjoyed by the Falangist syndical élite, however, depended strictly on their support for the regime. Thereafter, the Falangist syndical élite were the faithful servants of Francoism. Their subordinate and dependent status was reflected in the frequent reformulation of the ideology of the OS according to the needs of the regime, from the abandonment of the totalitarian project to the New Frontier of Syndicalism.

For all its formal power, the syndical élite failed to build a popular base among workers. Throughout the dictatorship, it attempted, through reform, rhetoric, and patronage, to shore up its declining influence within the regime. But it could meet neither the needs of workers nor those of employers. On the one hand, the OS's role as a repressive instrument of the state precluded any large base among workers. On the other hand, the hierarchical and paternalistic system of industrial relations in Spain was increasingly inappropriate to an expanding capitalism that needed to bargain directly with workers over productivity and new technology.

The most important reason for the failure of the syndical élite, like that of the regime itself, was that it was unable to contain working-class and popular struggle. Towards the end of the dictatorship, the OS became overwhelmed by the new labour movement and the project to prolong its existence into the post-Francoist democracy under another guise was swept aside by the emerging democratic unions.

Yet the Syndical Organization left a pervasive legacy to contemporary Spain. While Fascism was overthrown in Italy and defeated in Germany, there was no triumphant reversal of ideology in Spain. The ease with which the whole apparatus of the OS slipped away belies the deep imprint that it left on industrial relations in post-Francoist society. The majority of organized workers gained some experience of collective action in the last fifteen years or so of the dictatorship. But there were many others—workers of small or medium-sized plants, white-collar employees, technicians—who knew only the divisive, individual, legalistic system of labour relations administered by the syndical élite. And there were millions more who had no experience of unionism of any sort. It is this heritage that explains in part the weakness of union organization in Spain today.

13. THE 'TÁCITO' GROUP AND THE TRANSITION TO DEMOCRACY, 1973–1977*

Charles T. Powell

A remarkable feature of Spain's transition from authoritarian to democratic rule was the role played by some members of the Francoist political élite.[1] Its success is partly attributable to the presence of groups within the ruling coalition which observed the minimal possible adherence to the regime during the final years of its existence while simultaneously staking out a strong position in a future democratic system of government. This was done by formulating and publicizing a political strategy and programme—which we shall describe as reform-ist—which sought to guarantee a non-violent transition to democratic rule after Franco's death. In doing so, these sectors of the Francoist élite blurred the boundaries between those 'inside' and 'outside' the official political world (never very clearly defined in authoritarian regimes), which enabled them to exercise influence in both camps. During Franco's lifetime, these groups undermined the position of those within the ruling coalition who were opposed to democratic change by making the reformist alternative attractive to the sectors of Spanish society which had benefited most from the regime's existence. After his death, they provided leadership and an element of continuity which reassured these social groups and encouraged them to partici-pate in the consolidation of the new democratic system.

It will be argued in this essay that, among the varied contributions to

---

* This article is largely based on personal recorded interviews with the following persons, to whom I am greatly indebted: José Luis Alvarez (19 July 1984), Fernando Alvarez de Miranda (7 June 1983), Iñigo Cavero (30 Nov. 1984), Jaime Cortezo (3 Apr. 1986), Juan Carlos Guerra Zunzunegui (26 July 1984), Landelino Lavilla (22 July 1983), Marcelino Oreja (5 May 1983), Juan Antonio Ortega y Díaz Ambrona (27 Sept. 1984), Alfonso Osorio (29 Nov. 1984), José Manuel Otero Novas (27 Nov. 1984), Alejandro Royo Villanova (27 July 1984), José Luis Ruiz Navarro (24 June 1987). 'Tácito' articles published between June 1973 and April 1975 are collected in 'Tácito' (Madrid, 1975), which also contains their programme.

[1] The term 'authoritarian' is used to describe political systems which are neither totalitarian nor democratic. See Juan Linz, 'An Authoritarian Regime: Spain', in E. Allardt and Y. Littunen (eds.), *Cleavages, Ideologies and Party Systems* (Helsinki, 1964).

the transition made by the reformist élite, one of the most crucial was that of the group known collectively as 'Tácito'. Accordingly, it focuses on the composition, political programme, and performance in office of the group between 1973 and 1977.[2]

'Tácito' came into existence in May 1973, after a lengthy gestation period which had its origins in a meeting of the Asociación Católica Nacional de Propagandistas (ACNP) held at Manresa in 1968.[3] The more forward-looking members of the ACNP, led by its president, Abelardo Algora, wished politically aware Propagandists of different tendencies to come together in a new group in an attempt to reunite the Francoist and anti-Francoist wings of the organization. Algora's efforts did not impress the older generation of ACNP leaders, and neither its more prominent opposition figures, notably Joaquín Ruiz Giménez and José Maria Gil Robles, nor those who collaborated with the regime at a senior level, such as Federico Silva Muñoz, lent him their support. This did not deter some of the younger, more anonymous (though politically ambitious) Propagandists, who constituted the nucleus around which 'Tácito' was to develop. Though clearly launched under the auspices of the ACNP, the latter soon adopted a low profile, and non-Propagandists were also encouraged to join the group. Once 'Tácito' had been established, Algora ceased to attend its meetings, and by mid-1974 the group no longer made use of the ACNP's premises.

'Tácito' is perhaps best defined in terms of the age and the occupational and social profile of its members. With very few exceptions, 'tácitos' had been born shortly before, during, or after the Civil War (1936–9), and were therefore in their 30s or early 40s when the group was formed. (Politicians in this age group are sometimes referred to as 'the Prince's generation'; Don Juan Carlos was born in 1938.) Almost without exception, 'tácitos' were in possession of a university degree, often in law, and a small minority had later studied abroad at a time when this was still unusual. Most of them embarked on a career in the liberal professions, particularly those which were both financially

[2] The collective pseudonym appears to have been suggested by Marcelino Oreja, who had been struck by the parallels between the Roman historian's account of Nero's words to the Senate on assuming power after the death of Claudius and the type of speech Don Juan Carlos might make on succeeding Franco. See Tacitus, *The Annals of Imperial Rome*, xiii. 4 (e.g. in English tr. by M. Grant; Harmondsworth, 1977).

[3] The ACNP, a prestigious Catholic lay organization founded in 1908, had provided the Franco regime with much of its political élite in the late 1940s and 1950s, but gradually lost influence. See M. Jerez, *Elites políticas y centros de extracción en España, 1938–1957* (Madrid, 1982).

rewarding and socially prestigious. Virtually all of those who later played leading political roles were in the service of the Francoist state, or had strong ties with it. Marcelino Oreja, Rafael Arias Salgado, and several others were career diplomats. Landelino Lavilla and Juan Antonio Ortega y Díaz Ambrona acted as *letrados* (lawyers) to the Consejo de Estado, while Alfonso Osorio, José Manuel Otero Novas, and Eduardo Carriles belonged to the other élite corps of the Spanish civil service, that of 'abogados del Estado'. A significant minority of 'tácitos' studied economics or engineering, and were employed in the public sector or had become entrepreneurs and financiers. The vast majority had been brought up in Madrid, where most were based, but between them they had ties with virtually every Spanish region. Women joined the group in very small numbers, and did not play an important role in its development.

The more active 'tácitos' had often belonged to the same political organizations in the past. Many had joined the Asociación Española de Cooperación Europea, launched by the ACNP in 1954, a Europeanist platform which became an important forum for general political debate. In many cases, it was there that future 'tácitos' were first exposed to democratic and even socialist opinion. Some had also belonged to the monarchist groups which defended Don Juan de Borbón's claim to the throne, and were amongst those who regularly visited the exiled pretender at Estoril. Fernando Alvarez de Miranda had even belonged to Don Juan's Privy Council between 1964 and 1969, when it was dissolved after the designation of his son, Don Juan Carlos, as Franco's successor.

As Algora had noted with concern, these experiences had not prevented the future 'tácitos' from drifting apart in the late 1960s and early 1970s. A small minority had actively participated in official political life, though they were still regarded as very junior members of the Francoist political class. This was particularly true of Oreja and Osorio; the former sat in the Movimiento's National Council and the Cortes, while the latter, also a member of the Cortes, had briefly belonged to the Council of the Realm, the most exclusive Francoist institution of all.[4] Much to Algora's satisfaction, 'tácitos' also attracted some of those who had taken part in relatively harmless, 'alegal' (unlawful but semi-tolerated) forms of opposition to the regime.[5] The

---

[4] For an explanation of their position, see A. Osorio, *Trayectoria política de un ministro de la Corona* (Barcelona, 1980), 15–18.

[5] See Juan Linz, 'Opposition to and under an Authoritarian Regime: The Case of

latter were generally associated with Gil Robles and Ruiz Giménez, and could boast democratic—or at least anti-Francoist—credentials which served 'Tácito' well. Juan Carlos Guerra Zunzunegui, one of the few 'tácitos' whose family had not supported Franco during the Civil War, had helped to organize the 1956 student strikes in Madrid, for which he was briefly imprisoned. In 1962, Alvarez de Miranda, Iñigo Cavero, and José Luis Ruiz Navarro had been confined by the authorities for several months after attending a meeting with representatives of the exiled anti-Francoist opposition in Munich. These backgrounds, however, were not typical of the group as a whole; the majority of 'tácitos' had neither held office under the regime nor had they actively opposed it.

'Tácito's' early influence was largely determined by its ready access to the Catholic press. The decision—taken at the instigation of Cavero and Lavilla, with Osorio's disapproval—to publish a weekly article discussing current affairs or matters of general interest was thus decisive. For almost four years, between June 1973 and February 1977—with brief interruptions in August 1975 and 1976—'Tácito' met every Wednesday evening to discuss the article to be published two days later. The articles initially appeared in *Ya*, the Madrid daily owned by the Editorial Católica, whose board of directors included a number of 'tácitos'.[6] Within a year, they were being reproduced by some twenty newspapers throughout Spain. Although it is impossible to estimate how many readers 'Tácito' attracted, in 1975 the newspapers in question were selling over half-a-million copies a day.

Due to the nature of the group and the absence of an official register, accurate membership figures are not readily available. Routine meetings were generally attended by fewer than a dozen people, but forty or more would congregate to discuss a major political event. In all, some ninety different people belonged to 'Tácito' at various stages in its development. The group was therefore not much smaller than most of the proto-parties which constituted the 'alegal' opposition, and probably had more bona fide followers than some.[7]

Spain', in R. A. Dahl (ed.), *Regimes and Oppositions* (New Haven, 1973), 210–19.

[6] The ACNP founded Editorial Católica in 1912, and was closely associated with the Press thereafter. At least two 'tácitos', Luis Apostua (sub-director of *Ya*) and José Luis Alonso Almodóvar (director of *Diario Palentino*) were professional journalists. See A. Saez Alba, *La ACNP y el caso de El Correo de Andalucía* (Paris, 1974).

[7] Gil Robles's 'party', Federación Popular Democrática, claimed to have some 400 members in 1975. Ignacio Camuñas's Partido Demócrata Popular and Francisco Fernández Ordóñez's Partido Social Demócrata had even fewer.

'Tácito's' emergence in mid-1973 raises a number of questions concerning the role of dissidents within the ruling coalition of an authoritarian regime. Above all, why—and when—do élites belonging to social groups which have hitherto supported the regime and benefited from its existence begin to distance themselves from it?

One explanation would appear to be the regime's gradual loss of legitimacy. By the early 1970s, the Franco regime's legitimacy rested largely on the 'order' it had restored to Spanish life and on the socio-economic progress over which it had presided. In 'Tácito's' view, an excessively high price was being paid for the former, and the regime was no longer necessary for—and was possibly a hindrance to—the consolidation of the latter. The very nature of the regime had prevented it from achieving an effective national reconciliation after the Civil War, and had fostered anachronistic antagonisms. 'Tácito' believed the Francoist state had failed to assert the supremacy of civil over military authority, and held it responsible for institutionalizing an anomalous relationship with the Church. Furthermore, the regime's twin policies of political centralization and cultural repression had only served to exacerbate the regional question. In the sphere of labour relations, official legislation and institutions were questioned by workers and employers alike. Finally, 'Tácito' resented the fact that the regime's origins had prevented Spain's integration into Europe and her full acceptance by the international community.

Loss of legitimacy, however, may be a necessary but not sufficient condition for regime transformation; what really matters is the absence or presence of preferable alternatives.[8] Given Spain's geo-strategic position, her recent socio-economic development, and her political culture, the most obvious alternative to authoritarian rule was a Western-style democracy. By the early 1970s, even Spaniards who had supported the regime—as well as those who had passively tolerated it —had begun to believe that their socio-economic interests could be safeguarded in a democratic context as well as—or even better than— in an authoritarian one. Simultaneously, some of their self-appointed representatives in the ruling coalition—groups such as 'Tácito'— gradually became convinced that they could ratify (and even improve) their position via competitive elections.

Admittedly, many Spaniards had been aware of the democratic

[8] A. Przeworski, 'Some Problems in the Study of Transition to Democracy', in G. O'Donnell, P. Schmitter, and L. Whitehead (eds.), *Transitions from Authoritarian Rule: Comparative Perspectives* (Baltimore, 1986), 50–6.

alternative long before certain sectors of the official political class openly acknowledged its appeal. The emergence and development of these reformist nuclei was largely—though not exclusively—determined by the imminence of Franco's death. Attempts to institutionalize the regime also affected reformists' perceptions of the likelihood of success. The designation of a successor (Prince Don Juan Carlos, 1969), the appointment—and subsequent assassination—of a head of government, other than Franco himself (Admiral Luis Carrero Blanco, 1973), and his replacement by a civilian (Carlos Arias Navarro, 1974), are all examples of this. The more far-sighted sectors of the political élite were similarly conditioned by fluctuations in the distribution of power within the ruling coalition, particularly when these resulted in attempts to 'liberalize' the regime from within. Exogenous factors, notably the collapse of authoritarian rule in Portugal (April 1974) and Greece (July 1974) were also taken into account.

'Tácito's' very existence raises a related question, namely: why did those in power tolerate dissent within the ruling coalition? A possible explanation is that some of the advantages of the existence of an opposition in democratic systems of government also apply to authoritarian regimes.[9] As long as internal dissidents accept the regime—albeit temporarily—their participation could provide it with considerable flexibility by shifting blame, giving hope to emergent leaders, and broadening the base of recruitment. Significantly, at the time only the extreme hard-line sectors of the ruling coalition regarded 'Tácito' as a threat to the regime's stability.

'Tácito's' programme was conceived as an attempt to provide fresh answers to the many questions posed by the prospect of Franco's death. It was based on the premise that under Franco Spain had developed into a country not unlike her Western European neighbours, and that Spanish society was therefore ready for democratic rule. In effect, 'Tácito' was advocating far-reaching political change while at the same time accepting existing socio-economic conditions as fundamentally valid.[10]

'Tácito' came into being partly as a reaction to Carrero Blanco's appointment as head of government in June 1973. This was generally perceived as a victory for the regime's 'continuistas', those who wished

[9] See Linz, 'Opposition', pp. 226 ff.

[10] This is not to say that 'Tácito' was not critical of some of the consequences of the so-called Spanish economic miracle: the group advocated a far-reaching fiscal reform, the extension of welfare services and the socialization of education. See 'Tácito', pp. 35–8.

to uphold the status quo. 'Tácitos' were unanimous in the conviction that the Franco regime could not outlive its founder, and therefore regarded 'continuismo' as an irresponsible and ultimately suicidal attempt to postpone the inevitable. By opposing attempts to liberalize the regime from within, the hard-liners could only increase the likelihood of a sharp, possibly violent, break with the past, and would become its first victims. 'The option', a prominent 'tácito' declared, 'is not continuity versus change, but gradual change versus abrupt change.' This is not to say that 'Tácito' had no sympathy for those who thought of a future without Franco with apprehension. On the contrary, its message to them was a simple one: Franco's death would entail democratic change, but if anticipated and supervised by the General's lawful sucessors, the latter would be in a position to ensure that those who had prospered under the regime would have nothing to fear.

'Tácito' was equally critical of the anti-Francoist opposition's 'ruptura democrática' programme, which envisaged the creation of a representative provisional government (presumably at some point after Franco's death), a plebiscite to decide the republic vs. monarchy issue, and the immediate restoration of the Statutes of Autonomy granted under the Second Republic. Even if the opposition were sincere in their avowed rejection of the use of violence to further their cause, 'Tácito' feared that any attempt to break sharply with the past would inevitably lead to a military intervention. Furthermore, a non-violent 'ruptura' presupposed a spontaneous collapse of authority, and could only succeed if it enjoyed the active support of broad sectors of the population. 'Tácito' thought the opposition could take neither of these for granted. The Portuguese revolution had some useful lessons to offer, but comparisons should not be drawn too closely. Spain was not involved in a colonial war of long standing, the armed forces of the two countries had little in common, and Franco had named his successor. Above all, Spain had endured a civil war which made a lasting impact on its political culture.

'Tácito' believed the only viable alternative to the above was a democratizing process originating from within the existing political framework and respectful of the established constitutional order and its own systems of reform. Although it was generally agreed that this would only get under way in earnest after Franco's death, there was considerable debate within the group as to how the reformist programme could best be advanced during his lifetime. The more conservative wing of the group, represented by Osorio, advocated limited reforms which would free the hitherto undeveloped democratic potential of existing institutions. Osorio had been a 'procurador familiar' for the province of Santander in the Cortes, and believed the latter could be made more representative by increasing the proportion of directly elected members.[11] Similarly, he hoped office-holders at the municipal level would be made accountable to the electorate at large. These reforms, it was argued, could make the transition to a fully democratic system of government less traumatic. This optimism was not shared by the more progressive—or perhaps simply sceptical—'tácitos', such as Alvarez de Miranda and Cavero, who never believed those in power would make significant concessions. Most members stood somewhere in between these two positions, and favoured a pragmatic approach, advocated by the likes of José Luis Alvarez, which was to allow 'Tácito' to adapt to new circumstances as they arose.

'Tácitos' may have disagreed amongst themselves as to how much they should expect from reforms attempted during Franco's lifetime, but they never doubted the General's successors would be in a position to initiate the democratizing process. The most important successor was, of course, the future king, whom many 'tácitos' knew personally. Those amongst them who enjoyed easy access to Don Juan were generally on close terms with his son as well. Many of the younger 'tácitos' who did not share this monarchist background had been taken to La Zarzuela to meet the then prince by the head of the ACNP's University College of San Pablo, Jacobo Cano, and Don Juan Carlos often visited the institution. These visits became even more frequent when Cano left the college to become the Prince's personal secretary. These contacts proved useful for Don Juan Carlos as well as for the future 'tácitos', for it enabled him to counteract the popularity of his cousin Don Alfonso, a former student of the San Pablo. In spite of having been nominated Franco's successor, Don Juan Carlos continued to regard Alfonso as a rival, particularly after his marriage to Franco's granddaughter in 1972.

The group's ties with La Zarzuela proved decisive in the development of its reformist programme. 'Tácito' enjoyed the Prince's confidence to the extent that in the summer of 1974 he inspired an article

---

[11] Since 1967, every Spanish province was represented in the Cortes by two 'procuradores familiares', elected by heads of households and married women. They were the only directly elected members of the Cortes, and represented approximately 20% of the total.

of theirs which criticized the decision to make him temporary head of state on account of Franco's ill health. Ortega y Diaz Ambrona recalls that 'we knew, because he had told us so himself, that at the time he did not want to become head of state, and would only do so again if it was for good, which is why we wrote such a critical article'. Partly as a result of this mutual trust, leading 'tácitos' were confident that after Franco's death the future king would seek to legitimize the monarchy by leading the democratizing process from above. In Ortega y Diaz Ambrona's view, 'as far as we were concerned, particularly after the fall of the Colonels in Greece, this was absolutely clear'. The support of 'Tácito' for the Prince nevertheless remained conditional on his ability to become the constitutional monarch of a parliamentary democracy. 'Only D. Juan Carlos and the monarchy can provide a way out of the Franco regime,' an internal 'Tácito' document observed, 'and not for emotional or technical reasons, but for pragmatic ones.'[12]

The type of operation envisaged by the group required more than the future king's commitment to democratic change, however. The reformist strategy also presupposed the existence of mechanisms whereby the Francoist constitutional framework could be reformed out of existence without contravening the letter of the law. This could be done in a number of ways, depending on the political objectives chosen. For 'Tácito', the election by universal suffrage of a legislative assembly capable of initiating a constituent process if it so decided was the key to a reform of this type. What was more, 'Tácito' believed the creation of such an assembly was possible without contravening the Francoist constitution; this could be done under the terms of the Law of Succession, which stipulated that the modification of a fundamental law (that is to say, a law of constitutional rank) required the executive to hear the National Council of the Movimiento, obtain the approval of the Cortes, and consult the nation by means of a referendum. Tortuous though it seemed to many, 'Tácito' favoured this procedure because it did not wish the future king to risk his prestige and authority in a more daring operation. Furthermore, the strict observation of Francoist legality would dissuade those opposed to change—including the more politicized members of the armed forces—from rejecting it on constitutional grounds.

---

[12] The article in question was 'La interinidad' (26 July 1974). On the monarchy, see also Una Monarquía social (7 Aug. 1973) and Un príncipe leal y un pueblo libre (29 Nov. 1974). Internal 'Tácito' document 1 (no title, no date, but probably May–June 1975).

Above all, the faith of 'Tácito' in the viability of the reformist alternative was based on the assumption that it would prove acceptable to
the majority of the population. In particular, it was thought the reformist programme would appeal most to 'a very wide section of the labour-
ing and professional middle classes . . . moderate people with a voice
which must be heard and who, due to their very nature, have not been
organized or even appealed to'. Indeed the potentially disastrous
consequences of this political demobilization constituted one of the
group's overriding obsessions. Events in Portugal, it was argued, had
shown what could happen in Spain if these sectors of society failed to
make themselves ready for the unavoidable changes which lay ahead.
'In times of crisis', 'Tácito' warned, 'it is impossible to improvise
leaders and programmes capable of attracting and representing an
electorate which is understandably disorientated and highly critical of
the past.' The group feared that if the silent majority it wished to
represent failed to organize themselves politically, the immediate post-
Franco era would be dominated by two determined minorities, one
actively committed to the regime's overthrow, the other to its survival.
'The extremes', 'Tácito' concluded, 'always proliferate when there is a
vacuum in the centre, and the only antidote is therefore to strengthen
the Centre.'[13]

During the early stages of its development, 'Tácito' may be said to
have adopted an attitude of 'semi-opposition' to the regime. According
to Juan Linz, one form of 'semi-opposition' is that practised by 'dissidents within the élite favouring different long-term policies and
institutional alternatives, but accepting the top leadership—perhaps
somewhat conditionally and temporarily—and willing to hold office'.[14]
The ambiguity of the group's position is reflected in its first public
statement—debated at great length and finally issued in December
1973 which announced that it would 'adhere' ('se sujetará') to the
existing legal order. In spite of its criticism of Carrero Blanco's efforts
to put the clock back, at first 'Tácito' barely succeeded in irritating the
government. Indeed, Alejandro Royo Villanova, one of the younger
members of the group, has evidence that the Admiral was 'quite sympathetic towards "Tácito", because he believed there should be a
degree of opposition, but a respectable one, and one which was not

---

[13] *'Tácito'*, pp. 23–4. See 'El Reto' (8 Nov. 1974), 'Portugal, un nuevo rumbo'
(17 May 1975), 'Frente a los extremismos' (4 Oct. 1974).

[14] Linz, 'Opposition', pp. 191–9, and L. García San Miguel, 'Para una sociología del
cambio político y la oposición en la España actual', *Sistema*, 4 (January 1974), 95–9.

Marxist'. Seen in this light, 'Tácito' seemed 'a minor, necessary evil'. It is unlikely that this paternalistic benevolence would have continued for long had Carrero Blanco witnessed the group's later development, but it is nevertheless a surprising example of toleration of internal dissent.

The assassination of Admiral Carrero Blanco by ETA in December 1973 and the subsequent formation of the Arias Navarro government presented the reformist 'semi-opposition', and 'Tácito' in particular, with a serious dilemma. The new government's programme, outlined to the Cortes by Arias on 12 February 1974, represented not only the promise of a limited liberalization of the regime but also an attempt to bring the reformist 'semi-opposition' back into the fold. The reformists realized that their participation in a limited and ultimately ineffective liberalization could tarnish their democratic credibility, while their indifference was sure to condemn Arias's initiative to failure even before it was launched. What was more, the government's intentions were theoretically compatible with the reformist principle according to which the foundations of the transition to democracy would have to be laid—partially at least—during Franco's lifetime.

The so-called 'spirit of 12 February' was largely the creation of Pío Cabanillas and Antonio Carro, respectively the Minister of Information and the Minister of the Presidency. The 'tácitos' Oreja, Gabriel Cañadas, and Royo Villanova were invited to work under Cabanillas, while two others, José Ramon Lasuén and Luis Jáudenes, joined Carro's team. The latter could also have included Ortega y Díaz Ambrona, who preferred to become director of the Institute of Administrative Studies instead. Another 'tácito', Lavilla, accepted a senior post in the Ministry of Industry.

The centre-piece of the Arias programme was undoubtedly the long-awaited legislation regulating the right of political association. Arias's speech reopened the debate concerning the nature of the Movimento and the future role of 'political associations' within the Francoist political system. Since Spain's constitutional framework had remained virtually unchanged during the Carrero Blanco era, the reformists found themselves echoing the views defended by Manuel Fraga Iribarne and other 'aperturistas' (those in favour of 'opening' the regime) in the 1960s. 'Tácito' spoke for them all when it warned the government in June 1974 that 'the political associations must never be placed under the organized control of administrative structures parallel to those of the State. That is to say, we believe in associations which may exist within the framework of certain principles, but not within the Movimiento understood as an organization.'[15] Ortega y Díaz Ambrona, who had been asked to work on the project, set out to translate these views into concrete legislative proposals, but these were soon declared unsuitable by Movimento officials.

The reformist team at the Ministry of Information was initially more successful. In Royo Villanova's opinion, 'shortly after our arrival the Press began to say more or less what it pleased . . . ideas and opinions which had not been discussed in public before began to be aired'. This is a somewhat over-generous view of the situation, given that many publications still ran into difficulties with the censors, but there undoubtedly existed greater freedom of expression than hitherto. Significantly, it was this facet of Arias's programme which irritated the hard-line sectors of the Francoist political class most.

'Tácito' found it increasingly difficult to reconcile its support for Arias with its commitment to reformism. In March 1974 the government attempted to expel the bishop of Bilbao, Antonio Añoveros, for authorizing a sermon read in every church of the diocese which was interpreted as a defence of Basque national rights. 'Tácito' reacted with caution, to the extent that Alvarez de Miranda accused the group of having sold out to the government. Another 'tácito', Jaime Cortezo, went even further, and left the group altogether.[16]

By late October, Arias could no longer stand up to mounting pressure to put an end to Cabanillas's liberalizing experiment, and the minister was asked to resign. The crisis had immediate consequences for 'Tácito'. Royo Villanova and Oreja came under intense pressure from those who wished them to stay, but they paid no heed. Ortega y Díaz Ambrona waited for several weeks in the hope that the new Estatuto de Asociaciones would prove acceptable, but resigned when he realized this was not to be.[17] Their reaction met the approval of most fellow 'tácitos', particularly those who had been reluctant to support the government earlier in the year. Nevertheless, a small minority, amongst them Osorio and Jáudenes, insisted that Cabanillas's fall did not seriously threaten the viability of the Arias programme, and saw no

---

[15] See 'El reto asociativo' (22 June 1974) and 'El marco constitucional del Derecho de Asociación' (12 July 1974).

[16] See 'Dos semanas de preocupación' (12 Mar. 1974). Fernando Alvarez de Miranda, *Del 'contubernio al consenso'* (Barcelona, 1985), 78. 'Tácito' had already advocated a clearer separation of Church and State in *Relaciones Iglesia–Estado* (3 July 1973).

[17] To the embarrassment of 'Tácito', neither Lavilla nor Jáudenes resigned.

reason why 'Tácito' should withdraw its support. In Osorio's opinion, Oreja and others were wrong to regard Cabanillas as the champion of their cause, for 'it should not be forgotten that it was he who stopped our article on the Añoveros crisis, which is why we published a weaker version'. These arguments failed to convince his friends, however, and on 31 October 'Tácito' published a highly critical article, written by Cañadas, which concluded: 'there was an opportunity to follow the path which had been outlined in the speeches and which we had defended. A different one was chosen . . . a political alternative ceased to exist yesterday.'[18]

The fears raised by the October crisis were confirmed two months later when the new Estatuto de Asociaciones was made public. At a special meeting held on 25 January 1975, 'Tácito' decided that in view of the Estatuto's limitations it would not form an 'association'. Only a small faction, led by Osorio, objected to this resolution, and later left the group to form their own 'association', Unión Democrática Española.

'Tácito's' rejection of the Estatuto reopened the internal debate as to the nature of the group and its future role. As Oreja wrote in April 1975, it was necessary to decide whether 'Tácito' was 'merely a platform where like-minded people of different political backgrounds come together on an informal basis, or whether the time has come to articulate a political group with its own discipline, programme, and organization'.[19] A majority of 'tácitos' favoured the second option, largely because they wished to help bring together the constellation of independent reformist personalities which cluttered the Spanish political scene. In the summer of 1975 'Tácito' was to play a key role in the creation of FEDISA, a reformist platform whose very existence spelt the failure of the Estatuto. The decision to institutionalize the group, however, necessarily entailed the departure of 'tácitos' such as Alvarez de Miranda and Cavero, who already belonged to a political party.

In the wake of the January meeting, 'Tácito' ceased to behave like a debating society and adopted the trappings of an embryonic political party. In April 1975 the group published its programme and articles in book form. This allowed prominent 'tácitos' to travel throughout the country giving numerous talks and press conferences, which led to the

[18] *El Estatuto de Asociaciones* (6 Dec. 1974).

[19] Internal 'Tácito' document 2, entitled 'Breve reseña de Tácito y reflexiones en el momento actual', dated 8 Apr. 1975, signed by Oreja.

setting up of small branches in Barcelona, Valencia, Seville, and elsewhere.

'Tácito' modified its strategy in other respects as well. The most important of these was the decision to forge closer links with the institutionalized opposition. Between February and April 1975 prominent 'tácitos' exchanged views with leaders of the Socialist Party (PSOE), various Christian Democratic parties (amongst them Ruiz Giménez's Izquierda Democrática and Gil Robles's Federación Popular Democrática), Social Democratic groups, the Basque Nationalist Party (PNV), and representatives of Catalan nationalism. Secret talks were also held, on a more informal basis, with Communist Party leaders in Spain and abroad, and with representatives of the Workers' Commissions (CCOO). That summer, an internal 'Tácito' document concluded: 'even though they do not believe in it, and even dislike it, a large sector of the opposition will support the reformist solution if it advances, and would certainly participate if it succeeded. Indeed they might not oppose it if the necessary contacts are made and adequate explanations are given.'[20]

The public statements of 'Tácito' during this period also became increasingly critical of the Arias government and its inability to prepare for the succession. Ortega y Díaz Ambrona set the tone at the Club Siglo XXI in February, when he declared: 'a democratization is still possible, but it is unlikely and will soon be unattainable'. Three months later, their articles had become positively alarmist: 'If in 1973 there was still some hope of a gradual evolution, today it is evident that anything short of immediate reform will mean accepting unforeseeable risks.' In private, 'tácitos' were even more explicit. An internal document observed: 'It is clear that reforms cannot be put into effect under the present head of state, both because of him and the groups which influence him. The opposition will never agree to negotiate with him and it is impossible to obtain foreign support or acknowledgement with Franco in power.'[21] This led them to advocate a solution already proposed by certain reformists in the wake of Franco's first illness, in mid-1974, namely Don Juan Carlos's accession to the throne during Franco's lifetime. With hindsight, Ortega y Díaz Ambrona and others readily acknowledge that this would have been highly counterproductive, but at the time it enabled 'Tácito' to dissociate itself publicly from those in power. Less than a month before Franco's death, 'Tácito' had

---

[20] Internal document 1.
[21] Internal document 1.

an article stopped for the first time. Written largely by Ortega y Díaz Ambrona, it defended the view that 'a monarchy for all Spaniards has to be a democratic monarchy'; only then would Franco's true successors, the Spanish people, regain their sovereignty. This proved excessively daring for the censors, and the group was taken to court. The case was later dropped, but the incident allowed 'Tácito' to pose—however briefly—as a victim of the regime's repressive legislation. By late 1975, therefore, 'Tácito' had ceased to behave like a 'semi-opposition' group in order to adopt many of the traits of an 'alegal' opposition proto-party.

Franco's death and Don Juan Carlos's proclamation as King of Spain in November 1975 marked the beginning of a new phase for 'Tácito'. Although it never supported the second Arias government, formed in December, with the enthusiasm it had shown for the first, 'Tácito' was once again associated with those in power. Osorio, who still regarded himself as a 'tácito' even though he no longer attended its meetings, was appointed Minister of the Presidency at the King's suggestion. Leopoldo Calvo Sotelo, who had kept a low profile in the group, became Minister of Public Works. The new Minister of the Interior, Fraga Iribarne, asked the 'tácito' José Manuel Otero Novas to become his expert in domestic political affairs. Oreja, who remained one of the group's more influential figures, joined José María de Areilza at the Ministry of Foreign Affairs.

'Tácito' encouraged the new government to adopt a reformist strategy consisting of three successive stages. The first envisaged a 'liberalization' resulting in the recognition of all democratic rights and freedoms. This would be followed by a 'democratization', which would culminate in free elections to all representative institutions. The final stage, described as a 'substantive constitutional reform', would enable the newly elected (*de facto*) constituent assembly to consolidate a democratic constitutional framework.[22]

The group's optimism was such that at a meeting held in January 1976 it was agreed that in view of the imminent democratic elections the group's top priority should be the creation of a political party. In spite of the presence of prominent reformists in the cabinet, however, the new government did not perform as expected, largely due to the attitude of Arias himself. This induced 'Tácito' to become increasingly explicit as to the type of democracy it wished to see installed. The group's original programme, circulated in April 1975, had included

[22] 'La tarea del nuevo Gobierno' (12 Dec. 1975).

amongst its objectives a bicameral system with a lower house elected by universal suffrage. This suggests that at that stage it did not discard the possibility of an indirectly elected upper house (Senate). A year later, however, 'Tácito' explicitly rejected the constitutional reform contemplated by the second Arias government, which envisaged the creation of such a Senate. Similarly, although its programme had clearly stated that 'sovereignty resides in the people and only those who are its legitimate representatives may govern', 'Tácito' did not explicitly demand that future governments be accountable to the Cortes until the Arias reform failed to meet its approval on this issue. In private, 'Tácito' had given these matters a good deal of thought, however. By mid-1975, the group had already decided it wanted to see an electoral system based on principles of proportional representation, incorporating correcting devices to prevent the proliferation of small parties. The system adopted two years later met these requirements entirely.[23]

The second Arias government's policy towards the democratic opposition, which sought to isolate the Communist Party and the radical left from their more 'moderate' allies also forced 'Tácito' to take a stand. In an article published in September 1974, the group repudiated 'those who defend fratricidal violence, Communism and any other form of totalitarianism'. Similarly, an internal document circulated in mid-1975 advocated the temporary exclusion of the Communist Party from the official political scene during the early stages of democratization. In April 1976, however, precisely a year before its legalization, 'Tácito' announced its support for Communist participation in the first elections. True to form, this was defended as a necessary concession to political realities, rather than as a matter of principle.[24]

In view of the government's failure to make significant progress on the road to full democratization, Arias's dismissal in early July 1976 raised the hopes of 'Tácito' once more. On this occasion, they were amply rewarded. Following the King's advice, Arias's successor, Adolfo Suárez, relied on Osorio, whom he promoted to the vice-presidency of the cabinet, to help him pick his ministers. Suárez felt he could not call on his own friends and colleagues, virtually all of whom had made careers in the official Movimiento structure. In spite of

[23] *Tácito*, p. 46. See 'No, pero' (1 Feb. 1976); 'La piedra de toque del reformismo' (26 Mar. 1976); 'Qué reforma?' (30 Apr. 1976).

[24] 'Puntualizaciones' (20 Sept. 1974); internal document 1; 'Extrañas alianzas' (2 Apr. 1976).

earlier differences of opinion, Osorio even approached Alvarez de Miranda, though he was later turned down. In all, no fewer than seven of the twenty ministers in Suárez's first government were (or had been) active 'tácitos'. As Suárez himself has admitted, it was to be the most cohesive and effective government over which he ever presided.[25]

'Tácito' read the difficulties encountered by the second Arias government as proof of the need for a more daring approach. Under Arias, Fraga had sought to introduce limited reforms which would allow for the election of a democratic congress without modifying other aspects of the Constitution. This approach had failed, and as early as April 1976 'Tácito' had begun to think in terms of a single reform law which would lead to the election of a democratic Cortes conceived as a *de facto* constituent assembly. As we saw earlier, such a law would have to meet the approval of the existing Cortes before it could be put to the nation in the form of a referendum. In the final years of his rule, Franco had congratulated himself for having left everything 'tied and well tied down'; the response of 'Tácito' could almost be summed up in a single article heading: 'Consult the nation, and cut the knot' (23 April 1976).

'Tácitos' in office played a major role in the events leading to the first democratic elections in June 1977. Between July 1976 and the spring of 1977 Osorio was Suárez's most influential advisor. Lavilla, the cabinet's leading constitutional expert, played a major role in drafting the decisive law of political reform, passed by the Cortes in November 1976. As Minister of Justice, he also planned and carried out the delicate legal operation whereby the major political parties — including the Communists — were legalized in the spring of 1977. Otero Novas, one of Suárez's closest advisors during this period, acted as the government's middleman in its dealings with the democratic opposition, as he had already done under Fraga. Another 'tácito', Enrique de la Mata, Minister for the Sindicatos, established contacts with the leaders of the illegal trade unions which paved the way for their legalization and the recognition of fundamental trade union rights in April–May 1977. Throughout this period, Oreja, Suárez's Foreign Minister, displayed an intense diplomatic activity which helped to establish the government's credibility abroad.

[25] Those associated with 'Tácito' were: Eduardo Carriles (Treasury), Leopoldo Calvo Sotelo (Public Works), Landelino Lavilla (Justice), Enrique de la Mata (Sindicatos), Marcelino Oreja (Foreign Affairs), Alfonso Osorio (Presidency), and Andrés Reguera (Information and Tourism).

The presence of prominent 'tácitos' in a government committed to far-reaching reforms left the rest of the group free to pursue its other, complementary goal, namely the creation of a political party capable of winning the first elections and of contributing to the consolidation of the emerging democratic system.

In spite of its origins, 'Tácito' had long since dismissed the idea of creating a Christian Democratic party in Spain. Most of its members were opposed to the existence of confessional parties on principle, and it was generally feared that the Christian Democratic label would alienate many of the group's potential constituents.[26] Furthermore, the more influential members of the Catholic hierarchy, notably Cardinal Tarancón and his *alter ego*, José María Martin Patino, had publicly discouraged the creation of such a party. According to Osorio, who was in favour of uniting the large though divided Christian Democratic family, Martin Patino, a personal friend of Cabanillas, was largely responsible for frustrating his plans.

By April 1976, 'Tácito' was already working towards the creation of a centrist, mass-based party, capable of attracting support from all sectors of society. The main concern of 'Tácito' was to bring together the numerous existing centrist groups and 'parties', and it was not going to allow strictly ideological considerations to stand in its way. In keeping with the pragmatism of 'Tácito', the future party's ideological purity would have to be sacrificed in order to maximize electoral support. Though fundamentally inspired in the principles of Christian humanism, 'Tácito' hoped it would appeal to Liberals, Social Democrats, and independents, as well as Christian Democrats.[27]

These ideas weighed decisively in the formation of the Partido Popular, formally launched in December 1976. Two months later, the last article of 'Tácito' announced the group's formal integration in the new party. Ironically, the 'conservative' and 'progressive' factions which had left 'Tácito' in early 1975, and which had gone on to form Unión Democrática Española (Osorio, Eduardo Carriles, Andrés Reguera) and the Partido Popular Demócrata Cristiano (Alvarez de Miranda, Cavero, Ortega y Díaz Ambrona) respectively, had come together in the autumn of 1976 as a new Partido Demócrata Cristiano.

[26] *Tácito*, p. 28. The use of the Christian label was explicitly rejected in 'La familia y el matrimonio' (27 Feb. 1976). For an attempt to account for the absence of a Christian Democratic party in Spain, see C. Huneeus, *La Unión de Centro Democrático y la transición a la democracia en España* (Madrid, 1985), 175–90.

[27] See 'Un gran partido interclasista' (9 Apr. 1976), 'El gran Partido Popular' (11 June 1976), and 'Un partido para una situación nueva' (18 June 1976).

The latter joined the Partido Popular in mid-January 1977, thereby forming the nucleus of the future Centro Democrático. Indeed the only politically active 'tácitos' who did not join the new party were those who had left the group in 1974–5 but had remained loyal to Ruiz Giménez. The latter would also have joined Centro Democrático, had it not been for Gil Robles's party, their partners, who insisted they should fight the elections as a clearly defined Christian Democratic alternative.

With the full approval of the more influential ex-'tácitos', in March 1977 party leaders sacrificed Centro Democrático's independence as well as their most popular colleague, Areilza, in return for unlimited government backing and Suárez's leadership. This did not come as a surprise. The party identified fully with the government's achievements—as 'Tácito' had done—and Suárez needed a suitable electoral vehicle. What was more, most of its leaders, the ex-'tácitos' included, were no longer certain of winning the elections on their own. This pact led to the somewhat improvised creation of Unión de Centro Democrático, the party which was to govern Spain until 1982.[28]

'Tácito' was right to assume that a majority of Spaniards would support (or at least tolerate) a gradual, non-violent transition to democracy after Franco's death on the understanding that neither their physical integrity nor material prosperity would be seriously endangered. The group was also correct in anticipating the King's role as a 'modernizing monarch', and in assuming that the armed forces—as an institution—would not interrupt the democratizing process as long as it was undertaken in accordance with the Francoist constitution, and by members of the pre-existing political élite, accountable only to the King.[29] 'Lastly, it was quick to see that the anti-Francoist opposition forces would discover—if they did not already know it—that the 'ruptura' they had envisaged was beyond their reach and would therefore agree to collaborate with the King and his cabinet in establishing a truly democratic system of government. The idea of a 'reforma pactada' ('negotiated break') was already implicit in the group's programme and strategy by mid-1975. Unlike most of those who theorized about the post-Franco era during the final years of the

---

[28] Twelve ex-'tácitos' won a seat in the Cortes in 1977, including Alvarez de Miranda, who became president of the new Congress. Three others (Lavilla, Oreja, and Osorio) sat in the Senate as royal nominees. A total of 25 ex-'tácitos' were elected to the Cortes in 1979.

[29] The role of the 'modernizing monarch' is discussed in S. Huntington, *Political Order in Changing Societies* (New Haven, 1968), ch. 3.

regime, 'Tácito' saw its members rise to positions of authority and implement their ideas with considerable success. Having belonged to both the 'semi-' and 'alegal' oppositions, 'Tácito' was ideally suited for the task of bridging the gap between the pre-existing political élite and that which had been denied a lawful and public existence until 1977. In doing so, its members made a significant contribution to the climate of mutual respect and generosity which marked Spain's transition to democracy.

14. THE IDEOLOGICAL CONVERSION OF THE LEADERS OF THE PSOE, 1976–1979*

Santos Juliá

'When we say our party is Marxist, we have serious reasons for doing so.'
Felipe González, August 1976

'It's a mistake for a socialist party to declare itself Marxist.'
Felipe González, May 1978

'Basically, I haven't changed, and there are my statements to prove it.'
Felipe González, June 1979

During the 1976 Summer School of the Partido Socialista Obrero Español (PSOE), the Spanish Socialist Workers' Party, the party secretary, Felipe González, delivered a long speech to an audience composed mainly of Socialists who had joined the party before Franco's death in 1975, or, at the latest, before the initiation of the transition to democracy. González devoted his lecture to defining the identity of the PSOE.[1] He felt compelled to do so, for, from the beginning of the 1950s onwards, the PSOE had been losing prominence among the forces which had fought against the Francoist dictatorship until, in the regime's final years, it was far from being hailed as an organization with a political future. On the left, the PSOE's efforts paled into insignificance beside the halo which surrounded the Partido Comunista de España (PCE), the Spanish Communist Party, on account of the latter's longer and harder struggle against Francoism. In addition (and without going beyond the limited boundaries of the so-called socialist family) the historical initials of the PSOE now had to contend with serious competition from other options, such as the Partido Socialista Popular (PSP), the Popular Socialist Party, led by Enrique Tierno Galván, and others which, in recent years, had appeared all

---

* Tr. by Sheelagh Ellwood. I am grateful to Antonio García Santesmases for the help he has given me in allowing me to consult his unpublished study, 'La evolución ideológica del socialismo en la España actual'.

[1] Felipe González, 'Línea política del PSOE', *Socialismo en Libertad* (Madrid, 1976), 21–58.

over Spain. Thus, by 1976, it was necessary to re-establish the credentials of the PSOE on a firm footing; to define its identifying characteristics, what it was and what were its aspirations, with regard to both the Communists and the other Socialist groups and parties.

The PSOE's first secretary (or secretary-general) found no better way of establishing the party's identity than by appealing, above all, to its historical legitimacy: the PSOE was a party with a history behind it. However, hard on the heels of historical legitimacy came ideological legitimacy: the PSOE was defined as a 'Marxist party'. There was the bond with the *fons et origo*, and there the fidelity to the theory of the founding fathers. The PSOE was a party with a history and a Marxist party. It was other things, too. It was a democratic, mass party, which was class-based, pluralist, federative, and internationalist. But it was legitimated first and foremost by its theory and its history.

The most substantial parts of the analysis made by the first secretary of the PSOE in that speech were incorporated into the political report approved by the party's XXVII Congress, held in December of that same year. Still only semi-legal and in an ambient mood of anti-Francoist struggle and conquest of liberties, the PSOE defined itself as a 'class-based and, therefore, mass party, which is Marxist and democratic'. These selfsame adjectives had been used by Felipe González in the speech with which the PSOE was presented to its members and to public opinion. Thus, on the threshold of 1977, the PSOE defined itself as a Marxist party. No one appeared to disagree with, or to dislike, that identity, although not everyone was agreed about its meaning and implications.[2]

Eighteen months later, when the first general elections since 1936 had converted the PSOE into the leading opposition party and had routed the remaining members of the socialist family, Felipe González stated publicly that it had been a mistake to define the PSOE as Marxist. No other socialist party had done so and not even the PSOE, in all its hundred years of history, had ever before had the idea of defining itself as Marxist. There was no reason whatsoever to change that century-old custom. It had been a mistake. To undo it, the secretary-general was prepared to do battle in the bosom of his own party. How and why the PSOE switched from having serious reasons for calling

---

[2] *XXVII Congreso PSOE* (Madrid, 1977), 115–23. This was not simply the political motion adopted by the Congress. The majority of the party groups had presented motions along the same lines, or imbued with even more radical tones, as can be seen in *XXVII Congreso: Memoria de gestión de la Comisión Ejecutiva* (n.pl., n.d.), 7–68.

itself Marxist to considering such a definition a mistake, will be the object of our attention in the following pages.

THE SERIOUS REASONS FOR AVOWING MARXISM

In 1976, the Socialist Party's definition of itself as Marxist was no more than one element in a complex ideological edifice, in whose foundations lay the principle of the transition to socialism. The PSOE had few members then—scarcely 10,000—and the party lacked solid structures and organization.[3] The Socialists believed, however, that they already possessed the instrument capable of 'building a new model' of society, as yet not established in any country, and whose principal characteristic would be the combination of socialism and freedom. Far removed from social democracy, which limited itself to remedying 'the most brutal facets of capitalism', and from what they termed social dictatorship, or social bureaucracy, which was nothing more than state capitalism, the 10,000 Spanish Socialists were intent upon initiating a long march of 'transition to socialism'.[4]

In accordance with a long-established tradition, that march was envisaged as consisting of various phases, prior to reaching the new model of society, which would be 'self-managing socialism'. The first stage would be the transition from the existing state, defined as Fascist, to formal democracy. The next stage, still within the confines of democracy, would be to advance towards the implantation of the political hegemony of the working class and its allies. Finally, that same bloc of anti-capitalist classes would put an end to capitalist exploitation and would establish a classless society, in which the apparatus of the state would be entirely replaced by worker self-management at all levels. The Socialist Party, declared Felipe González to the XXVII Congress, would conquer 'irreversibly a society in which the exploitation of man by man will disappear: a classless society'.[5]

[3] For data on PSOE and UGT membership, see José F. Tezanos, 'Continuidad y cambio en el socialismo español El PSOE durante la transición a la democracia', *Sistema*, 68–9 (Nov. 1985), 24. At the time of the XXVII Congress, the total number of militants was 9,141.

[4] 'Resolución política', in *XXVII Congreso PSOE*. In 'Socialismo es libertad' (*XXVII Congress PSOE*, pp. 9–16), Alfonso Guerra defined socialism's task as 'the radical transformation of capitalist society; its replacement by a society in which relations between men are radically different to what they are at present'.

[5] And he added, in threatening tone, 'Let it be clear to one and all: the party will never renounce that goal'; 'El trabajo empieza ahora', *XXVII Congress PSOE*, p. 102.

Girt up with the Marxism ideology and with its sights fixed on the future society, the Socialist Party arrogated to itself the role of 'central axis of the progressive historical forces'. In this way, the idea of the unity of the left, or of all progressive forces, to achieve the liquidation of the Francoist dictatorship was reiterated, but with an important innovation. Until Franco's death, the would-be mainstay of that political line had been the PCE, architect of the Junta Democrática and of the first steps towards the formal co-ordination of the various sectors of the anti-Francoist opposition. The PSOE reaffirmed the validity of that approach and reproduced it in its own proposals. At the same time, however, it attempted to take upon itself the role that the long struggle against Francoism had assigned to the Communists.[6]

In order to achieve that position, it was crucial to have a large and powerful organization and to state the Marxist essence of socialism. No one who was not a Marxist could seriously hope to become the keystone of the opposition to the dictatorship, or to those who intended to be its continuation. Moreover, it was not simply a question of opportunist tactics. It was because the refusal to accept the society constructed by Francoism was inherent in the visceral rejection of Francoism and its heirs. To break with the dictatorship's political system was equivalent to repudiating the social system which had served as its underpinning. To disclaim the state was also, therefore, to disavow the society, and the construction of a new state appeared as merely the first step on the long road to the building of a new society. This, in the political context and climate of the time, was the heart, the kernel of Marxism.

Within the ranks of the political class which inherited Francoism, a reformist sector came to the fore and made contact with the forces of the opposition. As this happened, the avowal of Marxism acquired the specific function of dressing the negotiations with those in power in ideologized garb. This bargaining was, of course, carried on in accordance with the political strategy of combining pressure from below with dialogue above.[7] Such dialogue did not, however, imply

[6] See *XXVII Congress PSOE*, 'Resolución política', p. 108. Felipe González expressed a similar idea when he said that the party must 'jealously guard its independence' and, at the same time, 'put its shoulder to the wheel with all the organizations which pursue the same objective', momentarily or strategically.

[7] The policy of pressure and negotiation was proclaimed by Felipe González during the Summer School, adopted by the XXVII Congress, and reaffirmed by González in his speeches to the Congress. José M. Maravall has explained the transition as a mixture of reformist policy from above and social pressure from below, in J. M. Maravall, *La política de la transición* (Madrid, 1981), 17–31.

reneging on essentials, nor renouncing the final goal. Negotiations were entered into because this was the way to press forward on the long march to socialism. When all was said and done, the first stage laid down by the theory was, precisely, the conquest of democracy.

In addition to being the expression of opposition to Francoism as a political genre and the ideological alibi for what ultimately became known as the 'negotiated break' (*ruptura pactada*), the claim to a Marxist vocation also fulfilled a particular purpose in the PSOE's attempts to become the only socialist party and to talk to the PCE on equal terms. The self-definition of the PSOE as a democratic, Marxist party, and its proposals for self-managing socialism (upheld by such prestigious economists as Miguel Boyer), blocked the appearance of ideological competitors for the same political territory. In the jockeying for positions to decide which party was the most Marxist, the PSOE leaders did not allow themselves to be overwhelmed by their nearest neighbours, who, one after another, were gradually integrated into the PSOE. The last of them was incorporated just a few days before the definitive abjuration of Marxism.[8]

Above all, the avowal of Marxism allowed the PSOE to go to its inevitable rendezvous with the PCE without an inferiority complex. Everyone was on the same side, the heirs of the same traditions. Certainly, they each had different ways of interpreting those traditions—that much had to be clear—but, even so, they were not mutually exclusive ways. If they did not allow Marxism to be snatched from them, the Socialists could become the Communists' rivals in the struggle to attract a left-wing electorate which was, foreseeably, very ideology-conscious. The disdain with which the Communist leaders treated the new-comers, their young competitors, turned into bitter disappointment when they saw the results obtained by the PSOE thanks to a political line which linked references to Marxism with an emphasis on liberty.

Laying claim to Marxism as a characteristic of the socialist identity should thus be seen as the result, or the expression, of the political culture of left-wing, anti-Francoist opposition, which implied the rejection of Francoism's political system and the repudiation of its capitalist society. However, it should also be seen as the key ideological

---

[8] The unity of the socialists in a single party—rather than in a federation of parties— was one of the central concerns of the PSOE leaders in 1976 and 1977. Santesmases (loc. cit.) identifies four socialist groups at the beginning of the transition: the PSOE which was loyal to the leadership in exile, the PSP, the Federation of Socialist Parties, and the PSOE recognized by the Socialist International.

element in the PSOE's strategy of self-affirmation among the socialist groups and parties taken as a whole, and of competition with the PCE to achieve overall hegemony on the left. As the central concept of a proposal for the transition to socialism, and of the PSOE's becoming the kingpin of the democratic forces of the left, Marxism was not simply 'taken on board', but proclaimed and broadcast by Felipe González and his supporters within the Socialist leadership.

With this language on their lips, and with a political praxis of negotiation with the reformist heirs of the Francoist regime, the Socialists made far-reaching inroads into the new political system. Their first electoral success, in June 1977 (taking almost 30 per cent of the votes and obtaining 118 parliamentary representatives), meant that their status as a marginal force was at an end and placed them right at the centre of the party system which arose from those elections. In addition to initiating a tendency to what came to be known as an imperfect two-party system,[9] the 1977 elections had two basic consequences for the left as a whole. In the first place, the socialist groups or parties which had been the PSOE's rivals either went out of existence or were left heavily in debt. Secondly, of the hotchpotch communist world, only the PCE remained, albeit with results far below those they had dreamt of and a long way short of those obtained by the PSOE.[10]

So it was that, after the 1977 elections, the PSOE no longer had three of the serious reasons that had led it to declare itself Marxist in 1976. With its mass of voters and its 118 MPs, it was no longer on the margins of the political system; the crushing defeat it had inflicted on the other socialist parties had made it cease to be simply one among many; and thanks to its electoral success with respect to the Communists, the PSOE was no longer the party presumably condemned to play second fiddle in the leftist orchestra. At the same time, the PSOE found itself inside the system and in a position of strength. In addition, it was the only socialist party and occupied a clearly hegemonic place *vis-à-vis* and PCE. In short, the PSOE had totally subverted the expectations aroused by its appearance in the final years of anti-Francoist opposition. Not only that, but it had also completely altered its objective situation in the political system.

[9] In an interview published by *El País*, 15 Jan. 1978, Felipe González stated that 'the voters did not want to maintain so many initials . . . and turned in the direction of what we might consider an imperfect, clarifying, and efficient two-party system'.

[10] In the general elections of June 1977, the PSOE obtained 29.21% of the votes, whilst the PCE obtained only 9.24%, and the parties grouped together in the coalition Unidad Socialista PSP–FPS obtained a mere 4.46%. The respective numbers of

This modification of the PSOE's real position in the party system had the effect of changing the perception of the socialist leaders who were closest to Felipe González, with respect to the party's short-term objectives and the strategies required to achieve them. In a very brief period of time, the values of a leftist culture formed in opposition to Francoism gave way to those of a new political system which was the fruit of an all-party consensus. A culture which centred on the rejection of a given power system was replaced by one which fed on the conviction that it was necessary to consolidate the newly unveiled system. To express it in the jargon in vogue at the time, the struggle for the occupation of new spheres of power took over from the fight for the conquest of new areas of freedom. For the leaders of the PSOE, the new task was two-fold, on account of the Socialists' own vocation for using political power as an instrument for effecting social change, and because of the weakness of the governing party, whose fragility could, at any moment, result in a power vacuum.[11] For these two reasons, once they had conquered liberty (and given the way in which they did so), the Socialists had to prepare themselves for the mastery of power.

However, there was only one way to become the governing party, and that was by having sufficient electoral support. Once democracy had been established, and the freedom-fighting political line had been put aside, the party had to orientate its activities towards making itself more attractive to the electorate. The point from which it started was not bad and, indeed, it could be said to be considerably better than what could have been hoped for up to a very short while earlier. Nevertheless, whilst the party's initial position was not bad, it was not sufficient to enable it to achieve power. It was necessary to consolidate what it had already and, at the same time, expand into new areas. Tactically, the consequences of this were obvious: since there were no longer any competitors on the left, the only expansion possible had to be on the right. The adversary was not the PCE, now limited to the small patch that commanded its fidelity, but Unión de Centro Democrático (UCD), the Union of the Democratic Centre, which had obtained 34 per cent of the votes in the 1977 election.

---

parliamentary representatives were 118, 20, and 6. The results are detailed in J. de Esteban and L. López Guerra, *Los partidos políticos en la España actual* (Barcelona, 1982), 74.

[11] 'The fragility of the governmental coalition', said González in Jan. 1978, 'creates a permanent situation of governmental crisis which obliges us to think of a possible power vacuum in less time than was anticipated' (*El País*, 15 Jan. 1978).

THE ERROR OF AVOWING MARXISM

Felipe González appears to have been the first person to realize that the basic definition which he himself gave of the PSOE, to arm it for its struggle for freedom and for hegemony on the left, was precisely what had to be destroyed in order to adapt the party to its new goals of increasing its electoral appeal and achieving power. To define the party as Marxist, and in the next breath to deny that it was social democratic or social bureaucratic, might be useful for identifying the PSOE as the leading party on the democratic left. That definition, however, became excessively narrow and placed useless limitations on the party when the latter's aim was to occupy not only the entire space of the non-Communist left, but also part of that of a very motley centre, which lacked adequate structuring, suffered from factional in-fighting, and was not without reformist and social democratic currents.

González went straight to the heart of Socialist identity as it had been established during the XXVII Congress. In the course of a meeting with journalists, and with the intention of informing the whole country, including his own party and fellow-leaders, he stated that it had been a mistake to define the Socialist Party as Marxist.[12] He was thus attempting, in one fell swoop, to destroy the main shibboleth of the previous phase. All who were socialists in 1976 had been united in Marxism and no one who had been a socialist during the Franco regime could relinquish the direct connection with the Marxist tradition. Now, however, said the party's secretary-general, the PSOE must no longer define itself as Marxist. It was not, of course, that there was no room for Marxists in the PSOE, but, rather, that there must also be space for many other people from a wide variety of theoretical and ideological backgrounds.

The idea of abandoning this feature of the socialist identity was clearly related to a significant change in the definition of the party's top priority tasks. Prior to making so forceful an entry into the political system, the Socialists always spoke of *formal* democracy, with the object of arguing immediately afterwards the need to transcend the conquest of democracy stage and establish the hegemony of the working class. The post-1977 novelty consisted in dropping the word 'formal' and in silencing the idea of the implantation of workers'

---

[12] According to *Ya*, 10 May 1978, González said the previous day in Barcelona, 'It's a mistake for a socialist party to declare itself Marxist, because this term has been used pejoratively by the right' (quoted in R. del Aguila and R. Montoro, *El discurso político de la transición* (Madrid, 1984), 89).

hegemony, whilst insisting on the notion of making democracy deeper and more cohesive. Thenceforward, democracy in capitalist society would no longer be a stage to be surpassed on the road to the abolition of capitalism, but a political system to be consolidated and deepened, with a view to introducing reforms which would gradually change society.[13]

The change in priorities was accompanied by a clear shift away from the strategic line advocated during the first years of the transition from dictatorship to democracy. Between 1975 and 1977, without sacrificing its identity or its autonomy, the PSOE lost no opportunity to present itself as the unifying force of the progressive left. After the 1977 elections, appearing to be part of a coalition, or the ally of other forces, was not only uncomfortable, but might also prove to be counterproductive. Freedom had to be achieved in the company of others; government, by contrast, had to be attained alone. 'At the present time,' said Felipe González in January 1978, 'any alliance into which the party might enter would subtract, not add, votes.'[14]

Felipe González chose what might be called the German, or Nordic, socialist path to power. He was fully aware that that choice constituted a novelty for the so-called southern European socialist model, since it involved the rejection of a common left-wing programme, along French lines, and, at the same time, the rejection of participation in a government composed of centre or centre-right parties, in Italian style. 'Perhaps in Spain we shall see a break-away from the south European model, with the Socialist Party obtaining power by an absolute majority.' Such was the prospect opened by the 1977 elections and by the 'imperfect, clarifying, and efficient two-party system' which came out of them. The relative failure of the PCE made the PSOE unwilling to adopt a policy of left-wing unity which could only benefit the former. In this way, the Spanish Socialists repeated the same argument as that used by the leaders of the British Labour Party in the 1930s, when it was suggested to them (among others, by the Spanish Socialists) that they pursue unity of action with the Communists. At the same time, the limited success of UCD, which had proved unable to achieve an absolute majority and suffered from intrinsic internal weakness,

---

[13] The insistence on the fragility of democracy and the need for its consolidation became the main features of Spanish socialist thought from 1981 onwards and, particularly, from the XXIX Congress, held in October of that year. Cf. A. García Santesmases, 'Evolución ideológica del socialismo en la España actual', *Sistema*, 68–9 (Nov. 1985), 61–78, which constitutes a synthesis of more detailed research, as yet unpublished.

[14] *El Pais*, 15 Jan. 1978.

meant that there was little or no attraction for the Socialists in the idea of a coalition government, such as the Communist Santiago Carrillo never tired of proposing.[15]

Since its objective was to achieve power alone, the PSOE orientated itself towards policies which reaffirmed its character as a governing party. In the belief that the real possibility of forming a cabinet would result from the collapse of the existing governmental coalition, Felipe González tried to turn the PSOE into the only party capable of filling a 'possible power vacuum'. This required putting visible distance between the PSOE and the Communists and appearing before the electorate free from all Marxist connotations. It was shortly after the formulation of this tactical line that González expressed publicly his conviction that it had been a mistake to define the Socialist Party as Marxist; a mistake which, of course, he was prepared to correct.

The announcement of this intention fanned the flames of a certain opposition which was growing inside the Socialist Party itself, and which included some of its organizational bodies. The 1977 elections had enhanced the figure of the party's secretary-general within the socialist community, increasing his appeal and giving him an audience that none of the other leading figures of the PSOE had enjoyed. In the eyes of an increasingly critical sector, the party was fast heading towards personal leadership and electoralism. The custodians of ideological purity and collegiate leadership felt lashed and stung by González's new attitude to Marxism. Electoralism and personalism, plus the abrogation of Marxism, were proof positive of the transformation of the PSOE. From a political party whose goal was the construction of a new society via the conquest of political power by the working class, the PSOE was being converted into a party prepared to win elections in order simply to administer, and slightly to reform, capitalist society. The guardians of the doctrinal and ideological fundamentals duly prepared to put up a fight.

Foreseeably, the battle took the form of a debate on Marxism or, more exactly, on the definition of the Socialist Party as Marxist. The appearance on television of President Adolfo Suárez, on the eve of the 1979 general elections, and the results obtained by the PSOE in that electoral contest, prompted Felipe González to delay no longer his

[15] On the policies of the PCE in this period, see G. Morán, *Miseria y grandeza del Partido Comunista de España, 1939–1985* (Barcelona, 1986), 551–61. For the reception given to Carrillo's proposal for a 'government of democratic concentration', see F. Claudín, *Santiago Carrillo: Crónica de un secretario general* (Barcelona, 1983), 272–4.

decision to suppress the term 'Marxist' from the definition of the PSOE adopted by the 1976 party congress. Since that adoption could only be rectified by a new congress, the XXVIII Congress was called for May 1979, shortly after the general elections of March and the municipal elections of April.

The outcome of the confrontation between the so-called official and critical sectors of the PSOE is well known and will be only briefly summarized here.[16] The critical sector was inspired by Luis Gómez LLorente, Francisco Bustelo, and Pablo Castellano, all of whom were members of the party's executive committee, and spurred on by Enrique Tierno Galván, who, a year earlier, had dissolved his Popular Socialist Party to become an integral part of the PSOE. It entrenched itself in the defence of a political proposal whose principal merit was the reaffirmation of the Marxist character of the PSOE, in opposition to Felipe González. This proposal and definition were approved by the majority of the delegates who, on the following day, tried to elect an executive committee in which Felipe González would continue to be the secretary-general, but which would also give the critical sector substantial representation. The delegates wanted Felipe González to remain as secretary and the party to stay Marxist.

González, however, had expressed his intentions clearly: he would not be the leader of a party which defined itself as Marxist. Consequently, he did not stand for re-election—a move which caught his opponents unprepared[17] and provoked a leadership crisis amid much weeping, wailing, and gnashing of teeth. No one was capable of composing an executive committee without Felipe González. As the PSOE vice-secretary, Alfonso Guerra, commented later, with unconcealed disdain for the critical sector, the sceptre was left abandoned on the table, and no one was capable of picking it up.[18] Felipe González was to return for the sceptre a few months later.

From that time onwards, the party ceased to define itself as Marxist. What was equally, if not more, important, none of those who liked to define themselves as Marxists or members of the critical sector ever again formed part of the party's executive committee. After the Extra-

---

[16] P. Preston, *The Triumph of Democracy* (London, 1986), 153–7.

[17] 'We never even remotely imagined that incompatibility in Felipe González', explained Francisco Bustelo shortly afterwards, in 'Puntualizaciones al Congreso Socialista', *El País*, 3 June 1979.

[18] Cf. the recollections and impressions of Alfonso Guerra, contained in *Felipe González: De Suresnes a la Moncloa* (Madrid, 1984), 124–6. The same vol. also includes the reflections of Pablo Castellano.

ordinary Congress of September 1979, Felipe González truly did hold the sceptre in his hands.

THE TRIUMPH OF GONZÁLEZ AND THE MATURITY OF THE PARTY

In the summer of 1979, between the XXVIII and the Extraordinary Congresses, Felipe González began a political and ideological offensive which, this time, had as its objective his own party. Since he wanted to appear to be free from any kind of alliance with the Communists (in spite of working alongside them on many town councils), and to undermine the position of UCD (despite having signed the 'Pacts of the Moncloa' with this party), Felipe González had to have a party which was homogenous in its leadership, disciplined in its practice, and coherent in its ideology. That is to say, he needed what he called during that summer a mature party. The debate around the abjuration of Marxism must be situated within the context of this campaign to turn the PSOE into a mature party.

In the initial phase—the composition of a homogeneous executive committee—he met with little opposition. Felipe González did not lend himself to any kind of compromise solution with the critical or Marxist sector. He refused to allow his name to appear in an executive committee proposed by the critical sector, in which he would constantly have been up against internal opposition and the accusation of abandoning ideals or betraying principles. He was not prepared to be part of an alien candidature; at most, he would include some of the critical sector in his own. In the event, not even this happened and all the members of the new executive committee, as well as owing their inclusion in the list to the personal decision of Felipe González held the same ideological views as he did.

The second stage of the campaign—the achievement of a disciplined party—involved no particular drama, due, perhaps, to the fact that the PSOE grew larger as it occupied new spheres of power. After the 1979 local government elections, the PSOE had thousands of town councils to administer. There were Socialist mayors in the most important cities and Socialists at the helm of many *diputaciones* (provincial councils). In addition, there were more than 10,000 Socialist town councillors—that is, more than the total PSOE membership in 1977. For thousands of Socialists, joining the party and entering public office had been two almost simultaneous operations. Naturally, and despite the familiar protestations regarding the sacrifices involved in accepting a public post, thousands of these Socialists found that their début in political life brought with it a process of upward social mobility. For them, the party became the channel for their social promotion and for the improvement of their economic situation.[19]

Nevertheless, the crucial factor in the maintenance of central discipline was not simply that this process occurred, but that it took place before local or provincial interest networks could be established. The lists of candidates for public offices were not drawn up on the basis of stable local or provincial political structures, which the central leadership had to accept. Rather, the designation process worked the other way round. Since the party structure was of recent creation, no one was in a position to dispute the capacity of the party executive committee (or, in the final analysis, of those on the committee who had the power to decide its composition) to decree who would run as candidates in local government elections. In this way, and perhaps for the first time in the political history of contemporary Spain, the central structure of a party was not the mirror image of local interests. On the contrary, local interests were subordinate to decisions taken at the centre. Thus, discipline was guaranteed.

With the critical sector awash in its own ineffectiveness and with internal discipline assured, Felipe González also devoted his attention in the summer of 1979 to speeding up the party's ideological maturing process. To explain it, he used a very plastic metaphor which may well seem rather inapposite: those who are unfamiliar with country lore, said González, do not know that when fruit farmers want figs to ripen quickly, they rub 'a little oil on the fruit's arse'. 'Well,' he continued, 'this party has no choice but to put up with having a little oil rubbed on its arse and to shorten its maturing process to a few months.'[20] In order to achieve this, González was willing to prepare the unguent with his own fair hand and to apply it without delay.

The ingredients he used in the elaboration of the ointment are clearly indicated in the interviews given to Juan Luis Cebrián for *El País* and Fernando Claudín for *Zona abierta* between the two congresses held by the PSOE in 1979. Above all, González denied any 'basic change', on the grounds that he had done no more than adapt his

---

[19] For a wealth of interesting data on Socialist leaders, militants, and voters, see J. F. Tezanos, *Sociología del socialismo español* (Madrid, 1983). The present writer is not aware of any study which has broached the process of the formation of the new Socialist political class.

[20] F. Claudín, 'Entrevista a Felipe González', *Zona Abierta*, 20 (May–Aug. 1979), 8.

analysis to reality, in order to achieve 'the present political maturity of the PSOE as a party'. The recurrent idea was that the PSOE must mature and, to do so, it must perceive its dual function in Spanish social and political life. The first, well-known—or, at least, much proclaimed—function was to offer 'an alternative for change'. The second, more of a novelty, was to constitute a 'point of reference which makes people feel secure'.[21] Change and security: these were the two substances which Felipe González proposed to mix, in equal parts, to obtain the oil of maturity.

The blending was to be done by means of a 'valid synthesis, which implies a broad base of popular representation'. The PSOE was to become the party of the three syntheses or, to be more exact, of a single, tripartite synthesis: 'a synthesis of ideological, sectorial, and territorial diversity'. In the first of these three, the PSOE's capacity must range from those who remained 'rigorously Marxist' to those who embraced socialism through a Christian-based commitment or simply from 'anthropological positions', amongst whom González mentioned specifically 'ecologists, krausists, and humanists'. Ideologically, then, the PSOE did not define itself in any concrete way, other than as a melting-pot, as the synthesis of a broad spectrum of ideologies, capable of including a whole universe of Marxists, Christians, ecologists, humanists, and even Krausists, a species thought to be extinct.[22] The meaning of the syntheses of the sectorial and territorial diversities was exactly the same. The aim was to open the PSOE to the widest possible range of social and territorial groupings.

What was omitted in those interviews was every bit as important as what was said.[23] In the interview given to *El País*, González made no mention of the socialists' struggle being defined as the fight for socialism. The erstwhile obligatory reference to the final goal the implantation of a society different to the present one—and to the transitionary process which leads to that society by stages, gave way to a more generic definition of the struggle for socialism as a 'struggle for

---

[21] From the interview with Felipe González by Juan Luis Cebrián, *El País*, 14 June 1979.

[22] The Krausists were mentioned in the interview published in *El País*. In the interview published by *Zona Abierta*, it was said that the PSOE must reach those who considered themselves the heirs of the republican left.

[23] In truth, what González said in 1979, he also said in 1976. The crucial difference lay in the fact that, in 1976, he said things which he omitted in 1979. For example, the conquest of democracy to implant socialism after a stage of working-class hegemony, discussed in 1976, was reduced, in 1979, to the consolidation of democracy. González's ideology was like a garment from which strips were being progressively torn off.

freedom and equality through solidarity'. Clearly, these are the ideals of the French Revolution, whose mechanical and literal repetition was only avoided by replacing 'fraternity' with 'solidarity', a more or less identical concept. With respect to initiating the stages which mark the process of transition to socialist society, Felipe González stated, in response to a question posed by Fernando Claudín in *Zona abierta*, that, in reality, that process was already under way.

The results of the 1979 elections and the ideological campaign to accelerate the maturing of the PSOE reaffirmed two of the principal ideas enunciated in the previous year. In the first place, González emphasized that Socialism's goal was the consolidation of democracy. Without doubt, his insistence was closely related to the permanent crisis suffered by the governing party, UCD, immediately after winning the elections. A very influential sector of the Socialist leadership began to define alternatives as though it really were a question of taking the place of UCD: the latter's fragmentation endangered democracy itself, unless the PSOE made preparations to become an alternative in government. So it was that an idea with deep roots began its gentle penetration of Spanish socialism: a perception of the immediate task as the substitution of the bourgeoisie and its political representatives, on account of their manifest incapacity to consolidate a democratic political system.[24]

Secondly, the advance of this line of political thinking gave rise to a greater insistence on what was termed the 'autonomy of the socialist project'. According to González, the party 'must not be defined by its alliances, nor by a strategy in common with one or more other forces, but by its own project'. The appeal of the Socialist Party, said González candidly, diminished if it was linked by lasting agreements to other parties, especially to the PCE. In response to his interlocutor's insistence, Felipe González impatiently rejected as 'anti-Francoist' the notion of an 'alliance of democratic forces, in which the PSOE would be the central axis'—that familiar policy from the first stages of the transition to democracy. Neither the party nor the country could take any kind of common agreement between the political forces of the left.[25]

[24] The clearest exposition of this idea appeared after the period under consideration here, in an article by Javier Solana, 'La alternativa socialista', *Leviatán*, 9 (Autumn, 1982), 9. From that time onwards, the overriding images of the PSOE were those of a party which would be the 'backbone' of Spain and of its function as the 'modernizing' agent of society and the 'rationalizing' factor of the economy.

[25] F. Claudin, 'Entrevista', p. 8.

What was at stake with the desertion of Marxism as one of the Socialist Party's principal 'identifying marks' was, therefore, much more than simply a semantic dispute or a fight over the new executive committee. It was the preparation of the PSOE to make a final assault on the political system in such a way as not to appear to represent the threat of a change of society, or of the beginning of a process which would, ultimately, lead to a change of society. This new position necessitated a different conception of what a socialist party should be from that preached in 1976. It also required a new view of the party's priority goals and objectives and of its policy on alliances. A party of change and security; a party of ideological, sectorial, and territorial synthesis; a party which would consolidate and deepen democracy; which did not threaten to impose a change of society, or, as it was put then, a change of 'model of society'; and which, on its own strength, without any need for alliances, constituted an alternative for government. Such was the profile of a mature party and such were the reasons which prompted Felipe González to drop the epithet 'Marxist' from the Socialist identity.

There was, as we have noted, another reason. By suppressing the emblematic core of the previous socialist identity, Felipe González liquidated all internal opposition and decisively reaffirmed his own personal power. That was the most noteworthy result of the Extraordinary Congress held in September 1979. Naturally, when obliged to choose between Marx and González, the delegates—who, this time, had been elected by their respective federations—did not hesitate to opt for González. The PSOE ceased to define itself as Marxist. When this happened, all those who had previously defended the Marxist identity were either left out in the cold or excluded themselves voluntarily from the new leadership. At the same time, those who did not define themselves as Marxists—or who repented of having done so—broke into a vociferous chant of 'Fe-li-pe! Fe-li-pe!', showing with their enthusiasm who the real victor was. Whilst it had undoubtedly been crucial to redefine what the party was and, because of what it was, what it proposed to do, for Felipe González it was equally important to have at his disposal a homogeneous, seamless instrument with which to carry out the new tasks.

Thus, at the end of the Extraordinary Congress, Felipe González had reason to feel satisfied. He had been re-elected as secretary-general and acclaimed by a mass of cheering delegates. The PSOE was, at last, mature. Behind him lay a self-confessedly Marxist party which had managed to establish its hegemony over the left as a whole and which had won over a sizeable wedge of the electorate. That was sufficient to situate the PSOE in the prominent position it occupied in the summer of 1979, although not enough to enable it to govern, especially if it intended to do so alone. After the September congress, however, having recovered the sceptre and his position at the head of what was now an explicitly non-Marxist party, Felipe González could proceed, without internal opposition, to the elimination of all ambiguity with regard to the character and aims of the party. *En passant*, he could also jettison the leftist ballast which, in his opinion, impeded the ship's progress.

Here was a party which had successively overcome its inferiority with respect to the Communists, resolved the dispersion of the socialist clan, gained the allegiance of more than five million voters, established a solid internal homogeneity, and appointed an undisputed leader. All was now set fair for it also to achieve an absolute majority in Parliament. For this to happen all that was needed was the addition of disintegration of UCD to the conversion of the PSOE into what González termed the evocation of tranquillity and security for the man in the street. This did not really depend on the Socialists, but in the Spanish political system of the time, it was still possible for things that did not depend on the Socialists to happen. And that, in effect, was one of the things that occurred in 1981. The repercussions of the PSOE of the collapse of UCD were decisive for the former's conception of itself as the substitute party and for the definition of its modernizing objectives. The most important result, however, was that, in October 1982, Felipe González was able to see the efficacy of the oil which he had so diligently applied to his party during the summer of 1979.

SIR RAYMOND CARR:
A BIBLIOGRAPHY, 1945–1988

Robert A. McNeil

The present listing of Sir Raymond Carr's published works makes no claim to completeness; none the less it includes articles and reviews in forty-four journals published in England, Spain, and the Americas, as well as eleven monographs and numerous contributions to other works. Several interviews (and one tape-cassette) have been listed, as a further indication of the wide range of Sir Raymond's activities. It should also perhaps be mentioned here that a large number of his seminar papers and lectures remain unpublished. Sir Raymond has been — and, happily, continues to be — an indefatigable book-reviewer; the 150-odd reviews included here are given in chronological order under broad subject-headings.*

A. BOOKS WRITTEN OR EDITED BY RAYMOND CARR

Spain 1808–1939. Oxford, Clarendon Press, 1966. xxix, 766 pp.

España 1808–1939. Corregida y aumentada por el autor. Revisión de J. Romero Maura. Barcelona, Ediciones Ariel, 1969. 734 pp., 193 plates.

Spain 1808–1975. 2nd edn. Oxford, Clarendon Press, 1982. xxx, 856 pp.

Directorio de latinoamericanistas europeos/Directory of European Latin Americanists. Consejo de redacción: H. Hoetink, R. Carr, H. Blakemore. Amsterdam, Centro de Estudios y Documentación Latinoamericanos, Universidad de Amsterdam, 1969. viii, 96 fos.

Latin American Affairs, ed. Raymond Carr. (St Antony's Papers, 22.) London, Oxford University Press, 1970. 157 pp.

The Republic and Civil War in Spain, ed. Raymond Carr. London, Macmillan, 1971. x, 275 pp.

English Fox-Hunting: A History. London, Weidenfeld and Nicolson, 1976. xxi, 273 pp.

English Fox-Hunting: A History. Revised paperback edn. London, Weidenfeld and Nicolson, 1986. xix, 275 pp.

The Spanish Tragedy: The Civil War in Perspective. London, Weidenfeld and Nicolson, 1977. xvii, 336 pp.

---

* This bibliography could not have been completed without the aid and enthusiasm of Paula Covington, Malcolm Deas, Pat Kirkpatrick, and (not least) Sir Raymond Carr himself. Any errors are, of course, entirely the fault of the compiler. Spanish editions of works originally published in English are listed only when they are of special interest.

La tragedia española: La guerra civil en perspectiva. Versión española de Jesús Fernández Zulaica y Mauro Hernández Benítez. Madrid, Alianza, 1977. 279 pp. [Contains notes and references not in the English edn.]

The Civil War in Spain, 1936–39. New edn. [of *The Spanish Tragedy*]. London, Weidenfeld and Nicolson, 1986. xvii, 328 pp.

España: De la dictadura a la democracia, por Raymond Carr y Juan Pablo Fusi. Barcelona, Planeta, 1979. (Espejo de España, 51.) 323 pp. [Winner of the 1979 Premio Espejo de España.]

Spain: Dictatorship to Democracy, [by] Raymond Carr and Juan Pablo Fusi Aizpúrua. London, George Allen & Unwin, 1979. xxi, 288 pp.

Spain: Dictatorship to Democracy, [by] Raymond Carr and Juan Pablo Fusi Aizpúrua. 2nd ed. London, George Allen & Unwin, 1981. xxi, 288 pp.

Modern Spain 1875–1980. Oxford, Oxford University Press, 1980. xvii, 201 pp.

Fox-Hunting, compiled by Sara and Raymond Carr. Oxford, Oxford University Press, 1982. (Small Oxford Books.) vi, 112 pp.

Puerto Rico: A Colonial Experiment. New York, New York University Press, 1984. xxii, 477 pp.

Spain: Studies in Political Security. Joyce Lasky Shub, Raymond Carr, eds. New York, Praeger, 1985. (Washington Papers, 117.) xii, 134 pp.

B. CONTRIBUTIONS TO OTHER BOOKS

'Spain', in A. Goodwin (ed.), *The European Nobility in the Eighteenth Century* (London, Adam & Charles Black, 1953), 43–59.

'Spain: Rule by Generals', in Michael Howard (ed.), *Soldiers and Governments: Nine Studies in Civil-Military Relations* (London, Eyre & Spottiswoode, 1957), 133–48.

'Two Swedish Financiers: Louis de Geer and Joel Gripenstierna', in H. E. Bell and R. L. Ollard (eds.), *Historical Essays 1600–1750 Presented to David Ogg* (London, Adam & Charles Black, 1963), 18–34.

'The Castro Revolution', in Grant Samuel McClellan (ed.), *U.S. Policy in Latin America* (New York, H. W. Wilson, 1963), 143–5.

'Latin America', in Evan Luard (ed.), *The Cold War: A Reappraisal* (London, Thames and Hudson, 1964), 220–42.

'Spain and Portugal, 1793 to c.1840', C. W. Crawley (ed.), *The New Cambridge Modern History,* ix. *War and Peace in an Age of Upheaval 1793–1830* (Cambridge, University Press, 1965), ch. 16: 439–61.

'The Cold War in Latin America', in John Plank (ed.), *Cuba and the United States: Long Range Perspectives* (Washington, Brookings Institution, 1967), 158–77.

'Mexico 1910–1916: The Mexican Revolution', in the partwork, A. J. P. Taylor and J. M. Roberts (eds.), *History of the 20th Century* (London, Purnell, 1968), 240–7.

'Mexican Agrarian Reform 1910–1960', in E. L. Jones and S. J. Wolff (eds.), *Agrarian Change and Economic Development* (London, Methuen, 1969), 151–68.

Foreword to *Franco: A Biography*, by J. W. D. Trythall (London, Hart-Davis, 1970).

'Spain', in J. M. Roberts (ed.), *Europe in the Twentieth Century: Readings in 20th Century History*, i. *1900–1914* (London, Macdonald, 1970), 222–6.

'Orwell and the Spanish Civil War', in Miriam Gross (ed.), *The World of George Orwell* (London, Weidenfeld and Nicolson, 1971), 63–73. [See also section C.]

'Spanish History from 1700', in P. E. Russell (ed.), *Spain: A Companion to Spanish Studies* (London, Methuen, 1973), 145–90.

'Spain: Franco and After', in *History of the 20th Century* (London, Octopus Books, 1976), 442–5.

'The Regional Problem in Spain', in J. C. Boogman and G. N. van der Plaat (eds.), *Federalism: History and Current Significance of a Form of Government* (The Hague, Nijhoff, 1980), 267–87. [See also section C.]

'El ejército en la historia de la España contemporánea', in Fernando García de Cortázar (ed.), *Aula de Cultura* (Bilbao, Correo Español/Pueblo Vasco, 1982/3), 37–47.

Introduction to *Handley Cross*, by R. S. Surtees (Craddock, Devon, R. S. Surtees Society, 1983).

Introduction to the photographic collection *Images of the Spanish Civil War* (London, George Allen & Unwin, 1986); published in the US as *The Spanish Civil War: A History in Pictures* (New York, Norton, 1986).

'Testimonio personal: La España que conoció Raymond Carr', in the partwork *La Historia del Franquismo* (Madrid, Diario 16, 1986), 344–5.

'Introduction: The Spanish Transition in Perspective', in Robert Clark and Michael Haltzel (eds.), *Spain in the 1980s: The Democratic Transition and a New International Role* (Cambridge, Mass., Ballinger, 1987), 1–15.

Preface to *Franco: A Biography*, by J. P. Fusi (London, Unwin Hyman, 1987).

C. ARTICLES IN PERIODICALS AND NEWSPAPERS

'Gustavus IV and the British Government 1804–09', *English Historical Review*, 60 (1945), 36–66.

'Essays in Bibliography and Criticism XXXIII: Heckscher's Economic History of Sweden', *Economic History Review*, 2nd ser., 9 (1956), 132–3.

'New Ways in History: New Openings 1 — Latin America', *Times Literary Supplement* (7 Apr. 1966), 299–300.

'Cuban Dilemmas', *World Today*, 23 (1967), 37–42.

'Uneasy Inheritance', *The Times* (13 Sept. 1967); Supplement on Chile, Peru, and Bolivia, p. ii.

'Huntin', Shootin' and Fishin' ', *Spectator* (25 Mar. 1972), 488.
'Spain's Party Games', *Spectator* (11 June 1977), 7–8.
'Euphoria in Spain', *Spectator* (25 June 1977), 7–9.
'Solving Argentina's Problems', *Spectator* (8 Apr. 1978), 9–10.
'The Regional Problem in Spain', *Bijdragen en Mededelingen betreffende de Geschiedenis der Nederlanden*, 94 (1979), 639–59. [See also section B.]
'Spain: The Politics of Apathy', *Spectator* (24 Feb. 1979), 14.
'Cultura y política', *Política* (?Buenos Aires, 4 Nov. 1979), 9.
'An Old-Fashioned Coup', *Spectator* (28 Feb. 1981), 9.
'Fox-Hunters, Unite', *Spectator* (31 July 1982), 15–16.
'Capturing the Middle Ground', *Spectator* (6 Nov. 1982), 7–8.
'Orwell y la guerra civil española' (tr. Mervyn Samuel), *Revista de Occidente*, 33/4 (Feb.–Mar. 1984), 125–40. [See also section B.]
'Charm of a King Who Survived'. Article on Juan Carlos I in the *Sunday Telegraph* (20 Apr. 1986), 2.
'How Two Spains Were Created', *Illustrated London News*, 7054 (May 1986), 46–7.
'Isaiah Berlin, contra la corriente: Entrevista' (tr. by Carlos Darde), *Revista de Occidente*, 66 (Nov. 1986), 103–39.
'Reflexiones sobre la historia de España: Discurso inaugural de los cursos 1987 de la Universidad Internacional Menéndez Pelayo', *Vuelta* (Mexico City), 133/4 (Dec. 1987–Jan. 1988), 34–6.

D. SELECTED PUBLISHED INTERVIEWS WITH RAYMOND CARR

'Recrear el pasado', *La Opinión Cultural* (Buenos Aires, 21 Sept. 1975).
'Los consejos de Raymond Carr', *Arriba* (Madrid, 4 Apr. 1976).
'The Temptation of St Antony's (sic)', *The Guardian* (27 Mar. 1976).
'Esperaba el triunfo de la UCD', *Arriba* (Madrid, 17 June 1977).
Joint interview with Juan Pablo Fusi, *Solidaridad Nacional* (Barcelona, 30 Mar. 1979).
'La situación política de 1936 es irrepitible en nuestros días', *Tele-Exprès* (Barcelona, 30 Mar. 1979).
'Raymond Carr, política e historia', *La Vanguardia* (Barcelona, 1 April 1979).
Joint interview with Juan Pablo Fusi, *El Correo Espanol* (Bilbao, 3 Apr. 1979).
Joint interview with Juan Pablo Fusi, *Diario de Barcelona* (19 Apr. 1979).
'Raymond Carr revisited', the Sunday magazine of the *San Juan Star* (Puerto Rico, 11 Aug. 1985). Also cover-picture.

E. SOUND-RECORDINGS

The Origins of the Spanish Civil War and *The Politics of the Spanish Civil War*, [by] Raymond Carr and Hugh Thomas. [London], Audio Learning Ltd., [1973]. Mono cassette, with supplementary booklet by Kenneth Bourne.

F. SELECTED BOOK REVIEWS (ARRANGED BY SUBJECT)

I. Spain and Portugal

Review of *Spain in Decline 1621–1700*, by R. Trevor Davies, in *History*, 44 (1959), 64.

Review of *The Eighteenth-Century Revolution in Spain*, by Richard Herr, in *The Cambridge Review*, 80 1956 (16 May 1959), 509–11.

'See Those Bullfights', review of *Pagan Spain*, by Richard Wright, in the *Observer* (20 Mar. 1960), 20.

'The Graveyard of Ideals', review of *The Spanish Civil War*, by Hugh Thomas, and *The Grand Camouflage*, by Burnett Bolloten, in the *Observer* (30 Apr. 1961), 30.

Short review of *Die deutsche Politik gegenüber dem spanischem Bürgerkrieg*, by Manfred Merkes, in *English Historical Review*, 78 (1963), 206.

'Movements in New Castile', review of *La Campagne de Nouvelle Castille à la fin du XVIe siècle*, by Noel Salomon, in the *Times Literary Supplement* (10 June 1965), 472.

'The Spanish Tragedy', review of *The Spanish Republic and the Civil War*, by Gabriel Jackson, and *Journey to the Alcarria*, by Camilo José Cela, in the *New York Review of Books* (25 Nov. 1965), 23–5.

'The Spanish Tragedy', review of *Spain, the Gentle Anarchy*, by Benjamin Welles, and *The Siege of the Alcazar*, by Cecil D. Eby, in the *New York Review of Books* (20 Jan. 1966), 25–6.

Review of *The Spanish Republic and the Civil War*, by Gabriel Jackson, in *English Historical Review*, 82 (1967), 641–2.

'Hands Up for Franco', review of *Spain: The Vital Years*, by Luis Bolín, in the *Sunday Telegraph* (22 Jan. 1967), 14.

'Making Friends and Influencing People', review of *Los reformadores de la España contemporánea*, by María Dolores Gómez Molleda, in the *Times Literary Supplement* (16 Feb. 1967), 130.

'The Long Reign in Spain', review of *Franco*, by Brian Crozier, in the *Observer*, (29 Oct. 1967), 27.

'Another View of Franco', review of *Franco: The Man and His Nation*, by George Hills, in the *Observer* (31 Dec. 1967), 20.

'A New View of Galdós', review of *Benito Pérez Galdós y la novela histórica española 1868–1912*, by Antonio Regalado García, in *Anales Galdosianos*, 3 (1968), 185–9.

Review of *The Mines of Tharsis*, by S. G. Checkland, in *Economic History Review*, 21 (1968), 193–4.

'Franco and the Falange', review of *Falange en la Guerra de España*, by Maximiano García Venero, and *Antifalange* by Herbert R. Southworth, in the *Times Literary Supplement* (12 Sept. 1968), 996.

'Allí va! Rá! Rá! Rá!', review of *Iberia*, by James Michener, *Spanish Scene*, by Chandler Brossard, *Franco*, by Brian Crozier, and *Franco: The Man and His Nation*, by George Hills, in the *New York Review of Books* (19 Dec. 1968), 29–31.

Review of *The Origins of Franco's Spain*, by Richard A. H. Robinson, in *Bulletin of Hispanic Studies*, 48 (1971), 360–1.

Review of *Archives de Jules Humbert-Droz I*, in *Bulletin of Hispanic Studies*, 49 (1972), 195–6.

Review of *Transportation and Economic Stagnation in Spain*, by D. R. Ringrose, in *Economic History Review*, 25 (1972), 272–3.

Review of *Documentos del Reinado de Fernando VII, vol. 6*, in the *Hispanic American Historical Review*, 52 (1972), 502–3.

'A Revolution Betrayed', review of *The Revolution and Civil War in Spain*, by Pierre Broué and Emile Témime, in the *Observer* (6 Feb. 1972), 32.

'Raymond Carr on Histories of Spain', review of *The Spaniards*, by Américo Castro, *Spain*, by Richard Herr, *The Making of Medieval Spain*, by Gabriel Jackson, and *The Origins of Spain and Portugal*, by Harold Livermore, in the *Spectator* (18 Mar. 1972), 435–6.

Short Review of *Las relaciones entre España y Rusia en la época de Carlos IV*, by Ana María Schop Soler, in *English Historical Review*, 88 (1973), 914.

'Rape of Andalusia', review of *The Pueblo* by Ronald Fraser, in the *Observer* (19 Aug. 1973), 32.

Review of *Government in Spain*, by K. N. Medhurst, in *Public Administration*, 52 (1974), 126–8.

'Catholics on the Left', review of *Historia de la Democracia Cristiana en España*, by Javier Tusell, in the *Times Literary Supplement* (11 Apr. 1975), 393.

Review of *Carlism and Crisis in Spain*, by Martin Blinkhorn, in *European Studies Review*, 6 (1976), 526–8.

Review of *Sir John Moore's Peninsular Campaign*, by D. W. Davies, in *History*, 61 (1976), 301.

Review of *Church, Politics and Society in Spain*, by William J. Callahan, and *Spanish Catholicism*, by Stanley Payne, in *Journal of Modern History*, 58 (1976), 971–3.

'Viva España', review of *The Distant Drum: Reflections on the Spanish Civil War*, ed. Philip Toynbee, in the *Observer* (18 July 1976), 21.

'The Aftermath of Franco', review of *Spain in Crisis*, ed. Paul Preston, in the *Times Literary Supplement* (30 July 1976), 947.

'Goya and the Two Spains', review of *Goya and the Impossible Revolution*, by Gwyn A. Williams, in the *Observer* (19 Sept. 1976), 27.

'The Cosmetic Constitution', review of *Franco's Political Legacy*, by Jose Amodia, in the *Times Literary Supplement* (1 July 1977), 809.

'All or Nothing', review of *The Spanish Anarchists*, by Murray Bookchin, *Durruti: The People Armed*, by Abel Paz, and *The Anarchist Collective*, ed. Sam

Dolgoff, in the *New York Review of Books* (13 Oct. 1977), 22–7. Also correspondence engendered by this review: 6 Apr. 1978, pp. 40–1.

'A Version of the Past', review of *Américo Castro and the Meaning of Spanish Civilization*, ed. José Rubia Barcia, in *Encounter* (Nov. 1977), 62–6.

'Much Ado About Something', review of *Guernica, Guernica*, by Herbert R. Southworth, in the *Spectator* (26 Nov. 1977), 21.

Review of *La revolución de 1820 día a día*, by Rafael del Riego, in *Bulletin of Hispanic Studies*, 55 (1978), 68–9.

Review of *La política religiosa en España 1889–1913*, by José Andrés Gallego, in *English Historical Review*, 93 (1978), 883–4.

'Spanish Types', review of *The Franco Years*, by Jose Yglesias, in the *Observer* (30 Apr. 1978), 30.

'The Bursting of the Dam', review of *La cultura bajo el franquismo*, ed. J. M. Castellet, in the *Times Literary Supplement* (9 June 1978), 637.

'Fiery Souls', review of *Dictatorship and Political Dissent: Workers and Students in Franco's Spain*, by Jose Maravall, in the *Spectator* (24 June 1978), 18.

'Patched-Up', review of *Republican Portugal*, by Douglas L. Wheeler, and *Portugal: Birth of a Democracy*, by Robert Harvey, in the *Spectator* (4 Nov. 1978), 19–20.

'The Road to Franco', review of *The Coming of the Spanish Civil War*, by Paul Preston, in the *Observer* (26 Nov. 1978), 31.

Review of *El socialismo durante la dictadura 1923–1930*, by José Andrés Gallego, in *English Historical Review*, 94 (1979), 891–3.

'Catalonia', review of *The Catalans*, by Jan Read, in the *Spectator* (3 Feb. 1979), 19–20.

'The Red and the White', review of *Blood of Spain*, by Ronald Fraser, in the *New York Review of Books* (19 July 1979), 39–41.

Review of *El latifundio*, by Miguel Artola and others, in *English Historical Review*, 95 (1980), 917–18.

'Harmony of the Highest', review of *The Krausist Movement and Ideological Change in Spain*, by Juan López-Morillas, in the *Times Literary Supplement* (14 Aug. 1981), 936.

'Absentee Owners', review of *The Rio Tinto Company*, by Charles E. Harvey, in the *Times Higher Education Supplement* (5 Mar. 1982), 22.

'Purity and Danger', review of *The Anarchists of Casas Viejas*, by Jerome R. Mintz, in the *New York Review of Books* (23 Sept. 1982), 54.

Review of *Ejército y Política en España*, by Daniel R. Headrick, in *Journal of Modern History*, 55 (1983), 363–5.

'Moulding the Details', review of *By Safe Hand*, by Sybil and David Eccles, in the *Times Literary Supplement* (18 Mar. 1983), 260.

'Reverberations from the Motherland', review of *The Spanish Civil War*, ed. Mark Falcoff and Frederick B. Pike, and *Mexico and the Spanish Civil War*, by T. G. Powell, in the *Times Literary Supplement* (29 Apr. 1983), 435.

Review of *Spain and the Loss of Spanish America*, by Timothy E. Anna, in *Journal of Modern History*, 56 (1984), 747–9.

'Corruption in Vetusta', review of *La Regenta*, by Leopoldo Alas, tr. by John Rutherford, in the *Times Literary Supplement* (6 Jan. 1984), 607.

'Knight Life', review of *Tirant lo Blanch*, by Joannot Martorell, tr. by David H. Rosenthal, in the *Field* (8 Dec. 1984), 75–7.

Review of *Spain, the EEC and NATO*, by Paul Preston and Denys Smith, in *International Affairs*, 61 (1985), 287.

'Catalan's Last Stand', review of *Voices of the Old Sea*, by Norman Lewis, in the *Literary Review*, 79 (Jan. 1985), 26.

'The New New Spanish History', review of *Fascism from Above*, by Shlomo Ben-Ami, *Revolution and War in Spain 1931–1939*, ed. Paul Preston, and *La encrucijada vasca*, by Ricardo García Damborena, in the *New York Review of Books* (17 Jan. 1985), 39–40.

Review of *The Mad Pomegranate and the Praying Mantis*, by Peter Luke, in the *(London Evening) Standard* (13 Feb. 1985), 18.

'The Reign in Spain', review of *The Transformation of Spain*, by David Gilmour, in the *Observer* (31 Mar. 1985), 27.

'Death in the Evening', review of *That Dangerous Summer*, by Ernest Hemingway, in the *Times* (18 July 1985), 13.

'Self-Defeating Triumphs', review of *La España de la Restauración*, ed. J. L. García Delgado, and 7 other works on modern Spanish history, in the *Times Literary Supplement* (4 Oct. 1985), 1105–6.

Review of *Franco*, by Juan Pablo Fusi, in *El País* (Madrid, 21 Nov. 1985), 'Libros', p. 5.

'The New Spain', review of *The Spaniards*, by John Hooper, in the *Guardian* (20 Feb. 1986), 22.

'Wellington's Blind Eye', review of *The Spanish Ulcer*, by David Gates, in the *Observer* (23 Feb. 1986), 29.

'Revised the Same in Spain', review of *The Spanish Civil War* (new edn.), by Hugh Thomas, in the *Times* (20 Mar. 1986), 11.

'After the Caudillo', review of *The Triumph of Democracy in Spain*, by Paul Preston, in the *Observer* (20 Apr. 1986), 24.

'Averting an Enemy', review of *Diplomacy and Strategy of Survival: British Policy and Franco's Spain*, by Denis Smyth, in the *Times Literary Supplement* (30 May 1986), 582.

'The Don Quixote of Diplomacy', review of *The Count-Duke of Olivares*, by J. H. Elliott, in the *New York Review of Books* (20 Nov. 1986), 39–41.

'Of Spain and Bloomsbury', review of *The Best of Friends: The Brenan-Partridge Letters*, ed. Xan Fielding, in the *Times Literary Supplement* (28 Nov. 1986), 1333.

Review of *The Spanish Economy in the Twentieth Century*, by Joseph Harrison, in *Bulletin of Hispanic Studies*, 64 (1987), 266–7.

Review of *Palmerston vol. 1: Private Correspondence with Sir George Villiers as*

Minister to Spain 1833–1837, ed. Roger Bullen and Felicity Strang, in *International History Review*, 9 (1987), 158–60.

'Grandsons of Noah?', review of *The Basques*, by Roger Collins, in the *Observer* (4 Jan. 1987), 22.

Review of *Fortunata and Jacinta*, by Benito Pérez Galdós, tr. Agnes Moncy Gullon, in the *London Evening Standard* (5 Feb. 1987), 26.

'The Invisible Fist', review of *Aggression and Community: Paradoxes of Andalusian Culture*, by David D. Gilmore, in the *New York Review of Books* (28 May 1987), 41–2.

'Visions of Goya', review of *In Spain*, by Ted Walker, in the *Observer* (27 Dec. 1987), 17.

'How Franco Made It', review of *The Franco Regime 1936–1975*, by Stanley G. Payne, in the *New York Review of Books* (4 Feb. 1988), 26–9.

'Sailing to Victory', review of *Armada*, by Duff Hart-Davies, *The Campaign of the Spanish Armada*, by Peter Kemp, and *The Spanish Armada*, by Colin Martin and Geoffrey Parker, in the *Observer* (17 Apr. 1988), 42.

II. General and Non-Hispanic Europe

Short review of *The Scandinavian Countries, 1720–1865*, by B. J. Hovde, in *English Historical Review*, 66 (1951), 626.

Review of *Cavour and Garibaldi*, by Denis Mack Smith, in *Italian Studies*, 10 (1955), 81–3.

Review of *Gustavus Adolphus: A History of Sweden 1611–1632*, by Michael Roberts, in *English Historical Review*, 70 (1955), 283–6, and 75 (1960), 305–7.

Review of *Primitive Rebels*, by E. J. Hobsbawm, in *Economic History Review*, 12 (1959), 348–50.

'Italy: Unity and After', review of *Victor Emanuel, Cavour and the Risorgimento*, by D. Mack Smith, and *Italy since 1945*, by Elizabeth Wiskemann, in the *Spectator* (5 Feb. 1972), 197.

'Cobb: The Proust of Historians', review of *Reactions to the French Revolution*, by Richard Cobb, and *The Counter-Revolution: Doctrine and Action 1789–1804*, by Jacques Godechot, in the *Spectator* (15 July 1972), 95.

'Raymond Carr on a History of Mediterranean Europe', review of *The Mediterranean and the Mediterranean World in the Age of Philip II*, by Fernand Braudel, and *The Iron Century*, by Henry Kamen, in the *Spectator* (28 Oct. 1972), 674–5.

Short Review of *Anarchici e anarchia nel mondo contemporaneo*, in *English Historical Review*, 88 (1973), 239.

'Full-Blooded Historian', review of *Paris and its Provinces 1792–1802*, by Richard Cobb, in the *Observer* (4 May 1975), 28.

'No Resting-Place', review of *A Savage War of Peace*, by Alastair Horne, in the *Spectator* (22 Oct. 1977), 16.

'Going Up', review of *The Civilizing Process*, by Elias Norbert, in the *Spectator* (5 Aug. 1978), 18.

'History in the Raw', review of *This Land of England*, by David Souden and David Starkie, in the *Field* (18 Jan. 1986), 55.

'Hieratic and Human', review of *Kings, Queens and Courtiers*, by Kenneth Rose, in the *Field* (8 Mar. 1986), 57.

'The Daily Life of a Hooligan Race', review of *The English: A Social History*, by Christopher Hibbert, in the *Spectator* (28 Mar. 1987), 31–2.

III. Latin America

'Judgment on Cuba', review of *Castro's Revolution*, by Theodore Draper, in the *Observer*, (15 July 1962), 18.

'Brazilian Isms', review of *A History of Ideas in Brazil*, by João Cruz Costa, in the *Times Literary Supplement* (18 Nov. 1965), 1015.

'The Mestizo Republic', review of *Brazil and Africa* and *Plantation Boy*, both by José Honório Rodrigues, *A History of Modern Brazil*, by José Maria Bello, and *New Perspectives of Brazil*, ed. Eric N. Baklanoff, in the *New York Review of Books* (26 Jan. 1967), 23–5.

'Mexican Fireworks', review of *One Man's Mexico*, by John Lincoln, in the *Observer* (6 Aug. 1967), 17.

'Pro-Indian Priest', review of *Études sur Bartolomé de las Casas*, by Marcel Bataillon, in the *Times Literary Supplement* (7 Dec. 1967), 1192.

'Obstacles to Change', review of *The Politics of Conformity in Latin America*, ed. Claudio Veliz, in *The Economist* (16 Dec. 1967), 1149.

'Prospects for Christian Democracy in Latin America', review of *Latin American Christian Democratic Parties*, by Edward J. Williams, in *Journal of International Affairs*, 22 (1968), 139–43.

'Bolstering Brazil', review of *Reflections on Latin American Development*, by Roberto de Oliveira Campos, in the *Times Literary Supplement* (18 July 1968), 749.

'When Brazil Looked to Britain', review of *Britain and the Onset of Modernization in Brazil*, by Richard Graham, in *The Economist* (17 Aug. 1968), 42.

Review of *Fidel Castro*, by Enrique Meneses, in *Journal of Latin American Studies*, 1 (1969), 78–9.

'The Stagnant Continent', review of *Static Society: The Paradox of Latin America*, by John Mander, in the *Observer* (30 Mar. 1969), 29.

'Cautionary Tale', review of *Argentina*, by H. S. Ferns, in *The Economist* (20 Sept. 1969), 63–4.

'Slave Colony', review of *The Loss of El Dorado*, by V. S. Naipaul, in *The Economist* (8 Nov. 1969), Supplement, p. iv.

Short Review of *Mexico: The Struggle for Modernity*, by C. C. Cumberland, in *English Historical Review*, 85 (1970), 430.

'Mexico in Revolt', review of *Revolution! Mexico 1910–1920*, by Ronald Atkin, *Intellectual Precursors of the Mexican Revolution*, by James D. Cockroft, and

Zapata and the Mexican Revolution, by John Womack, in the *Times Literary Supplement*, (26 Feb. 1970), 225–6.

'Vodou Power', review of *Papa Doc*, by Bernard Dietrich and Al Burt, and *The Haitian People*, by James Leyburn, in the *New York Review of Books* (12 Mar. 1970), 47–9.

'The Toad under the Harrow', review of *The Abolition of the Brazilian Slave Trade*, by Leslie Bethell, in *The Economist* (11 Apr. 1970), 46.

'Decline and Fall', review of *Guerrilla Movements in Latin America*, by Richard Gott, in the *Spectator* (21 Nov. 1970), 642.

Review of *Crown and Clergy in Colonial Mexico*, by N. M. Farriss, in *Economic History Review*, 24 (1971), 130.

Review of *The Peruvian Industrial Labor Force*, by D. Chaplin, in *Economic History Review*, 24 (1971), 131.

Short Review of *University Students and Revolution in Cuba*, by Jaime Suchlicki, in *English Historical Review*, 86 (1971), 888.

'Sugar and Revolution', review of *Cuba, or The Pursuit of Freedom*, by Hugh Thomas, in the *Observer* (24 Jan. 1971), 26.

'Castro's Wonderland', review of *Guerrillas in Power: The Course of the Cuban Revolution*, by K. S. Karol, in the *Spectator* (17 July 1971), 101–2.

'What's Wrong with Latin America?', review of *Guatemala—Another Vietnam?*, by Thomas and Marjorie Melville, *For the Liberation of Brazil*, by Carlos Marighela, and *Capitalism and Underdevelopment in Latin America*, by André Gunder Frank, in the *Spectator* (1 Jan. 1972), 11–12.

Review of *Government and Society in Colonial Peru*, by J. R. Fisher, in *Economic History Review*, 26 (1973), 365.

Review of *Latin America: New World, Third World*, by Stephen Clissold, in *International Affairs*, 49 (1973), 162–3.

Short Review of *Cuba 1933*, by Luis E. Aguilar, in *English Historical Review*, 89 (1974), 466–7.

Short Review of *Essays in Population History: Mexico and the Caribbean* by Shelburne F. Cook and Woodrow Borah, in *English Historical Review*, 89 (1974), 472.

'Utopia in the Jungle', review of *The Lost Paradise*, by Philip Caraman, in the *Observer* (23 Nov. 1975), 30.

Review of *Argentina in the Twentieth Century*, ed. David Rock, in *History*, 61 (1976), 430–1.

'The Last Frontier', review of *Red Gold*, by John Hemming, *Victims of the Miracle*, by Shelton H. Davis, and *Assault on the Amazon*, by Richard Bourne, in the *Spectator* (15 Apr. 1978), 19–20.

'New World', review of *The Discovery of South America*, by J. H. Parry, in the *Spectator* (21 Apr. 1979), 24–5.

'The Spanish Style', review of *The Centralist Tradition of Latin America*, by Claudio Véliz, and *Public Policy in a No-Party State*, by Richard Gunther, in the *New York Review of Books* (19 Feb. 1981), 43.

'Our Colony', review of *Puerto Rico*, by Arturo Morales Carrión and María Teresa Babín, in the *New York Review of Books* (18 Aug. 1983), 14–16.

'Bestriding the Ocean', review of *The Pacific since Magellan*, vols. 1 and 2, by O. H. K. Spate, in the *Times Literary Supplement* (9 Sept. 1983), 952.

'Viva Scotia!' review of *From the Falklands to Patagonia*, by Michael James Mainwaring, in the *Spectator* (3 Dec. 1983), 28–9.

'Protecting the Enterprise', review of *Notable Family Networks in Latin America*, by Diana Balmori, Stuart F. Voss, and Miles Wortman, in the *Times Literary Supplement* (10 May 1985), 515.

'Still Some Unachieved Goals', review of *Argentina 1516–1982*, by David Rock, and *A State of Fear*, by Andrew Graham-Yooll, in the *Spectator* (26 July 1986), 31–2.

'Revolutionary Roles', review of *Latin America and the Comintern*, by Manuel Caballero, in the *Times Literary Supplement* (17 Apr. 1987), 406.

'What Price Progress?', review of *Amazon Frontier*, by John Hemming, in the *Spectator* (4 July 1987), 29–31.

'The Invention of Latin America', review of *The Cambridge History of Latin America*, vols. 1–5, ed. Leslie Bethell, in the *New York Review of Books* (3 Mar. 1988), 29–33.

'A Revolutionary Hero', review of *Inside the Monster, Our America*, and *On Art and Literature*, all by José Martí, in the *New York Review of Books* (21 July 1988), 26–8. Also correspondence engendered by this review: 8 Dec. 1988, p. 60.

IV. Country Life and Oxford

'Heated in the Chase', review of *The History of Foxhunting*, by Roger Longrigg, in the *Times Literary Supplement* (2 Jan. 1976), 8.

'A Sportsman's Journal', review of *The Hunter and the Hunted*, by Robin Page, in the *Observer* (27 Feb. 1977), 24.

'The Landed Virtues', review of *Auberon Herbert*, ed. John Jolliffe, in the *Times Literary Supplement* (18 Mar. 1977), 292.

'Institutional Passion', review of *Peculiar Privilege: A Social History of Foxhunting*, by David C. Itzkowitz, in the *Spectator* (23 July 1977), 23–4.

'Rich Men in Their Castles', review of *Life in the English Country House*, by Mark Girouard, in the *Spectator* (2 Sept. 1978), 18–19.

'Foes of the Fox', review of *Mr Sponge's Sporting Tour*, by R. S. Surtees, in the *Times Literary Supplement* (7 May 1982), 503.

'Ratcatcher and Hunting Pink', review of *The Sporting World of R. S. Surtees*, by John Welcome, in the *Observer* (8 Aug. 1982), 30.

Review of *The Epwell Hunt*, by Edward Goulburn, in *Oxoniensia*, 50 (1985), 298–9.

'True Pro', review of *Tom Firr of the Quorn*, by Roy Heron, in the *Field* (5 Jan. 1985), 67.

'Rain Check', review of *The History of the Eglinton Hunt*, by Bryce M. Knox, in the *Field* (10 Aug. 1985), 74–5.

'Muck is Your Man', review of *Hillingdon Hall*, by R. S. Surtees, in the *Field (21 Sept. 1985), 66.*

'Quick from the Covert', review of Riding Recollections, by G. J. Whyte Melville, in the *Field* (23 Nov. 1985), 97.

'Fallow Fallacies', review of *The Idea of England*, by Russell Chamberlin, and *The History of the Countryside*, by Oliver Rackham, in the *Field* (15 May 1986), 72.

'Wondrous Necessary Men', review of *The Most Obliging Man in Europe: Life and Times of the Oxford Scout*, by Christopher Platt, in the *Times Literary Supplement* (26 Dec. 1986), 1455.

'Run for Fun', review of *Hedges and Hurdles*, by Roger Munting, in the *Times Literary Supplement* (3 July 1987), 729.

'Up the Airy Mountain, Down the Rushy Glen', review of *In the Pink*, by Caroline Blackwood, in the *Spectator* (10 Oct. 1987), 34–5.

INDEX